Magazines
for
Millions

JAMES L. C. FORD

Foreword by
HOWARD RUSK LONG

Southern Illinois
University Press
Carbondale and Edwardsville

Feffer & Simons, Inc.
London and Amsterdam

The
Story
of
Specialized
Publications

Foreword

WHENEVER a number of people with interests in common find it difficult to say to each other in spoken conversation all the things they wish to say, there is need for a publication.

In our society, where this need perhaps is greater than ever before, we are served, however imperfectly, by a complexity of sources ranging from the electronic networks, national and regional periodicals, the daily and weekly press, all commercially oriented, plus a breathtaking variety of media supported either by the contributions from the readers themselves or by a patron concerned with facilitating the communication process. Beyond the thousands of titles listed and crosslisted in successive editions, since 1880, of the annual directories of N. W. Ayer & Son, there is an obscure non-professional journalism existing in such forms as the ship's bulletin, the club and class circular and even the handwritten family newsletter.

Just as all seem to come into being because the spoken word is impermanent, inconvenient, or limited in range, unless aided by mechanical devices, it seems that such elements as urgency, diversity within the special interest group, and an economic base are some of the requisites to the birth of a publication.

For Thomas Paine, writing the *Crisis Papers*, as well as the editor of the underground newspaper, published only today, urgency was the overriding factor. Diversity is paramount to those who seek large audiences, composed of people with varied tastes, and habits, distributed widely in space. The economics of publishing explains the fate of the thousands of titles in the graveyard of

American journalism, a shocking total of which never appeared beyond the first number. Benjamin Franklin, when he suspended the *General Magazine* after six numbers faced the same realities confronting the management of the Curtis Publishing Company when *The Saturday Evening Post* was consigned to oblivion.

The periodicals, commonly called magazines, constitute a massive segment in the secondary communications system that ties the American society together in a functioning, and sometimes malfunctioning system. Magazines are big business. The total number of magazines recognized by the compilers of directories is much greater than the total number of newspapers, daily and weekly, and the total number of radio and television stations. Combined magazine circulation is much greater than the total circulation of the newspapers. There is no way to prove it, but it is probable that the combined readership of all magazines, as Professor Ford defines the magazine in this book, comes very close to the total audience of the electronic media, if allowances are made for those who have not yet achieved functional literacy.

In this light, as well as in terms of such important contributions as record keeping and providing a source of information and interchange for the intellectual elite, the American magazine is of great social and cultural significance. It is amazing, therefore, how little information there is available either to the serious student or the casual observer. A great deal has been written about specific magazines and about personalities reflected in the development of the better known magazines, Bok, Lorimer, Luce, Wallace, Ross, and others, but otherwise the literature is sparse. With publication of the fifth and ultimate volume of Frank Luther Mott's definitive *A History of American Magazines*, the ground will have been covered in this perspective from the beginning through midpoint of the present century. Theodore Peterson, Roland E. Wolseley, and James Playsted Wood are the principal published authorities on the magazine as we know it.

There is a need, therefore, for an up-to-date analysis of the various types of American magazines and the way they operate, with insights for the student and for the practitioner. And this is what Professor Ford presents so well in the present volume.

Southern Illinois University, HOWARD RUSK LONG
Carbondale
January 4, 1969

Preface

WHILE astronauts and rocket vehicles are whirling through the outer limits of space, right here on earth is an unknown, unexplored universe—that of specialized publications. Most of our communications media are well known to the professional and to the average consumer. We get acquainted with newspapers and radio and TV and general magazines and movies. But although we know them early and late, the specialized publications are overlooked or ignored.

Perhaps it's because there are so many of them; no one can count them all any more than the stars in the sky. But we all know *Jack and Jill* and *Seventeen* and *Photoplay* and *The Wall Street Journal*—all specialized publications along with the internal and external of Monsanto or the industrial monthly issued by Chilton. We take them for granted like the air we breathe.

The pleasantest undertaking for any author is to acknowledge the help of those without whom, literally, this book could not have been written.

To try to tell the story of these specialized publications has been our privilege, never achieved except for the good will and cooperation of scores of editors and publishers who cordially put their knowledge and experience at our disposal. Without them, nothing could have been accomplished. Even as this is written, however, new publications are being added. Changes are a constant in this universe. That's why the circulation figures, based on the November, 1968 reports from Standard Rate & Data Service, may be different in detail before this page is printed. That's why specialized publications are fascinating —they're alive!

Impossible as it is to thank each and every individual who has contributed to the writing of this book, we're eager to express our appreciation. Reversing the usual order, my wife, Elsa Ford, has shared every page. Dean C. Horton Talley, of the Southern Illinois University School of Communications, made research time and money possible. Of my magazine colleagues, Walter E. Botthof and his organization, the Standard Rate & Data Service, supplied endless facts and figures.

Among magazine editors and publishers, many hours of help were given by members of the Meredith Corporation, Bert Dieter and Ken McDougall, Jim Riggs and Dick Hanson, Bob Jolley and Ray Deaton and Bob Clark, who dug up illustrations and credits, always with unfailing good will.

In New York, at McGraw-Hill, there were John R. Callaham and Bill Giglio and A. J. Fox and Richard LaBonte. At Fairchild, James W. Brady, and at Ziff-Davis, W. Bradford Briggs.

While the whole staff of Eastman Kodak in Rochester put themselves at my disposal, a special debt is owed C. E. Fitzgibbon.

In Chicago, Harold J. McKeever of Reuben H. Donnelley Corporation drew generously on years of experience as did the whole Creative Department of International Harvester. In Nashville, Tennessee, cordial conversation and floods of information from Helen Couch of the Methodist Publishing House and Lucy Hoskins of the Southern Baptist Convention. In St. Louis, many of my friends and fellow-members of the Industrial Press Association of Greater St. Louis gave aid, but especially Len Paris and Guy Spilman of *Monsanto Magazine* and Dave Park of Southwestern Bell Telephone's *Scene*.

Company histories were supplied and, amazingly, often specially written for this book by many corporation presidents and vice-presidents whom I have named in individual chapter acknowledgments. No amount of payment could compensate these busy executives who gave so generously of their time and unequaled knowledge.

Major publishing organizations and associations were incredibly cooperative. Geraldine Keating of the International Council of Industrial Editors and Dave Bennett of the American Business Press must be singled out for extra interest beyond the call of any duty. That invaluable freelance reference, Writer's Market and its editor, Kirk Polking, made its valuable material available.

Among my educational fellows I happily acknowledge the trailblazing of Roland Wolseley and Theodore Peterson, whose books on magazines, have brightened the way for me and all students and teachers of magazine journalism.

Happy is the teacher whose students reward him with their professional achievements—and share them with him and others. I proudly hail Bill Barbour, editor and publisher of *Hardware Age* for Chilton, and Gretchen Schmitz, associate editor of *Decor* for Commerce Publishing.

To all who contributed permissions for text and pictures, suggestions and information, my gratitude is deep. A detailed list of acknowledgments, permissions, and picture credits, for all of which we are most appreciative, appears at the end of the book. As a crowning glory for the generous spirit of the magazine world, let it be recorded that no request, no matter how peculiar or difficult, was unfulfilled. Beyond all my hopes and expectations, not only friends and colleagues but many a heretofore complete stranger in this wide, wide universe of specialized publications gave freely and abundantly of themselves and their wisdom to this book.

With their welcome and mine, enter this wonderful universe through our pages and make yourself at home in it, for it is yours.

July and December, 1968   JAMES L. C. FORD
Carbondale in Illinois
and Holland Lake of Montana

Contents

CONTENTS

CONTENTS

List of Illustrations

LIST OF ILLUSTRATIONS

xvi

LIST OF ILLUSTRATIONS

Magazines for Millions

The Story of
Specialized
Publications

1. The Spectacular Unknown

I N the whirling universe of communications, a great celestial system spins spectacularly but unseen and unknown to most men! It is the brilliant and ever-expanding phenomenon of specialized publications. Formed of giant galaxies, shining constellations, and splendid single stars, it influences all our lives and we see it every day but remain ignorant of its powerful and persuasive spell.

You yourself are familiar with half-a-dozen specialized publications, although you're undoubtedly unaware that they belong to a family with 22,000 members. You grew up with *Humpty Dumpty* or *Jack and Jill*, then graduated in your early teens to *American Girl* or *Boys' Life*. A few years later you began reading *Hot Rod* or *Seventeen*. As an adult, your job brought you in contact with *Iron Age* and your hobby led to *Skiing*. Or, as a housewife, you subscribe to *Parents* or *Flower and Garden*.

All these are specialized publications and they're old friends of yours. But when magazines are mentioned, it's the huge mass circulation giants such as *Life* or *Reader's Digest* which get the spotlight even though their number is dwindling and they struggle to survive. The specialized publications, however, expand and evolve with life itself, serving and entertaining men and women in every hour of every day, companions in every activity. Yet, to most of us, most of them are strangers!

Specialized publications have been neglected by all concerned, even their own publishers and editors when it came to recognizing their own importance. Doubly neglected, by historians—especially the historians of journalism—and by journalists who talked and thought only of newspapers and maybe once in

3

a while of magazines of so-called general circulation. And disregarded also by most schools of journalism, who thereby compounded the faults of the so-called working press by looking back over their shoulders like Lot's wife, and teaching for tomorrow only what happened yesterday!

Government acknowledges the vital influence of specialized publications and their service to the public. The United States Congress has established a Periodical Press Gallery. In the "Congressional Directory," names of 412 authorized correspondents for specialized publications are listed as compared with 81 for general consumer magazines. *U.S. News & World Report*, which we classify as a specialized business news magazine, has 75 men and women on its Washington roll, the highest by far, as contrasted to 28 for Time-Life. Other large specialized Washington staffs include 33 for American Aviation Publications and 28 for McGraw-Hill. Washington is the capital for news as well as government and all major specialized publications have their representatives there—men and women reporting and writing for *The American Brewer*, *Bakers Weekly*, *Billboard*, *Leather and Shoes*, *Medical Economics*, and the *Telephone Engineer*, to name a few.

Specialized publications don't need to take a back seat to anyone. They make profits, they have millions of readers, they often are more stable and enduring. They offer sparkling stories, dazzling pictures, fun and fact. With an aggregate single-issue circulation of at least a billion, they're produced by an enthusiastic army of 100,000 men and women. The *Journal of the American Medical Association* carries more pages of advertising than any other magazine, specialized or general. Nine of the top 10 leaders have consistently been specialized publications.

Getting to Know Them

Let's get acquainted—you want to know what a specialized magazine is? You've already met a lot of them, as we suggested. Definitions can be a bore but they also can be stepping-stones to understanding. Most magazine people divide publications into two great groups—the mass or general circulation magazines such as *Look* or *McCall's*, and all the rest united under the all-embracing name of specialized publications. Experts have tried to classify them, and one analyst says "the specialized magazine is any that does not fall into the general or consumer group."

In a sense, every magazine is specialized for they all deal, in some degree, with a selected, specialized audience to whom they address their articles and their ads. Some are more specialized than others—or for smaller audiences. In a professional sense, this book deals with the specialized publication as dif-

4

ferentiated from the publication of general circulation, sometimes called "consumer," sometimes "a slick." It would take an encyclopedia to describe all the specialized publications, and this book can form only the first volume.

So specialized publications include trade and technical publications, fraternal periodicals, scientific journals, farm magazines and those issued by business and industry, juveniles, and religious publications. Let's take a closer look by showing you some examples of the specialized periodical—which simply is a magazine which meets the *special* interests of human beings, whether making a living or at play on long weekends. Or it may be a tabloid newspaper doing a similar job.

There are nine major fields into which specialized magazines may be grouped for convenience in discussing them. You know one of man's earliest efforts was to find a different name for everything, as Adam had to do. So we invent new verbal pigeonholes to make communication more convenient and also because for many of us, it makes sense to be systematic.

In this book we'll consider these nine main fields of specialized publications into which we've arranged all the 215 classifications listed by Standard Rate and Data Service in its Consumer, Farm, and Business directories which form an invaluable reference authority on publications. Here are the fields and some of their stars:

There's No Place Like Home

The young bride joyfully sews the curtains for her new home, comparing them with the decoration scheme in *The American Home*. The experienced architect is designing a hundred houses for the suburban subdivision. Or maybe *you* just won a blue ribbon for your Garden Party rose at the recent flower show!

Then this is where you (and millions of Americans) come in, to the "shelter" of the home and garden family of specialized publications. Certainly you belong if you're one of the more than seven million subscribers of *Better Homes and Gardens,* or any of the other magazines devoted to making a roof and all under or around it more convenient and more lovely.

New houses are built, old ones remodeled. The battle of the crabgrass is eternal, fancy hybrid fuchsias are created. More Americans than ever in history are home-owners. And most of them are addicts of the specialized shelter publications which supply articles of advice and pages of pictures to woo the beginner and keep the veteran hooked.

Some of them go in for family service in a big way. They serve not only recipes but travel tips; they give budget advice and tell how to kill the aphids. Practical and alluringly dream-world at the same time, they keep the American dream buoyant while they keep the cash register ringing for the builder and nurseryman.

Your First Reader—the Juvenile

When Mom took you on her lap to read before bedtime, what gay pictures entranced your sleepy eyes? Ten to one, it was from the wonderful pages of *Humpty Dumpty* or the *Golden Magazine*. (If you belong to an older generation, it would have been the much loved and lamented *St. Nicholas* or *Youth's Companion*.) When you got a little older, perhaps you read *Boys' Life* or *The American Girl* for yourself—we hope, realizing that you might have gazed instead at the "comics."

In any case, juveniles opened the door for you into the wonderful world of magazines—and, significantly, juveniles are another kind of specialized periodical. Of course, there's some overlapping—many religious publications and some recreational magazines are for children. The religious juveniles, however, stress moral values as their primary interest, and the recreational juveniles stress a particular kind of recreation. The true juvenile is published to entertain and inform the young just because they *are* young, and there are about 20 of them today.

Top circulation for a genuine juvenile today climbs up to the 2 million plus of *Boys' Life*, with its built-in advantage of Boy Scout sponsorship. Other leaders in quality and quantity include the junior fashion books such as *Seventeen* and the *Scholastic* group which furnish news and comments as a classroom aid.

The epidemic of comic books, infecting the non-reader of 3 or 30, is variously estimated to range from 50 million to 90 million monthly. The first figure is from SRDS and may be conservative although more reliable. The depression of the 1930's brought the comics, which are seldom funny today, and the death of the fine old juveniles—which wasn't funny at all!

Fun and Games

Americans have more leisure than ever before and they work hard to enjoy vacation and recreation. And so they seek the specialized publications of sport and travel, of hobbies and entertainment, for suggestions to guide them on their merry way!

For most Americans, cars afford both the leading form of recreation and a means to other recreational activities. In addition, they're vehicles for major sports events and even collector cupidity. In 1965, 97 million Americans took at least one vacation trip by automobile, driving 140 billion miles in the 75 million registered passenger cars, and spending $22 billion en route.

While some recreational magazines such as *Sports Illustrated* conceivably might be called mass circulation, basically they appeal to very specific special interest in sports. So we have outdoor hunting and fishing and camping, skiing on snow and water, bird-watching, coin and bottle collecting, photography, skin-diving, you name it!—there's a specialized magazine.

Beside the magazines intended for the fan of baseball, football, pro or amateur, there is a swarm of specialized publications put out by commercial publishers to profit from fad or fancy. The entertainment area is prolific as a source of periodicals for the TV and radio audience for surely we must class them as fun and games—for most listener-viewers.

SRDS devotes 34 headings to out-and-out recreational categories. Circulations soar up to 14 million for *TV Guide*, and include quite a few with a million plus, such as *Field & Stream* or *Sports Afield, Popular Science Monthly* and *Popular Mechanics* for the how-to-do-it-er. For the movie fan, *Photoplay* provides a lure that catches more than a million, and a half-dozen other film books (as magazines are called by the trade) attract from 500 to 750 thousand buyers each.

All these specialized publications testify that Americans take their recreation seriously, spending billions on fun and games!

The Role of the Religious Magazine

Among the earliest American magazines we find the religious publication, seeking new converts and to furnish inspiration for those already in the fold. By 1825 more than 25 religious periodicals were flourishing in the United States. Today the number is close to 1,700, of which between 400 and 500 are Catholic, 200 Jewish, and the rest Protestant.

There are three major varieties of religious publications. There's the general magazine for all readers—or, at least, all Protestants, or all Jews, or all Catholics. Among such publications, dealing with news and views and stressing the latter, one would include *The Christian Century*, the *Christian Herald*, *America, Commonweal, Commentary, Catholic Digest*. Religious circulations range into the millions.

Then there's the denominational magazine such as *Presbyterian Life*, with its more than a million copies, and *Together*, the color-splashed Methodist monthly which reaches 600,000. Other leaders are *Columbia*, the publication of the Knights of Columbus, and the *Lutheran Witness*. These publications, while stressing their own creeds, all evidence modern layout and a wide variety of content—articles of opinion and interpretation, fiction and poetry, special departments.

When you went to Sunday School you got acquainted with the religious

7

juvenile, with its built-in convictions and circulation. Issued for every age group from pre-nursery to the upper teens, there is an almost infinite variety. For example, the Methodist Publishing House with its headquarters in Nashville, Tennessee, has nearly 20. It is representative of many denominational publishers, for each major church has so large a list of publications that it's efficient and economical to establish its own publishing facilities.

The Company Communicates

Company publications form the largest group of specialized publications. No man knows for sure how many company publications exist. The best current estimate would run as high as 17,000. They multiply like flies and range from little 2- by 4-inch leaflets accompanying your phone bill to "internals" for thousands of employees and "externals" for millions of customers and dealers. New companies create new products which in turn create new customers.

Among the earliest was *Harper's* which actually began as a company publication to sell books. Company publications trace their history back to the *News-Letters* of the House of Fugger, a potent financial empire of the 16th century with its headquarters in Bavaria. Internals were called "house organs" up to the 1930's—which didn't make much sense for they were neither concerned with houses or organs.

Internals often begin as little mimeographed one-page sheets and sometimes grow into highly attractive magazines with gorgeous four-color illustrations and fascinating articles about computers and kidney-beans, cabbages and kings. Large companies such as DuPont can have as many as 40 different publications. Not so incidentally, *DuPont Magazine* is one of the best to read and look at. Others which stand out include the colorful *Ford Times* and Southwestern Bell's *Scene* with its brilliant layout and spectacular design. On the beverage side, there's *Foam* of the Schaeffer Brewing Company which swirls gayly among its employees and dealers.

The Voice of Industry

Technology and industry are the twin king-pins of modern times and the industrial publications speak for them. For the vital intercommunication among the intricate complexes of industry, the industrial is essential. To inform society as a whole of the welfare and the progress of industry, the industrial furnishes a fundamental channel.

"Industrial" publication is a term which covers a multitude of periodicals basically connected with the manufacture of a product, its marketing, and all allied technical and service occupations. Often called "business" publications,

8

the industrial indeed may deal with merchandising and a wholesale or retail business—or cover the whole wide spread of a major industry.

The industrial covers the operations of an entire industry or one of its subdivisions rather than the activities of a single company. Whether relatively huge, such as steel or chemical, or small, as the toy or optical industries, each has its own specialized publications and trade association journals. Industrials probably total 2,600, command a circulation of 62 million and an even greater influence. Blue-chip advertisers crowd their pages which are produced with skilled and even lavish quality.

The Profit and Pay-check Publications

You have to be pretty specialized to earn a living in the modern world— and naturally there's a specialized publication for every specialized business and worker. Where once the self-sufficient early American chopped his own wood, drove his own horse, and butchered his own hog, nowadays he pays for someone else's skill to supply fuel, transportation, and food. So we have a host of profit and paycheck publications.

Banks and chambers of commerce keep the financial wheels turning. But there's more to business than dollars and cents; credit unions and loans are a major part of the investments and enterprise. World trade is inescapably geared to national trade. All of these, banks and business organizations, credit institutions, and international economic activity, all have their specialized publications—*The American Banker, Barron's, World Business*. Reporting on the news and trends which affect the whole spectrum of business are well-known specialized magazines such as *Fortune* and *U.S. News & World Report*. They compete with any mass magazine as the opinion shapers and leaders, they command respect in congressional halls and university classrooms. They speak for business!

Among the 80 million workers of America, labor unions have played a prominent part, although they have lagged in producing first-class magazines chiefly because their communication efforts have centered around the newspaper format. Consequently there are relatively few regular labor periodicals despite the 17 million union members.

Unions are responsible, however, for most of the labor magazines such as *The Carpenter* of the United Brotherhood of Carpenters and Joiners of America, with its circulation of nearly 470,000. Another national union, the American Federation of Musicians, publishes the *International Musician*, whose press run totals 245,000. The *Signalman's Journal* reminds us that trolley cars and trains were responsible for early specialized publications, and rail unions today publish at least six others with a total circulation of more than 600,000.

9

Professions and Occupations
Organizations and Associations

Most Americans work even if they aren't union members. They're doctors or merchants or nurses or stenographers. Most Americans belong to a social or fraternal organization. And all professions, occupations, and organizations have publications. That's Q.E.D.

One of the major qualifications for professional careers is that the individual pursue postgraduate education and lifelong learning. And one of the major means to this end is the regular reading of the professional magazines which serve the doctor, the lawyer, and every professional man and woman.

It's not surprising, therefore, to find that teachers, dentists, journalists, and all other professionals have their own specialized publications, hundreds of them, and follow them intently. Thus they keep professionally up-to-date, ever honing their skills to a keener edge. A side benefit comes with the columns of personal news—they keep in touch with former colleagues. A further advantage stems from the international content of their journals—they keep in touch with the latest Russian technique or Japanese research.

Each profession has its leading magazine, many issued by its own professional societies. Others come from major industrial research centers or are published commercially by reputable private enterprise. The physicists receive the *American Journal of Physics*, the mathematicians the *Bulletin of the American Mathematical Society*. For the lawyer there's the *American Bar Association Journal* and the state and city legal bulletins.

No profession has more publications than medicine which provides everything from *Medical Economics* to *Today's Health* to cover every facet of medical practice. More than 200 medical periodicals, many lavish in layout and ad lineage, are circulated and you'll have time to read them in your doctor's waiting room.

Every educational level from kindergarten to graduate school offers a multitude of magazines. As millions more attend school, the importance and size of the educational structure is growing like Topsy and with it, the number of educational periodicals.

The plumber may forget his tools but he doesn't forget his specialized publication. The logger and the radio repairman have their own magazines to keep up with their own jobs and today's new techniques in our fast-changing technological society. So they pore over the pages of *Plumbing, Heating, Cooling Business* or *The Northern Logger* or the *Electronic Technician/Dealer*.

"Big" government also means government publications pouring out of the Government Printing Office, for you and me, for workers in many specialized occupations, and for government employees. The Federal government employs more than three million civilians and the Armed Forces bring the total to six and a half million. When one includes specialized publications produced by and for city, county, and state employees, it's obvious that another major dimension has been added. Many private publishers also produce periodicals for civil and military personnel—for example, the *National Defense Transportation Journal, American City*, and *Public Works Magazine.*

It's often been said that Americans are great joiners. And also that they're generous. Certainly the number of social, civic, and philanthropic organizations would support any such claim. Which do you belong to—a fraternal order, service club, Greek-letter sorority, veterans group?

How many organizations do you support? How many of them publish a magazine? Here's a representative list: *The American Legion Magazine, The Elks Magazine, The Rotarian*, the *Record of Sigma Alpha Epsilon, Scouting, American Junior Red Cross News*, and the *Clubwoman* of the General Federation of Women's Clubs. Some have a million members and a million or more copies monthly. Some only a few thousand. But they all emphasize the special goals and interests which brought them together as an organization.

The Farmer and His Wife

Farm magazines were among the first specialized publications and today they number more than 200. They're published geographically, to cover state, regional, or national interests, and to meet the variations which climate and locale offer in growing tall corn or white balls of cotton. If you breed fat steers in Texas or contented dairy cows in Wisconsin, you'll want your own farm journal about folks raising critters like yours.

Leading and typical farm periodicals include *Farm Journal* and *Successful Farming, The American Hereford Journal* and the *Montana Wool Grower, Gobbles* and the *American Bee Journal*. Their circulations range from a few thousand to *Farm Journal*'s more than three million. Their content includes patterns to adorn the farm kitchen as well as highly technical formulas for artificial chemical fertilizers such as cyanamid which is composed of $CaCN_2$, $CaCO_3$, CaS, Ca_2P_2, $Ca(OH)_2$, C, R_2O_3, SiO_2, MgO, H_2O, and "combined moisture." No, you don't have to be a chemist to be a farmer but it might help!

Farm boys and girls keep active in their own organizations, and their own magazines tell the story of 4-H and Future Farmers and Future Homemakers. That's one way to keep them down on the farm!

Specialized Satisfaction

Stimulating, successful, the specialized publications we're writing about are the most vital and influential channel of American communication. Though you've not been aware of their variety and number, they've been with you,

11

part of you, daily. They shape your life and thoughts. They're part of your job. They entertain you when you relax. Sparkling, serious, satisfying your needs, spurring your dreams, the specialized publications accompany your best hours.

This is a world of constant change—therefore our circulation figures will have gone up or down while this manuscript was being printed. Some magazines may have died, others certainly will have been born. Some will come under new ownership or be merged into new groups. But this kaleidoscopic activity is one of the fascinations of specialized publications. They're alive, never static, always responsive to every change in man and his life.

We've visited briefly the nine chief continents in the whirling world of specialized publications and we hope your curiosity has been excited to explore them further in the chapters that follow. Important as they may be as a communicative cement which holds our society together, their economic and social contributions are not what you'll prize most in the long run. No, it'll be the warm memory of the glow you felt turning their pages in childhood, the thrill you knew as a teen-ager when they tantalized your thinking. Grown up now, you prize the ideas and information they furnish for your work—and at day's end, you lean back and enjoy them, relaxing in the companionship of old friends.

2. The Affluent Home and Family

THE spacious green lawn, shaded by flowering trees and cooled by the blue swimming pool, surrounds the split-level brick-and-white home. Turning smartly into the double garage is Dad, home from work and eager to get the barbecue going to begin the weekend relaxation. That's life for the affluent American family of today, stimulated to a more luxurious, lively life by the home and family magazines.

Today, with ever-upward spiraling income and the haven in the suburbs, Mr. and Mrs. Jones either have their dream house already or are dreaming of it. Five-day weeks and 8-hour days have given Bill Jones plenty of time for recreation and hobbies. Annual paid vacations and superhighways mean piling kids and gear into the car, and off they go, reeling off the scenic miles before it's home again.

Of the 58 million family households listed by the U.S. Census, 32,796,087 own their own homes. That's a high 56 per cent, and one of the best testimonials to American affluence. Another source, the 1965 Starch Consumer Magazine Report, gives an even higher percentage of 65. When you look at the home and family magazines, however, you're looking at a still more fortunate and special group of readers. *Better Homes and Gardens*, the circulation giant of the family, claims 85 per cent home ownership, with nearly 40 per cent of its families living in homes valued at $20,000 or more. Refer to the ABC audit on *Better Homes and Gardens*, illustrated in this chapter.

This especially favored class in the world's most prosperous nation has, in home and family desires, the ability to purchase quality living. With relatively

13

high income and educational levels, it can indulge in conspicuous consumption and the advertising men certainly are inclined to encourage it! And so the editorial and advertising staffs cooperate enthusiastically with each other, and the promotion department can blissfully perform merchandising miracles. To call these books "shelter" magazines, is a gross over-simplification. They deal not only with a roof and walls, but more, a great deal more as we shall see. With the ever-expanding circle of family activity, widening interests include travel and recreation as well as the more familiar home concerns of cooking, decorating, gardening. So the home and family magazines compete in content for circulation with many other specialized publications as well as the general women's magazines.

Dramatic witness to their skyrocketing rise to the circulation heights may be viewed in the performance of *Better Homes and Gardens*—150 thousand when founded in 1922, 3½ million in 1950, and nearly 7½ million in 1968. That's one of the most startling success stories of the magazine universe, comparable in every degree to the rise of *Life* or *Look*. Why did it happen? Because these home and family books not only satisfy present needs, they whet the appetite for more, and offer beautiful escape into what tomorrow will surely bring.

Better Homes and Gardens of the Meredith Corporation represents the most scintillating ascent among the four main magazines in its field, although all home publications have risen remarkably in the last 20 years. The other three are Downe's *The American Home* with 3,643,000 circulation; the Condé Nast *House & Garden*, 1,200,000; and Hearst's *House Beautiful*, 980,000.

There also are two regional magazines, covering similar content for a more limited geographical area—*Sunset* on the Pacific Coast, and *Southern Living*. More of a society than a home-family devotee, *Town & Country* still stresses house decoration and landscaped gardens, justifying its inclusion at one end of the spectrum. At $1 a copy, its price matches its intended status and 110,000 readers share its society.

Actually, to run the whole scale of home and family interest, we'd find considerable similarity in some content of *Family Circle* and *Women's Day*, as well as such outright women's magazines as *McCall's* or *Ladies' Home Journal*. They surely represent competitors for readers and advertising, but their editorial aims are more limited by sex.

Because a house is not a home unless it offers the perennial problems of black spot on the roses and crab grass among the blue, gardening becomes a natural and inevitable member of the family. As led by *Flower & Garden's* 625,000, the green-thumb boys and girls form a large and growing contingent which properly deserves consideration in this chapter.

Hobby-horse riders have all kinds of special publications of their own and

14

we've placed them in a category of their own, too, under the heading of Recreational Publications in Chapter 4. But two magazines, by name and content, are so closely allied with home and family that they deserve mention here. These are *The Family Handyman* and the *Home Craftsman*. Perhaps sewing is a similar obsession and the women's handiwork books also should be mentioned although some tend to consider it a spinster sport.

For our final notice, we've reserved a single pigeonhole for *Parents*, the huge George Hecht monument to monogamy. It has spawned a whole house of comic and juvenile publications, fittingly, with which we deal in our chapter on children's specials.

While fads and fleeting fantasies may make some magazine publication an ephemeral gamble, it seems safe to conclude that home and family are here to stay as long as man inhabits the planet, and therefore these magazines should be around quite a while.

The Big Four of Home and Family

The big four of home-family books are *Better Homes and Gardens, The American Home, House and Garden*, and *House Beautiful*. All are monthlies. The first two sell for 50 cents a copy on the newsstand; the latter two for 75 cents each. Thus there is a difference, supposedly, in income level and appeal, although in reality there is great overlapping in articles and advertising. Perhaps there's some significance in the titles—the two lower-priced magazines stress "home" while the other two use the impersonal "house."

The most venerable of the Four is Hearst's *House Beautiful* which has experienced many transformations in ownership since its origin in 1896. Notably, all the three others had their roots in the soil, for two began as garden books for the genteel amateur and the third had a horticultural devotee as its first editor (he also was a gourmet).

Editorial Content

What's the editorial content that's common to all four? Pages and pages of striking four-color photographs of beautiful kitchens, gorgeous living rooms, breathtaking bedrooms, plus a scattering of text description. Owners, in the lower-priced books, tend to anonymity, but "social names" (whatever society means today) are a most desirable criterion for the others.

Home plans are frequently woven in with the decorating interiors, and the emphasis is on the original and distinctive, definitely, rather than the usual and average. This applies not only to design, but also to the use of color—and prices. Even in the affluent society, much of the appeal for readers must be found in building fantasies akin to castles in Spain. A combination of escapism, day-dreaming, and voyeurism is smartly employed to upgrade the reader's desires.

Food is often next in space, and emphasis is on the exotic and the new—lemon-barbecued chuck steak, the avocado bacon open-faced sandwich. Nutrition is given some attention but it tends to get lost beautifully in the appetite appeal of mouth-watering, living, breathing color. Recipes, yes, but allow plenty of time and your herb shelf better be well-stocked. This observer doesn't recall any suggestions about using up the left-overs.

What red-blooded American doesn't annually imitate the Indianapolis Five Hundred, cram family and fixings into the car, and roar down Interstate 80 for the yearly vacation? Or fly off to Mexico or Paris on at least a 3-week tour? Travel and transportation are high on the editorial list, and it must be almost as tiring to think up new angles as to actually make the grand tour. But there's always home to come back to—unless you're a member of the jet set.

Purple iris and pink dogwood and white azaleas garnish the editorial pages, although humble grubbing for spurge and chickweed is less likely to command attention (weeds are big in the garden books). Again, maximum illustration and minimum text. Without four-color photographs, the editors would be bereft and nowhere is this more true than in the garden. Flower arrangements, dramatic plantings in concentrations and contrasts of massed color, but seldom much sweat.

Pages in the lower-priced books are dedicated also to home appliances and housewares, home and income management, and, a comparative few, to the child who seems to be somewhere out in the cold. In the higher-income bracket, antiques and art, music and assorted culture, are apt to be substituted. For all of these, words are frequently used as much or more than pictures. The service article is presented with serious intent. To build, buy, or rent? How much insurance? What kind of heating? "Service" is a big word in these magazines and it implies factual information of an expert nature on what, when, how much.

Unabashed merchandising tie-ins are a way of life for the home / family books. They range from elaborate full-page spreads to regular shopping guides which, sometimes, include such fanciful notions as full-length transparent black lace body stockings as well as more conventional items. Insofar as price and where-to-buy are legitimate queries to which the reader wants answers, one cannot fault this practice although it must raise questions sometimes as to where a line should be drawn.

Of editorials there is a void. If opinions are to be expressed, it'll not be in these books on any economic, political, or controversial subject. They're to supply ideas for the environment, the external, not the mind. You can't ruffle any reader by what you don't print, but the American home and family are seen in this mirror as mentally and socially unconscious.

Annuals Add

But the readers apparently can't get enough of suggestions for how they should live materially. In addition to the regular monthly issues, elaborate annuals are issued for more specialized help and comfort.

Better Homes & Gardens has seven "Idea" annuals, known as the Special Interest Publications Department and consisting of *Home Improvement Ideas* (published in August); *Home Furnishings Ideas* (September); *Christmas Ideas* (October); *Home Building Ideas* (December); *Garden Ideas* (January); *Kitchen Ideas* (February); and a federal income tax guide. These have the same size and layout, plus elaborate four-color, of the parent publication, and sell approximately 2,000,000 copies annually on newsstands only at $1.35 a copy.

House Beautiful has its "Specials:" *Building Manual, Home Remodeling, Home Decorating, House & Plans, Gardening & Outdoor Living.* They also supply house plans to readers for $25 the set, accompanied by a "Building Ideas Kit"—"a file of useful booklets from advertisers" who "qualify" for the kit if they place one-quarter-page or more advertising in three different specials within 12 months. All but *House & Plans* are semi-annuals, priced at $1.35.

The *House & Garden* "Guides" comprise three semi-annuals for building, remodeling, and decorating, plus two annuals, one for kitchen and bath and the other supplying house plans. These also sell for $1.35 and nearly a million copies are distributed of each edition.

Every potential home owner is hungry for information, while each current householder is looking for remodeling ideas, so the idea guides and specials roll continuously off the presses, with everybody happy. They supply a blend of both new and reprint material, can be produced by regularly employed staff members, and add considerable additional revenue.

How to Buy Beautifully

Looking at the ads is a pleasant pastime (and profitable, probably, to everyone concerned) for the home / family reader. They're magnificent with rainbow hues and full-page glory, and sometimes it's hard to tell where the articles end and the ads take over. Ad pages run as high as 70 per cent of total space. In fact, they're a substantial and important part of the reading appeal for these books.

Naturally the publishers know this and do their best to help both parties, the advertiser and the reader. Thoroughly, each editorial page is listed for buying data: Page 78, Teaspoon—"Belle Anne" by Anders, Linkcaster, Ind. 42810. Additionally, an advertising index often is supplied (just as in industrial publications), so you can turn to the exact pages where all the carpet ads appear.

Part of the editorial-merchandising service covers reprints and plans, from each issue, supplied at extra special charges which range from 25 cents to $25.

High in total advertising pages in all these home / family books will be found furniture, appliances, building materials, soap and detergent products, floor coverings, garden supplies, food, and beverages. Page costs range from $6,400 to $36,230 for one-page black-and-white, from $9,350 to $37,500 for four-color one-page.

Inasmuch as regional editions and split runs are provided by *House & Garden*, *The American Home* and *BH&G*, advertisers may buy for as many special regional interests as they wish, either singly or in multiple combinations.

Regional Editions Multiply

These regional editions provide not only the advertiser but also the reader with an à la carte menu to meet geographical conditions, climatic variations, and human tastes. Originating after World War II, regional editions (and split runs for advertisers, so media selection could be custom-tailored) were speedily adopted by the home / family and gardening publications. While most of the copy changed in the "regionals" was ad, some editorial pages were shifted, although relatively few.

A major advantage for the advertiser is selective placement to meet regional and seasonal preference and difference. California's ranch living and year-round flowers contrast considerably with Vermont's rugged weather and terrain. With regional editions, magazines now could compete toe-to-toe with local newspapers and radio-TV. So *Flower & Garden* blossomed out with Eastern, Mid-America, and Western editions. *Better Homes & Gardens* supplied nine standard regions and soon was offering 78 different "custom"combinations. *The American Home* also provides nine regional editions and a wide variety of split runs and combinations.

Meeting with Meredith

When meeting with Meredith prepare to be overwhelmed with facts, figures, and a cordial welcome. This major communications company on the banks of the Raccoon and Des Moines Rivers has a strategic location in the heartland of America, close to the people and convenient for distribution. The Meredith Corporation began when a 19-year-old youth, Edwin Thomas Meredith, received the "Farmer's Tribune" as a wedding present from his grandfather.

After seven years of publishing a paper, the young, energetic Iowan decided on a farming magazine and founded *Successful Farming* with the help of his wife. It *was* successful and made Meredith a national reputation, leading to his appointment as Woodrow Wilson's secretary of agriculture. (Two other Des Moines publishers of farming publications, the Wallaces, Henry C. and Henry A., also served as secretaries of agriculture. And Des Moines is the original home base for the Cowles interests who publish *Look*, *Family Circle* and *Venture*.)

A year after leaving the cabinet, in 1922, E. T. Meredith, as he signed himself, brought out a new magazine which he first called *Fruit, Garden, and Home*. Two years later, already well on its feet, the publication was re-christened *Better Homes and Gardens* and under that name it out-distanced its older competitors and climbed into top position among the home / family service books.

Today the Meredith company has become a multiple enterprise. In addition to its two magazines, it has extensive book publishing interests, a broadcasting division, thirteen book clubs, and manufactures geographical globes—a fitting product symbolic of its widespread activities. Meredith revenues in 1967 were $110,358,000, net earnings $7,007,000.

Success, however, has not spoiled Meredith or its executives. Service becomes warm hospitality when you visit Des Moines. A company car and driver were waiting for me at the airport and soon I was sitting beside the desk of Bert Dieter, editorial director of *Better Homes & Gardens*. After a hearty greeting, he had some correspondence to sign and I had a chance to look at the page and cover layouts for the current issue and 11 months to come—they covered two whole walls, a graphic daily check on what was done and what was still ahead (see the illustration for a *BH&G* lay-out).

"We're a *family* magazine," Dieter said emphatically, as he rejected my reference to "shelter" publications. "We're broader and rounder, and the description makes sense from the standpoint of editorial content and appeal. Also we're definitely interested in husbands and go after them as readers, along with their wives."

He waved a large yellow placard at me.

"This is what we try to do."

And I read, "*Better Homes & Gardens* editorial philosophy is to *serve* husbands and wives who have a serious interest in home and family as the focal point of their lives . . . and to provide this service in the form of ideas, help, information and inspiration to achieve a better home and family. INHERENT IN THIS PHILOSOPHY IS THE EDITORIAL RESPONSIBILITY TO MOVE THESE HUSBANDS AND WIVES TO *ACTION*."

I asked about that philosophy.

That brought out a memo from publisher Robert A. Burnett which stressed the way *BH&G* puts this publishing credo into practice. "People selectivity"—meaning high home ownership, above average income, high ownership of appliances and automobiles.

Of *BH&G* readers, 85 per cent own their homes. Ninety-four per cent possess one or more cars, 98 per cent an electric refrigerator, 98 per cent a TV set. More than a third live in the suburbs, and just less than another third in the city itself. More than half have children under 18. Median family income is $8,790, and 2 of every 5 *BH&G* families has an income of $10,000 or more. Women outnumber men as primary readers, 7,020,000 to 2,663,000.

BH&G families are frequent entertainers, 3 out of 5 entertain guests in a sample week, and it's very likely to have been a barbecue, for nearly three of every four have outdoor cooking facilities. They also like to travel—almost three-fourths take vacation trips, traveling a median distance of 1,770 miles.

This profile of the *BH&G* family comes from the active and energetic research division, which constantly produces questionnaires and surveys to supply editorial and advertising staffs, and the advertisers, with every drop of pertinent information.

For how it's translated into editorial content, I turned back to Bert Dieter.

"*Every* month, in *every* issue, we cover our 12 Family Service Editorial areas and that gives us the range and depth of coverage that makes *Better Homes* broader in reader appeal. Too, we think we differ from other books in the field by our stress on the *family*."

That emphasis on the family and its concerns has produced a phenomenal circulation growth for *Better Homes and Gardens*. It more than doubled its circulation between 1950 and 1968, skyrocketing from 3,509,000 to 7,250,000 copies, an increase of 206 per cent. Each decade, beginning in 1930, has shown a giant step up: 60 per cent higher from 1930 to 1940; 56 per cent gained between 1940 and 1950; 43 per cent increase from 1950 to 1960; and 50 per cent advance between 1960 and February, 1968. Few magazines can match such a record, although *House and Garden* is close with 192 per cent from 1950 to 1968. Refer to the circulation chart in this chapter.

But why—and how? That emphasis on family-centered activities must make the difference. And it does. Every month *Better Homes and Gardens* devotes extensive space to money management—the first major magazine to do so, the publishers believe. Each month there is a major section on the automobile, America's traveling home, and also on travel. Every issue furnishes information on family health and medicine. Each of the 12 main editorial areas gets this special treatment.

The editor explained how they plan it that way.

"Our 12 main areas are residential building, foods, furnishings and decoration, gardens and landscaping, kitchens and equipment, money management, family cars, home entertainment, family health, travel, sewing and crafts, education. Then we emphasize what we call 'Idea editing'—major articles which combine several of these areas. The result is a blend of ideas in architecture, decoration, landscape, kitchens, food—each flowing into the other, each benefiting the other. It's a logical, reader-oriented approach."

"We work hard at this inter-area mixing. Every month there's a meeting with each department and sometimes several, to see what they can contribute. A year in advance, the editor, managing editor, art editor, and I plan together for the succeeding 12 months. Here, these production schedules will give you the best idea how we go at it," and he handed me two sheets (which you'll find reproduced as Appendix A).

"What do you regard as your competition?" I asked.

"*Good Housekeeping, Ladies' Home Journal, McCall's,*" he said quickly, "on basic subject matter, all women's magazines. Then the service magazines —*American Home, House Beautiful, House and Garden.* Those last two surpass us in snob appeal and as escape reading."

Dieter, who was named editorial director while I was in Des Moines, is a veteran at Meredith and with *Better Homes and Gardens.* Considering his background in art and graphics, it's not surprising that *BH&G* is known as a handsome magazine. He joined the company in 1934 as a graphic designer, became art editor of *BH&G* six years later, served as art director for all Meredith publications for a number of years, then was named editor in 1960. His successor as editor, James A. Riggs, has held posts as associate editor, managing editor, and executive editor successively since 1951.

I asked Dieter how it worked to edit a magazine out in Des Moines, far away from the magazine mainstream of New York City.

"We think it's an advantage—we don't get bogged down in New York provincialism. Our staff live in their own homes, rather than apartments. They have lawns to mow, and time to work at keeping up their own properties. This is a great idea generator. We're closer together and closer to our readers."

"What do you want next?" Dieter looked at me quizzically.

"How about work from free-lancers as compared with staff . . . what proportion do you use?"

"Most of our writing is staff; they know what we want and how to go about it—it's specialty copy and that calls for specialists. We buy all our photography, using free-lancers on assignment. Many of our pictures are done here in Des Moines but we do buy much of our food photography in Chicago or on the Coast, either LA or San Francisco. And much of our art is assigned to

21

free-lancers. How about lunch? Here's Ken McDougall, our editorial promotion director, to tell you more while we eat."

So we went downstairs to the Meredith cafeteria, a bright place with chairs in bold crimson, orange, blue, and green. After lunch I carried on with McDougall and his young assistant, Robert S. Clark.

McDougall and a four-man staff have responsibility for editorial promotion of both *BH&G* and *Successful Farming*. From him, as you might expect, Meredith information flows easily and endlessly. But he's receptive to questions and I fired plenty at him.

"Primarily we try to reach the readers of advertising trade publications, through getting them to use written and picture material. We also work largely through personal contact—on my monthly trips to New York."

"How do you like that kind of long-distance commuting?"

"Oh, it's a way of life that you get used to in a hurry at Meredith. A lot of our people do it. Of course we also have regular staff people in New York. Our advertising director, Morton Bailey, is there and *Better Homes* has a seven-man editorial staff based there. But we do a lot of traveling."

McDougall's department has as its major responsibilities:

1. The corporate public relations of the Meredith Corporation.
2. The editorial promotion for *Better Homes & Gardens*, and *Successful Farming*.
3. "To serve as the catalyst for developing circulation and editorial promotion. . . ."
4. Promotion of special articles or issues of the magazines.
5. Support for advertising and circulation promotion.

"How does this work in actual operation?" I asked McDougall.

"Special arrangements have been made for us to obtain from *BH&G* or *Successful Farming* the specific editorial plans for forthcoming issues up to eleven months prior to issue date and then again six months prior to issue date. Using this information and working with the editors a detailed editorial promotion plan is developed."

This also involves planning promotion to be carried out in cooperation with circulation and advertising promotion divisions which, McDougall explained, are separate from his own.

"One of our major objectives," McDougall emphasized, "is building stature and authority for the magazines—effort's made to develop editorial excitement for each individual issue. In virtually all our promotion efforts a focused rifle technique, rather than shotgun, is used. Specific targets are selected and zeroed-in on."

My next visit was with Ray Deaton, research associate, surrounded by reports and surveys on all sides, alert and obviously absorbed in his work, eagerly anticipating my questions and answering them with enthusiasm.

"My job's information-gathering for the whole company—reader interest studies, non-reader interest studies, ad surveys on recent purchases, mail questionnaires, the whole works, you know, content and even suggestion surveys. Here, this will give you an idea—" and he handed me a sheaf of reports.

I glanced at them and put them aside to study more carefully when I wasn't interviewing. You'll see one reproduced in this chapter, a reader questionnaire with accompanying letter which ends, "We are counting on your help, and as a small token of our appreciation we are sending you a crisp new dollar bill." Then there was one, 57 pages long, on "Recent Purchasers of Power Lawn Mowers." The cover of another read "Facts . . . Facts . . . Facts . . . Facts . . . Facts . . . Facts . . ." and that's just what Deaton was pouring forth.

"Our field work is done by independent services although we do spot-checking ourselves by phone. And we get some results by tying in with promotion. For research on teen-agers, we offer reduced rates on our cookbooks through home ec teachers, for example."

After a lot more question-and-answer, I thanked this intensely curious man who gathers information so systematically (and statistically), and went to see Jim Riggs, the just-named *BH&G* editor. To my pleasure I found a man as interested in words and putting them together as I was, an editor vitally interested in writing.

"Fortunately, most of our articles are done by our own staff members and they're specialists and know what they're writing about and how to write it. Still, there's quite a bit of rewrite and revision, to tighten up, to get clarity, to fit. But that's what it's all about, of course. Any professional knows it and is prepared to work over his material."

"Where do you get your writers?"

Riggs shook his head as if perplexed and a little resigned.

"That's one of our real problems. Mostly we develop our own—we take them from colleges, from other magazines sometimes, sometimes from free-lance ranks. Each department is, of course, a blend of subject specialists (architects, interior designers, horticulturists, home economists, etc.) and writers who are there to put sparkle into the words. Some of the specialists write, others do not. Some of the writers become technicians in their fields after several years.

"Most of our articles are planned and written to carry out a theme or idea for a particular issue. It's got to tell something, to say it in words the reader will understand, and, hopefully, so he or she will do something about it in their own home. We have lots of lead time so our writers can work months ahead on an idea—but they're still writing against a deadline."

After lunch with Riggs, I was driven out to the huge Meredith printing plant, 11 acres of production under a single roof, on a green spread of 106 acres along the Des Moines River. The building with several additions already since 1959 represents a cost of $7,300,000 but the complicated equipment inside would take $30,000,000 to replace. Computers are extensively used to meet production and distribution. See the production schedules in the Appendix for an example of meticulous planning.

With the skilled guidance of Bob Jolley, production and purchasing manager for the magazine publishing division, I toured the plant, following the " U "-shaped production flow which makes possible the printing of 100 million books, magazines, and publications every year. Eleven hundred printers and pressmen work in the temperature-controlled rooms with ceilings 28 to 40 feet above the floor to allow headroom for the huge presses. Everything is color-keyed, including the walls, to pastel shades of gray, green, and tan.

The skill and efficiency of the Meredith printing division has necessarily kept pace with the expansion of the Meredith Publishing Company. *BH&G*'s ad revenues for 1966 were up more than 44 per cent over fiscal 1964, *Successful Farming*'s ad revenues reached a record high in 1966 also, advancing for the fifth consecutive year. But it all comes back to the readers whom they serve— and, the quiet, confident competence of the Meredith people.

The Competition

Bright with color, flourishing lavish full-page pictures, the three other chief contenders for home / family circulation offer the reader much the same menu—home building and decoration, good food and lovely gardens. While a cost differential does exist between *BH&G* and *The American Home* and the higher-priced *House & Garden* and *House Beautiful*, it's certainly not too apparent in content.

One of the differences is that "names" are used in *House Beautiful* copy; also in *House & Garden*. The house is that of Mr. and Mrs. Jonathan Lavolette of Greenwich, Conn. There tend to be more rooms and more provision for guests and entertaining. Merchandise carries more expensive price tags, although there is considerable duplication of advertisers.

Many magazines had served the American home, starting in the 19th century, although they really achieved wide acceptance in the middle of the next century. *Household* was a Capper Publication with a going circulation of more than 2,600,000 when it suspended. Curtis bought the subscription list from

Capper in 1958 and also purchased *American Home*, which had started out as *Garden Magazine*. Beset with financial problems, in 1968 Curtis sold *American Home* (and *Ladies' Home Journal*) to Downe Communication, headed by Ed Downe Jr. Downe also operates the Sunday newspaper magazine, *Family Weekly*, radio stations and CATV systems, and has a 32 per cent interest in Bartell Media Corporation.

The *American Home* proclaims on its cover that it's for "Active Young Homemakers," and the contents bear out the claim. There are always two or three features addressed especially to the youthful wife, and the general tone is lighter. Today it can be bought as an advertising combination with *Ladies' Home Journal*, but also affords multiple split-runs of its own and nine regional editions.

House and Garden plays up entertaining and party-giving, apparently in the Condé Nast manner of its one-time owner. It's an entertaining sidelight to note that it, along with most of the Condé Nast magazines, is printed at the mammoth Meredith printing plant in Des Moines under the same roof as *BH&G*. Royal blue presses distinguish the Condé Nast section from the pearl-gray giants which produce the host's publications. Here is a unique facet of modern competition, the sharing of costly production facilities by business rivals, a practice increasingly common among both magazines and newspapers.

Ideas for living are the appeal of *House & Garden*.

"You'll love the every-day usefulness of *House & Garden*!" runs the title of a promotional piece, which declares, "You'll use *House & Garden* when making your daily decorating decisions . . . when you plan a meal . . . when you remodel . . . every time you pot a plant."

Dating back to 1901, *House & Garden* was purchased by Nast in 1909. From the beginning it was intended for the well-to-do and Nast, himself of the social set, kept its content at a level of luxury. It offers split-runs and regional editions in six geographic areas. Today *House & Garden* belongs to the Newhouse communications empire which took control of Condé Nast Publications in 1959.

Major publishing interests are closely involved in the home family field with Hearst in contention with Meredith, Newhouse, and Downe. Founded in 1896, *House Beautiful* was published by The Atlantic Monthly Company until the 1930's when Hearst bought and combined it with *Home and Field*, a similar publication. *House Beautiful* "is a buying guide for the home, where quality families turn for ideas and inspiration. . . . Every issue explores the good life with timely, informative, imaginative features ranging from architecture and decorating to entertaining, music and travel."

Merchandising service is the aim of *House Beautiful*'s monthly *Advance*

25

Retail News which is distributed to six thousand stores. The magazine especially stresses its influence on trade channels of distribution, operating through advisory boards and panels which report on trends.

Its readership level may be seen in its advertising statements that *House Beautiful* readers own homes averaging $33,154 in value, that their median income is $11,895, that the median cost of their decorating projects is $1,944. That's on the upper rungs of the economic ladder, close to the high-living *Town & Country*.

Special Living

If you subscribe to *Town & Country*, you're one of the beautiful people, to use a phrase of *Vogue*'s, another but more fashion-oriented medium of high society . . . high primarily in conspicuous consumption. It's perhaps paradoxical that William Randolph Hearst, the popularizer of much mass journalism, also liked to dabble in class publications. Born way back in 1846, *Town & Country* came into Hearst's hands in the 1920's and, today as then, it follows its original design for the "well-born, the rich and perhaps the able."

While it's not a basic competitor of the home / family group, *Town & Country* co-exists on the upper fringes, for its pages show lavish homes and extensive grounds along with the journeys to exotic hideaways on Carribean islands, and candid shots of party life among the refugee princes. With a circulation range around 110,000, it illustrates how the one-time social four hundred have evolved in the late twentieth century.

Two geographical regions have developed their own ways of living into a special style in today's U.S.A., one by influence of climate and the other as an heirloom of tradition. So they have their own home / family books in *Sunset* for the American Far West, and *Southern Living* for Dixie Land.

Sunset was stimulated into success by L. W. Lane, who had learned his publishing at Meredith and sought to apply it for himself, as other one-time *BH&G* staffers have done. Originated as an external promotion by the Southern Pacific railroad, *Sunset* was purchased by Lane in 1928 and he built it into a regional home / family magazine which had won 863,766 circulation by 1968. *Sunset* calls itself "The Magazine of Western Living" and serves the residents of eight Western states and Hawaii through four editions "so that contents may be localized within the Western region. . . . The publication is staff written, with the active, higher-income Western homeowner always in mind."

Not only is *Sunset* Western-oriented, it even provides a subscription bonus for Western readers who pay only $3 a year compared with the $5 charged elsewhere. Lane's original policy was to "figure out a regional service . . . not compete with national magazines." *Sunset*, he said, would emphasize four fields of editorial content—Western gardening, cooking, travel, and home building. And in its own home, *Sunset* practices its preachment, occupying a rambling adobe dwelling in Menlo Park, California, which contains four test kitchens along with the customary offices, photo studios, and lunchroom. Around it are seven flowering acres, including a half-mile "Pacific Coast Garden," as setting.

Southern Living is allied with *The Progressive Farmer*, of Birmingham, Alabama, and reaches 411,408 readers in the deep South with its monthly articles and photographs. *The Progressive Farmer* had a women's department, titled "The Progressive Home" which was given a new name, "Southern Living," in 1963. Two years later, the board of directors set up a planning committee for a completely new publication which would make *Southern Living* a magazine in its own right. The charter issue made its debut in February, 1967, carrying 92 pages of editorial and advertising in an initial print order of 300,000 copies. A little more than a year later, circulation had climbed to 509,000.

As a regional family service book, *Southern Living* was an instant success, featuring Southern travel, cooking, fashions, homes and gardens, as well as Dixie personalities and cities. As the publishers declared, "The South has had no regional magazine of its own—no spokesman for its brilliant industrial progress, for those responsible for its accelerated programs of education, its bountiful endowment of vacation facilities, no widespread medium to tell of its homes, landscaping, history, and culture. There has been no voice to speak effectively and eloquently for it."

Southern Living has become such a voice—for the White South. You have to search to find any mention of the Negro. But the South where the living is easy and affluent has found a magazine to present this culture.

Home or interior decorating, one theme prominent in most family service books, also attracts commercial attention. *Decor* is one of three periodicals dedicated especially to decorating accessories such as picture frames, wall hangings and racks, plaques. One of the five Commerce Publishing Company Publications of St. Louis, *Decor* dates back to 1880 and has a 7,571 paid circulation. It's of special interest to us because its assistant editor is Gretchen Schmitz, one of our graduates who also has served as president of the St. Louis affiliate of the International Council of Industrial Editors and as an editor of Pet Milk Company magazines. Another Commerce Publications assistant editor for a while was Jo Rukavina, who also went to her duties directly from college and served on *Life Insurance Selling* and *Club Management*. *Decor* is edited chiefly for retail dealers as a "how-to" merchandising book of suggestions and ideas. Its competitors are *Gifts & Decorative Accessories*, a Geyer-McAllister periodical, and Haire's tabloid newspaper, *Gift & Tableware Reporter*.

Roses and Green Grass

Most homeowners succumb to gardening soon after finding their house surrounded by ground which, presumably, may support grass, flowers, and trees. Whether equipped with green thumb or no, either the man or woman of the house and sometimes both find themselves eventually possessed with an urge to grow. Your lawn must be greener than your neighbors or your trees higher or your roses redder. While it's not necessarily competitive with humans, it does become a constant struggle with mildew, mites, and crabgrass.

Herein lies one of the chief promotional values of the garden book—advice from experts on how to win the war. Or maybe you want to know when to prune the spirea. And certainly you hope to have the latest hybrid tea blooming in scarlet and gold magnificence in your rosebed. Garden books are how-to-do-it hobby publications and it's not surprising to find them wholly devoted to the joys of peat moss and compost heap when the home / family books emphasize gardening so prominently.

In circulation, *Flower & Garden* leads the seven magazines listed by Standard Rate & Data Service with its 625,000 circulation and three regional editions. It's natural to find these periodicals stressing special editions on the basis of geography and climate for, of course, the broad expanse of the United States offers many variations.

Relatively modern in birth, *Flower & Garden* began in Kansas City in 1957. Averaging about 52 pages an issue, the cover is a superb four-color photograph of purple-blue grape hyacinths bravely challenging the white crystals of a late snowdrift—or some similar flowering triumph. Inside will be seasonal features for spring or autumn and a variety of departments featuring trees, gardening books, the beginner. Always an article on sensational newcomers among the chrysanthemums or dahlias. Pictures run largely to black-and-white except for a single page in living color. Advertising is extensive and, ranging from lawn tractors to nursery paeans for fragrant carnations, attracts the aficionado's eye as much as the editorial copy.

A trio of garden magazines, all with more than 250,000 circulation, are closely grouped as contenders. *The Home Garden Magazine* actually claims more advertising pages than *Flower & Garden* and has a 444,352 circulation. It is one of the senior publications in this field, going back to 1914. *Organic*

Gardening and Farming stresses that it's primarily a man's magazine for gardeners with an average of 2.7 acres to till. *Popular Gardening & Living Outdoors* is published by Holt, Rinehart and Winston, the book people, and, as its title indicates, gives special emphasis to outdoor living.

Major organizations with thousands of members are devoted to gardening and naturally they publish magazines for these specially interested readers. Thus we have the *American Rose Magazine*, official publication of the American Rose Society; *The Gardener*, official publication of the Men's Garden Clubs of America; and *Horticulture*, the organ of the Massachusetts Horticultural Society ever since 1904.

All of these are, in a special way, hobby and recreation magazines and it is not by chance that *Flower & Garden* is a subsidiary of Modern Handcraft Publications.

Home How-To-Do-It

While much of the content of how-to-do-it books such as *Popular Mechanics* concerns the home craftsman, there are magazines which give primary attention to the handyman around the house. Actually one calls itself *The Family Handyman* and it guarantees 500,000 circulation for its tips and hints on how to make or fix anything in your home. Then there is the *Home Workshop* and the *Workbench*. That latter is published by a Modern Handcraft subsidiary as a companion to its *Flower & Garden*. Established in 1946, its circulation is 368,566 and its editors describe it as "a do-it-yourself home improvement and woodworking magazine edited primarily for do-it-yourself home owners." It includes a woman's page. They assert that their average reader spends $1,300 a year on additions, alterations, repairs, and replacements as compared with $283 by the usual homeowner.

The Folks

The ad says: "When making up your list, remember that families with children spend more for virtually all products than any other market! 135 per cent more for homes, 79 per cent more for food, 72 per cent more for home furnishings and equipment, 76 per cent more for cars."

This little reminder from *Parents' Magazine* that two cannot live as cheaply as one, if nature takes its course, constitutes the fundamental element in the home / family universe. It also is testimony to the triumph of George H. Hecht's idea—"There are magazines devoted exclusively to the raising of cattle, hogs, dogs, flowers, and what not, but until now none on the most important work of the world—the rearing of children."

29

Whereupon he promptly remedied that lack in 1926 by creating *Parents'*
Magazine (originally called *Children, The Magazine for Parents*). Child care,
marriage problems, housing, family entertainment, and travel—all are part of
the home environment. The line on the circulation chart climbed rapidly and
steadily until today *Parents'* guarantees two million circulation. It states that
the magazine, regarded as a scriptural must in many a home, reaches one of
every 10 U.S. homes with children, and that it has the highest percentage of
women readers in the 18–34 age group among all women's shelter, store,
general monthly, and weekly magazines.

Today Parents' Magazine Enterprises also encompasses children's magazines and toy-making, books and book clubs, all eloquent witness to the biological urge, and the strong likelihood that home and family will flourish so
long as the human race endures.

Serving the Family

Despite hippie revolts and rebels against conventional matrimony, marriage has been around a while and it seems likely that the family will endure for
some time as a social institution. Confident of this, the family service, the
house and home and garden books, are likely to be around for a while, too.
Few—if any—other general or specialized magazines have seen such soaring
circulation gains and, unless the bottom falls out of the birds and the bees and
the baby business, they'll continue climbing.

BETTER HOMES & GARDENS

(Established 1922)
PUBLISHED MONTHLY BY
MEREDITH PUBLISHING COMPANY
1716 LOCUST STREET, DES MOINES, IOWA 50303

Magazine Publisher's Statement

Subject to audit by Audit Bureau of Circulations, 123 N. Wacker Drive, Chicago, Ill. 60606

FOR 6 MONTHS ENDING DECEMBER 31, 1967
This publication is not the official organ of any association.

Class, Industry or Field Served: A home and family service magazine.

1. AVERAGE PAID CIRCULATION FOR 6 MONTHS ENDING DECEMBER 31, 1967:

Subscriptions:
Individual 6,433,923
Bulk - See Paragraph 14(a) 3,953
Mail Subscriptions Special - See Paragraph 14(b) 356
Average Total Number of Subscriptions **6,438,232**
Single Copy Sales:
Through Retail Outlets 836,494
Through Boys ....
Bulk and All Other ....
Average Total Number of Single Copy Sales **836,494**
AVERAGE TOTAL PAID CIRCULATION INCLUDING BULK **7,274,726**

Average Total Paid Circulation Excluding Bulk 7,270,773
Average Total Unpaid Distribution (audited as to total only) 110,024

2. PAID CIRCULATION (Total of subscriptions and single copy sales) & UNPAID DISTRIBUTION BY ISSUES:

Issue	Paid	Unpaid	Issue	Paid	Unpaid	Issue	Paid	Unpaid

(See reverse side.)

3. PAID CIRCULATION BY POPULATION GROUPS based on October, 1967 issue:

October, 1966 issue used in establishing percentages.   (For Canada, see reverse side.)
Total paid circulation of this issue was 1.21% less than average total paid circulation for period.

METROPOLITAN AREAS	Number of Areas	Subscriptions	%	Single Copy Sales	%	TOTAL	Copies % of U. S.	Population % of U. S.
1. New York Consolidated Over 10,000,000	1	360,259	5.70	51,356	8.13	411,615	5.92	8
2. Chicago Con., Los Angeles, Philadelphia, Detroit 3,000,000 - 9,999,999	4	694,605	10.99	89,510	14.17	784,115	11.28	12
3. 1,500,000 - 2,999,999	7	522,060	8.26	64,306	10.18	586,366	8.43	9
4. 750,000 - 1,499,999	19	768,553	12.16	76,498	12.11	845,051	12.16	11
5. 300,000 - 749,999	50	971,435	15.37	94,753	15.00	1,066,188	15.34	13
6. 50,000 - 299,999	132	845,661	13.38	85,278	13.50	930,939	13.39	12
Number of Areas	213							
TOTAL METROPOLITAN		4,162,573	65.86	461,701	73.09	4,624,274	66.52	65
Number of Counties	420							

NON-METROPOLITAN AREAS	No. of Counties							
Counties with population:								
7. Over 50% Urban	509	800,786	12.67	77,382	12.25	878,168	12.63	12
8. 37.5% - 49.9% Urban	418	494,882	7.83	40,744	6.45	535,626	7.70	8
9. 25% - 37.4% Urban	443	367,212	5.81	24,636	3.90	391,848	5.64	6
10. Under 25% Urban	1,313	494,882	7.83	27,225	4.31	522,107	7.51	9
TOTAL NON-METROPOLITAN	2,683	2,157,762	34.14	169,987	26.91	2,327,749	33.48	35
Unclassified								
U. S. TOTAL	3,103	6,320,335	100.00	631,688	100.00	6,952,023	100.00	100

Population data from 1960 Census. Metropolitan Areas are SMSA's as revised in 1964.

25

Miniature lay-outs for *Better Homes and Gardens*; courtesy of Meredith Corporation.

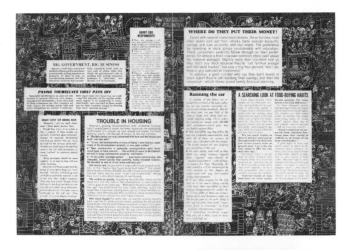

WE'D LIKE TO SEND YOU

A NEW DOLLAR BILL

WITH NO STRINGS ATTACHED

Reader interest questionnaire for *Better Homes and Gardens*; courtesy of Meredith Corporation.

BETTER HOMES & GARDENS - PAGES OF EDITORIAL

CLASSIFICATION*	February			CUMULATIVE YEAR TO DATE (Jan.-Feb.)				68 Goal
	1967	1968	Page Change	1967	1968	Page Change	1968 Percent	Percent
500 Building	20.2	7.4	-12.8	28.4	14.2	-14.2	11.0%	19.0%
510 Architecture	8.0	4.0	-4.0	14.1	10.3	-3.8	8.0	- -
520 Mat'ls, Mod'n, Maint, Repairs	11.9	3.4	-8.5	13.1	3.9	-9.2	3.0	- -
540 Financing & Insurance	.3	- -	-.3	.8	- -	.8	- -	- -
700 Children	.5	- -	-.5	.6	- -	-.6	- -	.5
801 Gardening & Flowers	8.8	8.0	-.8	10.0	15.7	5.7	12.2	9.0
900 Food & Nutrition	16.6	13.3	-3.3	26.7	26.6	-.1	20.6	21.5
1100 Home Furnishing and Management	13.5	27.0	13.5	38.9	44.2	5.3	34.2	29.0
1110 Appliances, Equipment, Housewares	3.0	10.2	7.2	4.4	10.4	6.0	8.0	6.5
1120 Tableware	1.5	1.2	-.3	2.0	1.7	-.3	1.3	1.5
1130 Decorating & Home Furnishings	7.6	7.2	-.4	30.3	23.7	-6.6	18.4	18.0
1150 Homemaking and Home Management	1.4	8.3	6.9	2.2	8.4	6.2	6.5	3.0
1300 Travel & Transportation	3.8	6.0	2.2	15.4	9.3	-6.1	7.2	9.5
1310 Travel	.2	4.1	3.9	10.8	4.1	-6.7	3.2	7.0
1320 Transportation	3.6	2.0	-1.6	4.6	5.2	.6	4.0	2.5
1322 Automobile, Trailer (inc. Highways)	3.0	2.0	-1.0	4.0	3.4	-.6	2.7	- -
600 Business & Industry	- -	.1	.1	- -	.1	.1	.1	- -
1000 Health & Medical Science	2.2	2.0	-.2	4.2	3.4	-.8	2.7	3.0
1200 Sports, Recreations & Hobbies	.2	.3	.1	.3	.5	-.2	.4	1.0
1500 Cultural Interests	.2	.2	- -	.2	.2	- -	.2	.5
1600 General Interest	7.3	3.6	-3.7	10.9	7.7	-3.2	6.0	3.5
1603 Insurance & Savings	3.8	1.9	-1.9	6.1	4.4	1.7	3.4	- -
1700 Miscellaneous	2.6	3.0	.4	5.1	5.8	.7	4.5	3.5
100 National Affairs	- -	- -	- -	- -	- -	- -	- -	- -
200 Foreign & International Affairs	- -	- -	- -	- -	- -	- -	- -	- -
300 Amusements	- -	- -	- -	- -	- -	- -	- -	- -
400 Beauty, Grooming,Toiletries	.4	- -	-.4	.5	.1	-.4	.1	- -
1400 Wearing Apparel & Accessories	1.2	.9	-.3	1.5	1.3	-.2	1.0	- -
1800 Fiction & Stories	- -	- -	- -	- -	- -	- -	- -	- -
TOTAL EDITORIAL	77.4	71.9	-5.5	142.6	129.1	-13.5	- -	- -
TOTAL MAGAZINE	167.0	158.0	-9.0	285.0	260.0	-25.0	100.0%	100.0%

* All main classes and sub-classes deemed worth listing - - there are many sub-classes not shown which have no entry or a very small one.

Source: The Lloyd H. Hall Company.

Cumulative summary of editorial content based on the survey by the Lloyd H. Hall Company; courtesy of Meredith Corporation.

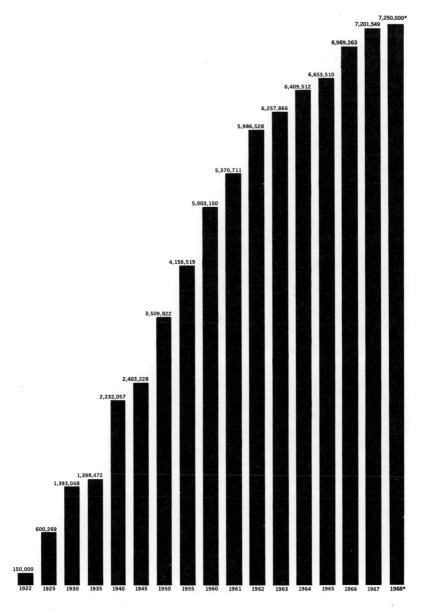

Circulation growth chart for *Better Homes and Gardens*; courtesy of Meredith Corporation.

Better Homes and Gardens cover. Copyright, June 1968, Meredith Corporation.

3. The Juvenile Revolution

TRANSFORMED more remarkably than Alice's world when she walked through the looking glass, specialized publications for children have undergone a sweeping twentieth century revolution. Once upon a time there were *St. Nicholas* and *Youth's Companion*, class magazines for children of the middle and upper middle class income and educational levels. Lovingly remembered, they have long since departed this life. Instead we have *Humpty Dumpty* and *Batman*, *Seventeen* and *Mad*.

Today's magazine Disneyland for children has six main regions—the true child's weekly or monthly; the teen-age guide to cosmetics, dress, and dating; the entertainment-fan publication; the youthful religious publication which chiefly stresses the church; the educational juvenile; and the so-called comic which rarely is comic. After briefly considering their ancestors, let's explore these regions and their main landmarks.

The religious juvenile of today, although increased in number and circulation, is the direct descendant of periodicals which flourished through the 19th century. Today's religious juvenile is most likely to be part of a carefully planned curriculum for church schools, efficiently organized to meet church and educational objectives, and so we defer consideration of them to Chapter 5, where they properly belong.

Glory That's Gone

Like many another nostalgic child of another generation, it's tempting to look back and recall fondly the wonderful stories and illustrations of

31

magazines that are gone. It may be realistic, at the same time, to realize that these were relatively limited in circulation—and the comic book of today reaches many more children, for good or bad, than the dear departed.

St. Nicholas was founded in 1873 and had a long and, chiefly, happy life until 1930 when, after going through a variety of ever-more-mournful vicissitudes, it began a death-bed scene which, like Camille's, dragged on for 13 years. In its good days, it was very, very good, with such firsts as Kipling's "Jungle Book" and "Little Lord Fauntleroy" and "Uncle Remus" and illustrators such as Frederic Remington and Howard Pyle. Its young readers, some of whom like Stephen Vincent Benet and Rachel Field would become famous in their own right, contributed verse and brief stories and *St. Nicholas* was a cherished member of the family.

While *Youth's Companion*, a New England sprout of 1827, never quite got over its Bostonian birth, it served outdoor adventure and historical tales that appealed to a wide age range and reached a top circulation of a half-million. It died in the depression year of 1929, sold to its chief competitor, *American Boy*, which, after a flourishing existence for 30 years, also succumbed to advertising malnutrition after struggling on for another decade.

Although modern juveniles have piled up mass circulation figures, do they command the love and admiration of their older cousins? However, an accurate observer must admit that teen-age girls religiously follow the ads of *Seventeen*, that comics are saved and traded, and that today's juveniles may be as mesmerized by their magazines as their parents were yesterday. The modern juvenile is efficiently and often, attractively, produced with a publishing formula and a market and computerized calculations. Too often the efficiency shows and all seems a little contrived.

If this is so, it is because the modern juvenile is part of a technological society in which mass communications pursue mass audiences, edit with an "editorial mix," and measure success by millines. The modern juvenile also suffers from a culture which pushes the sub-teen and teen-ager into adult modes and manners. The gradeschool girl uses her mother's lipstick and the mother her miniskirt—and the sub-teen and teen magazines participate in precocious mating.

Mass circulation magazines such as *Life* reach out and down for younger readers and successfully steal many of them away from the juveniles. Finally, in revolt against the premature and promiscuous mixing of the ages, the teen-agers seek to declare their independence and taste in their own esoteric world of *Mad* and hero worship of the current movie or "big beat" idol. All these cross- and counter-currents produce a publishing scene that shifts continually like a kaleidoscope. To understand this constant confusion, let's look at the magazines themselves. From them we may gain some understanding.

The Child's Magazine

In this topsy-turvy world, *Humpty Dumpty* reigns and *Jack and Jill* climb but never come tumbling down. These two, along with *The Golden Magazine* and *Highlights for Children*, are the publications which most parents choose for their children as first readers. The age range is 2 to 12, and some 17 magazines in all compete to entertain the child. These publications, with psychological guidance, put their trust in their child-like qualities and shun the quasi-adult world of their teen-age siblings.

Curtis Publishing of Philadelphia gave birth to *Jack and Jill* in 1938. It started off as a lusty infant with 40,000 copies, a monthly without advertising, and by 1968 had grown to 868,616 and had opened its pages to ads.

Along with *Highlights for Children* and *The Golden Magazine*, these publications with the nursery-rhyme names make a colorful show of rainbow-hued pictures, simple stories, catchy verse, and a variety of short articles. Typical contents will include a how-to-make a playful puppy from pipe cleaners and a wooden ice cream spoon, or plans for a circus party, or collecting insects. Plus lots and lots of pictures on every page. Painless learning is carefully stirred in by consulting educationalists. Chief problem is to have something for every age in the wide span of readers sought. Chief recipe is bright and light entertainment, with some spoon feeding, carefully sugared, of knowledge.

Back in 1926, a social worker named George J. Hecht, decided parents are people and deserved a publication. Oddly enough he first called it *Children*, "The Magazine for Parents," but changed the name more appropriately to *Parents' Magazine* three years later. Its success (see Chapter 2) spawned new members of the Hecht family. *Your New Baby*, one of half-a-dozen infant periodicals, begins with the cradle (or earlier). With the first steps and falling down comes *Humpty Dumpty*, and Hecht has built its circulation to more than a million.

Highlights, begun in 1946, is the most pedagogical in editing with an impressive chart of learning benefits as a guide to each issue, plus an accompanying roster of advisory editors. Parents have been impressed to the extent of buying it for almost a million children and its adless pages and non-newsstand distribution (and appearance in doctors' offices) are intentionally maintained to cultivate its prestige.

Golden Magazine, the youngest of the group, is a combined project of talents assembled through the years by its major owner. As a relative newcomer born in 1964, *Golden Magazine*, published by the well-known producers of the Golden Books, got off to a very fast start and four years later, its circulation was a half-million and climbing. Its parent firm is Western Publishing

Company, which also owns the Whitman Publishing Company and Gold Key Comics. *Golden Magazine* has picked the 7- to 12-year-old as its reader, whereas the other three also include a lower age level.

To establish the buying influence of their young readers and thus attract advertisers, *Golden Magazine* conducts a series of mail questionnaires to which boys and girls themselves reply, giving their brand preferences (see the sample quiz from "Cracky," a trade-marked character from the book).

These four also have quite a few companions, in publishing, of which the most prominent for the primary ages are *Child Life, Children's Digest* (also a Hecht product), and *Children's Playmate Magazine.* While strictly an organization publication, the *American Junior Red Cross News* is edited for primary readers although it reaches up to the 12-year group. Another juvenile organization periodical is *The Modern Woodmen Magazine*, issued bi-monthly for children 6 to 16.

From time to time, nature and wild life magazines for children have been issued by museums or organizations to satisfy the curiosity of youngsters about birds and bees. One of the most colorful of these is *Ranger Rick's Nature Magazine*, published by the National Wildlife Federation. With simple stories and full-color photographs, it appears 10 times a year. Another is *Nature and Science*, published 18 times annually by the American Museum of Natural History for fourth- to sixth-graders, which presents basic scientific theory and fact with attractive articles related to every-day life.

Forming a special family of juvenile publications are the Scholastics, eight magazines for junior-senior high school students. They're intended to mix learning with entertainment, featuring movies, records, TV, cars, hobbies, fashions, dating advice, and sports—and also supplying information on current events in world and national news along with such academic subjects as science, English, and the arts. Beginning with one publication in 1920, the group now includes *Senior Scholastic, World Week, Practical English, Scholastic Scope, Senior Science, Co-Ed, Junior Scholastic, Science World, Newstime*, and *Graduation Annual*. The publishers state that the magazines now are used in 80 per cent of the nation's high schools and have a paid circulation of 5,750,000. *Scholastic Roto* also is issued as a high school supplement for school papers and reportedly has a circulation of 1,785,550.

Bridging the sub-teen and young teen groups is another George Hecht publication, *Young Miss*, intended for girls 9 to 14. *Young Miss*, which formerly was "Calling All Girls," was founded in 1955 and has a circulation of 377,778. It features "Fun, Fashions, and Good Looks" and its exuberant cover personifies the message, along with articles on "How to Talk to Boys" and "You can be Miss Teenage America."

34

The Teen-Age Island

When you're in your teens, it's an island with its own customs and conventions or non-conventions, dress, language, and heroes. Nobody knows this
better than the 30-million modern teen-agers in the United States. They've also
had it impressed upon them by the modern merchandiser who seeks to capture
the $12-billion bonanza which he helps to create.

The island is divided by nature into two sexes, each of which follows to a
marked degree its own magazines. It also is divided demographically by family
background and occupation, income and educational categories.

The revolving island of teen magazines spins on two levels, upper, commercial and conventional, as contrasted with lower, sensational and full of
kicks. The upper level is chiefly for girls and is full of fashions, facial and
bodily, and the morals, modes, and manners of being a teen-age girl. The
sensational other world is inhabited by movie star fan books, recording
star fan books, confession stories, and was rocketed into whirling orbit by
Elvis Presley in the 1950's. Then it really took off into outer space with the
Beatles.

One authority (as a magazine writer of sensation) has estimated that 70
to 80 magazines with a total circulation of 21 million copies appear monthly
for the teeny-boppers. She figures that at 30 cents a copy, this works out to
$75,000,000 that teen-agers spend annually on magazines alone—not counting
the comics.

Bigger and Better

Teen-age girls from the middle class and up have pledged allegiance to the
Girl Scouts or Campfire Girls, even as their brothers or boy-friends are Boy
Scouts. Such organizations have active publications, *American Girl* and *Boys'
Life*. The Girl Scout monthly goes to a million early teens, and *Boys' Life* has
a circulation of 2,590,310. The Scouting magazines stress character-building
and youthful citizenship. Testimony to the economic nature of membership
may be found in *Boys' Life* promotional claim that 44 per cent of its readers
are in families with incomes of $8,000 and higher, with 78 per cent living in
privately-owned homes.

Seventeen sets the pace for girls (1,494,318 circulation), with *Ingenue* and
'Teen coming up fast. Somewhere in there also is *Mademoiselle* which, while
aimed at 18 to 25, has a very sizeable following among the younger teens, as
do *Glamour* and the other women-fashion publications. Listen to the *Seventeen*
story, as told promotionally (for it applies in some degree to the whole group).

"... edited for the nation's teen-age girls. Feature articles run the gamut

35

from reports on high school literary magazines and teen drinking to a discussion of getting along with parents. Regular monthly departments include fashion, beauty, entertainment, home, food, etiquette, 'You the Reader,' teen news and contributions, and a celebrity 'talk to teens' series. Monthly columns include reviews of new movies, TV shows, recordings and books, travel, college and careers.

"The Country is Growing Younger . . . Half the population of the United States is 25 years old and under . . . 40 per cent is under 20!!! . . . every issue is read by more than 5,700,000 teen-age girls in the U.S. . . . every other girl aged 13 through 19! . . . These girls have $6,800,000,000 a year of their own to spend as they please . . . the income of *Seventeen* reader-families is highest of all women's magazines analyzed in the 1965 Starch Report—58 per cent greater than the national average! . . . 800,000 teen-age girls become engaged every year . . . 700,000 teen-agers marry each year . . . a special audience —87 per cent attend high school and college—52 per cent work full or part-time . . . *Seventeen* reaches these girls during their greatest years of development as customers."

If that doesn't impress, just listen to your teen-age daughter or sister or girl-friend or wife.

Another aspect of this teen-age island is the speed with which it whirls. As *Seventeen* claims also, "Every year more than a million girls move from their sub-teens into their teens, and from their teens into their twenties." This must make for circulation and promotion problems—an annual 20 per cent turn-over, and a complete change in total readership every five years! "*Seventeen* carries more advertising" (it certainly does, it's loaded) and then lists 22 categories from accessories to footwear to hosiery to jewelry to movies to records to soft drinks to toiletries.

Some critics might hold that all these books put the emphasis on the material and external, and that they do, but generally in a perfectly proper way for today's teen-age girl.

Who carts the cash from this teen-age bonanza to the bank? Triangle Publications, the Annenberg empire, does the trucking for *Seventeen*. *Ingenue* belongs to Dell, which is big also with such teen trove as *Modern Screen* and *Modern Romances* and comics. Condé Nast has *Glamour* and *Mademoiselle*. '*Teen* is a Petersen property—Petersen also is very much involved with the boys who buy its *Hot Rod* and *Guns & Ammo* and half-a-dozen other leisure-recreational specialties.

What else are the boys reading? They form a basic market for magazines on sports, cars, the outdoors. Along with some of the girls, they buy nearly two million monthly copies of *Mad*, whose pictorial humor runs to the crude and sadistic which no mature adult can stomach. The teen-age male in the upper level, also, is a reader of general circulation magazines such as *Life* and *Saturday Evening Post* and *Time*, according to a *Journalism Quarterly* report. The sample of 259 boys and 173 girls was taken in a predominantly white, higher than average ability and income Wisconsin school. These teen-agers in grades 7 through 12 preferred adult general magazines to teen publications in listing their first three reading preferences.

Among the girls, those in grade 7 listed *American Girl* second to *Life*, with the *Saturday Evening Post* third. *Seventeen* placed second or third to the same two general competitors at every other grade level. Of the boys, those in grades 7, 8, and 9 gave *Boys' Life* as the second or third choice with *Life* first. Boys in the higher grades made it *Life, Post, Time* in that order. For girls and boys, the over-all ranking for general magazines was *Life, Post, Time, Look, National Geographic*, and *Reader's Digest*.

Although this obviously is a skewed sample, and hobby and school periodicals are not included, its conclusion that general adult magazines attract heavy teen readership is supported by many other studies.

Favorites among teen magazines, after *American Girl* for the younger and *Seventeen* for the older girls, were *Ingenue* and *16 Magazine*. For the teen girl below *Seventeen*, *16* is almost as sweet and simple as its name. Its editor explains that it doesn't play up scandal, plays down smoking, and runs only house ads. Circulation is mainly newsstand, half-a-million copies. For the boys, *Mad* was the only teen magazine to attract significant attention—most boys called the rest "trash." Girls, except in the lowest grade, ignored the screen, radio-TV, recording fan publications.

But—and it can't be emphasized too strongly—this is far from typical of teen-age America, particularly among less privileged youngsters. They are the avid readers, buying millions of copies of books which turn the spotlight and microscope on the rock-and-rollers, film stars, and the TV types.

Bargain Basement

Teen-age girls are the chief readers of fan magazines, just as they form the screaming, squealing audience for the heroes they sustain. Reader entertainment is the sole goal of these books; they deal naturally with entertainment personalities. The names are look-alikes—*Teen Screen, Teen Talk, Teen World*. The covers are cluttered with garish color and heavy black type. Cheap paper inside is dedicated to bold illustration, sensational titles, and imitation writing. Such advertising as exists is mail-order and bargain counter.

While the boys have a few titles, such as *Male* and *Stag*, which run to sex and violence, they mostly go for the drag-car, football specialties. *Sport*, for example, has more than a third of its readers among 10- to 17-year-old boys, a hefty 34.7 per cent.

Two monthlies designed for the upper teens, male and female, of the protest generation hit the newsstands in 1957 and 1968.

Hearst, capitalizing on the success of sexy editor, Helen Gurley Brown, with *Cosmopolitan*, made her supervising editor of *eye* with a lower-case "e." Starting with an initial press run of 500,000 in March, 1968, *eye* also dealt with the new "underground" in press, films, and music, plus political satire and adventure articles on the "exciting people." Its format of $10\frac{1}{2}$ by $13\frac{1}{2}$ inches, 120 and up pages, ran to eyecatching layout and big fold-out wall posters of pop-op art. It tried appealing to all sexes. Blinding color, blackest blacks, sans serif, ultra-narrow 8-pica columns with six to a page divided by stark rules, blast out from pages of semi-nudes, hair, yoga, and way-out everything.

Curtis made the scene in 1957 with *Scene*, a brand new idea in magazine merchandising, representing a tie-in with local radio stations for exclusive distribution rights under their own call letters in their own markets. Content features fan and photo stories on pop music and the stars who make it. Promotion stated that around 40 top-40 stations were participating—for example, *WAPE-Scene* in Jacksonville, Florida, and *WTRX Scene* in Flint, Michigan. Five pages in each issue are the local station's for local editorial, promotion, or advertising, while Curtis sells national ads.

Supposedly confidential stories about The Animals or The Rolling Stones, Ann-Margret and / or Bobbie Darin, plus pseudo-confessions about invented nobodies are the stock in trade of the recording, movie, romance, and confession publications. It's been estimated that there are about 20 movie magazines circulating 8 million copies monthly. Supposed adult books such as *Photoplay* (1,119,619), *Motion Picture* (456,941), and *Modern Screen* (823,332) top the list.

There are about 25 of the confession books—"Did She Stay All Night?" —with about 8 million monthly copies sold. Bernarr Macfadden started the trend probably and Macfadden-Bartell still capitalize on it. Their *True Story* and *True Confessions* sell 2,228,842 and 444,927 monthly, respectively, and are widely imitated down into the fly-by-night trade. The chief content is the girl who gets in trouble, chiefly by getting pregnant illicitly, and the ending is moral . . . repentance when it's too late. The lure is the lurid title which promises much more than the relatively prim but purple text delivers.

That text also is no more purple, either, than the perfume and after-shave ads and TV commercials, the publishers claim with considerable justice. Both certainly get plenty of exposure among the teen-agers. *True Story* attracts 29.2 per cent of its readers from among 13- to 19-year-old girls.

Macfadden-Bartell and its subsidiaries put out 15 publications. Other major names in the field are Dell, Ideal, KMR, Complete Women's Group, Secrets Romance Group, Sterling Women's Group. All together these seven love, sex, and screen entrepreneurs circulate nearly 12 million copies monthly.

While it might be claimed that these publications should be classed in the consumer-general category, their high degree of teen readership certainly also calls for special mention here.

The Not-So-Funny-Comics

The funny papers of the newspapers have grown into a monstrous family of comic books. Five hundred million copies are sold yearly, 80 per cent of them to teen-agers. What began with the katzenjammers of Hans and Fritz evolved into the adventure of "Terry and the Pirates," and "comic books" in the 1930's. World War II and the non-reading habits of GI Joe boomed the books into semi-adult picture serials of crime and sex, seldom funny and many without newspaper parentage of any kind.

After a peak period in the mid-century 1950's when nearly 400 different comic books were being marketed by some 50 different companies, TV and competition shook the total down until today 8 major publishers have pre-empted the major circulation figures. The National Comics Group has a 6-million-plus distribution and is among the leaders. This company describes its activities as follows:

"The National Comics Group is edited for 7–14 year olds—both boys and girls—with heavier emphasis on boys. The 42 magazines in the group deal with Adventure, Fantasy, Humor, Mystery, War Stories. Superman and Batman are the leading characters. While the editorial content is concentrated in these areas, emphasis is stressed on encouraging boys and girls to become active hobbyists."

While this redundant last sentence with its stressed emphasis is a propaganda effort for public favor, it's true that major businesses center around the hobby of selling Batman capes, hoods, masks, guns belts, flashlights, etc., to captivated youngsters. Now that TV serials have put Batman in orbit in your living room, sales of comic books and "hobby" items for young collectors have not suffered.

Other National Comics titles include *All American Men of War, Our Army at War, GI Combat, Hawkman, Doom Patrol, Our Fighting Forces, Sea Devils, Star Spangled War Stories, Superboy, Wonder Woman.* The major military content undoubtedly is testimony that the Armed Forces still are a fertile circulation field. While violence may be a daily ration in Vietnam, one wonders about its place in the 7-year-old diet.

Most of the competitors are also aiming directly at GI Joe—Charlton Comics, operating from Derby, Conn., devotes eight of its 21 "Adventure Group" to sanguinary exploits. True, its "Romance Group" ranges from *Teenage Love* to *Career Girl Romances*. The two groups have a joint circulation of around 3,524,147. There are several other major houses: American Comics, 4.36 million; Archie Comic, 5.6 million; Dell Comic, 3 million; Gold Key (the Walt Disney outlet), 6 million; Harvey Comics, 3.9 million; Marvel Comic, 7-plus million.

Gold Key Comics has a youth-publishing background—also true of books issued by *Boys' Life*, George A. Pflaum, and George Hecht's far-reaching enterprises. With 80 different titles owned by Gold Key, they run from "Yogi Bear" to "The Lone Ranger" and "Huckleberry Hound." According to promotion by Western Publishing Company (also owners of *The Golden Magazine*), average age of their readers is 10.2, 54.8 per cent boys and 45.2 per cent girls—which doesn't leave much room for the adults who peek! Yes, that figures, too—48.8 per cent of the mothers and 48.6 per cent of the fathers.

Comic publishers keep presses running around the clock, printing their 184 different books with approximately 40 million circulation monthly. With new babies being born and new wars being fought, demand seems inexhaustible, unaffected by literacy rates or social critics of the comics. These are today's novels and pulps and they have spread the range of non-reading appetites from three to thirty!

What Next?

If the juvenile revolution of the 20th century has supplanted the fond old familiars with "adventure" comics and teen-age cosmetic guides, it undoubtedly has extended the reach of the juvenile magazine, both in kind and number. The *Youth's Companion* and its companions could be counted on both hands and were restricted in circulation to a special clientele among the upper middle class. Today's juvenile has a different title for every age and interest, and it is truly a mass medium.

Considering the amazing changes achieved by the juvenile revolution, it would be suicidal to attempt a forecast of the next whirl of specialized publications for the young. It may be safe to say that, now that mass marketers have discovered this gold mine, there will be more and more money spent, both by consumers and advertisers, to reach the young reader and non-reader.

GOLDEN MAGAZINE Questionnaire

① How long have you been reading Golden Magazine?

_____ Years _____ Months

② Which of the following reading matter that you find in GOLDEN MAGAZINE do you like a lot, like somewhat, or dont like?

SUBJECT	LIKE A LOT	LIKE SOMEWHAT	DON'T LIKE
Drawing & Coloring			
Jokes			
Puzzles & Games			
Mystery Stories			
Adventure Stories			
Sports			
Crafts & Hobbies			
Science			
Nature			
History			
Geography			
Cooking			
Languages			
Music			

CRACKY'S COMING ATTRACTIONS

NEXT MONTH:

For bike riders
FUN ON WHEELS

For adventurers...
A GAME PARK SAFARI
and
A GLIMPSE OF INDIA

KNOWING ABOUT:
Shell Fishing
11 Beautiful Weeds
Navaho Sand Painting
Buccaneer Gold Coins
Delaware the 1st State

Be Sure You Don't Miss This Exciting Issue!

"Cracky" cakewalks for *The Golden Magazine* as its advance man for future fun; courtesy of *The Golden Magazine*.

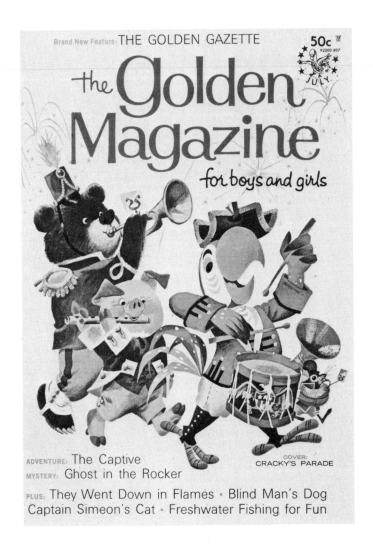

The Golden Magazine cover. Copyright, 1968, *The Golden Magazine.*

HOW
DO YOU
SPEAK
TO AN
ANGEL ?

You come into her world
of SEVENTEEN where...

Reader Reaction
Reader Involvement
Reader Participation
Reader Gratification
Reader Enchantment
Reader Dependence
Reader Loyalty

...to both editorial and
advertising are unparalleled!
She pays 50¢ for each issue
every month of the year—
newsstand or subscription.
SEVENTEEN carries more
advertising than any other
women's monthly magazine.

seventeen®
America's Teen-Age Magazine

Circulation: 1,457,348
(Single copies: 1,096,537)

Media/scope, March 1968   37

Trade advertising for *Seventeen;* courtesy of Triangle
Publications.

What would happen if 4¼ million Boys' Life readers suddenly discovered your product was their answer to good grooming?

You'd probably have to build another plant, that's all! It's surprising that many toiletry advertisers are letting the great untapped teen-age Boys' Life market go down the drain. Probably because they haven't seen the new Boys' Life. It's a kick! Lots of smart advertisers *have* discovered Boys' Life. Companies like Coca-Cola, Polaroid, General Electric, Columbia Records, Goodyear and Wilson. They know what can happen when 31 % of the young (10-17 year old) men in the country get excited. 4¼ million boys can buy lots of deodorant, shaving lotion, soap, hair dressing, toothbrushes, and electric shavers. Boys' Life has 'em. You should look into it.

Look into the new

BOYS' LIFE

July means swimming—"Suited For Swimming", plunges into the past, present and future of Olympic swim star, Don Schollander.

Arthur C. Clarke, foremost science-fiction writer, now spins a tale of conquering gravity—"The Cruel Sky".

Loads of special features—Autos, Nature, "Making the Scene", Chess, Water Skiing, etc.

Trade advertising for *Boys' Life*; courtesy of *Boys' Life*.

4. The Long, Leisurely Weekend

FISHING or a drive in the country, anyone? Load the picnic basket into the family car, and take off! For many Americans, with the advent of the five-day week, the long, leisurely weekend has become a way of life. Recreation, ranging from relaxed putting around the backyard to strenuous skiing, is a mystique with millions.

Multiplying magically, a multitude of specialized magazines serve the recreational activities of Americans, which range from bird-watching to boating, from airplane models to wildlife. At least 260 different publications whet the interest of fans and hobbyists, not counting the trade periodicals supplying the dealers and manufacturers of leisure-time goods.

Circulation gains bear joint testimony to a society with more money and time to spend on leisure and recreation. Outdoor magazines have quintupled their sales in the last thirty years, as has *National Geographic*, the dean of travel publications. The science-mechanic books have tripled, and a bevy of new recreation periodicals has been born. *TV Guide* comes a close second behind *Reader's Digest*, and there are ten recreation magazines in all with circulations of a million or more.

Although an incredible number of categories might be set up to provide for the infinite recreational variety, there are four main canopies which shelter the fun and play and relaxation. Crafts and hobbies provide for endless hours. Entertainment, visual and aural, comes through radio and reading, music and movies and television. Sports, vicarious and participant, offer competition, conflict, and conquest. Travel takes us through sky, across land and sea, offering movement for restless modern man.

41

Magazines give meaning and zest to recreation and stimulate the desire for more. They are, as one might expect, stimulating themselves in dramatic layout and an array of rainbow colors. They enlist writers of fame and fortune. They pyramid advertising dollars which sell ingenious, complex playthings, providing more advertising dollars to sell more toys for the adult hours of recreation.

Crafts and Hobbies

Buttons and bottles, coins and stamps. Wood-working, model-building. Antiques and telescopes, how-to-do-its and home movies. No matter what your hobby or craft, you'll share and read about it with the other zealots.

Catch them young is the effective endeavor of the all-purpose how-to-do-its, and many a boy, poring over the pages of *Popular Mechanics*, has grown into maturity in a life-long love affair with gadgets and gimmicks and the work of his own hands. Whether it's puppy-love in the sub-teen youngster or a senile last fling, what female can contend with the charms of making your own periscope?

Popular Science Monthly, the lively ancient with today's circulation of 1,624,250 started as a serious scientific journal back in 1872. Today *Popular Science* is part of the McCall magazine kingdom, controlled by the California conglomerate magnate, Norton Simon. In its great early days, it was a respected rival of *Scientific American*, and carried the writings of such scientific geniuses as Charles Darwin and Thomas Huxley when they were presiding at the origin and birth of evolution. Even in the mid-1930's, when I was a member of its editorial staff, one of my colleagues was Edwin Way Teale, later to become known as a classic modern writer on nature.

Of course, along with the years came considerable popularizing of the sciences, with picture items and diagrams on how to build an electronic treasure finder. Clear little photographs punctuated the pages and the age level went down. But the appeal for older as well as younger readers persists for in the 1960's the *Popular Science* reader had a median income of $8,844, a third were college-educated, and four out of five owned their homes.

This profitable, popular market drew more publishers. In 1902, *Popular Mechanics* was founded in Chicago by Henry H. Windsor and became an instant success in its first year, climbing from a weekly of only 16 pages to a monthly with more than a hundred. Before it passed into the Hearst magazine empire in 1958, it had won acceptance through French, Spanish, and Scandinavian editions as well as wide American readership. By 1968, its circulation was 1,654,373.

Popular Mechanics promotes its adult image, stressing that three out of every four are married, that 85 per cent are men, and emphasizing its high home readership. It claims "today's best reporting on automobiles, boating, fishing, camping, photography, home improvement, tools and home workshops, gardening, hi-fi equipment, electronics, aviation, science, and mechanics." While this may be pardonable exaggeration, it does carry editorial coverage in all these areas. Typical articles might be "Tips on Buying a Fishing Motor" and "Rotate to Better Television Viewing." Departments are the backbone, with regular sections devoted to aviation, science, new inventions, and a dozen more. While some pages give open and dramatic layout, others are the comfortable clutter of assorted items which have always been part of the magazine's main pulling power.

Hearst also publishes *Science Digest* which "reports and explains the news of the month in science and technology for the general public. About half of each issue is straight news, organized in a section called Science This Month; the other half, background information organized in two sections— Science Panorama and Science Miscellany. News stories, feature articles, columns and shorts are illustrated and written to appeal to readers of all ages." Circulation is 153,747.

The Fawcett entry is *Mechanix Illustrated*, at 25 cents priced a dime less than the two "Popular" books. It emphasizes youth, that its readers have a median age of 31, as well as a median income that rates close to the $8,000 figure of the "Populars." *MI*'s roto printing gives it a different look than its colleagues, and it stresses that "all articles are as non-technical as possible." It dates back to 1928 when it began as *Modern Mechanics* and, 40 years later, had grown to 1,489,135 circulation.

Science & Mechanics, produced by Davis Publication which also publishes more than a dozen other craft-hobby books, first appeared in 1930 and had reached 291,843 circulation by 1968. Fewer pages on cheaper stock don't help its competitive effort.

All the mechanics-science books make considerable use of photographs as illustrations, and devote some space to departmental tips for camera bugs, for photography is a modern hobby for millions, thanks to the famous Eastman Kodak Brownie which everybody could afford and operate.

The big three of the photography publications are *Popular Photography* with 445,354 circulation; *Modern Photography*, 281,490; and *Travel & Camera*, 197,923. The trio all seek to serve the beginning bug as well as the experienced professional, but the major stress is on the more advanced camera artist. Naturally they play fine color and black-and-white reproductions. Their content also covers picture-taking and developing techniques, product analysis of new equipment, critiques on readers' pix submissions. Readers also find much to study in advertising which also emphasizes fine shots.

The late 1930's were the birth years for these photography magazines, following close on the popularity of *Life* and *Look*. They add to their revenues and reader service by publishing annuals. Ziff-Davis has its "Photography Annual" and "Photography Buyers' Guide" to supplement its *Popular Photography*. U.S. Camera Publishing Corporation issues "U.S. Camera World Annual," which sells 250,000 copies, and also *Camera 35*, a bimonthly for 35-millimeter enthusiasts.

Professional organizations also promote their members' interest with *American Cinematographer* (matched in the amateur area by *Better Home Movie Making*) of the American Society of Cinematographers; *Infinity*, published by the American Society of Magazine Photographers; *The Professional Photographer*, of the Professional Photographers of America; and the *PSA Journal*, of the Photographic Society of America. Of these, *The Professional Photographer*, for commercial and industrial studios, has the largest circulation with 17,674.

Such publications for professionals and dealers, paralleling the journals for the amateur, are characteristic of the hobby-craft field which encourages cross-fertilization and the exchange of experience and expertise. Sometimes it becomes a perplexing question as to who is the real expert—the amateur who has made his hobby a lifetime labor of love, or the professional who has to devote part-time to the dollar.

All camera fans also are aware of the many fine manuals, guides, and publications of Eastman Kodak which devotes (in fulfilled expectation of reciprocity) much time and money to their production and distribution.

Kodak keeps its customers coming back, not only to buy and process film, but through clever and bright little externals such as *Kodak Movie News*—buy a Kodak movie camera and you're on the mailing list by sending in a card. Similar externals serve not only the amateur photographer but also serious professionals and technicians here and abroad. There's *Applied Photography* and *Studio Light* for professionals, *Kodak Bulletin* and *Commercial Camera* for commercial photographers and retailers, *Medical Radiography and Photography* for medical science, *Dental Radiography and Photography* for the dental office, and a bevy of similar books for foreign readers. The 4-H boy and girl and leader are given special instruction manuals for photography courses. And every book of course contains the most magical photography that ever graced a magazine!

This Natural World

While the photographer's life is a craft-hobby familiar to millions, it often is closely related to the landscape of forested mountain and reflecting lake, which inspires some of his best pictures. This world of nature is drawing more and more lovers for its own sake as the conservationists, the rod and gun enthusiasts, and the tourists contend for its protection and its use.

With most remarkable color photographs of flowers and wild animals, *National Wildlife*, published by the National Wildlife Federation every other month, promotes outdoor recreation through first-person narratives but most of all through its unsurpassed illustrations. Distributed to 215,000 members and associate members, it plays a low-keyed hymn to conservation, depending chiefly on the persuasion of beauty.

A close competitor in presenting the glories of America's flora and fauna is *Natural History*, the official publication of the American Museum of Natural History, which "is edited for the layman interested in nature beyond the field-guide level, and covers contemporary research in the natural sciences, including anthropology, archeology, and astronomy" and, naturally, conservation. Here also, photographs add tellingly to articles and attract a circulation of 178,000.

Similar in intent and sponsorship, *Frontiers* is produced by the Academy of Natural Science of Philadelphia, with five issues a year written for laymen on birds and mammals, plants and fossils. It uses black-and-white illustrations, often effectively, and covers the world.

As indicated by its name, *Audubon*, the magazine of the National Audubon Society, stems from the love of birds evidenced in the life of the great American naturalist. However, it also provides for wider natural interests, covering camping and hiking, other wildlife, and seeks the preservation of natural resources. Its bimonthly issues also carry many color photographs and go to a circulation of 77,184.

Appalachia, the *Sierra Club Bulletin*, and *Michigan Out-of-Doors* are exemplars of the wide-ranging and crossing lines of interest among the magazines devoted to conservation and nature. The first two are club publications of organizations dedicated to maintaining nature in its pristine beauty. The third represents the many periodicals printed by state governments through their departments of wild life and conservation, and intended for lovers of outdoor recreation.

These publications, often of digest size, are equally aimed at the hunter and fisherman, and are closely related to the outdoor and sports magazines. And, as they often appeal and are addressed to the tourist, some of them carry a considerable content of travel and camping material.

Collecting Mania

As one who has squirreled away stamps for a lifetime (sometimes defended as an investment although who would sell such a treasure trove?), it is easy to understand the fanatics who spend their time and substance on collections

45

of almost anything—an accumulating urge, practiced by two-legged packrats. For these, as for every kind of human being, there is spur and satisfaction in specialized hobby books.

Antiques, serving 55,265, collectors of the old, and *Spinning Wheel*, with 32,049 circulation, are leaders "for those who like antiques and want to know about them." The editors of the *Spinning Wheel* continue their description, declaring that it's for beginners, seasoned collectors, and dealers, covering "a wide range. . . . Regular features include calendar of antique shows, book reviews, decoration questions and answers, tours and exhibits, letters, news." In the same field is *The Antiques Journal*, using articles on glassware, chinaware, and furniture.

Closely related are other hobby magazines, covering wide ranges of intense interest. There's *The Dollhouse Newsletter*, official monthly publication of the Doll House Clubs of America, whose members also include collectors or builders of miniatures, and toys.

The acquisitive urge is strong among numismatists and philatelists. Among publications for the coin collector are *Coins*, a monthly reaching 84,387, *Coin World*, the *Whitman Numismatic Journal*, *World Coins*, and the *U.S. Coin Collectors' Quarterly*, *The Coin Digest*. The chief philatelic periodical is *Linn's Weekly Stamp News*, describing new and old issues, carrying biographical, geographical, and historical material on both collectors and stamp subjects, and circulating among 63,183.

Have you ever watched the darting flashes of light in a home aquarium? Then maybe you're a reader of the *Tropical Fish Hobbyist*.

Cultivating the Crafts

Where the hobby ends and the craft begins is fertile ground for debate. *Hobby News* "deals only with the type of hobby that can be purchased in scale model hobby shops—trains, model cars, slot racing boats." Each of these has its own literature. *Car Model* drives ahead with 170,000 circulation. *Flying Models* has 27,000. Then there are *Model Airplane News*, 71,740, and *Model Car Science*, 130,420.

Passenger trains may be vanishing with the passenger pigeon, but rail buffs keep 'em coming 'round the bend with *The Model Railroader*, which features articles "the modeler needs to improve and enlarge his 'pike.' . . . Keeps the hobbyist posted on methods of planning a model layout, building benchwork, laying track, forming scenery, installing the electric wiring system and how to operate his railroad efficiently and according to real train methods." Its 101,751 circulation has right-of-way, followed by *Railroad Magazine*'s 21,788, and *Railroad Model Craftsmen*, 47,868.

A. C. Kalmbach put *Model Railroader* on the right track back in 1934, with plenty of layouts (both magazine and railroad) and illustrations, chiefly in one color and black and white. A full-color cover shows a dream model for railfans. Abundant how-to-do articles (and outfitting ads) tell you to get busy on your own track scene. Realism is the order sheet for the day. Departments, and prizes for best models and best pix of models, fire the buff to get up a head of steam on his own system.

Sewing and wood-working have a traditional following among the home-crafts and so it's not surprising to find magazines encouraging these skills. The top publication with monthly frequency, *Workbasket*, goes to 1,495,852 women who "are modern active 'doers' who spend a larger percentage of income on the fine art of homemaking." "In a 12-month period practically all phases of needlework are included. Various crafts, general care and culture of house plants and foods section with tempting recipes . . . are featured each month."

Brother publication to *Workbasket* is *Workbench*, also published at Kansas City by Modern Handcraft Publications. Its 368,566 craftsmen "do more and spend more on projects than the general home-owner"—$827.18 annually on additions and alterations, against $138.67; $335.17 for maintenance and repair, compared with $96.22; $144.28 for replacements, contrasted with $48.11. That's an active, productive group of men who know how to do it. *Home Craftsman* and *The Family Handyman* are other guides to men who relax by using their skillful hands.

Although published only twice a year, *McCall's Needlework & Crafts* is purchased by 1,542,424 ardent seamstresses. Its tri-annual *Pattern* reaches another half-million. Similarly, *Modern Needlecraft, Simplicity, Vogue Knitting Book* are semi-annuals. *Vogue Pattern Book* is a bimonthly.

An art or a craft? It depends on the individual, but it's safe to say that many of the more than nine thousand readers of *Handweaver & Craftsman* are genuine artists, for it's intended both for the gifted amateur and the professional. Articles and departments deal with design, techniques, yarns and fibers, tools and equipment, occupational therapy, exhibitions, and the great weavers of antiquity and the present.

The Fine Art of Entertainment

When the films, radio, and TV entered modern life, the multi-million audiences were created and, in turn, gave rise to millions of readers who, first entertained by the live and electronic performance, hastened to read about the stars of stage and screen and air. At the mass peak of the entertainment magazines is *TV Guide*, with its soaring circulation of 14,040,775. Published by Triangle Publications, an Annenberg enterprise, *TV Guide* is second only to *Reader's Digest* in its sales and its regional editions have passed the 70 mark and are still spiraling upward.

Fan-fare, *TV Guide* spills the stardust around your living room with program features and listings, personal items, and personality profiles about the evanescent creatures of the idiot box. It's a service as a program guide, it's a melange of promotional puff.

Entertainment on TV, radio, and stage also is spotlighted in professional trade publications such as *Variety* and *Billboard*, and in theatrical program-periodicals such as *Playbill*. *Playbill* is distributed free to playgoers in the theaters of New York, Boston, Philadelphia, Washington, Chicago, Los Angeles, San Francisco, St. Louis, Cleveland, Atlanta, Dallas, and Great Britain. *Playbill* was purchased in 1968 by Metromedia, a major operator of radio-TV stations. From a program only, the magazine has expanded into pieces about the stage and its personalities, fashion trends, and even editorials. Metromedia also has a 10-million controlled circulation magazine, *Homemaker's Digest*. For news of the other-world of show business, *Variety* is a must, while *Billboard* performs a like function in the commercial music and recording industries.

Variety is a five-a-week specialized daily paper, issued in Hollywood with a circulation of 11,000. It has a Hollywood rival in the *Reporter*, with identical circulation days and figures. In New York City, there are three entertainment papers. They are the *Film Daily*, covering movies and TV, for 6,300 five-a-week readers; the *Motion Picture Daily*, going to 3,400 daily except Saturday; and *Radio-Television Daily*, five-times-weekly to 9,800. All are tab-sized and do their trade reporting in a Broadway-sho-biz language of their own. Also they're big with promotion ads.

For a short-lived time in the early 1960's, several theater magazines appeared in splendor. Hugh Hefner, the flamboyant founder of *Playboy*, came a cropper with his *Show Business Illustrated* which was swallowed up by Huntington Hartford's *Show* after a half-year of life. Even Hartford, heir to the A&P grocery millions, got tired of red ink and killed *Show* off in a few years.

While more elegant theater-goers apparently won't support a stage publication, the mass addicts of radio, rock-and-roll, TV, and the films have made their fan magazines prosperous. Most of these have a top-heavy teen-age following. The star system pays off, and one-shot ventures featuring the Beatles or Elvis cash in quick and big.

Eight million copies of 20 movie magazines move monthly, befitting their status as first and foremost to feed the ravenous fan appetite. Long a leader, since its creation in 1911, *Photoplay* was astutely edited by James R. Quirk and his successors have kept it on top with a circulation of 1,119,619. It's "edited for the young woman," and plays up "personalities" and personal chitchat about them. However, the publisher's research shows 42.4 per cent in ages 18 to 34 compared with 57.5 per cent in the range from 35 up.

Sharing high billing are Dell, Ideal, Screen Stars, Sterling, and Timely Women's Groups, publishing 12 movie fan books with a total circulation of 3,600,000. Macfadden-Bartell, the entrepreneurs of *Photoplay*, have four other film publications which add another 2,900,000.

Since radio-TV have become prime teen entertainers, magazines based on the big beat and its vocal-instrumental groups have burgeoned, playing up "star" performers. *TV Radio Mirror*, owned by Macfadden-Bartell, has the amazing circulation of 764,754. It is "edited for the young woman, and is devoted to the field of Radio and Television, particularly the home lives of the stars." Some publications such as *TV Radio Mirror* and *Movieland and TV Time* have double coverage. Others, such as *TV Star Parade*, concentrate on a single communications channel.

While most music magazines are not edited for the teen-ager, *Hit Parader* and *Song Hits* are aimed directly at the adolescent. The editorial profile for these two Charlton publications declares, "*Hit Parader* is edited for the young-at-heart popular music fan. An average of 40 top song lyrics appears in each issue, and features are based on taped interviews with music personalities in the Popular, Country, Folk, Jazz, and Blues fields. . . . *Song Hits* concentrates on popular singers who are in the limelight for the duration of one issue."

All the music books are in competition to some degree with each other, for many listeners have omnivorous ears when it comes to sound of varying descriptions. But they do exhibit preferences. *Hit Parader* concentrates on the latest hits, while jazz is *Downbeat*'s beat. *Hi Fidelity* emphasizes records. They all attract foreign readers as well as U.S. for music is a universal language. Nearly one-seventh of *Downbeat*'s circulation is abroad, fostered by its staff of 15 foreign correspondents. It's basically for the professional and serious amateur who'll know a "gig" is a performance and a guitar's an "axe." Its editorial layout is black and white, narrow and packed columns; advertising features musical instruments.

Music publications, closely related to records and the hi-fi-stereo syndrome, range from country and popular to "serious" jazz and classical. The title of *Country Songs and Stars* indicates its content. *The Harmonizer* is the official publication of the Society for the Preservation and Encouragement of Barber Shop Quartet Singing in America, Inc. *Bravo* runs the gamut of opera, dance, concerts, musical theater, and records, and is a quarterly, serving also as a program for concert-goers. Its circulation is 802,192.

Recordings attract many listeners today, who also read their special magazines such as *Audio*, *Hi Fi/Stereo Review*, and *High Fidelity*.

High Fidelity is a thick book running around 180 pages of detailed musical analysis, criticism, and equipment advertising. Produced by Billboard Publications, it carries 11 names on its masthead including audio, music, and art editors as well as six contributing editors. One fourth of its circulation is concentrated in the Middle Atlantic region with other highs centered in the Middle West and on the Pacific Coast. Special editions for the Coast and Metropolitan New York recognize and stimulate this distribution, while a third special edition, "Musical America," is devoted to opera and concert news. There also is considerable foreign circulation, amounting to one-sixth of the total.

Ad fold-outs of stereo components and sets alternate with many record and tape reviews. Then the main editorial section with articles on music in Red China or Petula Clark or the golden age of opera. Then back to the consecutive pages of discography and commercials for sound systems. Layout is conservative black and white touched up with one color.

Electronic sound has such a following that many general circulation magazines also devote regular departments to the latest releases. And in such high-level entertainment as *Saturday Review*, one may find special issues devoted to recordings, as well as columns on TV-radio, opera and the dance, and, of course, its original concentration on literary reviews and criticism.

Saturday Review made its final move out of the newspaper supplement sphere into the giddy, fast-moving world of big finance and big circulation when Norton Simon, the California food packer, took control of *McCall's* in 1956. Five years later, *McCall's* paid $3,000,000 for *Saturday Review*, a bookish weekly with ambitions for broader content. By 1968 the sales figure had climbed to 538,721 and the book reviews were part of a culture package which also included periodic sections on science, education, travel, mass communications, and the arts.

Once upon a time, the magazine had been the book review section of the New York Evening Post, edited by such critical and literary figures as Henry Seidel Canby, William Rose Benet, and Christopher Morley. In 1924 it acquired independence as the *Saturday Review of Literature* (and for a year or two was tinged with *Time*-invested money partially). It had financial ups and downs but finally came into the sunlight when Norman Cousins became editor in 1940. Cousins gave it liberal vigor and editorial drive, lifting it out of the doldrums of detached aestheticism and into the modern scene of life and strife.

For years, the *Saturday Review of Literature* supplemented book reviews with informal personal essays by Morley, light verse, satiric cartoons, and literary acrostic puzzles. Today its range is much wider, although it still continues the original fare. Articles by name by-lines deal with world politics and social issues—a new policy for Vietnam by Theodore Sorensen, "Can a Scientist Be an Optimist" by an Austrian physicist.

Its editorial staff lists John Ciardi for poetry, Katharine Kuh in art, Irving Kolodin in music, while the impressive roll of editors includes John Mason Brown, Joseph Wood Krutch, Granville Hicks, Elmo Roper. Regular columns of literary chitchat and humor appear, written by Goodman Ace, Herbert R. Mayes, Cleveland Amory. This galaxy is presented in black-and-white pages, three columns wide, occasionally relieved by pen-and-ink sketches and photographs. The *Saturday Review* today is serious, involved, the thinking man's companion to a worried world, a reflection of its editor, the concerned Cousins.

While the New York *Times* Sunday literary section of book reviews and the *New York Review of Books* offer, in newspaper tabloid format, reports and some criticism of books, they do not afford the scope of *Saturday Review*'s coverage. Such quality magazines as *Harper's* and *Atlantic Monthly* rival and even exceed its article range but, as monthlies, they do not compete in timeliness with the weekly *Saturday Review*. It has made a unique place for itself among the modern magazines, without any genuine competition.

A dozen magazines with a total circulation of around 430,000 arrange the palette of art for the American of taste, for the collector, for the professional artist, and the gallery. *Horizon*, which terms itself "A Magazine of the Arts," is the most lavish with its art-adorned, hard cover and rich color. Initiated in 1958 after the success of its senior sibling, *American Heritage*, *Horizon*'s quarterly numbers go to 154,000 subscribers.

In more customary magazine format, *Today's Art* leads in circulation with 90,225. The *American Artist* is second, purchased by 63,000 amateur and professional artists, covering fine and commercial art and techniques. *Art News* describes itself as "a magazine for artists, collectors, and the public interested in art." It runs reviews and previews of exhibitions, and its articles provide color illustrations. It is published by Newsweek Inc. Two other major art publications are *Art in America* and *The Artist*.

The activities of galleries and museums, and their professional curators are given attention by *The Art Gallery*, *Museum News*, and *Arts Magazine*.

Sport—a Way of Life

Sport has become a way of life for millions of Americans, active living, active participation in hunting and fishing and hiking, tennis and golf and bowling. Millions more take part vicariously in spectator sports, football, baseball, basketball. The variety of sport activity is limited only by man's ingenuity and imagination. The variety of sport magazines is identical, for there is at least one publication for every sport.

The swift flanker back races downfield, picks off a pass at his finger-tips, and dives in for the score. The crowd rises in a roaring crescendo and creates an instant hero. Hero worship is the secret to magazine sports—*Sport* especially has built its appeal by erecting pedestals to sport heroes. Since it was created in 1946 by Macfadden-Bartell, it has been dedicated to personality pieces about the star players and teams in the major sports, to depth profiles about their lives, their skills.

Sport is devoted to deification of the sports star. While its article authors, many from the newspaper sports staffs, often inject expertise and some analysis, they write chiefly for fans who want to admire and even worship the home-run king. It's no accident that more than two-thirds of the *Sport* audience are "young males under 35," for this is the age for hero worship. More than a third are in the 10 to 17 age bracket. Much of its monthly coverage is seasonal; it follows the sports calendar. Four-color photographs, some where the action is, others posed for posterity, dress up the pages with a portrait gallery of the greats.

The major spectator, professional sports of football, baseball, basketball are the concern of *Sport*. Other athletic activities may glean a few pages on occasion, but *Sport* smartly and mainly puts its emphasis on the main events. It has paid off with a devoted circulation of 1,120,424.

Looking around for more works to conquer, the sharp eyes in *Time*'s tower sighted in on a new target in 1954. *Sports Illustrated* was the result, a sports weekly which climbed surely and steadily to success. Its air of superiority stems naturally from the Luce manner which spurred the owner to write, "We have the H-bomb and we have *Sports Illustrated*. These are the two instant symbols of our fears and hopes. . . . Peace in American in mid-20th century means enjoyment of life, the pursuit of happiness. It means, in short, *Sports Illustrated*." Devoted to "excellence" as defined by *Time*!

Sports Illustrated had some early moments of truth when its first staffers fumbled a few times. They often were selected for skill in writing rather than sports knowledge. But publishing persistence and a bulging bankroll paid off in the long run, greatly aided by bountiful use of first-class action shots in color.

In its first six months, *Sports Illustrated* spurted to more than half-a-million sports readers. Since then its circulation has mounted in a continuous upward curve to the figure of 1,506,437 by 1968.

Editorial content is almost as wide as the range of sports, with many

52

editorial pages emphasizing upper-income participation in golf, sailing, tennis. There's an Atlantic-seaboard, semi-snob air, demonstrated in layouts devoted to sport fashions, fancy recipes for game, and society names.

Its trade advertising stresses its role as a newsweekly, claiming a leading position among all "newsmagazines" for readers with household income of $25,000 and over, who hold country club memberships, own foreign cars, hi-fi's, and color TV. Four regional editions, plus New York and Chicago metropolitans, California and Southern California, offer advertising assists and four editorial pages an issue of semi-localized interest.

As a "news weekly," of course *Sports Illustrated* is limited strictly to sports news despite its promotional claims. In sports it does a consistent job of covering the big game of the week, whatever the season, providing a scoreboard of results, and a miscellany of features. As its staff has developed, they have produced a surer, more competent coverage. Writing, skillfully professional much of the time, sometimes is superlative, sometimes infuriatingly smart-alecky. Week in, week out, *Sports Illustrated* sparkles with action caught in color shots, the real class of its content.

One of the top specialized sports books is *Golf* with a top circulation, 384,444, in its field, followed closely by such competitors as *Golf Digest*, *Golf World*, and *Golfdom*. It also claims first place in ad revenue and newsstand sales. Running about 100 pages per issue with many color pages, it's published by the Universal Distributing Corporation of New York which also produces *Golfdom*, *The Family Handyman*, *Ski*, *Ski Business*, *Ski Area Management*, and a number of vocational guidance and home plan books. It's primarily devoted to the serious golfer, with lots of tips on how to lower your score. Profiles of golfing greats and golf courses, as well as fairway fashions, humor, and regular departments complete the editorial content which is supplemented with a bonanza of ads offering golf equipment and golf resorts.

As golf has its devotees or skiing its zealots, so these and many other fans support their own periodicals, magazines exclusively edited and published for a single sport. Every activity is represented by at least one magazine. There are eight different golf publications, 15 for shooting enthusiasts. Magazine titles representing sports include: *Bow & Arrow*, 78,421 circulation; *Bowling Magazine*, 120,957; *Flying*, 287,534; *Hot Rod*, 787,233; *Guns & Ammo*, 252,820; *Skating*, 8,681; *Ski*, 254,840; *Skin Diver*, 73,853; *Surfer Magazine*, 102,743; *Swimming World*, 16,510; *The Water Skier*, 10,783; *World Tennis*, 72,200; *Yachting*, 112,896.

If your own recipe for the active life is not represented in this list, it's almost certain that there's at least one magazine published somewhere for you.

Maybe it's *Weight Watchers* so you can get ready for the active life!

While dieting and calorie-counting has itself become a kind of indoor sport for many Americans, it took the wide world of magazines to produce a special publication for those who seek to shed pounds. Springing into life in 1968, *Weight Watchers* is a glossy monthly with circulation of 440,000. It offers painless, poundless existence elegantly, in parties at El Morocco, recipes and menus, and even travel and fiction about the single girl who slims into romance.

Several publishers have specialized in sports. Davis Publications is a major recreation house with at least nine different magazines, four in sports. Fawcett has three titles and a half-dozen annuals. Hearst's magazine empire also has three sports titles and four annuals. Rajo Publications covers camping, "Trailering," flying, and foreign cars in four books. Ziff-Davis produces seven recreational publications plus four annuals. All of these are located in New York City, the magazine publishing capital.

A modern magazine success story has been the rise of the Petersen Publishing Company in Los Angeles. Robert Petersen started modestly in 1948 with a slim bankroll of $400. A one-time film PR man, he gunned *Hot Rod* into a fast start as a money-maker its first year, although for a while he sold subscriptions around the dragtracks. It was the beginning of a complete line of recreation magazines: *Guns & Ammo, Surfing, Car Craft, Motor Trend, Rod & Custom, Skin Diver, Sports Car Graphic*, plus a *'Teen* book for the teen-age crowd who drive the stripped-down, jazzed-up racers. Total Petersen circulation in 1968 was around 5,500,000.

In addition to the specialized consumer books in sports, SRDS Business directory lists at least 48 more different publications under eight classifications for sporting goods dealers and professionals. Among the sports magazines quite a few represent sports organizations—for example, the National Rifle Association's *American Rifleman* with a 1,042,813 circulation, chiefly among members. That's a pretty big business, except that it's tax-exempt although it earned more than a million dollars in advertising revenue in 1966!

First published in 1885, the *American Rifleman*'s editorial policy seems chiefly to serve as spokesman for one of the nation's most powerful lobbies—in opposing gun control legislation. Regular features include "Why I joined NRA," "A Court Case of Consequence," "The Armed Citizen," and "The Editor's Firing Point." Much editorial matter concerns competitive shooting, re-loading of ammunition, and amateur gunsmithing. "Dope Bag," a potpourri of reader letters and contributions, bulks big in number of pages and interest. Advertising, primarily of guns and gun supplies, is heavy, intruding into the middle of the book. Layouts are somewhat drab, with one-color leavening constant black and white.

Hunting and fishing probably claim more adherents than any other American sport, for the outdoor life has become the all-American activity for all ages.

Three major outdoor magazines monopolize the readership. They are running relatively close together in circulation: *Field & Stream*, owned by Holt, Rinehart and Winston (controlled in turn by Columbia Broadcasting System); Hearst's *Sports Afield*; and *Outdoor Life*, owned by Norton Simon who controls McCall's, and in the lead with 1,647,106. *Field & Stream* has 1,475,630 and *Sports Afield*, 1,370,123.

Sports Afield is the oldest of the outdoor publications, dating back to 1887 although it did not come under Hearst ownership until the 1950's. An outdoors man from Colorado, John A. McGuire, founded *Outdoor Life* in 1898, but it passed from his family (McGuire had been a big-game hunter and explorer) and into the hands of *Popular Science Monthly* in 1934 (still listed as its immediate corporate parent). A pair of duck hunters, patiently waiting in a blind, got the idea for *Field & Stream* in 1895. After vicissitudes it was acquired by Eltinge Warner who pumped money into its arteries along with other magazine properties. It was taken over in 1951 by Holt, Rinehart and Winston, the book publishers who also produce *Popular Gardening* and a couple of home annuals.

The backbone of the outdoor books is personal narrative of hunting and fishing triumphs, backed by judicious support for conservation, and regular departments devoted to guns, rods, dogs, and all the elaborate paraphernalia of camping, boating, and outdoor "roughing it" with the most modern gadgets. They are books for men, primarily, and fifty million fisher-hunters say they're fascinating. The editorial profiles of these magazines clue in on the content: ". . . number of hunting and fishing trips taken in the last 12 months per 100 copies of circulation—1,179. . . . highest percentage of households owning boats and . . . outboard motors."

While the outdoor trio occupy the top rung, more than one hundred other magazines blow tally-ho, urge on the dogs, or camp out. About half of them are state sponsored, fish-and-game publications, about half are commercial.

Twin goals inform the reader of state wildlife magazines that conservation supports and is supported by hunting and fishing. These publications for the most part are free-distribution, going to members of sportsman's associations who, in turn, contribute to fish and game departments by their license fees. Their content is composed of brief articles on wildlife, often illustrated by photographs, and their appeal is based on the enthusiasm their readers bring to them. *Nebraskaland*, published by the Nebraska Games, Forestation, and Parks Commission, and *Montana Wildlife*, produced by Montana Fish and Game Department, are typical examples of these state magazines.

55

Nebraskaland describes itself as edited "to promote outdoor recreation and vacation in Nebraska. Feature articles include hunting and fishing, boating and camping, old West history and general articles about Nebraska." It has a circulation of 65,840 copies.

The outdoors abounds in special interests and many profit publications concentrate on them. Each region has something unique to offer, from the *Alaska Sportsman* to *Fishing in Maryland*. Or it may be a particular breed of outdoorsman who seeks surfcasting or deep sea fishing. If so, there's the *Salt Water Sportsman* or *Sportfishing*. If he's enamored of riding to hounds, and lives with his horses and dogs, then *Hounds and Hunting* or *The Chronicle of the Horse* will be his favorite reading. There are 17 horse books listed in SRDS, eight about dogs, and a *Cats Magazine*. *Tropical Fish* and *Aquarium* are for finny fanciers. Pet lovers in general may buy *Pet Life* or *Our Dumb Animals*.

Many of these readers would regard animals as anything but dumb—in fact, might prefer them to humans. *Cats Magazine* seeks "to reflect the influence of the cat in our culture. About half of its editorial pages concerns breeding, selling, and exhibiting of cats. A fifth is devoted to care and health, and another fifth to the cat in art, literature, and history. . . . Show schedules, book reviews, veterinary column, letters, poetry, cartoons, and photo contest are regular features."

Animals, wild or domestic, hunted or petted, and their natural habitat—these are powerful forces, pulling man back to his own origins. Total circulation of the outdoor, hunting, and fishing books exceeds six million and no other recreational activity except travel has more adherents.

Specialized Sport Newspapers

Undoubtedly the best known of all sport newspapers is C. C. Johnson Spink's *Sporting News*, issued in St. Louis as a Saturday weekly avidly read by about 265,000 fans. Founded in 1886, it covers baseball as its first love, but also football, basketball, bowling, golf, and soccer in season.

There also are five horse-racing papers, mostly tabloids and issued six times a week. They are the Los Angeles *Racing Form*, 19,000 circulation; the Miami *Racing Form*, ranging from 5 to 7,000; the Chicago Daily *Racing Form*, with a weekly range from 50 to 60,000; and the New York *Armstrong Daily and National Program*, daily except Sunday to 32,000. Most of these carry form charts and race tips for the various tracks.

The Family Car

A hundred million Americans hop into the family car on the annual vacation and take off on adventure into the land of hotdogs and hamburgers, geysers and grizzly bears, flat tires and tents and trailers. Has there ever been such a nation of nomads, whizzing along the concrete interstates in search of scenery!

Travel books whet the appetite and form a memory book. No other magazine has ever captured the charm of strange and familiar lands more continuously than the *National Geographic*—or with more success. In 1966, the tax-exempt, Congressionally-chartered National Geographic Society had an annual income of $48.3 million, while the *National Geographic* magazine rang up $7,000,000 in advertising income. That's an impressive testimonial to the lure of far-away places!

The *Geographic*'s three regional editions were distributed in 1968 to 6,050,137 subscribers, "members" as they are termed in the Society's terminology, a magazine "family" steadily and consistently growing ever since its birth in 1888. As Frank Luther Mott observed, "There is really nothing like it."

Established as an educational institution "to increase and diffuse geographic knowledge," the National Geographic Society decided its first year to publish a magazine "as one means of accomplishing these purposes." However, it was not until 1896 that regular monthly publication began. Who started the society and the magazine? One hundred and sixty-five men, mostly scientists, who got together in the Cosmos Club in Washington, D.C. Gardiner Greene Hubbard was elected the first president, and his family has been closely associated with the *National Geographic* ever since.

That familiar yellow-bordered cover and the bouquet of rainbow photographs inside were early and distinct features of the magazine, as were the narratives of explorations which it sponsored. First-hand, often first-person, accounts of the discovery of the North and South Pole, the pioneering flights of a Lindbergh or Byrd, the capering naked bodies of African pygmies or a portfolio of American birds, these captivated boys and girls and entertained their elders in doctors' waiting rooms.

When Hubbard died, his son-in-law, Alexander Graham Bell, the inventor of the telephone, became president of the National Geographic Society. Bell's son-in-law, Gilbert Grosvenor, became a director and assistant editor of the magazine in 1899 just a year before he married Elsie Bell. Grosvenor *was* the *Geographic* for more than half a century, not stepping down as editor until 1954. His son, Melville Bell Grosvenor, took over in 1957.

The Grosvenor editorial policy has guided the *Geographic* all its modern life with seven principles:

1. The first principle is absolute accuracy.
2. Abundance of beautiful, instructive, and artistic illustrations.

3. Everything printed in the magazine must have permanent value and pertinent one year or five or ten years after the publication as it is on the day of publication.
4. All personalities and notes of trivial character are avoided.
5. Nothing of partisan or controversial character is printed.
6. Only what is of a kindly nature is printed about any country or people, everything unpleasant or unduly critical being avoided.
7. The content of each number is planned with a view of being timely.

Maps have been a major editorial feature of the *National Geographic* ever since it began in the '80's, and today its four annual map supplements continue this unique service. As the pioneer among American magazines of natural photography, the *Geographic* in 1910 not only became the first, but also maintained its position as the largest and most consistent user of many-hued illustrations. These wonderful photographs have been a magnet for readers of all ages and a model for magazine primacy in color and pictorial journalism.

The *Geographic* has been host to the famous. Distinguished bylines have included Presidents Theodore Roosevelt and William Howard Taft, General John J. Pershing, Admiral Chester W. Nimitz, and Nobel Prize-winners. Its art and editorial staff is large by any standards; nearly two hundred names appear on its masthead. The Society's Board of Trustees indicates the position and reputation of its backers. They include: Crawford H. Greenewalt, Chairman of the Board, E. I. duPont de Nemours & Company; William McChesney Martin, Jr., Chairman, Board of Governors, Federal Reserve System; Laurance S. Rockefeller, Chairman of the Board, Rockefeller Brothers, Inc., and President, Jackson Hole Preserve; Earl Warren, Chief Justice of the United States; Conrad L. Wirth, Former Director, National Park Service, U.S. Department of the Interior.

Prestige and tradition of this quality are carefully maintained in an advertising policy which carefully segregates all advertising, even though it consists of blue chips such as American Telephone & Telegraph, Eastman Kodak, the Northern Pacific Railroad, Hamilton Watches, and the Merriam Webster Dictionary. Travel by rail, sea, and air is promoted both by transportation companies and state tourist bureaus. The *Geographic* does not accept any liquor or tobacco advertising.

As a family magazine of travel, both arm-chair and actively en route, the *Geographic* has had few peers through the years. It is a convincing and heartening witness to the supremacy of quality.

Holiday, a natural name for a travel publication, first appeared in 1930 when the American Automobile Association, naturally, produced it as a travel monthly. But its triple-A existence was short. *Holiday* was reborn as a Curtis publication in 1946, just as World War II and the gas rationing ended. Its early years saw a slow start but then it found an accepted niche as a glamour book of travel. Despite the Curtis corporate financial difficulties of the early 1960's, *Holiday* still held a circulation of 1,135,425 in 1968 with its high-style articles often under distinguished names, and glossy pictures in giant color.

Although *Holiday* once described itself as a general monthly—and its contents for a time did cover a wide range of modern life, it devotes most of its pages to articles about foreign lands or scenic tours in the United States. It stresses, its editors say, "the active enjoyment of leisure." Departments also cover the theater and arts, dining out in fine restaurants, a bazaar of exotic gifts from abroad. It cultivates the offbeat approach; thus it commissioned Aubrey Menen, Indian-Irish writer, to do its lead-off piece in a special New York City issue. Menen had never been there before! It sent John Steinbeck on "Travels with Charlie" in a camper around America.

Holiday advertising is heavy on travel promotion for Europe, Asia, and Africa, with airlines and sea cruises offering their best inducements. Other ads run to fine cars, luggage, liquor, and similar appendages of luxury living. Page layouts are simple but elegant, with white space framing a bold use of typography, accompanied by dramatic color photographs full page and extended across the gutter into facing pages. Pages sized $10\frac{1}{2}$ by $13\frac{1}{2}$ make an effective setting for maximum effect.

Two other travel magazines tantalize the roving eye. *Travel* was an early bird, founded in 1901 and absorbing the original *Holiday* in 1931. *Travel's* editor, Malcolm McTear Davis, says that its editorial policy "is simply to talk travel and nothing else." As part of its promotional program, it also operates the National Travel Club, begun in 1910, for an annual membership fee of $7.50—which includes a subscription to the magazine!

Travel is particularly interested in out-of-the-way, off-the-beaten-path American areas, preferably trips that the reader can duplicate on his own vacation. Its editorial policy declares that it is edited "for active travelers" with articles emphasizing "where to go, what to see and do, with costs and prices worked in where appropriate. . . . Special sections each month include a digest of news of interest to travelers and one containing special columns from world capitals and resort areas." Content also includes notes on Broadway shows, hotel news, camera coverage, and travel book reviews. Its circulation in 1968 was 355,000.

Color is used extensively in *Travel's* format for headlines, and rules and borders. It is mainly one-color—four-color illustrations are reserved for special features, such as a four-page portfolio on Austrian lakes and Alps. A

59

straightaway story gives travel tips on a tour of the "Baltic States," while others cover "Ohio's New Lakes," the "British Virgin Islands," "Washington's Canadian Corner," and "Wisconsin's River Road." Style is simple and to the point; useful details are given on routes to follow, sights to see. *Travel* is basically a traveler's guide, with no fuss or fine feathers about de luxe elegance.

The Cowles Magazines, successful with *Look* and *Family Circle*, ventured into the travel field with *Venture* in 1964. Also affiliated with a travel organization (with a dollar reduction in its annual $12.50 subscription price for holders of American Express credit cards), *Venture* also sells through bookstores in keeping with its original hard-cover. It *is* aimed at the first-class, luxury traveler who goes first class. As the original prospectus stated, "Routine has made him [the traveler] blind to adventure, bored and blasé. But transport [him] to Paris. He is excited, enthusiastic.... What is *Venture*? The who, what, when, where, why and how of travel, photographed, written and wrapped in a package of personal experience. *Venture* is a new kind of magazine.... The contemporary and the classic will meet between its hard covers, the peasant and the prince, the factual and the fairytale."

Published six times a year, *Venture* is edited "for the affluent travel enthusiast" and a study of its subscribers reveals a median income of $20,450, that 77 per cent are college-educated, a median age of 50, and with two out of five from the ranks of administrative executives. As upper-bracket tourists, half of them have expense accounts, four out of five own stocks or bonds, 85 per cent have American Express cards, nine out of 10 took a 200-mile U.S. trip last year, and two out of three went abroad. For these comfortable travelers, *Venture* after a year changed from a hard cover to unique three-dimensional color photographs, something out of the ordinary to attract their jaded eyes.

Inside one turns to flamboyant scarlet end papers of a charity ball. The spotlight is turned on "Transopolis: London / New York," with rich full-color photographs and an equally rich prose, stylishly "in" while "slumming in the stews of Soho." Practically the entire issue plays, parallel by parallel, the entertainments, the social whirl, fashions and art of the metropolitan centers facing each other across the Atlantic. A lonely article on Crete, "Epic Island," and an African safari do offer change of pace for those bored by the urban scene. Another issue offers a special Canadian guide on heavy light blue book stock—or, "All the Riviera: The Yachtsman's Golden Odyssey." Or you may prefer "Prague—Castle Without a King," or "Skiing in the Alps: Always in Season."

If *Venture*'s 260,000 subscribers in 1968 were not jet-setters, at least they could qualify for the social register of special people. Travel ads and Lincoln

Continentals swarm among the editorial features, interrupting the swinging, if you want to go adventuring with *Venture*.

While *Holiday*, *Venture*, and *Travel* set the pace, other magazines of travel concentrate on a special scene for a select group. *Colorado* tells the story of the state whose name it carries, the tale of six million tourists to the "tourist cross-roads" of the Rocky Mountain West. *Desert Magazine* contrasts with *Down East*, as Maine faces Palm Springs across the continent. Every area offers its own appeal, from the Great Stone Face of *New Hampshire Profiles* to *Pictorial California* and the *South Illustrated*. Each cultivates regional pride and invites the visitor. Together they tell the story of our land, in prose and picture, in a thousand pages every month.

Travel is spurred by commercial interests such as car manufacturers and gas companies, both of whom have their own publications with tantalizing pictures of scenes to beguile the driver. Probably the best known is the *Ford Times*, the pocket-size tour guide with charming watercolors of what lies at the highway's end. Each major auto trademark has its own fascinating tripper. Among the oil and tire publications, the slim *Adventure Road* of the American Oil Motor Club leads you on and on. The airlines have gotten into the act; for example, National Airlines publishes *Florida*, a sightseeing special for passengers aboard its playground-bound flights.

As you travel, you need a stopping place for the night after covering miles and miles. That's where the motels and hotels come in, and that's where magazines like *Hospitality* make their pitch to lodging managers. *Hospitality* can be found near most registration counters. There really are two *Hospitalities*, one edition for rooms and the other for board, to use the old-fashioned terms for lodging and restaurants. The motel-hotel-resort edition claims coverage of 27,518 motels and 7,366 hotels with its controlled circulation of 79,252. The restaurant combination totals 60,966 non-paid copies going to restaurants, cafes, dining rooms, supper clubs. Both offer how-to-do-it better articles for owners and managers, plus news of the trade, and feature articles about top operators. Their competition includes *Hotel & Motel Management*, *American Hotel Journal*, and *Institutions Magazine*.

Trailers and camping both are big with Americans on the go. Among the trailer magazines, the *American Trailer News and Camper Trends* combines both activities, naturally. It is published by the Travel Trailer Clubs of America. Also for those who like to take their traveling home with them, to a campsite on a mountain lake, are the *Mobile Home Journal*, *Mobile Living* (of the National Association of Trailer Owners), *Trailer Life*, and *Trailer Topics*. Circulation runs around a total of 450,000 for the trailer and camper families, a gregarious clan in a warm friendly way.

Whether you do your camping in a luxurious rolling caravan or prefer a bedroll by a blazing camp fire, you're a modern American pioneer adventuring on the national park frontier and a present or potential reader of a camping magazine. A trio of camping publications finds *Camping Guide* leading at 68,750, with departments on camping recipes, nature lore, vehicle safety tips, news on new campsites, camping equipment. The others include *Camping Journal* and *Better Camping*.

Automobile clubs naturally have their national and state periodicals for their members. *The American Motorist* is the official publication of the American Automobile Association Motor Clubs. Then there are a multitude of state triple-A publications such as *Keystone Car* and *Minnesota AAA Motorist*. There's *The Automobilist*, for the Automobile Legal Association. Should one mention the National Safety Council? Yes, it has its magazines too!

Recreation or Relaxation?

Seldom in history have so many had so much time to amuse themselves either by relaxing in the living room before the TV screen, schussing wildly down a mountain, or spinning around the curves of an interstate. In these pages we've found a kaleidoscopic assortment of magazines, each calculated to spur the veteran or trap the beginner into new adventures. Hobbies at home or afield, the lacy fragile wing of a butterfly or the burning rubber of a drag-racer, these are the quiet or clangorous moments of recreation—and sometimes relaxation—for the modern American.

Applied Photography. Inside front-cover spread. Copyright, 1964, Eastman Kodak Company.

Kodak Bulletin cover. Used by permission of Eastman Kodak Company.

If this is Sports Illustrated's idea of the average sports fan, we'd like to know what happened to Yankee Stadium, hot dogs, and beer.

There's nothing wrong with a sophisticated, blue-blooded sports fan. There just aren't very many of them.

The real American sports fan is either glued to the TV or down at the stadium watching his favorite team in person. Not standing around a polo match or boasting his yacht for a cruise.

And besides, it costs you twice as much per page to advertise to the young male market in Sports Illustrated or any other competitive magazine as it does in Sport.

Cost per thousand, (males under 35)
Sport Magazine 1.03
Sports Illustrated 1.55
Playboy 2.83
Esquire 3.10

So if you're looking for sports-minded young men, you can reach more of them per dollar in Sport than in any other competitive magazine.

We may be the only bargain left in advertising. SPORT

MACFADDEN BARTELL CORPORATION • NEW YORK (212) 532-9090, CHICAGO (312) 263-2400, LOS ANGELES (213) 655-6055, SAN FRANCISCO (415) 981-2241.

Trade promotional advertisement for *Sport* magazine; used by permission of Macfadden-Bartell Corporation.

FEBRUARY/MARCH, 1965

National WILDLIFE

DEDICATED TO THE WISE USE OF OUR NATURAL RESOURCES • PUBLISHED BY THE NATIONAL WILDLIFE FEDERATION

National Wildlife cover. Copyright, 1965, National Wildlife Federation.

5. The Role of Religious Magazines

THE story of religious publications is the earliest story of American publishing for our colonies were largely settled by exiles for faith—Puritans and Pilgrims, Catholics and Huguenots, Quakers and Mennonites. In today's theoretical separation of church and state, it may be difficult to realize the impact of the theocratic society of New England where Harvard College was founded in 1636 to train ministers—and where the Harvard Press began two years later to print sermons, hymnals, and the Bible.

From 1757, when the *American Magazine* was edited by the Rev. William Smith, through all the history of American journalism, religious men and religious publications have had wide and deep influence, from the abolitionist journals to voiced dissent against war in Vietnam. Mainly the religious magazine has been the voice of conviction and faith, often a particularized denominational faith, but seldom only a still, small voice. While estimates vary, there is general agreement that more than 1,700 religious magazines exist today and tiny indeed is the religious group which does not possess and publish at least one.

There have been various efforts to estimate and classify religious publications. By organized church or doctrine—150 to 200 Jewish, 400 to 500 Roman Catholic, a thousand Protestant, maybe 1,700 in all. Those are today's figures but there never has been a time when religious periodicals did not play a major role in American journalism.

Frank Luther Mott, the great historian of magazines, estimated that approximately a hundred religious weeklies, Congregational, Episcopal,

Methodist, and Presbyterian, were appearing in the 1830's. Some of them evolved into general magazines, as did the *Independent*, a Congregational weekly founded in 1848 and edited by Henry Ward Beecher, famous and controversial New York preacher.

Early also came the growth of denominational multiple publishing, with major churches distributing dozens of their own different publications through their own publishing houses. This trend has continued and grown and concentrated today, so that in Nashville the Southern Baptists, the Methodists, the Seventh-Day Adventists have giant printing and editing plants. Other centers are Philadelphia for the Presbyterians and Episcopalians, Minneapolis and St. Louis for Lutherans and Disciples of Christ.

What is a Religious Magazine?

What is the religious magazine? The voice of religious belief. What is its role? To express and reinforce religious faith, to win new believers. To achieve these goals, however, the area of religious publications has become broad and complex. The range is from the major area of concentration, church school publications, to such peripheral periodicals as church construction and comics.

One major division is composed of denominational magazines, founded early due to non-ecumenical divisions, which include publications for clergy and the laity, for adults and for babies. In fact, there actually is pre-natal anticipation, with the Southern Baptist *Your Baby-to-Be*. There are non-sectarian family publications such as *Christian Herald*, the journals of opinion as *Christian Century* or *Commonweal* or *Commentary*, and the technical specialized periodicals for the church library, the leaders of the church children's choir and church finance.

Not only are the numbers and varieties of religious magazines high, but their circulations also are impressive when taken either as a total or in individual cases. *The Watchtower* (of Jehovah's Witnesses) is near the 5 million-mark and circulates in more than 70 countries. Methodist's *Upper Room* has 3 million and its monthly *Together* is pushing 600,000. The *Catholic Digest* reaches 600,000, *Presbyterian Life* 1,000,000. Efforts to estimate the millions of children reached by church school "story papers" would be just guess-timates —but the Catholics alone count more than six million students in their parochial educational system. The "World Almanac" cites reports from 233 religious bodies which list a Sunday or Sabbath school enrollment of 46,856,391. When one considers that each one of these children may be receiving at least one religious periodical every week, the figures become almost astronomical!

One must realize, however, in assessing size of circulation that church school circulation is free or "give-away" circulation, with distribution to the youngsters in Sunday school classes. In addition, the "every-member" plan used by such periodicals as *Upper Room, Together*, and *Presbyterian Life* also amounts to controlled circulation, for each individual church subscribes at reduced rates for each family—sometimes for more than one member of a family.

Editorial Goals and Content

Objectives and the content of church periodicals certainly differ widely as is evident from examining some editorial statements of policy—and also from looking at the magazines themselves.

A representative statement might be that of James L. Sullivan, executive secretary-treasurer of the Sunday School Board of the Southern Baptist Convention. In the elaborate 52-page "Church Literature Guidebook," Sullivan writes:

The printed truth enters doors

through which spokesmen may never go. It is as sound as the spoken truth, but has the potential of reaching multitudes who may never hear it.

Spreading the printed truth through its church literature and related materials is one of the objectives of the Sunday School Board. These objectives were adopted by the convention in 1965, though in practice they have been adhered to since the Board was established in 1891.

Each church literature publication has its specific purpose. Publications dealing with theological matters are firmly based on clearly stated doctrinal positions, totally consistent with the historic beliefs of the denomination.

Publications dealing in such fields as teaching, training, family ministry, or recreational topics are based on an unswerving adherence to the truth and on the soundest of ethical and moral standards. At every stage of their preparation and distribution, the guidance of the Holy Spirit is conscientiously sought.

May God speak through this church literature, and may Christ be honored through the response of individuals to the truth they find therein.

A closer look at individual church magazines shows policy in practice.

Storytime (Southern Baptist): "Primaries and Beginners will delight with this illustrated weekly. Its simple stories about other boys and girls will help the youngsters learn the basic principles of Christian life—sharing, loving, giving, and being thankful. Poems, puzzles, how-to-do-it articles, and occasional game suggestions give this storypaper variety and readability."

Words of Cheer (Mennonite)—"Published weekly for children, 9–14.

65

Nonfiction: Articles, 800 to 1,500 words, designed to increase the child's interest in Christianity, his understanding of the Bible, his identification with the church; human interest sketches of noteworthy children; creative approaches to personality improvement, nature and hobbies.

"Fiction: Wholesome stories for the modern child. 1,500 to 2,300 words, encouraging Christian attitudes toward himself and others and the situations in which he finds himself. Unconventional treatment welcomed if handled discreetly. Character-building emphasis should be inherent in stories. Serials to five parts.

"Verse: Avoid religious and poetic cliches. Semi-humorous verse with an unexpected twist often used. Wants some nature verse, 4–20 lines.

"Fillers: Quizzes and puzzles, especially on biblical themes."

Presbyterian Life is described by its publishers, The United Presbyterian Church in the United States of America, as a "religious family magazine which covers a broad editorial scope: current events, history, theology, philosophy, medicine, literature, music and the arts and recreation." Broad scope indeed! As with most religious publications, advertising policy bans liquor and tobacco advertising. Color photographs are used frequently on the cover; inside, one color is the rule.

The Catholic Layman—"Nonfiction: Want practical (not theoretical) articles that concern people in their everyday life, having at least some reference to them as Christians. Should be factual articles bearing on current events, social and personal problems, family life, Catholic-Protestant cooperation; topics of interest to Catholics as citizens and parishioners; controversy, apologetical, popular explanation of moral theology. Matters of U.S. interest. (Very little that would have European or other locale.) No devotional articles. Material should be written in reportorial style with magazine flair. See 'Counseling: Couch or Confessional?' in a recent issue."

We see in a Winter copy of *Christian Adventure*, a Christmas poem within the modern duochromatic cover with its old white church surrounded by dingy tenements. Then comes a feature story of a teen-ager and his religious credo, accompanied by snapshots. This in turn is followed by a serious discussion on "Prayer." Then there's a Christmas story on "The Case of the Thin Chocolate Man," and after that an article on "Affluence and Poverty: Dilemma for Christians."

America, the Jesuit weekly of opinion, devotes one issue to "Prague in Metamorphosis," an analysis of the Communist satellite; the use of "Modern English in the Mass;" an ecumenical discussion by a Methodist layman on "Protestant Mergers;" as well as editorials, letters from readers, book reviews, and current news items. Ads total six pages out of 32, and include books,

Catholic colleges, and General Motors. The cover is a "shocking pink" ball almost seven inches in diameter, catching you between the eyes, against the flat white cover with its Gothic nameplate in black. Only black and white line cuts inside.

Format in religious magazines runs the gamut of the possible. Methodist's "ultra-liberal" *motive* is full of abstract drawings within bold abstract covers, incorporating two or three flat colors, on good text paper and with layouts utilizing ragged right copy, much reverse typography, and a determined "modern" design. For its college-age readers, it may be just the right touch.

Inside *motive*, the article and verses are even more determinedly modern, mirroring the supposed "revolt" of the college student against the world. In a page-long poem, James den Boer writes,

IV

The Asian Wars happened at last.
When the rifles were given out
on streetcorners, the black men
and the white men lined up for them.
Once in their hands . . . .

XII

I did not want to go into the white light.
The Negro broke his gun, then turned
his harsh eye. My father kissed his mother.
The harsh lies did us all in, in time.
Once in our hands, the birds sang lovely
songs, opened scarlet wounds, told love: Go.

Immediately following is a piece on "When Stokely Met the Presidents: Black Power and Negro Education," which states,

The dominant concern was embodied in a set of questions which Black Power advocates have been burning into the ears and consciences of all who will listen: How will these schools and their students relate to the residents of America's black ghettos? What will be their posture towards a society that has broken the lives of its Negroes, both in and out of the ghettos? What is their loyalty to a nation which solemnly promises to crush non-white rebellions all over the world from now on?

Aimed at college students, *motive* focuses on its concept of their problems—the next article deals with "Higher Education: Social Adjustment or Human Liberation?" Nat Hentoff, the voluminous writer on all that's new, considers next, "Overturning the School System at I.S. 201." Perhaps, the dissonant chords which *motive* sometimes strikes are sounded most clearly in another title, "New Left Man Meets the Dead God." The Negro, education, sex, art, poetry—these are the mainstay, reiterated in issue after issue.

Nursery-age picture periodicals have big type, pastel or bright primary-colored drawings, simple short stories and verses. These children's magazines basically do not differ very much from the commercial juveniles such as *Humpty Dumpty* or *Highlights*. Their stories are sweet, short, and simple—really words filling in the edges around the bold, splashy pictures. They will carry a simple moral and draw more frequently from Biblical sources. But they are carefully oriented to the proper age with the right vocabulary and level of interest.

The *Christian Century* might be *Nation* or *New Republic* with its unrelieved black-and-white text on rough coarse paper, minus pictures, and with the usual table-of-contents typographical cover in constant black and white. Subjects range over the whole human condition with one recent six-months index listing: Abortion, 7 items; Advertising, 9; Armed Forces, 29; Catholicism, 84, and Church and arts, communism, education, international relations, politics, race, etc. totaling some 390.

Together is full of four-color pix, both photographs and drawings, feature articles and stories with "punchy" writing, and a few house and book ads—sometimes it's been criticized as "slick-paper Christianity" and certainly is an earnest effort to compete, as a Christian magazine, with secular slicks for readership. But the editors are aware of their problem for a colorful back-cover house ad is headlined, "IS YOUR HOME DELUGED WITH READING MATERIAL?" And leads off with, "A reader recently noted, 'I like *Together* but it is just one of SO MANY magazines coming to our home each month.'"

Contributors to *Together* seem chosen, by design or accident, from the ranks of lay leaders and from the clergy. Their writing is oriented to socio-religious questions that perplex the church member's conscience today. "Teaneck's Success Story" deals with integrated residential housing in the suburbs. Next comes a personal first-person narrative of a woman's second marriage and the difficulties which arose between her teen-age son and her new husband. Will man destroy his natural birthright, the good earth, is another first-person piece in "The View from Mt. Nebo." Interspersed with these varied articles are regular departments such as "People Called Methodists," "The Church in Action," "Teens Together." It's a scatter-gun technique in the hope that there'll be some member of the family hit by some story in each issue.

Together also distributes with each issue a four-page insert such as "Together/News Edition—ILLINOIS Area," chiefly carrying brief and timely stories about churches and events of timely interest.

From its beginnings in England in 1861 until today, the Salvation Army has mingled with the people where they live and its colorful magazine is just as simple and colorful as the Salvation Army girl on the corner. *The War Cry*, appearing weekly since 1880, has regional editions as well as regional editors in addition to the main staff. Full-color and one-color are used generously throughout the slim publication which carries short stories and articles, by-lined by well-known names, with a spiritual theme.

Structure of Major Denominational Publishing Houses

Many of the major denominations have large and carefully organized magazine and book publishing houses, controlled by the church and supervised by selected publishers and editors. The Christian Board of Publications, for example, is affiliated with the Christian Churches (Disciples of Christ).

The Methodist Publishing House is, as the name indicates, the over-all roof for eight operational divisions of this, the largest Protestant Church. While more complex than some, its structure will provide some understanding of the nature of religious publishing.

The Board of Education is a vital part of the picture, for the United Methodist Church, like the majority of religious groups, is a mammoth religious educational system. And the majority of its publications are designed for use in educational enterprises conducted by each local church. The Board of Education establishes the policy which guides the editorial functions of the church school curriculum publications.

The Methodist Publishing House, which is the operating arm for the Board of Publication, is closely tied to both the individual local church and to the national administrative organization. The local church does, at some distance, participate in the election of delegates to conferences which in turn, elect members of the administrative bodies of both the Board of Education and the Board of Publication. The accompanying charts, reproduced in this chapter, show clearly the involved and detailed nature of the links in the chain of responsibility.

The Board of Publications, is the policy-making body for general United Methodist Church periodicals, for Abingdon Press (book publishing), and for the production and business divisions known as publishing, manufacturing, sales (Cokesbury is the name given the retail bookstores), accounting and personnel-public relations.

A considerable number of religious publishing houses do their own printing and the United Methodist Church will have three major printing centers, in Nashville, Tennessee, and Dayton and Cincinnati, Ohio, as its merger with the Evangelical United Brethren becomes effective. Its editorial offices likewise include not only the three cities named, but also New York and Chicago. Such denominational mergers as the Methodist—EUB not only have become the trend of the ecumenical 1960's but the unity movement has extended to other areas of religious editorial and advertising agreements. Nine Protestant periodicals, with a combined approximately three and a half million readers, have decided on joint publication of editorial articles—there is, of course, little risk of duplicating readership. In advertising solicitation, The Interfaith Group, composed of Catholic, Jewish, and Protestant magazines, has been formed to sell space to national advertisers.

Talking with the Editors

While charts of organization are helpful in understanding the mechanics of magazine publishing, the editor is the heart of the magazine. Let's visit, therefore, two representative editors of two different church magazines. Both are in Nashville, Tenn., only three blocks apart.

You enter a modern office building, with elaborate entrance hall and blonde receptionist, when you walk into the publishing headquarters of the Southern Baptist Convention. There I talked with Lucy Hoskins, the editor of *Church Administration*, slim and cool in green in her pastel office with African violets on the window-sill.

"Perhaps I can take a clearer look at our Sunday school periodicals because the magazine I edit, *Church Administration*, is in a different field," Miss Hoskins commented. "But first let me just tell you about the Baptist home and leadership magazines.

"We have three basic home and devotional periodicals—*Home Life*, a monthly for parents' use in the home to promote daily Christian living. Then there are *Open Windows*, and the *Bible Reader's Guide*, two quarterlies organized for daily personal reading of the scriptures."

She held up a copy of *Church Administration*.

"This, of course, is my favorite which I've worked on since it began. The other eight leadership magazines include five for church music—the choirs and their directors; *Church Recreation*; and the *Church Library Magazine*. I think their names are pretty descriptive. *The Quarterly Review* is designed to keep pastors, school workers, and church officers aware of our church progress and history."

Miss Hoskins pointed to a long row of magazines on a shelf.

"There, that should give you some idea of the number of different Sunday school publications we have—I think there are almost 50 of them, including special magazines in Braille for the blind, for the deaf, and in Spanish. We have graded materials for all age levels—and the staffs of these periodicals are carefully trained in curricular organization and development, as well as educational principles.

"Our Sunday schools are divided into seven major departments—Adult; Young People, 17 through 24; Intermediate, 13 through 16; Junior, 9 through 12; Primary, 6 through 8; Beginner, 4 through 5; and Nursery, birth through 3. Each age level has its own weekly, monthly, and quarterly magazines—and the teachers for each level have their own periodicals, too."

She gave me copies of the different magazines—attractive formats, chiefly 5½ by 8 inches in size, printed in fine four-color on good quality enamel-coated papers. I admired them and told Miss Hoskins so.

"Thank you—we do try."

"How about the stories and articles—who writes them? Who does the art work and layouts? And do you handle your own printing?"

"Eighty per cent of our material is assigned or staff-written, which leaves about a fifth of our space for the free-lance to fill. We have a central art department which provides practically all of our layout and art. And we contract for all our printing. How's that for answers right to the point? You know, some people say women talk too much."

I assured Miss Hoskins that talk with her was rewarding, indeed, and she told me about her own training which includes a master's degree in journalism. Then we said goodbye and I went down the elevator and walked a short distance in the sunshine to the equally handsome building which houses the Nashville headquarters of The Methodist Publishing House and the Editorial Division of the Board of Education.

There I was ushered into the office of another experienced woman editor, Mrs. Helen Couch, who heads the staff of *The Christian Home*. (Yes, there are men, many of them, who edit church magazines—but it *is* wide open in opportunity for women.)

"*The Christian Home* is a magazine for parents chiefly in their relationships with their children and each other. *Together* deals more widely with all areas of Christian concern," Mrs. Couch explained. "Yes, I guess our church magazines do demonstrate how thoroughly we cover the whole range of human experience."

I had commented again on the large number of church publications, Methodist ones in this case. While *Together* and *Christian Advocate*, for Methodist ministers, are edited in Chicago, the Nashville offices concentrate on book publishing (Abingdon Press) and church school periodicals for the Board of Education—all the way from *The Kindergartner* and *Three/Four* (3rd and 4th grades) up through *Accent on Youth* and *Face-to-Face* for high-schoolers.

"Church school publications are issued by the General Board of Education through the Graded Press, which is the curriculum publishing department of The Methodist Publishing House. All of them are prepared carefully to meet age interest and church goals."

I asked about the other Methodist magazines.

"Oh, yes, there are periodicals, such as *Youth Leader* for Church School teachers of youth, or *Christian Action* for young adults with leaders' helps in *Adult Leader*. Then there is *The Church School*, for church school teachers and superintendents, and finally *Mature Years*, for older adults.

"Of course you already know about our general Methodist magazine, *Together*, but how about *The Methodist Woman*, which is edited in New York in the Board of Missions?"

I admitted that was a new one to me.

"Well, we sometimes have trouble ourselves keeping in touch."

How about editorial or advertising taboos?

"As you might expect, we don't accept liquor or tobacco propaganda, and in church school publications we advertise only Methodist materials. *Together* and *Christian Advocate* accept outside advertising. Editorial policy is set largely by particular periodicals, depending on their individual objectives and age groups. For free-lancers, we offer a steady market, although I suppose a majority of our material is by assignment. As you can see," and she handed me mimeographed suggestion sheets, "we do try to help the free-lance writer understand our needs."

I nodded as I looked over the four or five pages of carefully prepared specific tips and hints (see Appendix). Here was an editor who certainly met her writers more than half-way.

Editorial procedures are affected by Methodist operation of their own printing plant; helpfully, Mrs. Couch believes. Art and layout is handled through one central art department also, although some individuals may be assigned personally for work with certain publications.

But as I glanced over the detailed production schedule Mrs. Couch handed me, I could see that each step was carefully planned, with work on the January issue, for example, beginning in mid-April, nine months in advance. There are 12 check dates for each story, as may be seen from the chart illustrated in this chapter.

When Mrs. Couch gave me another sheet, I was even more impressed. Editorial themes for emphasis are planned, on a month-by-month basis, years ahead. This was *methodical*, even for Methodists!

Independent Protestant Periodicals

"We want articles on all subjects of public questioning and controversy to which religion is related" is what the *Christian Century* tells the free-lancer. Controversy, in its journalistic sense, means reader interest to the editor and reader-interest means circulation. This may be a crass interpretation but it's a realistic one.

Protestant but non-denominational today, *Christian Century* was started in 1900 by the Disciples of Christ. But when Charles Clayton Morrison bought it eight years later, he soon moved it into a wider arena of liberal inquiry. This editorial policy continues today. Its circulation is 44,000.

Also involved in controversy is *Christianity Today*, which publishes "essays written from an evangelical (Biblical) Protestant perspective on crucial contemporary issues and indicating the driving relevance of the Christian revelation to the modern scene." Its combined paid and controlled circulation runs around 170,000.

Less addicted to argument but active as a family magazine since its founding in 1888, *Christian Herald* publishes short stories and articles, characterized as wholesome and inspirational by one experienced observer. This content has been popularly received, the magazine claims, offering as proof its frequent reprinting in *Reader's Digest* and a circulation of 400,000.

Catholic Magazines

Decentralized publishing with more single magazines issued by many different organizations are the two points which distinguish Roman Catholic from the major Protestant operations. "Writer's Market" lists, under "Religious," 56 different Catholic magazines. These are edited at 50 different addresses, ranging from Stockbridge, Mass., to St. Benedict, Ore. Twenty-two different Catholic orders of priests, nuns, and brothers are listed among the editors of these magazines.

Controversial subject matter is another characteristic of much modern Catholic publishing, or perhaps a better adjective would be questioning. While editorial diversity undoubtedly plays a strong part in producing such debate, monolithic publishing such as that of some Protestant churches is not apt to encourage argument within the ranks. The Vatican Councils I and II certainly encouraged question-asking by Catholics, and some Catholic editors have led in pointed queries.

Today, articles in Catholic family magazines range over such topics as freedom of conscience, birth control, sex education, civil rights. A recent issue of *Ave Maria*, a national Catholic weekly, included pieces on "The Plight of the Unwed Father," "Terrorism in Viet Nam," and "The Sideshow of the House Un-American Acitivities Committee." Although devotional and religious articles still occupy much space, especially in the more conservative periodicals, Catholics and non-Catholics alike have been startled, sometimes

73

pleased, sometimes horrified, by the new freedom of Catholic editors. Of course, the religious orders edit many periodicals intended for their own members, and these continue to concentrate on inspirational messages, spiritual and theological issues, organizational activities, and personal news items.

Opinion, world affairs, and criticism especially occupy the pages of some Catholic publications which appeal to the liberal or conservative intellectuals. *Commonweal*'s debate often is carried on with its conservative Catholic relative, William Buckley's *National Review*. *America*, edited by Jesuit fathers, describes itself as dealing with "current events in the light of Catholic thinking and scholarship. It serves the clergy, religious, educators and business, professional and political leaders interested in a serious Christian outlook on national and international affairs including social, economic, political, and technological problems plus education, religion, literature, and art. Current comment and editorials constitute 25 per cent of each issue; contributed articles, about 50 per cent; book reviews, 12 per cent; columns on arts, religion, the press, films, theatre, the balance."

While circulations are not large, ranging from 35 to 90 thousand, these magazines are quoted and influential to a degree—they influence the opinion-makers, as do their Protestant colleagues, *Christian Century* or *Christianity and Crisis*.

Catholic juvenile magazines stress devotional activity through stories and articles. A relatively small number, only seven of a total of 77 religious juveniles listed in the "Writer's Market," are identified as Catholic. Three of these originate with the George A. Pflaum Publications in Dayton, Ohio, as commercial ventures. They are: *Treasure Chest*, issued in comic book form for elementary parochial students; *Junior Catholic Messenger*, for both parochial boys and girls in the lower grades; and *Young Catholic Messenger*, for 11 to 14 year-olds and also intended for parochial classrooms. The two *Messengers* have circulations of 830,177 and 544,659, respectively.

Two additional Catholic publications may be mentioned which might conceivably be listed under Association periodicals, which also is true of the various journals issued by the different orders. They are *Columbia*, the official publication of the Knights of Columbus with more than a million circulation, and its junior version, the *Columbian Squires*. (See Chapter 9.)

Another widely circulated Catholic magazine is the *Catholic Digest*, which says its editorial policy is to provide "a condensed review of what is currently being published in magazines, books and newspapers in the U.S. and abroad—edited especially for Catholic families. Approximately 20 per cent of the content is 'religious' and 80 per cent is devoted to subjects of broad general interest—health, sports, education, travel, hobbies—in short, the business of living." This parochial version of *Reader's Digest* has a 582,500 circulation.

Partly digest, partly opinion, *Extension*, founded in 1906, is designed for popular taste, and uses Catholic personality features, articles of family appeal, and romance and mystery fiction. It is published by the Catholic Church Extension Society of the U.S.A. and has a 380,000 circulation. Similar magazines although less popular and more religious in tone, are the *Sacred Heart Messenger* (Jesuit), the *Saint Anthony Messenger* (Franciscan), and *The Sign* (Passionist) with circulations of nearly 150,000 for the first, and 305,000 and 212,000 respectively for the last two.

Jewish Magazines

Among the best known magazines edited or published by or for American Jews (and, in several cases, the general reader), there are *Commentary*, *American Judaism*, and *The National Jewish Monthly*. *Commentary* is a national journal of opinion which deals with controversy and current affairs and declares it is edited "for people with a belief in the power of the critical intelligence to locate and comprehend the issues playing beneath the surface of contemporary life. It is a magazine that aims primarily at clarifying these issues rather than at merely providing information; at encouraging original thought rather than reiterating known positions; at analyzing problems and discontents rather than engaging in pious celebrations; at keeping alive a 'utopian' sense of human possibility rather than settling for the world as given. Too, *Commentary* is a Jewish magazine edited to avoid parochialism and apologetics." It was founded in 1945 by the American Jewish Committee and has consistently carried the bylines of well-known contributors on a wide variety of social and cultural subjects. Circulation is 65,188.

While writers, editors, and publishers of Jewish ethnic origin are many and influential in the magazine world, the number of strictly Jewish periodicals is relatively small. Only eleven are listed under the religious categories of "Writer's Market" and the two SRDS magazine directories. Not one of these has an editorial address identical to the others. One or two others, edited for a more specialized clientele such as Zionist women or Jewish juveniles, also have different editorial offices. Diversity rather than denominational solidarity would seem to characterize the Jewish publishing world.

The National Jewish Monthly announces that its "editorial policy is to keep American Jewry informed on issues which concern them as Americans and as Jews. The magazine is a family publication for the major observances of American Jewry—Orthodox, Reform, Conservative. Contributors and correspondents for *The National Jewish Monthly* range throughout the globe to provide readers with reports and comments on world affairs, Jewish history, philosophic issues, social and cultural developments. Feature articles also cover

75

music, literature, arts, sports, travel, community affairs, and personalities in the news." It is the monthly national magazine of B'nai B'rith (and therefore might also be classed as an Association magazine), circulating to a paid list of 215,767.

Dimensions in American Judaism likewise is an official publication, founded in 1873 by the Union of American Hebrew Congregations (Reformed). A quarterly, it stresses all aspects of Jewish life and uses poetry and fiction as well as articles.

Jewish juvenile publications, as listed in "Writer's Market," are only two in number—*World Over*, for ages 9 to 14, and *Young Judean*, which covers the same age range and concentrates on American-Jewish and Zionist-Israeli history, holidays, legends, and poetry. Another Zionist and organization magazine is *Hadassah*, the official publication of the women's Zionist Organization of America with circulation concentrated among 332,966 members.

Commercial Religious Publications

While a large number of religious publications are produced chiefly for religious goals, other specialized publications seek their profits from church-related business. For example, there are *Church Management, Protestant Church Buildings & Equipment* (a *Christian Herald* publication), *Catholic Building and Maintenance, Christian Life, Your Church,*—all concerned commercially with the tremendous church investment in buildings and their care.

Bookstores have their commercial publications in the *Catholic Book Merchandiser* and the *Christian Bookseller*. Clergymen have their own professional magazines in *The Homiletic and Pastoral Review* (a Joseph F. Wagner Publication) for Catholic priests, and *Pulpit Digest* for Protestant pastors.

The $ in the vast religious market is stressed in the professional advertising of these publications. *Your Church* proclaims "learn how to reach and sell the Pastor / Architect team . . . the important decision makers in today's BILLION $ CHURCH MARKET for products like these: acoustical materials, air conditioning, audio-visual equipment, flooring, kitchen equipments, lawn maintenance, office furniture." *Your Church* claims its controlled circulation goes to 186,707 Protestant pastors, 3,503 synagogues, and 5,315 architects.

Church Management talks about a 2.4 billion dollar market reached by its 8,585 paid and 3,290 non-paid circulation and says the average annual budget of its subscriber churches is $169,031 compared with an average for Protestant churches of $9,156.

Catholic Building and Maintenance, one of the three Wagner magazines, gives a "business analysis" of its 38,392 circulation as including 5 cardinals,

76

34 archbishops, 235 bishops, etc., and claims "an almost 2-to-1 margin" over *The Catholic Market*, its competitor published by the Catholic Publishing Center of the Archdiocesan College of St. Thomas in St. Paul.

Christian Life, published monthly by Christian Life Publications, Inc. of Wheaton, Ill., which lists three other commercial church magazines, states in SRDS that it "is prepared for those who buy or influence purchasing in the Protestant church, Sunday school, Christian educational institute, and home. The majority of these are pastors, church or Sunday school officers. Editorial areas include building plans, financing programs, kitchen equipment, floor coverings, projectors, screens, pews, chancel furniture, auxiliary seating, sanitary equipment and supplies, organs, pianos, choir vestments, books, Bibles, recordings. Editorial content covers: church building and development (12 per cent), family counsel (18 per cent), equipment and supplies for church and Christian educational activities (22 per cent), trends in church and Sunday school development (26 per cent), new products (17 per cent), religious recordings, radio, etc. (5 per cent)." Wheaton also is home editorial base for several other religious publications in the juvenile field.

When one considers the extent of the market, it is surprising there are not more publishers for commercial gain joining the denominational presses in printing magazines about church construction, church libraries, church music, and church book-selling. Religious memberships in the United States totaled 125,778,656, according to the "World Almanac" for 1968.

Religious Newspapers

While most people today may not think of the *Christian Science Monitor* as a religious newspaper, it was established in 1908 by the Church of Christ, Scientist, and still continues as the publication of that denomination. However, its excellent foreign and national coverage of general news and reporting on literary, music, and art developments have brought it a deserved reputation outside the religious area. With a circulation of 192,000 in several American editions and an overseas edition distributed in 120 countries, it utilizes modern electronic transmission and printing facilities.

Several small and large Catholic papers exist which are specifically Catholic also in content and style. One of the larger Catholic weeklies is the *Register*, printed in Denver, Colorado, and issued in several editions around the country. Another is *The Witness*, a weekly printed in Dubuque, Iowa, but also circulated nationally. Both are in standard newspaper size and *The Witness* especially is noteworthy for its printing quality and good halftone photographs.

How to Get a Job

If you'd like to work on a religious publication, if it's denominational, be sure you're a member of that church. Interviews and other contacts indicate that this rather natural requirement of religious background and mutual interest is almost universal. If you're going to work in one of the educational periodicals, get training in education. Some theological training may be helpful also, both in landing a job and keeping it. Finally, it helps to have some journalistic training.

In Closing

Church and synagogue complement their active institutional life in school and sanctuary with the circulation of millions of magazines to their members. These publications represent the complete range of modern life, and in content and goal seek to develop man socially and spiritually.

CHURCH SCHOOL PUBLICATIONS — THE LOCAL CHURCH TO THE LOCAL CHURCH

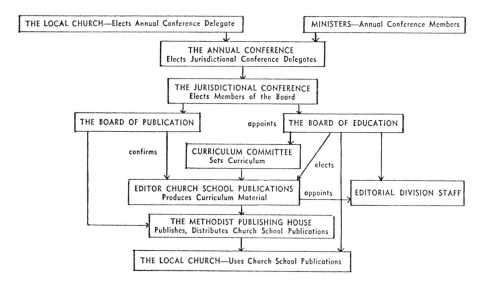

THE BOARD OF EDUCATION AND THE CURRICULUM COMMITTEE

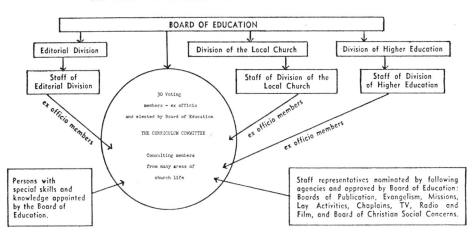

Chart showing relation of church-school publications to local organizations; chart showing relationship of the Board of Education and the Curriculum Committee; courtesy of The Methodist Publishing House.

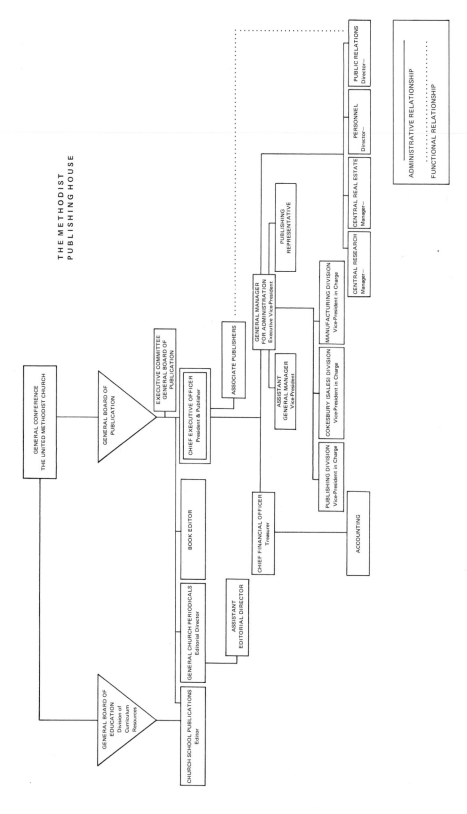

Organization chart of the Methodist Publishing House. Use by courtesy of the Methodist Publishing House.

DATE DUE SCHEDULE

Issue	PP. Due From Writer	Stories Due For Illust. Art D.	Manu't Due	Copies To Study Guide Writer	Engrav's Copy Due	Copy Due F'm Canada	To Press	1st Proof Received	1st Proof To Can.	1st Proof Returned	2nd Proof Received	2nd Proof Returned
Jan.	Apr. 15	May 1	June 1	July 15	July 24	Aug. 1	Aug. 28	Oct. 5	Oct. 5	Oct. 13	Oct. 21	Oct. 23
Feb.	May 15	June 1	July 1	Aug. 15	Aug. 24	Sept. 1	Sept. 28	Nov. 5	Nov. 5	Nov. 13	Nov. 21	Nov. 23
Mar.	June 15	July 1	Aug. 1	Sept. 15	Sept. 24	Oct. 1	Oct. 28	Dec. 5	Dec. 5	Dec. 13	Dec. 21	Dec. 23
Apr.	July 15	Aug. 1	Sept. 1	Oct. 15	Oct. 24	Nov. 1	Nov. 28	Jan. 5	Jan. 5	Jan. 13	Jan. 21	Jan. 23
May	Aug. 15	Sept. 1	Oct. 1	Nov. 15	Nov. 24	Dec. 1	Dec. 28	Feb. 5	Feb. 5	Feb. 13	Feb. 21	Feb. 23
June	Sept. 15	Oct. 1	Nov. 1	Dec. 15	Dec. 24	Jan . 1	Jan. 28	Mar. 5	Mar. 5	Mar. 13	Mar. 21	Mar. 23
July	Oct. 15	Nov. 1	Dec. 1	Jan. 15	Jan. 24	Feb. 1	Feb. 28	Apr. 5	Apr. 5	Apr. 13	Apr. 21	Apr. 23
Aug.	Nov. 15	Dec. 1	Jan. 1	Feb. 15	Feb. 24	Mar. 1	Mar. 28	May 5	May 5	May 13	May 21	May 23
Sept.	Dec. 15	Jan. 1	Feb. 1	Mar. 15	Mar. 24	Apr. 1	Apr. 28	June 5	June 5	June 13	June 21	June 23
Oct.	Jan. 15	Feb. 1	Mar. 1	Apr. 15	Apr. 24	May 1	May 28	July 5	July 5	July 13	July 21	July 23
Nov.	Feb. 15	Mar. 1	Apr. 1	May 15	May 24	June 1	June 28	Aug. 5	Aug. 5	Aug. 13	Aug. 21	Aug. 23
Dec.	Mar. 15	Apr. 1	May 1	June 15	June 24	July 1	July 28	Sept. 5	Sept. 5	Sept. 13	Sept. 21	Sept. 23

Editorial schedule for *The Christian Home*; courtesy of Mrs. Helen Couch, editor. Used by permission of The Methodist Publishing House.

Curriculum Units -- THE CHRISTIAN HOME

	1964-65	1965-66	1966-67	1967-68	1968-9	1968-70
Sept.	The Family Deals With the Pressures of Society	Keeping Up With Children of Tomorrow	The Family and the World of Work	The Family and Higher Education	Discipline -- What? How?	When There's Work to Be Done
Oct.	Teaching Religion in the Home	The Health of the Family	Impact of Mass Communication Media on the Family	The Family and Vocation	Still a Member of the Family	The Question of Authority
Nov.	Christian Citizenship	Family Economics	Planning and Parenthood	Our Changing Knowledge of the Bible	Our Family and the Joneses	Money and the Family
Dec.	When the Family Entertains	What Love is in the Family	The Family Observes Christmas	Family Rituals -- A Way to Deeper Meaning	Friends of the Family	From Generation to Generation
Jan.	Faith for the New Year	The Family Faces Its Conflicts	Too Little--Too Much	A Nation of Cities	Parents -- Keepers of the Faith	All God's Children
Feb.	The Family's Relation to Persons of Varying Social Background	The Family Enjoys Art	Facing Family Feelings	What Happens As Children Grow	Learning to Cope	The Scriptures
Mar.	Togetherness and Solitariness	The Family and the Church	When Your Children Ask	The Meaning of Christian Marriage	Teaching of Values in the Home	Parents and Report Cards
Apr.	The Family Discovers the World of Nature	A Family Makes a Difference	The Family as Neighbors	The Kingdom of God and the Kingdom of This World	Too Busy!	In Times of Trouble
May	Faith in God for Today's World	What Determines Your Standards?	National Family Week Theme	National Family Week Theme	National Family Week Theme	National Family Week
June	Private Property	Changing Roles of Family Members	The Home in Your House	Mom and Dad: Who Are They	Before the First Birthday	Experiencing Forgiveness
July	Creativity vs Conformity	Outwitting Boredom in Family Living	Instant Happiness	Authority and Freedom	Christian Citizenship Begins at Home	Freedom/Responsibility
Aug.	The Scattered Family	Creative Learning in the Family	Home and School	The Family and Politics	God's World -- Our World	Love -- A Universal Need

Curriculum plans for six years for *The Christian Home*; courtesy of Mrs. Helen Couch, editor. Used by permission of the Methodist Publishing House.

three four

CHURCH STORY PAPER FOR BOYS AND GIRLS
IN ELEMENTARY III-IV
SECOND SUNDAY IN LENT
CHURCH COLOR: PURPLE
FEBRUARY 19, 1967 VOL. 3, NO. 6

ILLUSTRATED BY JIM PADGETT

The Boy Who Wrecked Things

by Virginia Calkins

Tina's grandfather lived alone in a little white house just half a block from where Tina lived. This made Tina glad for many reasons. It was fun to visit Grandfather and talk things over with him. Besides, he was good at fixing things that got broken.

One day Tina brought her detective kit over to Grandfather's house. It was a wooden box in which she kept her detective equipment, her magnifying glass, her secret code book and her ink pad for taking fingerprints. One of the hinges on the box was broken and Tina wanted Grandfather to fix it.

"How did you manage to break this?" Grandfather asked.

"I didn't break it," Tina answered quickly. "It was Jack West. He grabbed the box out of my hand and threw it down on the playground. It's a good thing I had

1

Cover of *Accent*, a church-school magazine for teen-agers. Copyright, 1968, Graded Press. Used by permission of The Methodist Publishing House.

6. The Giant Galaxy of Company Publications

A S soon as early cave man began drawing pictures on an animal skin, he started the process of communicating. When Abe traded his extra berries for Noah's surplus fish, then began also the future for company publications. For, as barter led to business and two men multiplied to four men, then came the need to tell each other how many berries you had to give for a big fish.

As the map unrolled and the Fuggers of the 15th century set up their agencies through Europe, their letters, telling of prices and trade, set the pattern for company publications of today.

What is a company publication? For years they were called house organs, a clumsy tag certainly. Then, probably in the 1930's, their editors began calling themselves "industrial editors" although actually they were producing publications for a single company. This confusion compounded confusion because periodicals also were produced by industrial trade associations and publishers, such as today's *Iron Age*, published by Chilton. For those who've gotten used to calling themselves "industrial editors," as do many members of the International Council of Industrial Editors, we have understanding. It's difficult to switch names after being accustomed to one for years—even if women do it every time they get married!

Man has seldom used words as labels in a more misleading fashion. Though "house organ" still appears, though "industrial editor" is a frequent misnomer, we shall refer to any periodical, for employees or customers of a single company as a *company publication* and to its editor as a *company editor*.

Already there is considerable evidence that "company publications" is a term used when clarity is desired. In Baird and Turnbull's "Industrial and Business Journalism," they call one of their two main sections "Company Publications." S. D. Warren Company in its excellent series of handbooks for customers (also company publications) titles one booklet, "The Company Publication."

When a company, then, such as Standard Oil of California, edits and publishes *The Standard Oiler* regularly for its employees, *that* is what we call a company publication. When Chevrolet circulates *Friends* regularly among its customers, that's a company publication. When Cities Service Company regularly sends *Service* to both its customers and employees, that's a company publication.

In all three cases, it's a periodical, published by a single company or corporation to communicate with its employees and salesmen, or dealers and people who might be interested in its products or services. *That's* a company publication by our definition.

As we've seen already, there are different kinds. The employee type is what is called an "internal." When you publish one for wholesalers or retailers of your company's products, that's an "external." And naturally, a combination of both audiences means that you're producing a "combination."

Internals dominate the company publication field with 66 per cent of the company publications measured in "Operation Tapemeasure No. 3," the survey of its editor-members conducted by the International Council of Industrial Editors. While this primacy has remained fairly constant since the first such study was conducted in 1956, the relative popularity of externals and combinations has fluctuated. After a dip to 12 per cent in 1963 from 18 per cent seven years earlier, externals climbed back to 17.4 per cent in 1967. This renewed popularity was largely at the expense of combinations which dropped to 11 per cent in the latest survey, after having spurted to 26 per cent in 1963 from 14 per cent in 1956.

Two centuries passed after the *News-Letter* of the great House of Fugger before its first successors as company externals and internals appeared on the American scene. Fugger, based in Augsburg, Bavaria, circulated its mercantile reports among its branches from mid-1400 to the middle of the 17th century, capitalizing on this inside information to become a financial empire.

Although the earliest American papers carried commodity prices, mercantile, and financial news, they were private rather than company enterprises and intended for anyone who could pay the price for reading them in the coffee-houses. It's hard to draw a hard and fast line between early newspaper and pioneer magazine, as Frank Luther Mott, journalism's historian, remarked. But using a paraphrase of his own definition, let us say that any magazine, company or not, is a bound periodical containing a variety of reading material. And a periodical is a publication which appears regularly under the same name.

Getting down to cases, several sources credit the *Lowell Offering* of the Lowell Cotton Mills in Massachusetts as the first company publication. It was an internal, first published in 1840, printing the creative efforts of the textile company's women workers. Another, and long-lasting, company publication was *The Mechanic*, published from 1847 to 1914 by the H. B. Smith Machine Company of New Jersey.

Certainly *Harper's Monthly*, promoting the books published by the Harper brothers in New York City, was a pioneer external founded in 1850, to sell a publisher's list. Volume one, number one, of *The Traveler's Record* appeared in Hartford, Connecticut, in March, 1865. It still is published, now under the name of *Protection*, by the Travelers Insurance Companies. Perhaps it's no coincidence that the oldest continuous daily newspaper in the United States, is the *Courant* which also began in Hartford in 1764.

The Traveler's Record carried verse in the first column of the first page of its first issue, parodying the marriage troubles of Enoch Arden whose wife took a second bigamous husband when Enoch didn't show up. It followed the doggerel by the following little anecdote—intended to sell insurance to travelers through Travelers, no doubt.

A Troy alderman got married the other day and had rather a thrilling time on his wedding tour. He was two days in getting to Buffalo on account of the snow, was in the American Hotel of that city when it burned down, and on his way to Chicago was thrown over an embankment twenty feet high by a railroad accident, badly bruising him and his new wife. The couple are now in Chicago, recovering from their injuries and getting courage to try the return trip.

After this came two full columns reporting on railroad accidents and noting "it is a wise and safe precaution to obtain insurance against accidents, in the Travelers." Page one closes under the headline "Too Late," with a poignant note.

Dr. F. T. Hurxthal, Examining Surgeon for the Travelers Insurance Company at Massillon, Ohio, was instantly killed on Tuesday, January 31st, by falling upon a piece of iron which penetrated his skull. Dr. H. had one or two beneficiaries under his charge at the time but had neglected to take out a policy of insurance for himself.

Fifty thousand copies of this insurance internal and external made it a circulation leader in the 1860's when its distribution exceeded that of such general magazines as *Leslie's, Godey's Ladies Book, The Police Gazette,* and *Saturday Evening Post. The Record* was distributed not only through the Traveler agencies but also in hotels, barber shops, and clubrooms. James G. Batterson, founder of Travelers, is credited also with founding its *Record.* The first issue said modestly of itself, "It has one thing to recommend it; it costs its readers nothing."

In its hundred-plus years of life, the *Record* has had only six editors and has included such illustrious contributors as Mark Twain, Josh Billings, early humorist, and Thomas Nast, the cartoonist who created the Republican elephant and Democratic donkey. Today it's a monthly for the company's agents, brokers, and salaried agency personnel.

Hartford was the birthplace also for *The Locomotive,* issued in 1867 by the Hartford Steam Boiler Inspection and Insurance Company. Today's Massey-Ferguson Company had *The Triphammer,* a true internal, circulating in 1885, and another pioneer employee publication was National Cash Register's *Factory News,* issued in 1890 and still published today as the *NCR Factory News.*

A single year, 1908, in the first decade of the 20th century is noteworthy for the founding of three major externals still flourishing today as leaders. They include *Ford Times* whose circulation of a million and a half made it a real competitor of the Ford Model T which was born the same year.

World wars and the hosts of new workers which accompanied the overnight mushrooming of industry brought boom periods for the company publication which the depressions of the '20's and '30's could only momentarily discourage. Indeed the impetus of World War II created a momentum which still is evident, and an estimated 17,000 company publications form the largest branch of the magazine family.

Profile of an Internal

What is an internal?

Basically, it's a monthly or weekly periodical, published by management and distributed to employees. Those employees may be all types of workers, from white-collar and managerial to semi-skilled and part-time. The internal may attempt to cover this complete wide range and serve all plants and operations of the company. Or, there may be an internal for each separate plant, or for each different type of employee—the managerial, the clerical, the researcher, the salesman, the foreman. The variety is endless and governed by the nature and structure of operations in that particular business.

If a company operates a chain of groceries and its employees are stock boys and check-out girls, their interests and management's will call for a certain type of publication in content and style. If the corporation chiefly operates in mining and employs thousands of hard-rock miners, that will predetermine the kind of internal designed for their reading.

Many large corporations have a cross-section of employee occupations—stenographers, accountants, salesmen, machinists, electricians, maintenance men. If so, it's quite an undertaking to find a common denominator for all of them. In fact, it may be desirable to have several different internals, one for each major occupation represented on the payroll.

Exhibit of an External

When the company looks outside, it's looking for sales, promotion, public relations, customers old and new. And that's just what the external considers as it plans to win readership. While some observers draw a line between the external which emphasizes selling and the external which stresses buying, this seems an artificial distinction. The sellers may be the company, or its wholesalers and retailers, and the salesmen or dealers they employ. The customers, new or old, are buyers, and may be found either at the wholesale or retail level. It's simpler and perfectly accurate to define external readers as those outside the company itself.

Of course, the same company may publish several different specialized externals. So we find some of them concentrating on the wholesaler, others on the retail store, some on the individual customer. And the salesman, whether the girl behind the counter or the traditional traveling man with his sample case, is the reader sought by other special externals.

Externals may be directed to various geographical regions of the United States or published internationally in Spanish, Italian, or other foreign languages.

Another form of specialized external reports to the stockholders of the company. Not only through annual reports but also by means of monthly or quarterly periodicals, it gives them special information about expansion, new processes and products, management changes—all the fundamental facts to keep them convinced they are wisely sharing in the company's life and profits.

In some cases, the wholesale distributors of a company's products publish an external for retail dealers.

The second major function of externals, in addition to their responsibility for selling, is public relations. The two goals, of course, are closely allied, with reciprocal benefits arising from their reinforcing relations.

Many externals extend their circulation to achieve public relations benefits. Their mailing lists will include the officers and members of major trade organizations and the editors of industrial publications in common or allied fields. On the lists also will be found the names of important and influential leaders in government, in business, in education, in communications—because they are considered makers or leaders of public opinion.

This public relations function is one of the chief goals of the combination also. Whether considered as public relations, promotion of a favorable image and response, or communications to convey information and influence other social institutions, the external and the combination both are edited and published with the realization that sales and prestige are Siamese twins.

Today, more and more corporations have widely diversified their products and services. In keeping with this diversification, for example, Eastman Kodak publishes one external for dentists, another for medical radiologists, one for retail processors and developers, one for commercial photographers, at least 20 different externals in all, 13 domestic and seven international.

As matters stand today, more money probably is spent proportionately on an external than the internal. The external is printed on heavier, slicker paper, the cover and much of the inside is run in attractive four-color, with plenty of eye-taking photographs and effective use of white space. Plus a high degree of human interest colorfully spotlighted in the articles. There's no reason the internal should be duller or drabber—many can and do hold their own in any competition. But somehow there's a tendency to dress up more when it's not just family.

Composite of a Combination

A combination is what its name implies, a combination of internal for employees and external for dealers and customers. In many cases, this double objective makes the choice and treatment of content difficult. It's hard to use the same language and subject matter for readers with such widely varying interests. In fact, the content and writing may have to be quite different.

In one case, Edna Greene who works in the traffic department of the Goodstrong Rubber Company is personally involved when Mary Boslow gets promoted from filing clerk to secretarial assistant. A thousand miles away, Joe Wiechowski gets a flat and wants to buy a new tire. He wants to know about Goodstrong's new no blow-out guarantee and he couldn't care less about Mary's promotion.

It's true, however, that an article may be written about Goodstrong's purchase of Famous Star Films which will be read with interest by both Edna

84

Greene and Joe Wiechowski. Then the editor of a combination has solved one of his problems. It boils down to this—some companies offer goods or services which have a wide base of appeal and use. If the editor chooses wisely and carefully, and the article is written to appeal widely also, then you have some essential ingredients in the recipe for your combination.

Combinations lean to the relatively more costly and attractive format of the external. If generalizations are ever safe, it might be safe to generalize that combinations should focus primarily on the outside reader. Their contents may be more eye-catching for the employee than the relatively low-keyed treatment of his internal. There's nothing, of course, which says that an internal has to be dull. In most cases, the internal is still necessary and vital. No combination can really take its place. At its best, the combination is an extra benefit—for the company and its employees—probably well worth the relatively small extra cost of a few thousand more copies from the same press run.

Vital Statistics

Estimates vary as to how many company publications exist, although there's considerable agreement that they number at least 17,000, making this the largest field by far among all magazines or specialized publications. A single major corporation may issue as many as 40 or 50 although there are many more instances of one company, one publication. And that one publication, if there's only one, is most likely to be an internal. Very probably you have received some form of internal whatever job you've held.

Externals are extensive today, also. With your monthly bills from the phone or electric company, you very likely have found little four-page leaflets about their new services. Or a monthly magazine from Chevrolet if you drive a Chevrolet. Your insurance agent sees that you get a regular publication, all about Northwestern Mutual and its advantages.

While estimates vary, it seems reasonable to believe that the circulation figures may run higher than a half-billion copies per issue for the company publications in the United States. Total cost for these single issues runs to more than $100 million. Annually, it's a billion-dollar business. That's not surprising, inasmuch as some 70 million Americans every month are receiving at least one company internal or external—that's more than double the combined circulations of *Reader's Digest, Life, Look,* and *Saturday Evening Post.* The staffs of company publications probably total 15,000 men and women.

Along with this size goes considerable stability. The ICIE "Operation Tapemeasure" in 1963 showed that 95 per cent of the 1,600 editor-members who replied, worked for companies more than 25 years old.

Slightly less than half (46 per cent) of company publications were issued on a monthly basis in 1967. Other frequencies were: bimonthly, 17 per cent; quarterlies, 13 per cent; biweeklies, 9 per cent; and weeklies, 4 per cent. Obviously the company publication is not primarily regarded as a newspaper, carrying all the news hot off the press—if it were, it couldn't afford to appear more infrequently than once a week. And newspaper format, except in tabloid size, is used today by less than a third (28 per cent) of the company publications, the other two-thirds preferring magazine size and format.

Frequency of production is closely related to time necessary for production. Seventy per cent of the publications take from 50 to 400 hours to produce editorially. One out of ten took even more time. Less than 10 per cent were edited in fewer than 20 hours.

Of course, staff size has a good deal to do also with time required for editorial work. One out of three editors has one or more full-time assistants, while 60 per cent had at least one part-time helper. Some staffs run as high as 15 or 20 for the larger publications.

Staff time is devoted to editorial work—writing, editing, layout. An advertising staff is not needed for there's no outside advertising except for a minority of externals. Again, circulation is a relatively minor problem. While most internals used to be handed out in the plant, today's circulation is by mail (3rd class is used by 46.7 per cent) with only one publication in eight distributed at work. With mail delivery, the worker can have it handy at home to read, at his leisure—and so can the members of his family, particularly that major decision-maker, the missus.

Most externals or combinations are distributed by mail. Either envelope or self-mailer may be used, the postage rates are identical. There's a saving with the self-mailer due to elimination of the envelope, plus time for stuffing. There are four methods for 3rd class postage: use of ordinary stamps, precanceled stamps, postage meter, printed permit imprint. Savings also may be achieved by use of 3rd class bulk mailing rates, which are lower.

Circulations are most frequent in the range 1,000 to 10,000 with almost two-thirds represented. But 13 per cent distribute up to 25,000, 6 per cent to 50,000, and nearly 6 per cent are 50,000 or more.

Mechanical production exhibits a major swing to offset printing, from less than a third of company publications in 1956 to more than 61 per cent today. All but eight per cent of the balance are letterpress jobs. Pictures command considerable space, from 20 to 40 per cent the available total. Color also has added its pulling power, with two-thirds of the published company magazines using one color or more in addition to black. Of these periodicals, more than three-fourths use two colors. One of every eight goes in for regular use of three, four, or five colors and company publications today often make a masterful chromatic display!

If one could arrange a composite of all company publications, it would be a 12-page monthly internal, measuring $8\frac{1}{2}$ by 11 inches, with a two-color cover and plenty of photographs. There is an important minority which prefers the 6 by 9-inch size.

Costs of publication? On a single-copy basis, in 1963, slightly more than a third cost from 21 cents to 50 cents per copy to produce. The second largest group, spending from 51 cents to one dollar, totals nearly 18 per cent of the group surveyed. The company publication is certainly no cheapie.

The company is the publisher. It pays the bill and determines basic policy. In actual practice, the publisher's regular title may be executive vice president, or the vice president for public relations, or the vice president for industrial relations. These are the three operational posts most likely to hold top authority over company publications. Or it may be an executive heading a subdivision under one of the top trio—with a title of director of communications or publications. In a few situations, the editor may be his own policy-maker, and rise or fall accordingly.

Some writers on company publications suggest an "advisory board" consisting of the directors of public and industrial relations, managers or superintendents of major operating and production divisions. This system, while impressive on paper and perhaps sometimes helpful as a source of suggestions, does not always prove realistic and practical. Personal and informal conversations with pertinent executives on specific stories are apt to be more useful. One editor of a large external has an advisory board, 30 names on paper. How often does he consult them, how often do they advise him? "Practically never," he says.

Actually if the editor is responsible to one top executive, that's likely to work better. Different companies vary in their tables of organization. Eastman Kodak has the director of industrial relations coordinating the work of its internals, while the director of public relations and the various marketing divisions divide responsibility for share-owner, dealer, technical, and customer publications. This decentralization may be desirable, even necessary, for a large corporation.

ICIE's 1967 survey asked, "To whom does the editor report?" The answers came back: to the public relations manager, 25.9 per cent; a vice president, 19.1 per cent; the industrial relations manager, 16.1 per cent; the president, 12 per cent. One out of eight respondents said the editor is his own boss—still responsible presumably to the man who hires and fires!

Sample Staff Situations

Whether the editor makes policy or not, he'll certainly be busy carrying it out—by planning forthcoming issues, by writing and editing, by conferring with the artists-photographers about illustrations and cover.

Except for major corporations, most companies have relatively small staffs for their internals—as already mentioned, in two-thirds there's at least one full-time or part-time assistant. The typical situation might be the editor, one or two assistant editors, photographer, and stenographer. This means a good deal of doubling up. Everybody has to be able to gather information and write it, often take photographs too. Again, editing and layout are necessary duties for every staffer. Versatility and teamwork are essentials; no room for prima donnas.

Special duties mean staff specialists: art editor, production manager, contributing editors, women's page editors. The company publication has efficient men and women on its staff; its professionals carry out its assigned duties with verve and style.

We should remember, however, that plant reporters, divisional correspondents, and other part-time or special staff members channel a flow of stories to the central editorial office. *Consol News* of the Consolidation Coal Company lists 10 divisional editors.

NWB of Northwestern Bell names five area associate editors for Minnesota, Iowa, Nebraska, North and South Dakota. This system is followed by all the highly professional Bell periodicals. It was no accident that 10 telephone periodicals took ICIE awards in 1967. An elaborate extension of this method is *General Motors World*'s staff of correspondents in Uruguay, Portugal, Melbourne, Singapore, and 26 other exotic locations served by this overseas internal.

If we examine some representative situations, we can see that staff size is closely correlated to company size and, more vitally, to the format and frequency of the publication. At Stix, Baer & Fuller, St. Louis department store, an editor and a secretary put out a 6-page weekly, *The Associate*. The *Telephone Times* for the Arkansas Area of Southwestern Bell lists an editor for its bimonthly 4-pager. *Chain Links*, the bi-monthly of Goldblatt's, a department store, has an editor and a secretary, plus a part-time reporter for each of its 32 stores or divisions in Illinois and Wisconsin. Granite City Steel Company in Illinois employs an editor, assistant editor, and secretary for its 12-page monthly, *The Mill*.

A five-man staff handles *Kodakery*, the 8-page Eastman Kodak internal, issued every week by an editor and assistant editor, plus three editorial assistants—and really expert help from company photographers for the top producer of photographic materials.

Chrysler has one of the more ambitious internal and external programs of communications. Of it, C. J. (Mickey) Dover, manager of communication, remarks, "We have tried to emphasize quality rather than quantity. We have approximately 50 communication people as part of the personnel function at corporate, group and plant levels, a total figure much lower than companies of similar size with comparable programs."

These Chrysler communicators are headed by 17 managers or administrators, all with bachelor degrees and several with master's. They and their staffs not only handle periodicals but also films, recorded telephone messages, handbooks, the whole range.

Chrysler's colleagues demonstrated their respect in 1964 for the quality of its publications and editors when the ICIE Awards of Excellence in two categories, for internals of more than 10 thousand circulation and for management, went to *Chrysler Views* and to *Newsletter for Management*, both edited by Alfred J. Knight.

Ford has 30 plant internals, mostly 4-page biweeklies, each with a local editor; a 20-page bimonthly, *The American Road*, for all salaried employees (with a 4-page insert four times a year for retired employees). Most of you know *Ford Times*, the digest-sized external with the giant-sized circulation, the attractive water-color paintings, and the effective travel articles. But you'll also know the *Ford Owner Newsletter* if you drive a descendant of the Model T— for the postman will bring you the Newsletter in its bright four-colored envelope every month.

Ford's 30 editors, all college graduates, are responsible to the manager of the Employee Information Department, a sub-division of the Editorial Services Department. The manager in turn directs three supervisors.

The ICIE Awards of Excellence gave recognition in 1964 also to the *Wayne Ford News*, editor Hal Watts, in the two to five thousand circulation group, and to The *Ford World*, edited by Warren B. LeBaron, in the more than 10 thousand category.

Seven editors head the 13 internal-externals of Pittsburgh Plate Glass Company, assisted by a production staff of three, and four secretary-proofreaders who handle typesetting, layout, and paste-up for eight of the periodicals. PPG's magazines range from a 4-color, 32-page quarterly with 100,000 circulation to the 40,000-employee *PPG News* coming out every three weeks, and go to a combined annual circulation of 1,500,000.

PPG Products and editor Walter M. Leuzinger received an ICIE Award of Excellence in the category for "Special General Public Publications" in 1964 and again in 1967.

With 40 thousand employees, the Allis-Chalmers Company is publisher for more than 50 regular periodicals. A. R. Tofte, its advertising manager, describes how his corporation tries

to reach as many different levels of interest as possible with communications media designed especially for those levels. At the employe level, there is a monthly magazine, carrying general company news of interest to all employes, and mailed to the homes of all employes. In addition, each separate plant has its own periodical, carrying local plant news. Then, too, because the company's seven operating divisions are divided into two separate groups, each has a monthly News Letter going to all the employes of that group.

Salesmen in the Industries Group get a monthly magazine covering general news of sales interest.

Other distinct A-C internals are addressed to its field service staff, the foreign exports division, young graduate engineers in an orientation program, all employees with responsibility for safety, management news letters for its industries department and tractor division.

So you see there's a different set-up for every situation but it's safe to say that the staffs of company publications do a remarkably competent job, professional by every standard.

Get All The Help You Can

Employees take pride and enthusiasm in what they help to produce. Plant reporters and part-time correspondents need careful selection, a simple training program, and recognition. They are usually doing this extra chore for free and without prior experience. Therefore they deserve all the aid they can be given; they'll return it a hundred-fold.

How do you recruit such a staff?

Get management approval first. Ask them to send a memo down the line. If you're launching a new company periodical or revitalizing an old one, you need a little promotion piece to hand out yourself as you make your visits. Philip Morris used a simple and effective 6-page fold, breezy copy and colorfully humorous sketches. Take a look at it in this chapter's illustrations.

Then approach plant managers, division or department heads, and check with them. Ask them and foremen or other supervisory personnel to suggest reporters—alert men or women with reporting potential—getting the news is more important than writing it (you can dress it up—but don't edit too much or you'll make your cub reporter unhappy). You need reporters who are

90

popular with their fellow-workers and, most of all, have the desire to do the job.

Give your new reporter a head start with a highly and quickly readable booklet, which tells him what's news, the five W's of getting and writing it, deadlines, the importance of getting names and facts right, proper identifications, the effectiveness of good quotations. There's a compact model for such a booklet issued by Crucible Steel Company in 1953 and, if you want to see some of its high spots, refer to the illustrations.

If possible, arrange for your reporters to use a company typewriter. Supply them with a simple camera (Polaroid, Kodak Instamatic) and a few suggestions about what makes a good photograph (action, unposed, focus, black-and-white contrast, and glossy prints).

See that they have stories as samples of what you want: features on different jobs; human interest stories on hobbies, promotions, retirement, new employees, vacations, marriages, births, engagements, weddings, deaths, accidents; articles about winners of safety or courtesy awards, or bonuses paid for useful suggestions; coverage of company employee social and athletic events.

Thank-you notes are good, actually necessary, to keep your reporters happy and on the job. But more tangible recognition is desirable. There are a variety of ways by which the company and you can express your appreciation. Here are some which have worked well:

1. Count reporting time as work time at regular wage scale. Set a specific number of hours per week or month.

2. Or count reporting time as extra vacation time, if they use their own time as your reporters. Or, for using their own time, pay them at their regular rates.

3. Supply with special company press badges.

4. Give merchandise prizes for the best story and best photo used in each issue. Make the prizes company products if possible.

5. Invite them to attend special staff dinners, either in their plant towns or at company headquarters.

6. Hold annual staff conferences, with annual service awards.

7. See that they get bylines on good stories, credits on good pix, listing with the staff in the masthead.

8. Set up special company tours of company plants or scenic and tourist centers.

9. Play them up, one to an issue or in an annual feature, as the backbone of your publication.

Always remember that your own success depends on their willingness to help you do your job.

91

Knowing your reader is essential for the company editor. As a new editor, it's a desirable first step to get carte-blanche from management to tour the plant frequently, poking your nose into every corner, getting to know the other workers—and giving them a chance to size you up! Not only will you learn about your hoped-for readers, but you'll also learn more about the structure and operation of the company. Of course, it'll help if you have a detailed organizational chart, including names of key personnel.

The editor may be semi-suspect at the beginning until he establishes a first-name rapport with his fellow-workers. (Yes, you're a hired hand, too, though aligned closely with management.) Many of them may be blue-collar (to use the old and somewhat obsolete dichotomy) and the editor is white-collar. And they think (correctly) that he represents management. Much of his success will depend on the warmth of his personal relationships—is he snooping or paying a friendly call? And what he gathers as raw material for his articles will depend on the voluntary cooperation of his fellow-employees. Management hires you, the workers can make or break you. As the middleman, you may have the traditional troubles of the in-between position. But if it's sometimes a hot seat, it can also be the chair of responsibility.

Made—the Editor

Company editors are made, not born. No matter how good their college training, they join a company needing to learn the ABC's of its history, its organization, its executives, its operations, its products and services, and perhaps most important of all, its employees. Instead of having to learn by osmosis, they can benefit from a period of in-service training.

With the aid of a company's personnel division and his new boss and colleagues, the new staff member absorbs perspective and begins to comprehend the company for which he works. He realizes the responsibility of representing a company to the customer and to the employee, attractively, accurately. Each day is a continuing seminar of enrichment for the challenging career he has chosen.

Years ago an anonymous genius (whom we'd gladly credit if we knew how) etched, with a few deep scratches, a portrait of the company editor, who may bleed as he grins as he reads—

Whenever the task can't be done, the company editor is called in to do it. He's expected to pull rabbits out of non-existent hats!

He has the curiosity of a cat . . . the tenacity of a mother-in-law . . . the nervous system of a taxi driver . . . the digestive capacity of a goat . . . the diplomacy of a wayward husband . . . the hide of a rhinoceros . . . the speed of a jet . . . the good humor of an idiot.

92

Nobody has been given the run-around so often, has been passed so many bucks, is left holding so many bags, has cut his way through so much red tape.

The company editor keeps the coffee plantations, aspirin plants, liquor distilleries, and midnight oil companies in business.

He finds his job interesting but speaking for management from the Ivory Tower and then running down 36 flights of stairs to hear how it sounds makes it just a bit tiring. He must keep his head in the brass . . . his feet in the grass, a bit difficult position to keep from falling on his . . . back!

Maybe this is the place to remind you that 90 per cent of the ICIE editors surveyed said they liked their jobs!

If top management gives the editor access to the top councils of the company and a chance to participate—and it should—*then* professionally it seems sensible that the editor should be treated as the professional expert in his area, the man most capable of making decisions for that area. That's the viewpoint of Ed Shardlow, former director of Area 11 of the ICIE (Southern California), and the veteran editor of Southern California Edison Company's *Edison News.*

Shardlow says, "Top management doesn't review and check every action by the auditors, personnel manager, or the janitors. Why should they check everything the industrial editor does?"

Shardlow is worth listening to (partly we point with pride as he's one of our products).

The most an employee publication can do is reflect the company. It can't pass on any more of the whole than actually exists. In other words, an editor can't fool an intelligent reader; he must show the logic of his editorial conclusion. The closer he comes to explaining and interpreting the whole corporation, the better job he is doing.

A publication's primary objective is to convey management's philosophy and knowledge to all employees. Because the editor imparts the information through his publication or other media, the employees react to the editor, putting him in that ideal position for measuring that reaction.

An editor has as much responsibility to employees as he does to management. To establish an overall balance, and to build the necessary trust as the basis for effective communication, an editor should seek to build a "third" identity with his publication.

There's considerable agreement that the internal is intended to be the voice of management. There's less agreement on *how* that voice should speak, what it should say—and . . . how many are listening. And with what results?

The editor writes and edits. The publication's printed and distributed. Who reads it?

Keeping the Readers Happy—and the Boss

The internal reader, *if* he's the figurative, non-existent, typical American adult, wants to work and does work. In fact, he *probably* likes to work. He (or she—for one-third of U.S. workers are women) is between 18 and 54 years old, has finished the second year of high school, and was earning $6,928 a year in 1968. And, if the company is engaged in manufacture, he's probably a union member.

In earlier days, pioneer internals were informal in origin, informal in production, informal in content. One day the president thought it might be a good idea to have a plant paper. So he told his secretary to gather some news items and put them out in a two-page mimeograph sheet. Unprofessional and casual about editing and production, so were the contents—sometimes gossipy, corny jokes, and often a little piece by the president about "one great big happy family."

As internals grew up, more was expected of them, both in appearance and in accomplishment. They had always aimed, hopefully, at improving management-worker relations. More stress was placed on Madison Avenue "image." News items centered on management. The president's picture popped up on every page. Then public relations for the company somehow became a propaganda organ for "the American way of life."

The argument waged long and furiously, and still continues. Many editors, with their feet on the managerial ladder as "part of the managerial team," became more Catholic than the Pope and regarded the simple company editor who concentrated on information as simple without doubt but considerably less than pure. Here is part of the debate as reported in *Reporting:*

Stephen N. Bowen and Albert M. Reese exchange viewpoints, Bowen as communications manager of the Lubrizol Corporation; Reese, public relations director of the United Community Services of Boston.

REESE: I would guess the majority of industrial publications are designed (if they have any conscious design) as public relations tools. As such, the publication should be considered as one part of an integrated public relations program and the editor should be part of a smoothly functioning public relations staff.

BOWEN: The point that most public relations people fail to grasp is that the editor's primary mission is to communicate with employees and employees only. Any public relations advantage resulting from his work is strictly an incidental byproduct and should be considered as just that.

To ask the editor to fulfill a public relations and employee relations function is to ask him to serve two masters whose purposes, at time, are diametrically opposed. This may (and often does) lead to a communication disaster, especially in the twilight zones of labor negotiations, government affairs and shareholder relations.

94

Notice that Reese is titled "public relations," Bowen, "communications."

Prominent corporations and business leaders have insisted that the American company (and company executive) must act forcefully, through company publications and other channels, to win converts for its own social, economic, and political viewpoints. They have declared accurately that union publications have boldly declared their convictions on public issues. This corporate right undoubtedly exists—the question remains whether a corporation loses or gains by using strenuous methods of persuasion in a company publication.

Today the swing seems toward more subtlety and less pushing to the polls to vote for "free enterprise" and the business candidate. "Psychological motivators" are being retired. We witness the return of the experienced editor.

"If the editor is successful," says Carlton E. Spitzer, assistant director of information services for American Cyanamid, "his formula will be simple. He will regard truth as the standard for accuracy and home work as a requirement for every assignment. He will think in a positive way for and about his company but he will not publish ridiculous pap or ignore the facts, even if his management would. He will be a good reporter, a fair editor and a genuinely-respected spokesman for his employer."

The whole historical cycle has been sketched by Robert Newcomb, veteran company editor and now, with his wife, Marge Sammons, consultant to his colleagues. Introducing a specialized publications issue of *The Quill*, Newcomb says:

Since the internal or employe type of industrial publication far outnumbers the external type, it is reasonable to look first in that direction. Although it would be heartening to record that the unusual growth of the employe publication has resulted purely from management's wholesome new interest in better employe relations, it isn't quite the fact. For the long strides made by the industrial editing craft in twenty years the editors must credit the growth of unions with an assist.

This is no stark tragedy. For years many industrial managements cherished the view that the good employe was the uninformed employe. They assumed not only that the employe had no interest in the conduct of the business, but that the employe had no particular right to know about the business.

All the time the employe was cloaked in his mantle of ignorance, his employer happily took for granted his devotion to the corporate cause. Some of these managements have now been fitted with new glasses, with the rose-tint gone from the lenses.

The modern publication for employes has point and purpose. It talks company business—not always to the final penny of income—but in terms of what's going on. The progressive management now acknowledges the natural, healthy interest of an employe in the concern for which he works.

. . . .

The good employe publication editor hasn't dropped out his columns of personal news. He has simply improved the quality. He insists that news items about personnel be *news*, not a rehash of shop chatter.

95

Our summary has compressed the movements of decades into a couple of pages. Evidence abounds that all the evolutionary stages are still taking place today on different publications. But there is a demand for a return to fundamental information rather than indoctrination.

The Reader of the External

Definition of the external reader is difficult because of the many different kinds of externals. It is fairly safe to assume that an external for stockholders will be for readers with better-than-average educations, with better-than-average incomes, and with skilled or business or professional ties. The external reader is likely to range in age from 35 on up, including a significant segment of the retired. We must not forget, either, that many employees these days are stockholders also, taking advantage of stock options.

Externals which have their chief goals in selling are directed to businessmen—wholesale distributors or jobbers, retail dealers who operate service stations or stores, agents for insurance firms, purchasing agents for manufacturers. One great category also is the external directed primarily to the individual customer as consumer—the car-buyer, housewife, amateur gardener, parent. Direct mail carries a host of such externals to offer service to the old customer, to keep him sold so he'll continue to buy your product, to allure and attract new customers. These externals emphasize reinforcement for present buying habits, and the cultivation of new ones.

Then there are other externals which never mention selling (unless in a very subtle soft sell) but which endeavor to present the company in the best possible light. These are the public relations publications which build and maintain that favorable reaction which not only will aid selling, but also will manifest the company's reputation for civic and social consciousness, for fair dealing and integrity.

The Combination Reader

Can there be such a thing as a combination reader? Some editors think not—they argue that it's an impossible task to run stories which interest the employee by touching on intimate aspects of the work-day in the same book as articles about a window display in a retail store. Granted, the double-barreled approach *is* bound to have a certain scatter-gun effect. Perhaps some content ammunition is wasted. On the other hand, there may not be such a definite cleavage between the employee and the outside world. The employee is a stockholder sometimes, he is interested in the way the company looks to the customer and citizen—for he's both of those also. The wholesaler or retailer also will react favorably to skillfully written stories of expansion and new products which the worker definitely reads with special interest as a company employee.

This may be said with some certainty. The combination's concentration on the broad-gauge lifts content from routine to a larger dimension. From that, and from its human-interest appeal, its up-styled format, the employee can get a lift, a sense of pride and belonging. Then there's that added plus; for a relatively small added cost, you get employee circulation as well as the benefits accruing from the external's usual selling and promotional function.

Prime Policy

With this backdrop, it's time to swing the spotlight to what policy means for the company publication—internal, external, combination. What are the broad aims? Communication. Information. Persuasion.

Policy for Internals and Their Objectives

"Management wants to persuade employes," says John Earl Davis, a former ICIE president and editor of *Shell Progress*, "to certain lines of action: good work habits, reduction of waste, constant regard for safety, honest workmanship to protect the integrity of the product, and a readiness to speak well of the company wherever the employee happens to be.

So management invests in a mouthpiece known as the *internal* or *personnel* or *employe* publication. If it's good, it tells the employes the things they need to know and want to know about the company, its policies, its products, its manufacturing operations, its outlook for this year and the years to come.

It may—and usually does—give them significant news of their fellow employes: achievements on the job and in their communities; important milestones in their lives, so far as these are interesting to large groups of readers. The theory is that news of this kind is good for employes' morale— and that high morale makes for productive workers.

Finally, the internal publication tells employes *why* good work habits, reduction of waste, regard for safety, and so on, are profitable both for the company and for the employes themselves.

Dover, the Chrysler communications manager, sums it up succinctly in *Reporting* for December, 1954, "Chrysler management believes that there is a definite mutuality of interest between employee and employer; that attitude and performance are improved when employees are well informed; that effective, multidirectional communication must be seen as, *and used as*, an essential aspect of good management."

Good management—yes, in more ways than one! Here's a wise saying from the fine series by S. D. Warren Company, "An employee publication cannot be made to serve as a substitute for a sound policy."

Progressive policy calls for the fundamental premise that a successful company comes from the work of satisfied employees, that the sensible company shares its problems and its profits with these employees, and that the company publication is an important means of communicating with them.

Some companies provide such forums—in the form of Q. and A. columns, departments for letters to the editor, recorded or direct telephone calls, meetings, the inquiring photographer. But they are not numerous and, sometimes, there's evasion or timidity.

Communication does not necessarily mean debate, although there should be a place for useful dialogue.

Persuasion, si; indoctrination, no!

No amount of wordy propaganda can erase the impact of action. It is by deeds that the company will be known. Good management can make itself better with a good company publication.

Let's consider two contrasting statements from two company editors, participating in a Cornell University conference:

Editor A: "In our company, management is striving all the time to increase profits by increasing productivity and minimizing costs. This means that every worker must be encouraged to improve his job performance."

Editor B: "We try to write to the employees as people first and as employees second."

For which company would *you* prefer to work?

Finally, broad policy means agreement of management and editor on a statement of major objectives for his publication. These should be realistic in terms of time, money, and human nature. They should be specific, preferably in writing. They should exhibit the insight that success means dreams as well as dollars. They should express a values system which considers material well-being as a means to human dignity.

Objectives are established by broad policy. Here are some from three different company editors at the Cornell conference.

Our publications, taken together, have three objectives regularly in mind: 1) to establish a warm personal relationship between all members of the company, 2) to make clear to everyone our company policy and product information, and 3) to keep before the work force a picture of the company's role in the life of the community.

Our purpose in the employee publication is stated in every issue, at the bottom of the editorial page: "to report the way our people work together, to show the superior products they produce, to record a part of their lives; and to speak up for 'Made in America' opportunities and freedoms."

Our first desire is to make every employee feel that his job is important and needs doing well. As part of this we want to give every person with a stake in the company—employee or stockholder—a sense of identity with the company, a belief that the company's fortune and his personal fortune are as one.

To translate these objectives into the copy that goes into the internal, these suggestions may help:

1. Inform, explain, and interpret a company's policies and plans clearly and simply so that the employee may see where he fits into the over-all program. Give the news first and fast—before he reads it in a local newspaper.

2. Give specific information on company rules and procedures (this also can be done effectively through an employee manual) in relation to wages and pay scales, vacations and holidays, safety regulations, first aid and medical service, fire and emergency measures, job security and seniority, steps to promotion, absenteeism, personal counseling.

3. Encourage the employee's pride in his own job and his performance.

4. Reward achievement in that performance by giving it public recognition. And call his attention to the achievements of his fellow-workers.

5. Relate the employee's job to his department, his division, his plant, and his company so he establishes relationships and loyalty.

6. Personalize management, its problems, and its accomplishments.

7. Report on new processes and products, expansion and diversification, marketing and use, operating costs, taxes, profits—so the employee will appreciate the company's growth and achievements. *Tell the bad news as well as the good.*

8. Discuss the worker's own economic stake in the company—benefits such as group insurance, retirement and pension plans, accident-prevention, profit-sharing, special discounts on company products, increased productivity.

9. Show his own social benefits from the company—in social and recreational opportunities provided directly and indirectly, through athletic leagues, dances and picnics, community action for better government, better schools, better housing.

10. Tell the story simply, truthfully, accurately, and with imagination, conscious always of your reader, his pocketbook, and his heart.

And you'll have a full-time job!

Policy and Objectives for the External

Recalling that the external goes to many different kinds of readers—stockholders, wholesale and retail merchants, past or prospective customers, opinion leaders, it's easy to see that a single publication would have to have a policy and objectives that resemble an umbrella. Of course the situation's simplified considerably if the external is directed to only one or two of these reader groups, and sometimes this is the case. But generally it's free for all—and then the editorial task can baffle while it challenges!

Most magazines carry a masthead, generally on one of the first pages—although there's a growing tendency to switch it to one of the last pages. The masthead gives the name of the company which publishes the book, names of at least the top staffers, and often a succinct statement of its purpose. Here are some examples which illustrate some of the goals for the external.

R. G. LeTourneau, Inc., *Le Tourneau Co-Operator*—A swapping of on-the-job earth-moving ideas for and by outstanding operators, mechanics, supervisors, service engineers and field engineers . . . published monthly to help all of us dirt-movers do better work faster and at lower cost.

Socony-Vacuum, *Oil-Power*—A magazine of industrial romances, published for users and prospective users of Socony-Vacuum industrial products.

Mergenthaler Linotype Co., *The Linotype News*—Published at Linotype headquarters in the interests of all workers in the graphic arts.

Hoover Ball and Bearing Co., *The Hoover Sphere*—Published by the Hoover Ball and Bearing Company, to bring inspiration and friendly thoughts to present and future users of Hoover Balls, Ball Bearings, and Roller Bearings.

Pittsburgh Plate Glass Co., *Columbia—Southern Chemicals*—Purpose of this magazine is to make the services, products, plants, facilities and people of the Chemical Division of PPG better known throughout industry, in the educational institutions where America's future leadership is emerging, and wherever there is interest in the dynamic role of chemicals in the modern world.

These mastheads typify major policy aims of the external—information and the exchange of ideas, improved efficiency, the humanizing and glamorizing of industry, inspiration and friendly contact with customers. You can, if you wish, call it the soft sell. We might list other objectives more specifically:

To report new developments in a company and in its field.

To bring suggestions to dealers of selling aids—window and counter displays, advertising tie-ins and tips, promotional campaigns.

To discuss business conditions, present and future.

100

To aid the salesmen who represent the company.

To create interest in new products and services.

To provide case histories from contented customers.

To show the efficiency and skill of the company's executives and other employees.

To furnish suggestions for maintenance, replacement, and repair.

To increase the prestige of the company and enhance its public relations.

Policy and Objectives for the Combination

To define policy and objectives for the combination is challenging. To start with, all the objectives for the external apply. And if you consider your employee a customer—and indeed he is, also many objectives of the internal. But you can't write first and only for the employee—about minor departmental promotions or news items just for Suzy Cue of the steno pool and her fellow typewriter-jockeys. Nor can you do a how-to article on economical upkeep of a tractor—which may be fine for the farmer but a headache to one of the company's elevator pilots.

Make it broad-gauge. That's the single rule. Plus, human interest and good writing. That's a winning combination for any combination.

Inside the Internals

You *can* put anything you want in a company publication. But that's no guarantee that the reader will read it.

Without regurgitating the controversy, no sugar-coating can wholly disguise the pill. Remember your reader, *his* reactions—unless you want your company's parking lots carpeted with copies of your internal (and the "round file" is available at home too).

Most company editors today feel that internal copy should stress major company policy, promote productivity, reduce absenteeism and accidents, and develop employee loyalty. Many of them also believe the internal should interpret economic and political theory. All of these aims, with the exception of the last, have a close and obvious relation to the worker's job and his self-interest.

There has also been a reaction, perhaps natural, to the early tendencies of some internals to run gossip items of a highly personal nature about employees. Because of this reasonable revulsion, however, frequently company editors felt they should eliminate all human interest stories and personal references. This is throwing the baby out with the bath water.

Today there is a revival among editors of selecting copy to meet reader interest. Early texts on journalism preached that names make news—it's still true today. Self-interest and self-respect still are psychologically important values to men and women. The pocket nerve reacts strongly. So do emotions. And with the increasing competition of television and popular magazines, company publications have to be better than ever. Workers in their leisure time want entertainment and relaxation, not lectures. If content is closely concerned with their jobs, it will win attention but that's no excuse for dull, didactic writing.

Let's remember that most internals are mailed to homes. That means picking up additional readers—wives, sisters, mothers. Their reactions may keep a man happy with his work as well as his home. Or they may put the kiss of death on the employee's attitude towards his job. How do home readers feel about the company? It's the woman who buys . . . and this particular woman is one of the company's best potential customers.

Of course, many employees themselves will be women, single or working wives. That's the reason for running some feminine-angled copy such as fashions, recipes, home decoration. And writing *all* stories for women as well as men—after all, one-third of U.S. workers are women. Home readers also are going to include children, from those just old enough to look at cartoons up to the age when they themselves will go to work. What does the company say to them? Will they want to work for it? Or buy from it?

Dun's Review and Modern Industry made a selected sample of 256 company editors, asking, "What does *your company* consider the most worthwhile and useful types of news or feature material for employees appearing in your publication either regularly or intermittently?" In summarizing replies, William C. Lewis, editor of *Dun's Bulletin*, wrote, "The most popular topic was checked as employee progress—promotions, service anniversaries, distinguished achievement awards, and so." The two runner-up topics were these: "announce new developments and policy changes" and "describe company products or services." Next in order of management emphasis, but ranking far below the previous topics, came these two: "explain company benefit plans," and "promote efficiency—suggestion system, safety program, good housekeeping campaign, and so on." Fewest votes went to the objectives: "to present financial information about the company employees," and "to describe sales methods, sales programs, sales outlook."

Or read these comments by George Scriven, managing editor of the *United Rubber Worker*, a union periodical. As published in ICIE's own *Reporting* (eminently useful specialized magazine for company editors because it deals with their *own* problems as *employees*), Scriven suggests:

If you're putting out what you call an employee publication and you want employees to read it, then make sure you feature the employees in the stories and photographs. There are hundreds of good stories that have happened, are happening or will happen to employees. Write about them and you'll get the readership you want and need to justify your positions.

Remember Scriven is an editor for employees, hired and paid by them. Here are some more Scrivenisms:

Inquiring reporter columns—Excellent.

Labor-management relations column—Must reading.

"... encourage workers to buy the products they make ... it means job security."

"You're going to build a plant. ... What's going to happen in the existing plant—as far as the workers go. That's what they want to know and that's what they'll read."

"After all—you do call them employee publications—not employer publications. Mean what you say then."

Scriven quotes some worker reactions.

"We don't expect it to be a union paper, but about the only time they use anything on the union is when United Fund collection time comes."

And—

"We've got some interesting guys in the plant—they have some interesting hobbies and you'd think the paper would have something about them, but instead you see something in there about one of the wheels making a speech in New York."

Content not only must fit the company but also the type of employee in that company. Internals are even issued for *retired* employees. There are specialized internals, as well as the great majority intended for all employees.

One of the major varieties of internals is for the salesman—often on the road, sometimes in need of a morale-booster or selling suggestions, representing the company, often its chief image-builder and ambassador to the customer, and always confronting the competition. Here are hints for internals directed to company salesmen: current company advertising and promotion campaigns, new dealer helps, news of installations and big orders, sales opportunities, inspirational articles, suggestions for merchandise displays, reports on recent and upcoming conventions, notes on outstanding businessmen in the same field—their promotions and accomplishments, company contests—prizes or bonuses and honor rolls, sales training programs.

Corporations have realized that communication must be *up* and *sidewards*, to reach *management* at various levels, as well as *down* from management to other employees.

Success Stories

Every story that reaches out and catches readers—and holds them—is a success story for the internal. Let's look at some blue-ribbon examples.

The Shield of United Air Lines had a perfect follow-up on Christmas.

It shaped up as a sad and somewhat lonely Christmas for Michael Figielewski of Buffalo.

Michael, 10, wouldn't be spending the holidays at home but in a New York hospital bed, undergoing treatment for a serious eye ailment. Because two earlier confinements in the hospital and other visits by his family had strained finances, only his mother (already in New York) would be able to share Christmas with him. Dad and two younger brothers would have to stay in Buffalo.

That's the way things stood on December 21 when the *Buffalo Evening News* carried a story about the youngster's plight.

On December 23, the News carried another, happier story. Michael's dad and brothers (Paul, 7, and David, 3) would make the trip to New York, thanks to the warm-heartedness of another Michael—Mike Levorchick, United reservations agent at Buffalo—and his co-workers. With Levorchick spearheading the drive, the UALers had contributed the $70 needed to buy round-trip Buffalo-New York tickets for Mr. Figielewski, Paul and David.

Look at the *Scene* of Southwestern Bell Telephone, a repeated award winner, and you look at superlative use of tremendous four-color and photographs in an obviously happy marriage with written copy. Here's a lead from one of their spectacular spreads.

Speak of the Astrodrome and you must speak in superlatives. It's the largest indoor arena ever constructed. No clear-span structure yet erected can match its size. It boasts the world's biggest electrical scoreboard. The list of "firsts" and "largests" goes on and on. It's no wonder the stadium's builders wanted the best communications services possible, nor is it surprising that a lot of telephone people worked long and hard to see they got just that—the best.

An inquiring photographer or reporter can ring a bell, just like *The Ohio Bell* of Ohio Bell Telephone did when it asked women employees "What is the Biggest Peeve You Have About Men?"

Sample answer:

Oh, boy, I could write a book on the subject! To begin with, men are far too moody and temperamental. And when they're in one of their moods, they're as grouchy as old bears and exaggerate everything way out of proportion. One day they're all sweetness and light, and the next day, no matter how you try to please them, every little thing irritates them and they bark and growl like a petulant puppy. They're completely unpredictable. And on top of all this, they don't begin to appreciate the working woman.

Followed of course by a similar query to male employees about women, and here's one comeback:

When a woman makes an appointment for a meeting, she expects the man to drop everything and break his neck to make it on time. But if the man wants to be somewhere on time, you'd think he was asking for the moon. And he's usually late because the little woman simply won't be hurried. I have three daughters. I had to install my own bathroom so I'd get to use it occasionally. And they're continually monopolizing the phone. I may be old fashioned, but my real peeve is short skirts. After all, they ought to leave something to the imagination.

Then *Ohio Bell* tried, "What does Your Mom or Pop Do at Ohio Bell?"

Brenda Miller, 4 (Mrs. Sonja Miller, Operator): "I think my mother's some kind of an operator. She makes connections."
Becky Mangold, 12 (Charles Mangold, Combination-man): "He puts telephones in houses. He has an interesting job. He gets to see a lot."
Charlene Jones, 8 (Mrs. Florence Jones, Operator): "When people make calls my mother switches them."

Readership troubles, anybody?

Say "internal" today and you're talking of a publication which can do a practical, desirable, and essential job—and perform it with success based on the work and know-how of professionals.

Externals that Reach Readers

With the external, we are trying to reach those who are not employed by the company but whose relations with it are close—or, we hope, will be close! Among the first group, there are the dealers and distributors; secondly, we have individual customers who have bought our products and those other consumers whom we'd like to convert to our brand. The dealer wants details and techniques, the customer looks for more general information about what he can get for his dollar.

A fact of life for both the external and the combination is that they have competition. Other companies are competing for their reader's favor with other company publications. Therefore yours has to be more interesting, more useful, more attractive—and you've got to know what your rival editor is doing.

Readers in the wholesale and retail field will welcome coverage on new products and processes, new applications for old products, case histories of what other distributors have accomplished—and how they did it, suggestions to increase sales and profits, expansion and important developments in the company which they represent, major promotional and advertising campaigns with local tie-ins, reports on trade associations and their conventions, analysis of market conditions and trends.

External editors are ingenious in format as well as copy. As a convenience to the reader—maintenance man or dealer—new pages on new products and inserts on new processes come already punched with holes for insertion in leather folders with loose-leaf or spiral binding.

For the old and prospective customer (concentrating now on the individual consumer), your articles will feature how his car can perform better with greater care. Or you'll try gently to persuade her that it's time to exchange her 10-year-old refrigerator for your glamorous new model. Are there new ways for her electric beater to turn out delicious dishes—or new gadgets which make it do new tricks? How did the Browns (next-door or in the next state) add a barbecue pit to their outdoor patio? Tips, hints, suggestions—and how a particular brand or model can make life more economical, easier, pleasanter.

Community service is a constant with both externals and internals. They long have donated quantities of valuable white space and fine printing to improving and supporting civic action—Community or United Funds, Red Cross, vote registration and voting. If it's a worthy cause, company publications are always in the van.

There are special situations also in which they demonstrate their knowledge of social responsibilities. National Cash Register issued and distributed to a circulation amplified at least 10 times, a 64-page brochure supporting and explaining the activities of the United Nations. Extensively and expensively illustrated, it carried an endorsing foreword by S. C. Allyn, chairman of the board.

Wyandotte Chemicals Corporation issued "Community Study—Blueprint for Action," also to an expanded circulation. It dealt with water and air pollution, city shopping facilities and appearance, the amount and adequacy of city taxes, and attitudes toward Wyandotte Chemical itself.

Patriotism and products combine in a *Monsanto Magazine* lead article (October, 1964):

"All hands man your battle stations!"
The loud-speaker lashed the crew members of the nuclear missile cruiser U.S.S. Long Beach out of their late-afternoon quiet. By the time the command had been repeated in the twittering code of a bosun's pipe, men were racing down companionways or working their way into life jackets and huge helmets, outsize to accommodate the telephone headsets they wore.
Within seconds every man on the ship was at his battle station.

Why in a Monsanto magazine? An unobtrusive footnote on page 3 of the lavishly illustrated article gives the clue:

The neutron source for the Long Beach's water-cooled reactor, like those used for the N.S. Savannah and all U.S. atomic submarines, was made by Monsanto Research Corporation at Mound Laboratory, Miamisburg, Ohio. The laboratory is operated by Monsanto for the Atomic Energy Commission.

Monsanto Magazine not only received ICIE's Award of Excellence in 1965 as a "Customer Service and Sales Publication" but also won the top honor, receiving the Sweepstakes Award as the best company publication in all categories in the United States.

Its editor, Leonard A. Paris, and art director, Guy Spilman, deserve due credit. They are among the many fine professionals who frequently share their talent with college students preparing for careers on specialized publications.

This is the way Paris and his staff plan and edit their magazine for its 120,000-circulation—and an estimated audience of at least twice that number. Their challenge is keeping articles fairly general, with broad appeal, and yet to have that Monsanto product mentioned with some subtlety. In the illustrations, you can see their publication schedule, the article plan for one issue, their flow chart, and layout plan.

International Harvester's *World* and *Today* magazines are among the tops and one big contributing reason is not only their excellent editors but the wonderful work of Angus McDougall, their full-time staff photographer whose imaginative visual creations would enhance any book.

The honor roll could continue almost endlessly for here are experienced hands editing publications which have to compete with the best of mass circulation magazines—and the long and continued existence of the externals is witness to their winning qualities and excellence.

Contents for Combinations

Appealing to outsiders and insiders in the same magazine may seem difficult at first glance—until you think of them all as customers. The insiders are very special customers, of course, but their compelling interests and needs are those of all buyers.

While many of the reader interests of the internal and external will apply to the combination's contents also, there are several special guides for the combination editor. He'll look for articles which establish the reputation and integrity of his company and its products. Colorful human interest features, involving the excitement of new scenes and new experiences, will be high on his list—plus, very decidedly, effective illustrations.

Combination Choices

If you'd like to see what the combination editor chooses, here's an article called "Bell, Gong and Whistle," all about the activities of the U.S. Coast Guard. It appeared in *Service* (Jan., 1960) of Cities Service and starts off, "As a nation whose history is salted by the deeds of seafaring men, we give special

107

status to those who go to sea in ships. Many the motorist or railroad passenger who has been delayed while a drawbridge was raised to let a boat go sailing by." This lead introduces a four-page piece, accompanied by two four-colored photographs, four black-and-whites, a one-color plus black-and-white, and a two-color illustration showing different buoy and signal systems. Why run it? Cities Service sells gas and petroleum products and in mid-article, the reader is told, "Boating enthusiasts will spend upward of $2 billion this year for their maritime needs . . . including more than 400 million gallons of gasolene, 22 million gallons of diesel fuel, and 20 million gallons of lubricating oil."

Fluor-o-scope is published quarterly by the Fluor Corporation and one of its issues carried "Frozen Frontier" about new lows in low temperatures; "Panhandle Helium Factory," concerning research by the company to meet U.S. defense needs; and "War Achievement" which said:

The American Navy faced a critical challenge in 1940. Axis submarines lurked everywhere. To meet this threat, the Navy turned to a half-forgotten craft, the non-rigid airship—more commonly called a blimp.

At the recommendation of fleet admirals, Congress approved a bill expanding the airship fleet by 200. This meant that new supplies of helium would eventually be needed.

. . . .

One of the installation's most significant features was an improved gas treating process developed by Fluor. A license for this process, as a matter of fact, had been given to the Bureau of Mines in 1942 to help the war effort.

The Dow Chemical Company issues *Dow Diamond* for its customers, stockholders, and employees. In "Dow Fibers in Detroit," the article begins:

One of the most exciting stories being told in Detroit is the story of automotive styling and its expanding impact on the public. Color, texture and design play the most important roles in the drama. And since no tale is complete without a "fairy godmother" to add the necessary magic, the textile fibers department of The Dow Chemical Company has supplied one . . . Latex Metallic Yarn.

The combination creates readership by imaginative editing!

Publications Praised

When the Association of National Advertisers polled 300 employees of six major companies, 97 per cent said they believed what they read in their company magazines. Four out of five said they read them regularly. Nine out of 10 said they read some specialized department news—but the report didn't indicate whether the department was their own or another division. Personals commanded 55 per cent readership, sports 55 per cent, cartoons 69 per cent.

108

When the Warren Paper Company issued a book on company publications as a service to its customers, it quoted management officials on why they believe such periodicals are worthwhile.

The Chase Bag Company: *Bagology* is one of the oldest house organs in America. It has been published continuously every other month since 1901. The nature of the material used and the format have varied little since the first issue.

While it is difficult to assess accurately the value of this type of advertising, we are constantly aware, in a business such as ours where frequent friendly contact is an important factor, that Bagology is a valuable asset.

The demand for the magazine in recent years by people outside our range of business has been so great that we have been forced to ask a subscription price of $1.00 to defray the cost of this added circulation.

The Gulf Oil Corporation: *The Orange Disc* is an internal company magazine distributed bi-monthly to Gulf employees and stockholders. It is felt that the publication serves a very useful purpose in unifying the widespread Gulf organization and has helped create an unusual esprit de corps.

E. F. Houghton & Co.: *The Houghton Line* has been published continuously by E. F. Houghton & Co., manufacturers of oils, leathers and metal working products, Philadelphia, since 1908, being rated as the eighth oldest industrial house magazine in the United States.

Its present circulation numbers about 165,000. It is published in five editions: General, Metal, Textile, Foundry and Leather. These editions all contain the same topical section and vary as to technical articles and advertisements.

The Line was started by Charles E. Carpenter as an internal house magazine but, when shown to customers, created so many requests for outside distribution that, within a year, it had a circulation of 5,000. At one time, in the 20's, circulation climbed to 250,000.

. . . .

E. F. Houghton & Co. regards this publication as so essential to its publicity and advertising program that it devotes about 25 per cent of its advertising budget to this publication alone.

The plant manager sometimes pays part of publication cost out of his allocated budget. Robert E. Soden, a Monsanto plant manager, says in that case you take a careful look to see if an internal is worth the cost. Plus the benefits in productivity, in morale, in personnel training. Soden expects the plant's internal to improve safety records, and factory housekeeping. As to upgrading quality of items produced, Soden says "we've seen some real good examples when the publications have been real helpful." He acknowledges a debt also to articles which increased employee knowledge of their contract responsibilities. He records the values arising from motivation:

What can you better do to lift the morale of a man, to make him feel that you recognize him as an individual, that you know he exists, than to see to it that his name does get in print or that his picture does get in the paper?

109

When we consider the millions of dollars invested every year in company publications by management, we have the final answer as to their usefulness. The man who pays the bills for them is sold on their value.

Channels of Communication

Company publications are not the sole means of communication. There's many a company editor who, through the personnel, advertising, or public relations divisions, will participate in other channels. Some of these are unusual enough to warrant special mention. Chrysler's Operation Better Communication set up the following program as described in *Reporting* (December, 1964).

A Chrysler Corporation foreman named George Robertson picked up a plant phone recently and dialed 2 - 2 - 2 - 2. *His was the millionth such call in one year.* What George Robertson heard on the phone was a message taped personally by President Lynn Townsend, for PIP (Phone Information Program)—part of Chrysler's Operation Better Communication Program.

. . . .

Fifteen seconds after Chrysler Board of Directors announcement was flashed to wire services in New York recently, key Chrysler executives throughout the nation began hearing a pre-recorded message on another OBC phone network (called EXCOM, Executive Communication Program)—giving details in depth on Chrysler's record sales and earnings report.

Angela Gram tells in *Reporting* (April, 1963) how radio has been made a company communications channel.

We at Jewel Tea Company must communicate with some 8,000 people in 250 stores in four states. We use periodicals, bulletins, and person-to-person communication to keep our scattered and widely different types of people informed. But often speed of communication is essential. To communicate swiftly, we use radio. We have been doing so for the past 15 years.

We talk to Jewel people via radio every morning from 8:45 to 9, when employees are alone together as they prepare to open the store. Our program—it is called the Jewel Round-Up—is carried over a local FM station. Receivers in each of our stores are tuned to this station and are so arranged that the station setting cannot be changed. After 9 a.m., the station carries music, public service announcements, and Jewel commercials. The entire day's time is purchased by our company.

Buick is on the air too, as *Reporting* (February, 1964) reports:

At six o'clock on a gray November morning three years ago, the roar of a mighty factory whistle was boomed out over the radio to an industrial community of 400,000 people.

110

Neither the station, WKMF, which went on air half-an-hour early to do it, nor Buick Motor Division of General Motors, which sponsored it, realized that the Buick public-relations staff was about to discover how to use with great effectiveness a channel available many years for management communications *with* the employes of a single industrial plant.

That roar, a recording of Buick's own factory whistle, opened the first challenge over commercial radio for Buick's home-plant employes in Flint, Michigan, to settle down on time at their factory stations and build better automobiles.

The challenge long since has become the Buick day shift's alarm clock, and every workday a constant companion during the whole hour of shaving, dressing, breakfasting and going to work.

It is a radio program, a radio show. There's nothing else to call it, except its name, *Factory Whistle*.

Results from *Factory Whistle?*

Employes at once accepted the program, and with enthusiasm;
Genuine two-way communications evolved promptly, with frequency, warmth and volume;

. . . .

The Flint public listened, too, adding community-relations benefits;

. . . .

Eight large employers adopted the concept, put their own communications for employe relations a total of 13 times a day on nine commercial radio stations in nine other cities.

Annual reports have been transformed from the drab, sober, managerial secrets of yore. Today they are high-styled booklets, simply written, but with four-colored illustrations, art work, and circulated to all employees and the public. They're titled "Progress of Our Company," or "The Story of 1969" or "The Year in Review." Eastman Kodak produces one of the most handsome and beautifully illustrated yearly reviews, a double dividend in public relations and profits.

Of course, no company editor or publications staff can begin to carry out all communication activities. But they're often called in for aid or advice. And it's more than likely that, if interested, they may move into allied operations by promotion to managerial responsibilities embracing many channels of communication.

Achievement and Challenge

In the magazine universe, the giant galaxy of company publications is expanding in quality and responsibility to unite four major groups in modern society—management and employees, merchandisers and customers—into a homogeneous force with shared goals. No other publications reach so many readers. No other group of publications has as many different publications. No other publications have more complex problems or more challenging possibilities. The communication established by company publications may well contribute more than any other medium to a life in which man uses his intelligence to achieve meaningful personal existence and social welfare for all.

ISSUE	Color Art in Hand	Copy Due	B & W Art in Hand	Color Art to Printer	Final Copy to Type-setter	B & W Art to Print-er	Negs to Print-er	Mailing Strips delivered	On Press	Mail-ing Starts	Mail-ing Com-pleted
March	Jan. 4	Jan. 8	Jan. 11	Jan. 12	Jan. 25	Feb. 2	Feb. 11	Mar. 3	Feb. 24	Mar. 8	Mar. 12
May	Feb. 26	Mar. 1	Mar. 8	Mar. 10	Mar. 15	Mar. 23	April 5	April 22	Apr. 20	Apr. 27	Apr. 30
Summer	May 10	May 13	May 20	May 21	May 28	June 9	June 18	July 5	July 1	July 8	July 13
Oct.	July 19	July 30	Aug. 3	Aug. 6	Aug. 13	Aug. 20	Sept. 2	Sept. 21	Sept. 16	Sept. 24	Sept. 30
Dec.	Sept. 20	Sept. 24	Oct. 1	Oct. 6	Oct. 13	Oct. 20	Nov. 2	Nov. 18	Nov. 16	Nov. 23	Nov. 27

Monsanto Magazine publication schedule; by permission of *Monsanto Magazine*.

Editorial schedule for *Monsanto Magazine*; courtesy of *Monsant Magazine*.

	Title	Division	Color	Pages	Assigned
	MAY				
*	Merck, Aldomet	Org.	1	3	LP
*	Cord-Duesenberg	Multi	3	4	GR
	Gunboat	Org.			GM
	Olives	Org.			GR
*	Soil Conservation	Ag.	5	3	GR
*	Oil Recovery (later scratched)	HC-Org.	1	3-4	GR
	Ham Radio	Inorg.			GR
*	Operation Crossroads	Corp.	3	3	LP
*	Hershey Fair (later scratched)	Org.	5	3-4	LP
*	Acrilan Flags	Chem.	3-(4)	4	LP
	Florida Blasting	Ag.			LP
*	Safety (later scratched)	Corp.			LP
	Beer Bottle Labels (later scratched)	Org.			LP
	Phos-Check	Inorg.			LP
	Boeing Anniversary (inactive)	Org.			LP
	Plastic Paints	Pl.			GS
	Egg Factories	Ag.			LP
*	Mass Transportation	Pl.	3	3-4	GM
*	Corsets	Chem.	(1)	2	GM
	Hope Ship	Org.			GR
	Calgon	Inorg.			GR
*	National Open	Ag.	3	4	GR

112

Monsanto Magazine cover. Copyright, 1965, Monsanto Magazine. Used by courtesy of Monsanto Magazine.

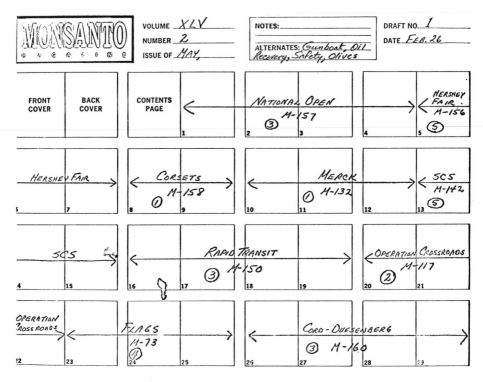

Page dummy for *Monsanto Magazine*; by permission of *Monsanto Magazine*.

In the very early days of our company, Mr. Philip Morris had only to walk to the back of his tobacco shop and talk to the man who hand-rolled the cigarettes. They would exchange ideas and he would give this employee his views on how the company — both of them — should operate.

This personal chat made for a happier employee. The man knew without question that Mr. Philip Morris was interested in him, and he also knew what Philip Morris — the two of them — were trying to accomplish.

These chats were important and took little effort.

But obviously, in over a hundred years, our company has changed.

Internal promotion for *The Call*, a company magazine by Philip Morris. Used by permission of Philip Morris, Inc.

Lay-out dummy for *Monsanto Magazine;* by permission of *Monsanto Magazine.*

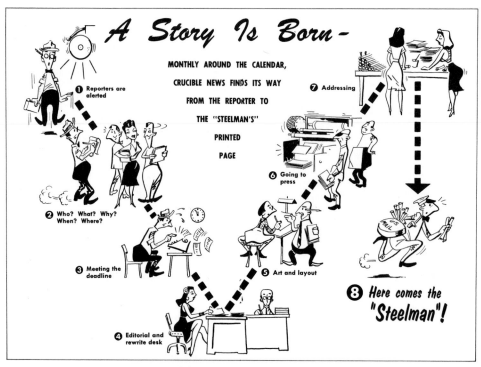

A Story Is Born —

MONTHLY AROUND THE CALENDAR,

CRUCIBLE NEWS FINDS ITS WAY

FROM THE REPORTER TO

THE "STEELMAN'S"

PRINTED

PAGE

❶ Reporters are alerted

❷ Who? What? Why? When? Where?

❸ Meeting the deadline

❹ Editorial and rewrite desk

❺ Art and layout

❻ Going to press

❼ Addressing

❽ Here comes the "Steelman"!

FIVE W's

A news story must be accurate and complete. In gathering the facts, the reporter should apply the five W's to the situation. These are Who? What? Where? When? Why? For example:

WHO: C. K. Baer, Sanderson-Halcomb Works

WHAT: was honored

WHERE: at a farewell party given by the Met Lab gang

WHEN: April, 1952

WHY: upon his promotion to the Tool Steel Sales Division

These answers fitted together, make up the following opening paragraph:

C. K. Baer, of our Sanderson-Halcomb Works, was honored in April at a farewell party given by the Met Lab gang upon his promotion to the Tool Steel Sales Division of our company.

Important facts should be stated first, with other facts and side lights following.

Pages from "A Guide for All Reporters," prepared for employees who cover stories for *The Crucible Steelman*, an internal publication, 1953. Used by permission of Crucible Steel Company.

7. The Voice of Industry

LOOMING ever larger in the communications sky, twin to the galaxy of company publications but serving *all* companies in a single industry and sometimes all industry, are the clustered constellations of more than 2,600 industrial publications.

Industrials cover manufacture and marketing and the intricate complex of technological activity. They include the journals of news and comment and opinion which represent the industrial community. Also called trade or business publications, the industrials are of three main types—manufacturing, merchandising, and trade association. The term "business publications" has gained considerable acceptance through its use by such associations as the American Business Press, whose membership includes merchandising periodicals. According to the estimate of one ABP member, 87 per cent of the American Business Press publications are properly classified as "industrial." Although tradition sometimes creates emotional reactions, rational consideration can agree that these magazines represent the technical production and distribution activities of a giant industrial society.

Looking at the paper industry as an example, we find *Pulp and Paper* "edited for the pulp, paper and paperboard manufacturing industry." Then there is *Paper Sales* "edited for printing paper and paper product wholesalers-distributors and their salesmen," Finally there is *Paper Industry* which concerns itself with "current management and production problems, innovations, new thinking, market development and sales" as well as "paper technology highlights." It is published by the Paper Industry Management Association.

113

Familiar to casual readers as well as lifelong industrialists are the industrial news magazines such as *U.S. News & World Report* or *Business Week* while opinion and analysis are blended in *Fortune*. Some, such as *Nation's Business* published by the United States Chamber of Commerce, speak with a potent and official voice. They compare favorably with their mass circulation cousins and their influence is great among the decision-makers of industry and government.

Industrials have multiplied in the industrial twentieth century, by the advance of technology, with the spread of the industrial revolution among undeveloped and new nations, by spin-offs due to demand for more information about detailed developments.

Perhaps some definition of the industrial publication is due. As noted in the last chapter, nowhere is confusion more current than in assigning names to periodicals produced by individual companies and those designed to serve industry. Despite a somewhat tortured attempt to refer to "businesspapers," "industry" is wider in scope and more modern than "business" as a term descriptive of modern manufacture and marketing. Most industrials are magazines in format, only a comparative few follow newspaper styles. Finally, even those who refer to "businesspapers," in subsequent usage refer to "company publications" when they seek clarity.

For many years executive vice president of McGraw-Hill's publications, John R. Callaham defines the industrial publication as "one that is devoted to the technical, industrial, and business interests of its readers—in other words, work-knowledge for application to their jobs. This definition is a broad one and naturally includes what is commonly known as trade, professional technical, merchandising and institutional publications."

Two extensive writers in the field, Russell N. Baird and Arthur T. Turnbull, describe the industrial as "a periodical published independently for profit, which provides a business, industry, or specialized profession with information. . . . the publication is intended for representatives of many companies."

Long associated with industrials as a Haire editor, Julien Elfenbein coined the term "businesspaper" and characterizes it as "a specialized periodical of editorial opinion, technical know-how, and news information, independently owned and operated." This has the disadvantage of being too broad and too inclusive. It might apply with equal effectiveness to skiing magazines.

For ourselves we would say the industrial publication deals with the manufacturing and marketing operations of modern industry.

But enough of definitions. How many industrials exist? Whom do they reach? What keeps them running?

Industrials have been growing at a rapid clip. Today, American Business

114

Press estimates, they number 2,600—that compares with 1,800 in 1950, and 800 in 1900. Circulation is greater than that for daily newspapers, with the industrial publication reaching 62 million in 1966. More than 70 thousand persons are employed, of whom 14,000 are journalists. The industrials are advertising pacesetters; of the top 10 publications in ad pages, industrial publications occupy the first rung and eight of the nine other positions. They've climbed from 788,000 pages of advertising in 1950 to 1,254,000 in 1966. In total advertising dollar volume, the 1966 figure was $820 million, fifth among major advertising media. This represents an increase of 215 per cent over the 1950 figure. Their staffs range from a single man or woman to as many as 42 editors, producing 800 thousand editorial pages.

Industrial and other specialized publications take second place to nobody when it comes to enterprise in getting news at the source. At Washington, world and national capital, the Congress has an accredited "Periodical Press Gallery." Of the 493 periodical correspondents listed in the Congressional Directory, 411 represent specialized publications, with the great majority of these on hand for industry. *U.S. News & World Report* has 75 correspondents as compared with 28 for *Time-Life-Fortune*. McGraw-Hill employs 28, American Aviation Publishers, Inc., 33.

When and how did all this communications activity start?

The fifes of the American Revolution were still echoing in the ears of the Patriots when merchants proclaimed they were open for business again and astute publishers realized that the price of sugar and tea and flour was news. Indeed, the earliest Colonial newspapers had carried shipping news and quotations on cargoes the ships had brought over the Atlantic. Even during the Revolution, *Philadelphia Prices Current* appeared in 1783. In 1795, there came *New York Prices Current* and the *New York Commercial*. More industrial publications followed fast—the *Butchers' and Packers' Gazette* in 1808, the *American Journal of Pharmacy* in 1825, the *American Railway Journal* in 1832 (it still lives as *Railway Locomotives and Cars*). One of the important characteristics of the industrial press, the multiple publisher, developed with transportation—in the 1880's, a young upstate New York high school teacher named James H. McGraw began working on a trolley car magazine. Less than a century later, the great publishing house which bears his name is the producer of more than 40 industrials.

Multiple publishing became a way of life by natural evolution of the industrials. Editors and advertising men got to know their opposite numbers throughout an industry. Not only did they become familiar with the men, they also were among the first to know of new developments and processes which in turn resulted in diversification and more developments. New departments

115

in the publications became complete new magazines, and multiple publishers reproduced themselves like the amoeba, by division and sub-division!

As men associate in joint enterprises they form organizations for mutual benefit. So it was with the industrial publications. Today the one major association is the American Business Press, representing 500 of the leading industrial magazines. In chapter 11 we'll deal in detail with its activities and those of other pace-setting periodical associations.

As industrials multiplied, they began developing in as many different directions as industry itself. Some of the earliest had chiefly been the communicators of price changes, financial news, and business activity—financial newspapers in reality. This variety exists today in the *Wall Street Journal*, a true financial paper, as well as in magazines such as *Business Week*, reporting on major events in the world of industry and finance. Some of these publications are limited, as were the pioneers, to coverage of a single city. Many others take entire states or regions for their territory, or are national or international in scope.

This geographical emphasis is one major characteristic of the industrials and accounts in considerable degree for their number. Localized news and information is a prime commodity in communication.

Concentration on a single industry or product is another important trait of industrials. Thus we have *Steel* or *The Paper Industry*. Within these individual industries we observe both horizontal and vertical tendencies and also in the publications which cover them. *The Oil and Gas Journal* blankets the petroleum field from geophysical surveys to government regulation. Other oil publications may be technical and professional, such as the *Bulletin of the American Association of Petroleum Geologists*, or engaged with the marketing of a single petroleum derivative as the *Butane-Propane News*. They may stress processing as in *Hydrocarbon Processing* and *Petroleum Refiner*, or emphasize distribution as does the *National Oil Jobber*. Every aspect, every trade, every product, every occupation of an industry has its publications, giving detailed, informed, comprehensive reports for knowledgeable readers who read for profit.

Multiple Industrials

Undoubtedly there are more multiple publishers among industrials than in any other specialized publishing field. Such giants as McGraw-Hill are known to almost everyone, but you have to be in the business, probably, to recognize Chilton or Reuben H. Donnelley. There are other top companies, too, which should command any publisher's respect—such as Cahners and the American Chemical Society, Harcourt, Brace or Haire, and Cowles' Magazines for Industry. We'll present a quick dossier on them here and examine them in more detail in Chapter 11.

Cahners

Cahners publishes 36 publications and directories itself and through its five subsidiaries, Conover-Mast, Industrial Publications, Inc., Medalist, Watson, and Rogers. Its main fields are building, metal-working, plastics, food, purchasing, boats, aeronautics—an across-the-board complement of modern industrial activity. Cahners itself is 40 per cent owned by International Publishing Corporation Ltd., of Great Britain, largest publishing company in the world with an interest in more than 200 industrial publications.

American Chemical Society

This is a paradox, a scientific association which also acts as a major publisher. The American Chemical Society has 19 journals of its own or issued by cooperating sub-divisions. While handling all editorial matters itself, the advertising for 16 ACS publications is taken care of by the Reinhold Publishing Corporation, also a chemical publisher. Oldest ACS periodical is the *Journal of the American Chemical Society*, founded in 1879.

Harcourt, Brace & World

Harcourt, Brace & World was one of the world's largest book publishers before it entered the magazine world in 1967 with the purchase of five state farm publications and two other allied periodicals and grouped them under the name of The Harvest Publishing Company. Then in 1968 it made a second major acquisition, buying Ojibway Press of Duluth, Minnesota, and three Ojibway subsidiaries, publishing 27 properties in 13 industries. The same year it acquired two more farm publications when it bought the Nebraska Farmer Company. The oldest Ojibway magazine is *Gas Age*, founded in 1883, the largest, *Electronic Technician/Dealer* with 83,359. Other specialized publication companies taken over by Harcourt Brace & World in 1967–68 include Byrum Publications (medical), Brookhill Publishing, F. A. Owen Publishing (educational), Scott Periodicals, and four books from Haire Publishing (novelties and apparel), for a total of more than 40 different magazines.

Haire Publishing Company

Ranging from women's apparel to accessories and notions, the Haire Publishing Company, of New York City, began industrial publishing in 1910 and today has 11 books and at least an equal number of directories and convention papers. Their first publication, *Dress Essentials*, was issued in 1911.

117

Their circulation leader is *Profit Parade*, 71,300 copies. They have an unusual arrangement with The American Express Company for joint publication of *Product News International* which is circulated on five continents.

Magazines for Industry, Inc.

Cowles Communications, Inc., is the conglomerate owner of almost every type of medium you can imagine from newspapers to radio-TV stations to magazines of general circulation to machine-learning. It also is very active in Magazines for Industry, Inc., which issues 18 magazines, 3 international periodicals, 4 newsletters, 6 annuals and directories, and has a half-interest (with Chilton) in two others. Its specialized publications chiefly concern consumer-oriented products and services—candy, soft drinks, food, drugs, medicine. Cowles itself of course operates *Look, Family Circle,* and *Venture.*

Specialized Industrial Newspapers

There are at least 18 specialized industrial newspapers, issued on a daily or semi-weekly basis, in such areas as apparel and textiles, with 3; building and construction, 8; home furnishings, 2; metals, 1; petroleum, 1; real estate, 3. This does not include other specialized newspapers which we list in the entertainment, business and financial, legal, and sports fields. Among the leading industrial newspapers are Fairchild Publications' *Daily News Record*, circulating 24,800 copies, and *Women's Wear Daily*, with 69,327. The same New York City company operates the *Home Furnishings Daily*, 40,000. All are tabloid in size. The building and construction papers are concentrated in California. *American Metal Market* distributes 14,600 copies from its New York office, while the 6,400 circulation of *Oil Daily* is from Chicago.

Constant Change

Industrial publications live in a world of constant change. As technology develops new trails, new publications explore them. The old ones continue—if in no other form, as hobby or collectors' journals! Often what begins as a department in the parent publication, spins off into a publication of its own which, in turn, may produce its own children. The 60-year-old *Office Appliances* of Business Press International gave birth to *Business Automation* and to *Office Design* after those upstarts got too big for their departmental pants. And *Business Automation* precociously spawned *International Business Automation*, printed in English, French, and German in parallel columns. Meanwhile papa itself has a lusty double life for his annual *Buyers Index* totals 322 ad-packed pages. These directories and other service by-products demonstrate another vital facet of the industrial's vigorous personality.

Who Are The Readers?

On the decision-executing level, we find *Modern Machine Shop* "read by men who specify and buy: works managers, superintendents, tool engineers, general foremen" . . . 64,000 circulation in 40,000 plants.

Among the *World Oil* readers, are the "key men in companies responsible for 98 per cent of the $5 billion purchases by world-wide gas and oil industries." *Farm Power Equipment* claims 29.2 per cent readership at International Harvester, 26.7 per cent at John Deere, 10.8 per cent at Massey-Ferguson and so on, calling the roll of agricultural implement manufacturers. *Hardware Retailer* sends 31,211 copies of its total 43,100 circulation to hardware retailers and employees.

The *kind* of readership is the vital blood stream which keeps the industrial publication alive. So it is no surprise to find BPA circulation audit reports stressing a detailed breakdown, as in this audit on *Business Automation* for six months ending December 31, 1967:

	Total Qualified Copies
Manufacturing Industries	15,225
Finance	3,113
Insurance	2,327
Government	3,643
Educational Institutions	4,429
Service Organizations	5,792
Retail & Wholesale Trade	2,151
Transportation, communication, printing & publishing firms	2,857
Utilities	781
Mining, construction & agric. organizations	601
Total	40,919

What Keeps the Readers Reading?

What keeps the readers reading these very specialized publications of industry? Here is Julien Elfenbein's explanation: "The good businesspaper is the continuous textbook of adult education for managers." Although Elfenbein's assumption that textbooks are continuously read may be questioned by some teachers, his phrase "adult education" may be more fortunately chosen.

Although the industrial publication has to operate in the competitive structure of modern business, it has set standards for itself. Here is the American Business Press Code of Publishing Practice:

ABP CODE OF PUBLISHING PRACTICE

As a condition precedent to membership, and as a condition for the continuation of membership, each member of American Business Press, Inc. agrees:

1. In the interest of the reader:
   A) To give equal consideration to all qualified readers and to agree to work towards and ultimately maintain either a preponderantly paid or preponderantly non-paid circulation service to readers in the field served by each publication.
   B) To publish no editorial material either as a consideration for advertising space or in return for monetary or other consideration.
   C) To maintain absolute editorial independence from the advertiser, and from government.
   D) To vigilantly and forcefully fight for the constitutional right of freedom of the press.
   E) To refrain from infringement of the trademarks and copyrights of others.

2. In the interest of the advertiser:
   A) To submit its publications to regular circulation audits by an independent, non-profit, tripartite auditing organization, and to encourage similar auditing practices by all presently unaudited business publications.
   B) To make available to advertisers and advertising agencies, directly or through a recognized published source, all the prices which publications charge for all units of space and services, including, but not limited to, such charges and services as—preferred or specified positions, colors, bleed, inserts, merchandising and research services, etc., as well as the terms of payment thereof; and to afford no advertiser an opportunity to purchase such space or services at a rate more advantageous than is available to any other advertiser.

3. In the interest of independent publishing:
   To encourage support of publications owned or controlled by independent, tax-paying organizations in the belief that such publications represent the basic principles inherent in a free press.

4. In the interest of improved postal service:
   To cooperate with the Post Office Department in its efforts towards improved service and modernization so as to prevent those rate increases which may be inimical to a free and independent business press, recognizing at all times that without an efficient postal service, business publications cannot effectively serve their readers. In furtherance of these objectives to accept rate differentials for the various classes of mail, and to take no action as a representative of, identified with, or in the name of the Association either to equalize those rates, or to maintain any differential.

5. In the interest of truth and decency in advertising:
   To refuse to accept, in its opinion, any obscene, vulgar, profane or libelous advertising material; to refuse to run any advertising in which any statement or representation is made which disparages or attacks the goods, prices, services, or advertising of any competitor or any other industry, or which contains statements or claims about an advertiser's own products or services which the publisher knows, or has reason to believe, are untrue or inaccurate.

120

6. In the interest of ethical publishing:
   A) To promote and sell its own publications solely upon their merits.
   B) To employ no advertising or personal selling methods which are unfair to other publications or advertising media.
   C) To make no misrepresentation either in the use of research data and survey results or otherwise by fully disclosing all research methodology.

The Editors Talk

What do editors of specific magazines set as the goals, the formulas, for their magazines?

Media/scope, published by Standard Rate & Data Service, says its editorial purpose "is to help the buyers of advertising invest their money more effectively and efficiently. . . . The principal subjects which its readers are concerned with are budgeting, selection of markets, selection of media to match markets, efficient techniques in the use of media, organization for media planning, buying, and control of expenditures in both national and local media— and in both print and broadcast. *Media/scope* presents a balanced coverage of all media, showing how marketing and advertising problems are solved by the intelligent mixing of media to achieve specific goals of coverage, frequency, and audience reach."

Media/scope analyzes its editorial content for the 12 months of 1966 to show how it achieves its aims:

Agency-Advertiser-Media Organization, Personnel and Buying Procedures	12.2
Advertising Media Effectiveness; including measurements not dealing with specific media	14.4
Planning, Budgeting, and Automation	8.6
Media Mix	0.9
Markets	8.3
Consumer Magazines, Farm Publications, Newspaper Supplements	4.0
Business Publications	10.6
Newspapers*	3.3
Radio: Spot* and Network	9.9
Television: Spot* and Network	12.3
Direct Mail	0.5
Transit	0.8
Point-of-Purchase	0.1
Outdoor	1.7
Specialized Media	0.8
Miscellaneous, Covers, Indexes, Announcements	11.6
	100.0%

Total Editorial Pages: 869
Total Magazine Pages: 1994

Analysis by Lloyd H. Hall Co. Inc.
*Covered in greater depth in Markets and Media Mix.

121

It is worth noting, additionally, that this survey showed a total of 869 editorial pages out of a total of 1,994 pages, or 43.6 per cent.

Missiles and Rockets says it "is published for the entire engineering and scientific community of the defense and space industries. With its systems-oriented editorial approach, *Missiles and Rockets* is written for defense / space research, scientific, engineering, design, management, production, operations, purchasing and procurement personnel."

The *NTDRA Dealer News*, published weekly by the National Tire Dealers and Retreaders Association, "is edited primarily for members of the National Tire Dealers and Retreaders Association who are independent tire dealers and retreaders. Material fits into three basic categories: Is material of value to members? The news and feature stories on advertising, sales training, industry trends, labor negotiations, marketing trends, new tire line, price changes, sales outlook, etc. Is material of interest to the dealer? Newsmakers, personnel changes, new products, legislative activities. Is material related to association news, convention coverage, local association news, new services?"

These specific statements are typical of thousands of others, clearcut definitions of goal and function. The industrial publication has to hit its target on bull's-eye to survive and succeed. Significantly, SRDS directories, which offer a unique and invaluable reference for the communications world, lead off each entry with a "statement of editorial character and objectives."

Interviewing the Editors

Turnabout is fair play, and also the way to find out what the editor says about his job. So we went to the editors.

Reuben H. Donnelley

At his desk in Chicago's busy Loop, the veteran editor-in-chief of *Road and Streets*, Harold J. McKeever, leaned back in his swivel chair and talked about his work.

"As you know, *Roads and Streets* is published by the Magazine Publishing Division of The Reuben H. Donnelley Corporation, a member of the Dun & Bradstreet Group. The Magazine Publishing Division is composed of six divisional groups with a total of 21 publications and one separate single publication, *Control Engineering*. The six groups are Municipal, Textile, International, Yorke Medical, Construction, and Transportation. Some of our main offices are in New York, some in Chicago. Do you want any more detail on our administrative structure? All right, take a look—"

And with a copy pencil on yellow paper, McKeever diagramed organization and chain of command, first for Dun & Bradstreet and then for *Roads and Streets*. It is worth noting the relationship between Dun & Bradstreet, major financial news service, and the six areas of industrial publishing. Financial news furnishes a foundation for all industry. McGraw-Hill has a similar relationship with Standard & Poor.

"We have four main departments for *Roads and Streets*—production, editorial, marketing, and sales management. Like many publications under multiple publishers, some functions such as research and control are centralized.

"But maybe I'm getting ahead of myself—do you know about *Roads and Streets*?

"No? Our editorial job is to give information on a national scale to heavy construction contractors, engineers, and government officials who carry out highway programs. That runs from planning and design through construction to maintenance and operation. Roads, streets, bridges, airfields—they are our territory."

McKeever leaned back, stretching his arms as if to take in all that territory.

"We have an active group of outside writers, as well as field offices in the East, South, Southwest, and Pacific Coast. Our editorial work here is divided into two main departments—editorial, and administrative. We have a Washington editor, two field editors and three contributing editors, and a staff of six writers and editors here in the home office.

"It takes coordination, a detailed schedule, and a determination to run on time to get a book like this out every month, with 150 to 200 pages. Color pages have to be planned and in hand 60 days before press time. Other editorial copy has a 30-day lead time. Our editorial content covers the general industry, with meeting and convention reports and a monthly newsletter; the engineering and highway department; the largest department called 'contractor interest' and dealing with equipment, earth-moving and excavation, paving, grading and foundations, drainage and culverts. Then there's a section, joint contractor-engineer interest, which involves specifications, quality control, contractor work conditions.

"Sound pretty technical?"

We nodded, and asked where he found his staff.

"Two main sources—journalism schools for our starting writers and most of them come in as editorial assistants. For professional coverage we look for a civil engineering background, and a skill with words."

While offices of industrial publications are spread out in many major cities more than the mass circulation magazines, New York still is the center.

123

Fairchild

Conferences with editors there brought back personal memories, especially when visiting Fairchild Publications and talking with James W. Brady, publisher of *Women's Wear Daily* and the *Daily News Record*. Brady, tall and slender, young-looking indeed for his executive responsibilities, has his desk in an alcove off the main editorial room, close to his writers and editors.

Fairchild was begun in 1890 by E. W. and Louis Fairchild and specializes in clothing and textile coverage, with its eight publications served by 1,582 full-time employees. It stresses news and spends more than $8 million a year in gathering news.

"Of all our employees, more than 600 are full-time staff writers and another 400 are correspondents," Brady brought us up to date. "Yes, it's mushroomed since you were an editor here. Now we have 41 bureaus in the United States and 33 foreign countries. We hire most of our people right off the campus, starting them around $110 a week. No, no sex distinctions. They get a 3-month trial and then they're given a $10 raise or else they're out. We look for writing ability first. They can learn our specialties on the job. Our turn-over rate is very low and we're moving more and more towards full-time rather than part-time correspondents. The St. Louis bureau hires for St. Louis, New York for New York, and so on.

"Our publications have followed a natural course of evolution, with departments growing into full-sized independent periodicals. The only exceptions perhaps have been *Electronic News* and *Metalworking News*. For now we've no plans for regional editions although we certainly use lots of regional reports. Our new departures have been a syndicate service for newspapers and a radio program in 11 major cities, sponsored by Celanese, and scripted by us.

"But our main job is news—news of clothes, fashions, wholesale and retail," Brady emphasized, his own well-cut suit underlining the point. "We run half-a-million news stories a year and print on our own presses more than 900 thousand copies a week. That keeps us busy—remember?"

McGraw-Hill

In midtown Manhattan in the turquoise-blue skyscraper, McGraw-Hill headquarters its empire, and there John R. Callaham, vice president in charge of editorial for its 48 publications, described them.

"Find a capable publisher and an effective editor and put them in charge. They'll establish a skillful staff and then it's a matter of giving the reader the dependable information he wants.

"With our growing family of publications, we've tried to help out. Here's the preliminary draft of our new Editor's Manual—," and Callaham reached out the black-bound book of 30 pages. "That was prepared by our Editorial

Board, the standing committee of our chief editors. As I say in the Foreword, 'This Manual is a working tool. Its aim is to help you write better articles, write them at higher efficiency, get them onto the page at optimum cost, and get them off the page and into the reader's mind at the highest level of impact and at least expense of effort on his part.'"

The table of contents read like a reporting text—how to get a story, how to write a story, how to illustrate a story, how to process copy into type, what you should know about libel, what you should know about ethics in journalism. Plus detail about McGraw-Hill and its policies and organization, and specialized hints on specialized publications and their editing.

One of the effective McGraw-Hill editors interviewed was A. J. Fox of *Engineering News-Record*, which goes weekly to more than 97 thousand construction engineers, designers, and contractors. Established in 1874, *Engineering News-Record* is one of the enduring pioneers among industrials.

Fox, lean, enthusiastic, pointed through the glass partitions surrounding his office.

"Right outside there are the top editorial people," and he waved to six or seven men and women closely grouped around several large desks. "They ride herd on planning and execution. It's an old phrase but it's true here—this is a team operation.

"And out there," he waved again to the rows of files and desks spreading out over a wide sweep of skyscraper floor, "there are the rest of our 40-man staff. They're backed up by more than 200 reporters and correspondents around the world. We try to cover everything that's news for our readers—that means legislation, labor, finance, prices, trends. It includes design developments and all major construction connected with buildings, transportation, water resources."

The coverage must do the job. *Engineering News-Record* has won 10 national awards for editorial excellence. Its circulation has grown by 57 per cent over the past 12 years, with renewals by two-thirds of its subscribers. In 1964, four cost issues brought 169,494 reader requests for further information. And *EN-R* in 1964 carried 4,179 advertising pages, 1,375 more than were carried by any other national construction publication.

Then Fox escorted me on a tour around the floor, showing me endless rows of files and their contents.

"Facts. Records. That's what backs up our editors when it comes to nailing down detail. Plus our regular deadlines. The presses start rolling every Monday. We've got to be in the mail every Tuesday. But you know what a deadline means to a news publication and that's what we are."

Those growing files are one reason McGraw-Hill is moving to a new skyscraper in 1970.

125

Chilton

One of the fastest-growing industrial publishers is Chilton in Philadelphia. One of the industrial giants in its second century (yes, it was founded in 1855) is *Hardware Age*, a Chilton publication, which in its vigor, its influence, and its size might serve as an outstanding exemplar. While its circulation totals 39,019, it's a circulation of maximum concentration among hardware retailers, wholesalers, and manufacturers. Its advertising leadership is evidenced by its 50.9 per cent share in 1966 of the 4,460 total advertising pages carried by the three national hardware publications.

Not content with age and size, *Hardware Age* constantly pushes ahead. It has 10 specials planned to meet hardware seasonal buying and selling needs, four regional editions, and a mammoth annual directory. Its publisher and editor is William A. Barbour, whom we claim also with personal pride as one of our graduates. He is also publishing vice president.

Here is what Barbour said about his company and his job.

"We publish hardware news with the emphasis on news. We don't try to educate our readers but we go all out to keep them informed. They're experts and they want to stay that way. We process thousands of reader inquiries a year—that means using computers to keep up. Our annual directory issue is a basic trade reference book—here, look at it—"

I hefted it, a real block-buster filled with vital data on all phases of the hardware industry.

Barbour believes in his job and is proud of his company.

"Chilton has made an all-out approach to modern publishing by clearly defining its purposes and policies. Using the printed word in which it so strongly believes, it has enlisted the cooperation of its editors and publishers through formulation of clear goals. Then these have been expressed in written guides by which we operate."

Leaning over, Barbour held out several booklets, his eyes serious and intent.

"Look at them!"

Four of them especially demanded careful attention with their effective coordination of colored stock and typographical symbols. The first, a slim blue booklet, is titled "Chilton Responsibilities and Policies." Inside, these are divided into responsibility to readers, to advertisers, to employees, to stockholders, to the national interest. As representative of their nature, here is what Chilton says about editorial policy:

> To put our responsibility to readers above all other considerations.
> To edit each magazine in the best interests of the field it serves.
> To make each magazine a vital, continuous force for adult education, presenting

126

news, and marketing, technical, merchandising and management information that will help readers in their business or profession.

To attain by all ethical means a position of leadership in each of the fields we serve.

To select editorial material only on the basis of reader values. Advertising considerations must not be a factor in determining the acceptability of editorial matter.

To respect the rights and dignity of all individuals in the editing of our publications.

To prohibit editorial personnel from accepting payment in any form, for material appearing in our editorial columns.

To use scientific and ethical research for evaluating editorial acceptance and for determining the kinds of information readers want.

To require each Chilton editor periodically to review and evaluate his publication's performance as it relates to these statements of policy.

To acknowledge our responsibilities to Chilton book authors. We will present their works to the widest possible audience, in accordance with the market potentials. We will account to them for each copy sold.

To give all contributors of articles to Chilton magazines prompt reports on their material; to use accepted material as promptly as circumstances permit; to pay going market rates.

Barbour carries his company's public interest into practice with his enthusiastic work on the ABP education committee, working to aid and improve college journalism training. He also sits on the Chilton editorial board, composed of each top Chilton editor.

"Chilton believes in cooperation by its own in policy-making. That's why we have the editorial board and also the Chilton board of publishers. You can see their organization and their work outlined in that booklet you're holding, 'The Chilton Publisher.'"

The foreword to the "Publisher" is worth attention as a statement of the duties of top management for modern industrial publication. This is what it says, in part.

The Chilton publisher should thoroughly understand the basic elements of a magazine: Editorial, Circulation, Advertising, Sales and Production. He must be able to build a staff and keep it running efficiently. He has to know and use modern marketing and research techniques to keep in tune with readers and advertisers.

The annual budget is his master control plan: It keeps him in touch with all phases of his operation. The degree of control he exercises is reflected in the company's profit statement.

Yet he spends as little time as possible in the office. He uses the rest for visits with his own staff in the field and with the leaders of the industry or profession his publication serves. He accepts committee appointments and speaking engagements; he attends meetings where his counsel may be sought. In short, he knows that a good part of the success of the publication depends upon his personal knowledge of the field and its leaders.

The other two booklets were a slim black one, "This is Chilton," with succinct descriptions of the 25 Chilton publications, and "The Annual Report," an open letter to its stockholders and the general public. The annual report demonstrates that clear and complete communication produces profits —a net of $1,756,287 for 1967.

Organization of the Industrial

Considering the care given by industrial publishers and editors to their work, it is essential to note the organization and operation of the industrial publication. Like most magazines, and differing from company publications, the chief business of the industrial is its own profitable operation. Additionally, it is self-supporting and therefore depends on advertising to furnish major revenues.

Under top administration, generally designated as the publisher, the over-all policies are determined and personnel selected for their execution. The publisher, as a rule, supervises the business side of the publication, including the budget and accounting controls, the setting of revenue ratios for advertising and circulation, the allocation of editorial space, the choice of top personnel.

Advertising Bankrolls the Industrial

Advertising and circulation are the two direct revenue-producing divisions. Advertising furnishes more than 90 per cent of industrial publication income. Sixty-five major advertisers spent a million dollars or more on industrial publication advertising in 1966, with blue chips topping the list with American Cyanamid, General Electric, General Motors, Borg-Warner leading in expenditures. See the illustrations, this chapter, for an illustrative bar chart of income for an industrial publishing house, The Penton Publishing Company. In the Appendix may be found a 10-year summary of financial data for the same company.

Advertising space in industrials ranges from 50 to 80 per cent of total available, and could rise even higher if publishers did not hold the line. A one-time insertion of a black-and-white full-page ad in *Coronet*, a mass magazine with a circulation of 413,668, costs $1,500. *The Oil and Gas Journal* with a circulation of 47,431, 11.5 per cent of *Coronet*'s, charges $940 for the same space, 62.7 per cent as much. Industrial publication advertising is premium quality advertising and commands premium prices.

For instant reference and comparisons of advertising costs and the circu-

128

lation being bought, Standard Rate & Data Service offers up-to-date and accurate figures, serving as a bible for all types of media.

One of the most important selling points for industrials is the research and service they offer advertisers and readers, both in the regular publication pages and in directories and surveys. Much of the advertising which industrials carry is for specific products and services. However, the promotion of institutional prestige is the focal point of a large volume, also. Classified is an important item in many industrials, although display furnishes the bulk business and revenue.

Advertising is solicited both by salesmen employed full-time by the industrial and also through advertising representatives who operate on a commission basis in key cities. Standardized order forms and regular rates, providing for discounts according to volume of advertising purchased, offer consistent and dependable figures to the advertiser.

Circulation Means Customers

Ad rates are adjusted, of course, to circulation. The more circulation, the higher your rate structure can be. As a consequence, bonafide guarantees of circulation are essential. Industrials have attached increasing importance to the authenticated audits of the Audit Bureau of Circulations for not less than 70 per cent paid circulation, and of Business Publications Audit for "controlled" circulation by distribution to a select list. Several multiple publishers produce some publications which are ABC-audited as well as others verified by BPA. Post office regulations permit paid circulation periodicals to circulate at 2nd-class postal rates, considerably less than the postal cost for those with controlled circulation.

Different advantages may be gained from either system, depending on the nature of the publication and its audience, and its competition. Factors that have to be considered include advertising income, the cost of production, the cost of securing subscriptions and renewals, actual and potential circulation. There is no iron-clad rule to determine which is better in any specific case. Paid circulation does provide additional income, better cues to reader interest, an active circulation with positive interest clearly indicated, lower mailing charges. Controlled circulation chosen for quality can mean a selective group of readers, and the elimination of the high cost of securing subscription renewals.

Circulation calls for more organization for the industrial than the internal company publications, although the external or combination company periodical almost always is set up on a basis of controlled circulation. The company publication does not need to consider any ratio of circulation to advertising, for it seldom carries ads. However, this proportion is a matter of vital significance to the industrial.

Swift accuracy is fundamental in circulation. Lists must be up to date with daily maintenance and change. This requires computerized operation for any sizeable circulation. The circulation department must cooperate closely with both editorial and advertising to promote and check on reader response, and to follow through.

This record-keeping and constant action become a major challenge when we view the 62 million circulation of industrials for 1966, only 3 million less than daily newspaper circulation.

News and Information Means Readers

Essentially the editorial content of the industrial publications is their bread of life. They provide news on each industry and all events which affect it directly or indirectly. This means action or plans by labor, by government, by other industries, civil or military happenings. Developments in science and technology, the research lab and the working day, bring ideas and information for the attentive reader. The editor looks for news of industrial organizations, industrial leaders, mergers, promotions, retirements, news of imports and exports.

Editorial content also includes editorials and interpretation. The editorial pages provide a forum for the expression of opinion, for discussion. The industrial publication is a public spokesman for the industry and, if intelligently and ably directed, a respected leader.

Often the best read editorial content is found in editorial departments which specialize in major divisions of the industry and give them all their attention. These specialized departments often develop such followings that they eventually spin off into new and separate publications.

What are the sources of news and information?

First and not to be forgotten, the expert and accumulated knowledge of the editorial staff itself. They have followed, gathered, and reported industrial activities often for a lifetime. They know its leaders and its history. They provide a wide-ranging, comprehensive, and impartial fund of information.

Then from the meetings, conventions, trade shows, councils of associations and organizations of the industry or related to it.

The industrial plants, laboratories, offices.

Interviews with industrial leaders and workers.

Surveys of the publications' readers.

130

The publications of the industry and its companies, of government-bureaus and departments.

Editorial staffs are composed both of full-time writers and part-time correspondents. They include editorial executives, layout and production men, contributing editors, and editorial assistants. Many beginners start as editorial assistants and many of them come direct from the journalism school. Wade Fairchild, of Fairchild Publications, says, "We much prefer reporters who can learn an industry rather than industry experts in whom we are supposed to develop a nose for news and writing ability." American Business Press estimates that, in 1966, of the 70 thousand employed by the industrial publications, 14 thousand belonged to the editorial department. Salaries as a rule run higher than those paid by consumer magazines. A *Printer's Ink* survey reported "in most cases, business papers pay the highest salaries for a similar dollar volume of work."

And well they may if we consider the Chilton code for its editors as a criterion. Here is what is expected of the editor.

The Chilton editor accepts leadership in facing industry problems. He serves as friend, critic, and counselor to his industry.

His knowledge of the industry is broad and deep. Such knowledge comes only from intimate, first-hand observation. Hence, the Chilton editor travels extensively.

He is also a skilled professional editor. He uses his experience and research to find new and better ways to get ideas off the printed page and into the reader's mind.

Research and experience are constantly opening up new and improved methods of communication. To maintain his magazine at maximum effectiveness, he keeps abreast of new concepts and techniques. The full development of the professional side of his staff is always of keen concern to him.

The Chilton editor is a businessman. He must run an effective staff, develop the skills and enthusiasm of all its members. He knows the importance of an operating budget. He understands the need for close liaison with the circulation, sales, and promotion departments; and he knows he must be a recognized personality in his field.

The editor's relationship with his publisher is of special importance if the magazine is to be effective and profitable. He must be a loyal, competent, forthright advisor to the publisher. Yet, he always recognizes the final authority of the publisher.

Above all, the Chilton editor knows that to best serve his company, his publisher and his magazine, he must first serve his reader. This he does by building the best editorial product he can.

If any editor lives up to that, you'll agree he earns his salary!

The typical industrial publication is published monthly and its staff may run between 12 and 15 men and women—the editor, managing editor, art editor, four staff writers, a photographer, a couple of copy and layout editors, two editorial assistants, two secretaries, a production editor. Of course, the number on a small publication may be correspondingly small, only three or four. On a major industrial it may range as high as 60 or 70 full-time and 200 part-time field or string correspondents.

These correspondents are a valued and essential news channel for many industrials. Fairchild has considered them so important that it issued a 64-page special manual for its 383 field corps. This manual includes such headings as, "What We Publish" and "News Policy" which gives guidelines on confidences, protecting news sources, printing rumors, no politics or religion. After advising how to cover news for Fairchild and where to find it, the manual details "The Kind of News Fairchild Wants." This totals 25 different categories ranging from fires or acts of God through strikes, obits, and retail promotions to financial statements. How to cover and write the news is the subject of 30 pages dealing with fashion shows, art, accuracy, style, legal data, and—rates of pay for the correspondent!

Some of the best known industrial news sources are weekly news magazines such as *Business Week* or *U.S. News & World Report*. Industrials run bureaus in Washington and major national and international centers. Their production problems, competing in time with daily newspapers and consumer magazines, are pressing. But all publications have to meet that ever-crowding deadline.

Research and Directories

Often the industrial directs an impressive volume of research—sometimes directly promotional, often as a reader service. Surveys of reader interest, merchandising aids, industrial trends—these not only are highly appealing to the reader, but they also furnish much profitable benefit to the publication itself. Research departments are not just brain boxes; they also are dollar-diggers.

Directories and special reports, sometimes annual, are the harvest of this research and in great and constant demand by the industry. Each industry has one or more of these invaluable references—and they not only are a desirable publications byproduct but often exceed the parent in profit and prestige. In the communications area, there are *Editor & Publisher Yearbook* and *Broadcasting-Telecasting Yearbook*. The national baseball weekly, *The Sporting News*, has a real big brother in *The Sporting Goods Dealer*, which in turn sells "How to Sell Sporting Goods" for $5 as just one of several added merchandising guides. Other promotions include "Let's Play Ball," "Let's Go Fishing," "Let's Play Golf," and " Let's Go Hunting." These suggest window and newspaper advertising contests and provide prizes, furnish advertising mats, solicit manufacturing and jobber support, and special mailings to sporting groups.

National Home Month was a promotion of the *American Builder* and within two years after its launching developed the showing of 12 thousand model homes valued at $98 million. *Office Appliances* provides an annual *Buyers Index*, providing manufacturers' addresses, product catalogues, classified product listing, and product trade names. It runs to more than 300 pages.

These directories are only part of the reader services which the industrial publications are providing. Many industrials include keyed reply cards in each issue so the reader can circle a number, corresponding with a number on an article or ad, mail the card, and receive special letters or booklets of information.

With such service, we can understand why the industrial publication has become a necessary partner for every industry. We also can appreciate that the promotion department is a necessary and valued auxiliary of every industrial publication, cooperating constantly with editorial, advertising, circulation.

Editorial Excellence

The variety of industrial publications is evidenced in the ABP awards given annually for editorial excellence. In 1966, in Class 1, circulation to 15,000, top recognition for an editorial went to *Bakers Weekly* for a series on "Drop the 'Bread Tax' from the Administration's Farm Bill." *Book Production Industry* received the award for the best special issue. In Class 2, circulation to 40,000, *The Modern Hospital* won for a series on Medicare; and *Interiors*, for a special issue on Sweden. For Class 3, circulation 40,000 or more, *Building Construction* won the editorial award, while *Fleet Owner* was selected for an "All-Safety" issue. Other prize-winners included *Pulp & Paper, College and University Business, Hospital Management, Undersea Technology, The Boating Industry, Automation, Missiles and Rockets*—12 different publications serving 12 very different fields of activity.

In use of color, in writing style, in layout, these and many other industrials will hold their own with any magazine. They *have* to!

Associations for Action

While most industrial publications are issued primarily for the profits derived from their publishing, others serve trade associations of many companies or individuals active in the same industry. For example, *The Wooden*

133

Barrel published by the American Cooperage Association or the *American Agency Bulletin*, official publication of the National Association of Insurance Agents.

Many of these publications derive their financial resources from the membership dues of individuals and companies, although they also receive advertising income—often from institutional or prestige advertisements as well as from those selling a specific product or service.

In major industries, these association journals often have state or regional representatives as well as national. In the beverage industry, for example, there is the *Illinois Beverage Journal*, and *Host*, of the Oregon Restaurant & Beverage Association.

Basically such publications have one clear purpose—to further the interests of the industry they represent. They cover industry-wide news. They act as a voice of beer or steel or logging. Therefore they not only are information channels but also public relation amplifiers.

Industrials and Modern Society

Back in the opening years of the 1800's it was necessary for the early merchants of New York to get commercial information, and the first industrial publication, carrying prices and news of trade, appeared. In our modern industrial society, the amazing diversity and complexity of technological civilization have placed an even greater premium on the industrial publication as a communications channel. Thus it carries news and information not only among the manufacturers or processors of similar products, but it also acts as a medium of understanding among allied or competing industries. It tells the industrial story to other agencies of society and especially to government. It acts as a spokesman for the industrial point of view.

The more complex and diverse a society, the more it needs such channels of communication. The industrial publication serves as interpreter and ambassador, spokesman and critic, but most important, to provide the essential news and information to industry itself and for the modern world.

134

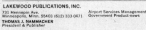

LAKEWOOD PUBLICATIONS, INC.
731 Hennepin Ave.
Minneapolis, Minn. 55403 (612) 333-0471
THOMAS J. NAMMACHER
President & Publisher

Airport Services Management
Government Product-news

LOCKWOOD TRADE JOURNAL CO., INC.
551 Fifth Ave.
New York, N.Y. 10017 (212) 661-5980
GEORGE E. LOCKWOOD
President & Treasurer

La Papeterie
Paper Trade Journal
Tobacco

MACLEAN-HUNTER PUBLISHING CORP.
300 West Adams St.
Chicago, Ill. 60606 (312) 726-2802
JOSEPH J. O'NEILL President

Boxboard Containers
Coal Mining & Processing
Concrete Products
Inland Printer/American
Lithographer
Rock Products

MACTIER PUBLISHING CORP.
820 Second Ave.
New York, N.Y. 10017 (212) 661-0450
BRYCE GRAY, JR. President

EEE-Circuit Design
Engineering
Electronic Procurement

MAGAZINES FOR INDUSTRY, INC.
(subsidiary of
Cowles Communications, Inc.)
777 Third Ave.
New York, N.Y. 10017 (212) 759-5245
DON GUSSOW President

Candy Industry and
Confectioners Journal
Candy Marketer, The
Food & Drug Packaging
Glass Industry, The
Glass Packer/Processor
Hard & Soft Goods Packaging
Ice Cream Field & Ice Cream
Trade Journal
Soft Drink Industry
Soft Serve & Drive-In Field

McGRAW-HILL, INC.
330 W. 42nd St.
New York, N.Y. 10036 (212) 971-3333
JOSEPH H. ALLEN President
McGraw-Hill Publications

American Machinist
Architectural Record
Aviation Week & Space
Technology
Business Education World
Chemical Engineering
Chemical Week
Coal Age
College & University
Construction Methods and
Equipment
Electrical Construction
and Maintenance
Electrical Wholesaling
Electrical World
Electronics
Engineering and Mining
Journal
Engineering News-Record
Factory
Fleet Owner
House & Home
Industrial Distribution
Metals Week
Modern Hospital, The
Modern Nursing Home
Administrator
Modern Packaging
Modern Plastics
National Petroleum News
Nation's Schools (Regular &
Board Member Editions)
Power
Product Engineering
Purchasing Week
Scientific Research
Textile World

AMERICAN BUSINESS PRESS INFO/FILE '67

TEAR OUT TO FORM
8-PAGE BOOKLET

Table of Contents

Business press advertising volume in terms of: Per cent of total business advertising, 1; Growth, 2; Different fields, 3; SIC classification, 4; Frequency/distribution type, 6; 1966 "millionaires," 7; Top 10 cities, 8; Investment by SIC in 30 states, 8.

Last year, business press advertising accounted for 40.6% of total dollars invested in business advertising, which also includes catalogs, exhibits, direct mail, films, etc. Estimates indicate this percentage should rise to 41.8% in 1967.

All the figures and factors relating to the growth of business press advertising are detailed in this special eight-page, tear-out booklet prepared for you by American Business Press and INDUSTRIAL MARKETING. It is a first-of-its-kind statistical analysis made possible by computers, and is designed to serve as a basic reference work throughout the year.

The results of two ABP studies are uniquely combined in this state-of-the-industry report: (1) Business press advertising page and dollar volume, derived from the association's annual survey of 2,259 business publications; and (2) geographical and SIC analyses, taken from ABP's 16th annual survey of 2,424 leading advertisers in the medium.

TABLE 1

JUNE 1968

SUN	MONDAY	TUESDAY	WEDNESDAY	THURSDAY	FRIDAY	SAT
						1
2	3	4	5	6	7	8
9	10	11	12	13	14	15
20	21	22	23	24	25	26
27	28	29	30	31		

NUMBER OF PUBLICATIONS

1950	1,772
1955	1,974
1960	2,310
1961	2,356
1962	2,435
1963	2,496
1964	2,559
1965	2,548
1966	2,395
1967*	2,350

*ESTIMATED

"BUSINESS PUBLICATIONS" DEFINED

WE'RE TALKING HERE ABOUT SPECIALIZED BUSINESS PUBLICATIONS SERVING SPECIFIC INDUSTRIES, BUSINESS, SERVICE OR PROFESSIONAL AUDIENCES, NOT INCLUDING GENERAL BUSINESS OR BUSINESS NEWS MAGAZINES.

THERE WERE ONLY 10 IN 1850, 900 BY 1900, 1,649 IN 1925 AND 2,395 IN 1966.

38% OF ALL PUBLICATIONS TODAY HAVE ABC OR BPA AUDITED CIRCULATION.

ANALYSIS OF PUBLICATIONS BY TYPE — 1966

INDUSTRIAL	1,168
MERCHANDISING	493
EXPORT, IMPORT & INTERNATIONAL	139
FINANCIAL	114
MEDICAL	318
RELIGIOUS	15
EDUCATIONAL	91
GOVERNMENT	57

Aids to members, and selling tools for American Business Press. Used by permission of American Business Press, Inc.

BUSINESS PUBLICATION CIRCULATION TOPS 61 MILLION

1950	24.3
1955	33.8
1960	47.6
1961	50.3
1962	51.7
1963	55.0
1964	56.2
1965	60.0
1966	61.3
*1967	64.0

°ESTIMATED

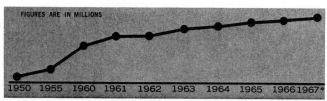

FIGURES ARE IN MILLIONS

1950 1955 1960 1961 1962 1963 1964 1965 1966 1967*

1966 CIRCULATION, ALL BUSINESS PUBLICATIONS ... 61,306,151
1966 CIRCULATION, ABC-BPA PUBLICATIONS 34,095,087

BUSINESS PUBLICATION ADVERTISING VOLUME

(Production Costs Not Included)

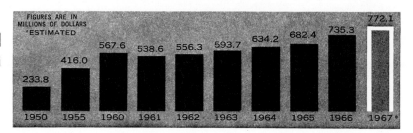

FIGURES ARE IN MILLIONS OF DOLLARS
*ESTIMATED

| 233.8 | 416.0 | 567.6 | 538.6 | 556.3 | 593.7 | 634.2 | 682.4 | 735.3 | 772.1 |
| 1950 | 1955 | 1960 | 1961 | 1962 | 1963 | 1964 | 1965 | 1966 | 1967* |

Publishing for industry thrives and grows as can be seen from these charts from "Fast Facts" produced by American Business Press. Used by permission of American Business Press, Inc.

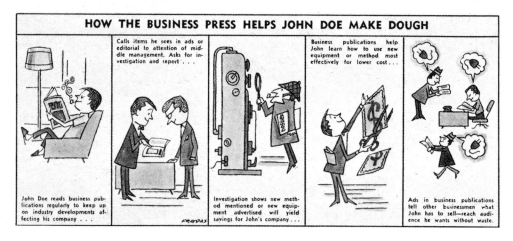

HOW THE BUSINESS PRESS HELPS JOHN DOE MAKE DOUGH

John Doe reads business publications regularly to keep up on industry developments affecting his company . . .

Calls items he sees in ads or editorial to attention of middle management. Asks for investigation and report . . .

Investigation shows new method mentioned or new equipment advertised will yield savings for John's company . . .

Business publications help John learn how to use new equipment or method most effectively for lower cost . . .

Ads in business publications tell other businessmen what John has to sell—reach audience he wants without waste.

Industrial publications produce dollars. A cartoon appearing in *New York Times* supplement; courtesy of American Business Press.

Trade advertisement showing publications of the Haire Publishing Company. Used by permission of the Haire Publishing Company.

PUBLISHER'S STATEMENT

For 6 Month Period Ending

DECEMBER 1967

BUSINESS PUBLICATIONS AUDIT OF CIRCULATION, INC.
420 Lexington Avenue, New York, N.Y. 10017
Established 1931

BUSINESS AUTOMATION

Business Press International, Inc.

288 Park Avenue West, Elmhurst, Ill. 60126

OFFICIAL PUBLICATION OF   None

ESTABLISHED   1958   ISSUES PER YEAR   12

FIELD SERVED

Business firms, institutions and government agencies that use business automation/data processing systems, including data communication, microfilm systems, data collection, data display, information retrieval and office reproduction systems.

DEFINITION OF RECIPIENT QUALIFICATION

Qualified recipients are: Data Processing Managers, Systems and Procedure Managers, Systems Analysts, Controllers, Presidents, Vice Presidents, Treasurers, EDP Educators and Administrators, and other Management, as indicated in paragraph 3a, of organizations that must either:

1. Use a computer, punched cards, punched tape or magnetic tape or
2. Employ 100 or more white collar workers (executives, supervisors, salesmen, and office employees).

Execeptions to the 100 white collar workers qualification are banks, insurance companies, hospitals, advertising agencies, management consultants, schools and government agencies.

AVERAGE NON-QUALIFIED DISTRIBUTION	Copies	**1. AVERAGE QUALIFIED CIRCULATION BREAKDOWN FOR PERIOD**	Qualified Non-Paid Copies	Qualified Non-Paid Percent	Qualified Paid Copies	Qualified Paid Percent	Total Qualified Copies	Total Qualified Percent
Advertiser and Agency	1,259	Single	40,789	99.9%	14	0.1%	40,803	100.0%
Non-Qualified Paid	1,366	Group	–	–	–	–	–	–
Rotated or Occasional	–	Association	–	–	–	–	–	–
Samples	133	Gift	–	–	–	–	–	–
All Other	655	Bulk	–	–	–	–	–	–
TOTAL	**3,413**	*See Par. 11 **TOTALS**	40,789	99.9%	14	0.1%	40,803	100.0%

U.S. POSTAL MAILING CLASSIFICATION   Controlled Circulation

2. QUALIFIED CIRCULATION BY ISSUES WITH REMOVALS AND ADDITIONS FOR PERIOD

1967 Issue	Qualified Non-Paid	Qualified Paid	Total Qualified	Number Removed	Number Added	1967 Issue	Qualified Non-Paid	Qualified Paid	Total Qualified	Number Removed	Number Added
July			40,182	231	204	Oct			42,762	703	3,311
August			40,171	393	382	Nov			40,919	1,843	–
Sept			40,154	323	306	Dec			40,632	287	–
						TOTALS				3,780	4,203

Publisher's statement for *Business Automation* for a six-month period ending in December, 1967. Used by permission of Business Publications Audit of Circulations, Inc. and courtesy of Business Press International, Inc.

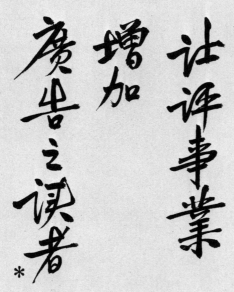

McGraw-Hill has just opened a Hong Kong news bureau. Assignment: translate Southeast Asian developments into American business talk. Overseas bureau No. 12.

McGraw-HILL
market-directed ®
PUBLICATIONS *Translation: Editorial enterprise builds advertising readership.

Advertisement for McGraw-Hill; courtesy of McGraw-Hill Publications.

Magazines produced by McGraw-Hill; courtesy of McGraw-Hill Publications.

Promotional advertising for *Hardware Age*; courtesy of *Hardware Age* and Chilton Company.

Arthur J. Fox, editor of the *Engineering News Record* confers with James B. Sullivan, managing editor, on the next issue.

THE CORPORATE RESPONSIBILITIES OF CHILTON COMPANY

Responsibility to Readers

Our first responsibility is to serve the many hundreds of thousands of persons who read Chilton publications.

We will spare no effort to provide helpful news and technical, marketing, merchandising and management information for our readers. Our responsibility is to contribute to their business or professional success.

Unless we fulfill this responsibility, and thus hold the respect and goodwill of our readers, we are without the foundation essential to a successful publishing enterprise.

Responsibility to Advertisers

Most of the revenue of our magazines comes from advertising. We have a great responsibility to our advertisers. The more effectively we meet the interests of our readers, the more certain is our ability to attract advertising.

It is our responsibility to advertisers to maintain the highest editorial standards and thus insure regular and thorough readership of our magazines.

It is our responsibility to use circulation procedures which place our magazines in the hands of the greatest possible number of potential buyers of advertised products.

We must use the most efficient methods available in meeting these responsibilities.

Responsibility to Employees

Our management has the responsibility to conduct our business so that employees may enjoy security and the opportunity to advance in accordance with their ability, industry and loyalty.

The best way to assure ourselves of the means of providing for the welfare of our employees and their families is by meeting our obligations to readers and advertisers.

Responsibility to Stockholders

The investment of our stockholders makes our enterprise possible. We have a responsibility to give them a fair return for the use of their money, and to make their investment increase in value.

We serve the best interests of our stockholders when we meet our responsibilities to readers, advertisers and employees. Our obligations to stockholders must always be kept in mind when making business decisions.

Responsibility to the National Interest

Specialized business publications, such as we publish, play a vital role in advancing America's growth, technology and living standards. We recognize a responsibility to uphold and promote the American system of free competitive enterprise. We firmly oppose communism, socialism and other forms of totalitarianism. We oppose confiscatory taxes and government competition with private enterprise.

Chilton considers its responsibilities, as seen from this page of a Chilton booklet. Used by courtesy of Chilton Company.

Financial and Operating Review

Distribution of Income
THOUSANDS OF DOLLARS

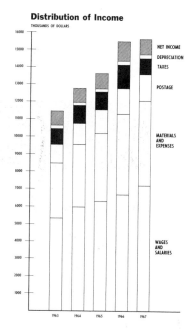

As you study the accompanying financial statements, you will note that 1967 was an unusually busy year from the standpoint of financial planning.

During 1967 the Company's total sales and revenue for the year were $15,643,926, compared with $15,402,994 in 1966 —an increase of 1.6 percent. This is the sixth consecutive year of record income. Net income in 1967 was $859,307 compared with $1,109,526 in 1966, a decrease of $250,219 or 22.5 percent. These figures are equivalent to 5.5 percent of total income in 1967 and the 7.2 percent in 1966. Earnings per share of 90 cents based on the average number of shares outstanding in 1967 compare with $1.16 in the previous year.

STOCK SPLIT

On May 29, 1967, the Board of Directors declared a two-for-one stock split payable, in the form of a stock dividend, September 1, 1967, to shareholders of record August 4, 1967. Net income per share for 1966 was adjusted for the two-for-one stock split. Other data in this report on earnings and book value for prior years also have been adjusted to reflect that split.

Financial and operating review from Penton Publishing Company. Used by permission of Penton Publishing Company.

Dial for industrial know-how from Penton publications; courtesy of the Penton Publishing Company.

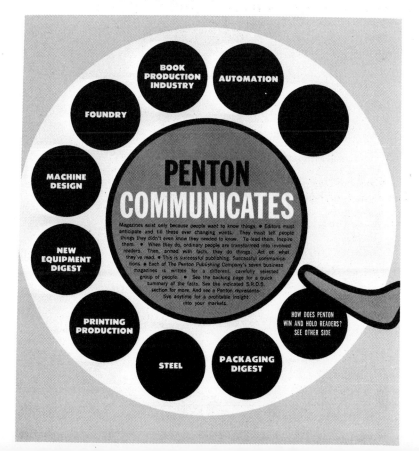

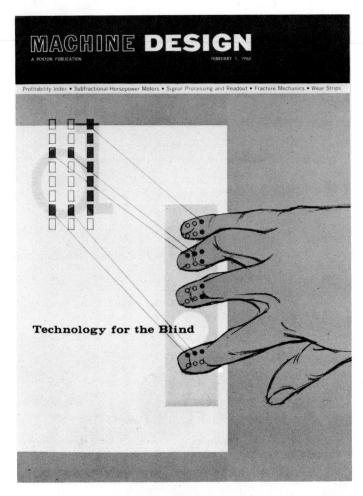

Machine Design cover; courtesy of Penton Publishing Company. Copyright, 1968, by *Machine Design*.

8. The Siamese Twins—
Business and Labor

B USINESS and Labor have been the twin preoccupations of American men—and many women—since the United States based its constitutional planning on equal opportunity in an open society. The earliest printed news covered commodity quotations under such headings as " Prices Current. " Ship arrivals and departures—and their cargoes—received detailed reporting. " Help Wanted " and " Job Wanted " ads in classified columns emphasized labor's hunt for work—or the business search for workers. Trade and commerce were big stories in the colonies, where economic conditions played a major role in creating the American Revolution.

These Siamese twins, sometimes struggling, more often cooperating, have constantly engaged publishers and readers with all the news of their incessant, changing activities. Although occupying opposite sides of the same coin, their fortunes are inseparably related and reported together. Other chapters have dealt with the publications of individual companies and industry (see chapters 6 and 7) but business and finance, with at least a hundred magazines concentrated on money-making, and labor, with nearly 80 million employed men and women, are enterprises of such importance and magnitude that they warrant a chapter of their own.

135

Business and the Profit Motive

Fortune and *Business Week, U.S. News & World Report*—these are big names among the business publications which accumulated an annual advertising volume of $18,000,000 in 1966. Their story is as spectacular as the supposedly humdrum but really breathtaking romance of American business.

The general health, the daily ups-and-downs, the monthly swings, and the annual trends of the business community—this is the big story, the continuing assignment, of the business magazine. National and international trade mingle and intermingle to such a degree that it's impossible to divide them clearly, although certain publications do concentrate on world trade. Intimately associated is the river of finance, its currents swirling and running fast or slow. Closely related are the organizations and associations in which businessmen join at the weekly Rotary lunch or meet in annual convention.

U.S. News & World Report

The familiar blue and white cover of *U.S. News & World Report* identifies it each week for a million and a half readers, many of whom buy it in preference to *Time* or *Newsweek* for its more thorough and complete coverage of economic events. Even the political and social developments of the day are seen through the business lens, and it devotes itself with single-minded attention to the economic viewpoint. Therefore it belongs among the business publications although many view it as a newsmagazine.

David Lawrence was the founder of *U.S. News* (as a Washington correspondent in 1933) and his conservative views and news for many years were identified with the magazine. During and following World War I, Lawrence had special entree into government circles as a personal friend of President Woodrow Wilson. This, plus his ability to deliver the major news of the Federal government, captured a national reputation. Even before *U.S. News*, he had published the "U.S. Daily," furnishing official texts of Federal departments, and *U.S. News* was a natural successor. In 1946, when World War II ended with the United States thrust into the role of the world's leading power, Lawrence initiated *World Report*—two years later he married the two magazines.

Its own statement of its goals clearly indicates the orientation of *U.S. News & World Report*: "... emphasis on original news reporting and the economic and social effects. ... It is for those whose business and personal plans and decisions are most likely to be affected. ... people in business, industry, finance, government, and the professions."

The concentration of this magazine is stressed by its own promotion which claims more than four million of its readers do not read *Time* or *Newsweek*. Its interviews in depth with major personalities of the establishment, coupled with its weekly breadth of economic coverage, have endowed *U.S. News & World Report* with a circulation of influence amounting to 1,699,984.

Business Week

Inability to see around the corner (and prosperity was not waiting there for American business) was McGraw-Hill's lot in September, 1929, when, just before the Great Depression, that major industrial publishing house decided to launch a new business weekly, *Business Week*, "keyed to the new tempo in business!" Despite the economic weather, the new venture rode out the storm and climbed to the largest circulation of any commercially operated business publication. By 1968, it reached 578,600 sales.

Its editors state that *Business Week* is "published for management. Each week it reports the news, the ideas and the trends that have an impact on the economy or on an industry—or that can provide new insights for the business executive." Its regular departments include the ubiquitous Washington report, production, marketing, labor, finance, management, transportation, and a half-dozen others.

Apparently it succeeds well in attaining its objectives for the leading magazine research firm of W. R. Simmons and Associates reported 8.1 readers per copy of *Business Week* for a wider response than *Life* or *Time*. This type of pass-along or bonus readership is particularly characteristic of many specialized business and industrial magazines, for they serve as circulating libraries in offices and manufacturing plants.

Below its maroon, black, and white nameplate, *Business Week* features a gay color cover which may be adorned with Pucci-clad air hostesses or a cartoon of suburban swimming pools in proliferating sub-divisions. One-color, the art device of the business weeklies, is splashed boldly in charts and graphs, occasional pen-and-ink sketches, and as borders for boxes. The standard three columns are used, but in a larger 10-point type set off by a generous white space between the columns, a bonus for the tired businessman.

"April brings smiles to Detroit" runs one article title. Other subjects include nuclear weapons and NATO, world fairs and corporate mergers, a profile on a new Federal Reserve governor, or a piece on GOP political maneuvering—all written to the big business beat and looking at the big picture. World trade and statistics occupy foreground and background. The writing moves, in short pointed sentences.

Fortune

A second hostage was *Fortune* itself which hit Wall Street just as the Big Bust delivered its knock-out punch in the cold Fall and Winter of 1929–30. Priced at a premium $1, *Fortune* literally dared the fates—successfully. Its generous proportions in portfolio pages, $10\frac{1}{4}$ by 13 inches, imaginative and artistic use of color in paintings, and distinguished typographical design combined in a format which fittingly dressed a magazine of distinction. Its publishers, Time Inc., made daring and investment pay off on the long pull, although the start was rough. Circulation in 1968 was 495,388.

Fortune paints its own portrait promotionally in these terms, "an unmatched concentration of higher paid, better educated men who not only have a taste for quality, but more importantly, set the standards and styles in their communities." This audience, *Fortune* asserts, had an average income in 1966 of $27,400, seven of 10 were college graduates, nearly 85 per cent owned their own homes which had an average value of $39,100, more than 88 per cent owned stocks or bonds with an average value of $135,100.

This fortunate family of subscribers is served in *Fortune* by carefully researched articles, examining an individual corporation or a whole industry under a microscopic lens. However, although financial and economic detail receives thorough examination, the whole is surveyed from the perspective of the broad social structure. Although the article is anonymous, the *Fortune* staff has been star-studded with such names as Russell Davenport, John Chamberlain, and Charles J. V. Murphy.

It became a cachet for a company or financier to be written up in *Fortune*. International finance and a roundup of domestic business, plus investment advice—these are the usual services performed by regular departments. Five regional editions—including an international—supply special merchandising for the advertiser.

Fortune's air of quality and elegance has had an impressive influence on both editorial policies and format throughout the magazine universe. And its own triumphs in attracting readers and advertisers have put a seal on fine performance which has set higher standards for all publishers and editors.

Dun's Review

Patriarch of the general business magazines is *Dun's Review*, whose controlling ownership is the equally imposing Dun and Bradstreet Publications Corporation which operates more than twenty municipal, textile, medical, construction, and transportation periodicals, some of them under its subsid-

138

iary, Reuben H. Donnelley Corp. Dun & Bradstreet of course is best known as the authority on credit rating.

To give its full title, *Dun's Review and Modern Industry* is "edited for decision-making executives throughout business. . . . It helps management improve business planning and operation with new information on key trends, developments and problems in corporate administration, marketing, technology, finance, labor relations, national economics, and international business." Annual reports are furnished on transportation, office, factory, packaging, management services, while regular departments treat business trends, Washington, the "Executive Investor," "President's Panel," marketing and labor conditions.

Its monthly issues go to a circulation of 167,322 of whom half are corporate officers and two-thirds in top management. *Dun's Review* states that "special attention is paid to attracting subscriptions from management in industry, especially manufacturing" and claims two-thirds of its circulation in this area. Five regional editions are printed.

Dun's has a red-black-white nameplate on its cover which also embodies symbolic graphic color in dignified design. Inside one-color is utilized in headlines and rules, along with considerable white space, to contrast with well-leaded type blocks. Photographs run to executives at their office desks. The half-dozen articles an issue tell "Why Britain Froze Wages" or about "The Muddle in Management Motivation." Writing style is quite lively—"managerial Geritol for tired truckmakers"—and highly readable despite the necessarily heavy cargo of facts and figures.

Dun's sells for 75 cents a copy, an amazing price for a relatively slim book but many of the business publications are able to command premium figures from their well-heeled customers.

Barron's

Barron's is a member of the prestigious Dow Jones family of financial wire services, *The Wall Street Journal* with its national newspaper circulation of a million-plus, and up-to-the-second stock quotations on "the ticker." Founded in 1909, *Barron's* features portraits of individual companies and analyses of stocks. "Each issue devotes 20 pages to performance records of 5,500 securities." Its editorial content stresses "industry-wide studies and individual company analyses" for the benefit of three interested groups—private investors, investment counselors, and corporate managers. Its 239,478 paid readers hold nearly 67,000 corporate directorships.

The format of *Barron's* is austere, a black-and-white typographical front page of an $11\frac{1}{2}$ by 15 tabloid in the style of an old-fashioned English literary or economics review. Across the top runs "*Barron's*" in 108 point and under it, "National Business and Financial Weekly." Then a heavy rule and the emphatic head, "Forbidden Fruit" superimposed above "Florida Orange Growers Should Resist the Lure of Subsidy." Or, "Paper Lion—That's What the Labour Party Has Made of Great Britain." At the bottom, boxed by rules, among the four wide 14-em columns, is the index of articles and 18 regular departments. The lead article *is* "a leader," in the British sense of an editorial. The articles, under disarming heads such as "Lambs or Lions," are larded with fact and written with verve. Then twenty pages of investment quotations make a solid finale.

Forbes

Forbes is the third publication which bears a family name. A biweekly, its promotional matter terms it a "capitalist tool" and observes that more of its readers earn $10,000 a year or more than those of *Fortune* and *Business Week* with which it contends for circulation. Its 1968 figures were 518,820 giving it second place among its self-chosen rivals.

Established in 1917, *Forbes* has the cover of a newsmagazine with a color portrait of a business leader, and similar news stories inside although its reporting naturally concentrates on the profit motive. Layout is given some life with one-color rules although the page-long type columns, one-column "mug" shots, and small heads don't lend themselves to dramatic effect. A cover story, half-a-dozen regular departments, and then detailed handling of the top business stories of the fortnight—that's *Forbes*.

Writing is a blend of news style plus editorializing—"Why did Clark feel more qualified than the ICC to judge what is an adequate provision for the orphan lines in the Penn-Central case? How does he justify the waste involved in delaying the merger—which will be no less monopolistic when it finally occurs?" There's a strong tendency to play up the personality, whether a corporate president or Washington cabinet member.

Nation's Business

Nation's Business, the official monthly of the United States Chamber of Commerce, naturally can be expected to serve as its spokesman and it does, with vigor. Its circulation of 854,712 is one-sixth to members and the remainder by outside subscription. *Nation's Business* is edited "for top management."

Policy objectives are "to make businessmen better informed, more active in national, regional and local affairs, and more successful executives." Three areas are reviewed monthly: national issues, government, business.

Typically a news magazine in layout design, *Nation's Business* appropriately is business-like in appearance, relatively staid typographically, using little color and modest heads. Top management is heavy among its subscribers, with more than 111,000 company presidents and board chairmen, 585,000 with major executive titles. Average personal income is more than $20,000. Relying on subscription sales only, *Nation's Business* provides service in spades —during one nine-months period it mailed out 579,456 requested reprints of its articles!

More Business Publications

The half-world of business reports is supplemented by a blizzard of bulletins and news letters from government and university, from banks and fiscal organizations, as well as from private services operating for profit. One of the latter has achieved a considerable following in its *Kiplinger Washington Letter*, which sells for $24 annually and consists of a mixture of prediction and analysis. Founded in 1923 by Willard M. Kiplinger, a Washington correspondent, it was the eldest sibling of five reports and a monthly magazine. The other Kiplinger bulletins, each bearing the founder's name, are the *Kiplinger Agricultural, California, Tax,* and *Florida Letters.*

Changing Times, the Kiplinger monthly, came out with its first issue in 1947 to supply a panorama of business-oriented articles for businessmen. Its circulation topped 1,316,500 in 1968, promoted by direct mail for subscription delivery only in the Kiplinger policy, and with its editorial content later revamped to sight in on the young married and family group.

Management and investment interests are comprehensively represented among the business publications. *Finance*, "All the News of the Hire of the Dollar," sells for $1 the monthly copy and has attained a 1968 circulation of 41,120 since it began in 1941. Basically, it's directed to bankers, who number more than three-fourths of its readers. Its red-and-white cover, sometimes accompanied with appropriate gold metallic inks, contains articles on metropolitan financing, mutual funds, the history and biographies of big banks and bankers. Of special interest, it should be noted that the two top officers of *Finance* are women and several other feminine names are listed in its masthead. Perhaps this is allied to the frequent statement that American women own 85 per cent of American wealth.

The *Financial World* is for the investor himself, and 99 per cent of its

141

readers own common stock. This weekly publication of the Guenther Publishing Corporation dates back to 1902. Its editorial profile declares, "*Financial World* content is gathered, researched, written and edited to serve one man— the investor. The stock market is an accepted . . . barometer of future business conditions. He is alert to change. Studies of Current Trends, therefore, may cause him to take a second look at conditions in his own industry. Selected Issues—here he learns how his competitor is doing. News and Opinion on Active Stocks—they tell him how his own company rates today." Circulation in 1968 was 76,264.

Trusts and Estates, a monthly published by the Darnost Publishing Company, seeks to serve the trust departments of banks as well as lawyers, estate managers, life insurance underwriters, and accountants. Established in 1904, its article titles accurately reflect its editorial interest: "Liability for Unpaid Federal Taxes," "Dealing with a Declining Asset," "Plan Estates for People." Regular departments cover the institutional investor, the operation of trust departments, yield tables, and legal counsel. All is written in a rather formal style, quite different from the familiar, informal, and even breezy manner of the business news weeklies.

Banking

Banking is the business of finance and is thoroughly represented by publications. There is the *Bankers Monthly,* established in 1883, and reaching more than 14,000 bank presidents as well as an equal number of other banking officials. It "is *edited expressly for the men in banking who make the important dollar decisions* whether it be in regard to correspondent relationships, the financing of business, stocks and bonds, or bank equipment." In its three-columned pages, embellished by occasional one-color and Gothic heads, articles review the automation revolution, the personnel plans of senior management, the interrelationships of government and the financial community. Rand McNally is the publisher.

Among its colleagues there are the *Burroughs Clearing House* and *Banking.* The latter is the official publication of The American Bankers Association. Founded in 1908, this monthly goes to 41,865 readers and members, of whom seventeen thousand are board chairmen, presidents, and trustees. Its articles deal with major news events which affect banks and economic conditions, whether in the United States or throughout the world.

The *Burroughs Clearing House,* begun in 1916, has the largest circulation of the three, with 82,409. It says its editorial aim "has been to publish a magazine of banking so informative, so interesting, that it is MUST reading for

142

executives in the banking and related financial fields, the world over." As proof of its service, "one editorial department alone, 'Booklet Counter,' receives over 12,000 requests for literature each year."

Many other bank periodicals are issued on a state and regional basis, concentrating on the banking activities of the South or Midwest, or those of a particular division, such as savings or loans.

Closely akin are the publications of credit unions which include the *Credit Union Magazine* and *Everybody's Money*. *Everybody's Money* is a quarterly for credit union members. Within its gay colored cover is an even more sprightly double-spread contents page. A recent issue showed a husky youngster, in blue trunks, holding his nose as he plunged through a bright yellow sky into the green waves below. And layouts for the articles are as lively, with a big bull moose asking "Does a Freezer Really Pay?" and a lemon-colored center spread featuring consumer tips and a "By George!" hair spray for men in a light note.

There were 22,500,000 members of 27,568 credit unions in the U.S. and Canada in 1968, handling $10,239,221,269 in savings and $8,518,966,348 in loans. So it would seem that this would qualify as big business, along with the bankers! The *Credit Union Magazine* is the association publication of the CUNA International, which serves almost all of this activity. Its circulation in 1968 was 80,539, primarily credit union managers.

The Office

The management of business enterprises, the operation of the business office, these involve daily and constant challenges to be met by planning, proper personnel, and modern equipment. And, as usual, there are publications to keep the files filled, the typewriters and computers clacking and whirring, the paper work pyramiding. Among the magazines may be found such titles as *The Office, Modern Office Procedures, Systems*, and *Business Automation*. More than 30 magazines with a total circulation of some 700,000 copies cultivate this field productively for themselves and their readers.

Specialized families develop—Business Press International, Inc., of Park Ridge, Ill., has *Office Appliances*, which dates back to 1904. From editorial departments in *Office Appliances* there have developed *Office Design* and *Business Automation*, as reader interest and demand induced spin-offs, and the departments grew up and became independent periodicals in their own right. This is a common characteristic of the specialized publications, a constant process of evolution with each new growing activity stimulating new interest and new magazines.

143

Foreign and Domestic Trade

World affairs and trade have become a major concern of the modern businessman in the small world of the twentieth century, when foreign plants and imports-exports play a vital role in the balance sheet. That firm with far-flung interests, Dun & Bradstreet, publishes *Business Abroad* every other Monday for U.S. owners and managers interested in international operations. The Chase Manhattan Bank has its *World Business*, produced every other month by its economic research division. *Business Abroad* has news magazine form and content; *World Business* is of a more analytical nature.

A long train of business periodicals, some of academic origin, some regional or municipal in scope, some devoted to specific segments of the commercial community, march along the broad highway of business. In St. Louis, there is *Saint Louis Commerce*, issued by the Chamber of Commerce. Cambridge has its *Harvard Business School Bulletin*, a bi-monthly combining alumni news and management analysis within a dramatic four-color cover. The Graduate School of Business At Indiana University publishes *Business Horizons*, a dignified and serious quarterly. Cornell University serves both business and labor with its bright, compact *Newsletter* from the New York State School of Industrial and Labor Relations, which also prints the *Industrial and Labor Review* as a quarterly. The U.S. Department of Defense issues the *Defense Industry Bulletin* every month to serve that most mammoth of all business activities. It goes to defense contractors "as a guide to industry concerning official policies, programs and projects."

Ever since the Sinclair Lewis' caricatures in "Babbitt," the service club and its weekly lunch have become a familiar part of the American scene. While we shall consider associations, organizations, and their publications in the following chapter, certainly we must mention here *The Rotarian, The Lion*, and all the other magazines which are read by the American retail businessman, the final link in the long chain between manufacturer and consumer—which Coolidge described when he said, "The business of America is business."

Financial and Business Newspapers

One of the best and most favorably known American newspapers is the *Wall Street Journal* which, despite its name, covers general as well as the financial-industrial-business area which solely concerned it originally. Published in eight printing plants across the country tied together by electronic typesetting equipment, the *Wall Street Journal* has pushed its circulation to 1,129,987 from around 30,000 in 1941. Its news weekly in tabloid size (the parent paper is standard newspaper size), the *National Observer*, was established in 1962 and competes for general circulation with *Time* and *Newsweek*.

Many other, smaller commercial newspapers are published around the country. Ayer's Directory lists 73 "court, commercial, financial, and legal," although 39 of these are primarily legal. The others, some weekly and some five or six times a week, deal with stock and bond quotations, current prices on grain, metal, and other commodity markets, and various other types of business news. One of the larger specialized papers of this type is *American Banker*, published in New York City five times a week for a circulation of more than 13,000.

Labor—and a Living Wage!

Intimately involved with business is its Siamese twin, labor. Where once the working man had to sweat for a living wage, today many unions are a form of big business in their own right. And the labor press has grown from a pygmy into a man with muscles.

Oriented toward newspaper format and style from its early days when it sought to provide a balance to the daily newspaper, today the weekly newspaper still is the basic form for much of the labor press. Growing with the expanding size and power of the union, however, there are notable labor magazines which serve many of the 17 million members. Standard Rate & Data Service estimates there are "166 labor newspapers or magazines with 4,000,000 circulation which accept advertising."

When one considers that some unions do not publish either newspapers or magazines, the printed voice of organized labor has not achieved full expression. And, while various professions and occupations are publishing periodicals (as considered in the next chapter), a host of men and women who formed the nation's total work force of 80 million in 1968 were without an adequate press of their own.

Today's unions have come a long way since the long and arduous struggle for recognition which culminated in the 1930's. Today almost half of all union members live in the suburbs and have annual family incomes between $7,500 and $15,000. Again, half of union's membership was under 40 years old, according to the 1967 survey conducted for the AFL-CIO Committee on Political Education, and another one-fourth was under 30. This youthful group is the force which will want—and get—magazines of its own, fully comparable to other specialized and general publications.

But today the average union member does not turn to the printed page of any consumer magazine for information or entertainment. Television is termed their "most reliable news source" by 47 per cent, while 31 per cent depend on

145

the daily newspaper and only nine per cent on the weekly news magazine. Obviously an immense audience awaits the editor with the right formula!

Their own union publications get "a lot of attention" from two-thirds of union members who are more than 30 years old. The under-30 union man or woman was less interested; less than half in that age bracket paid "a lot of attention," said the survey findings as reported in the AFL-CIO magazine, *The American Federationist*.

As the official publication of the American Federation of Labor and Congress of Industrial Organizations, serving its multi-million members, *The Federationist* is a relatively slim magazine which carries no advertising and runs to 24 pages containing five or six articles. Typical titles are "The Rise of a Farm Workers Union" and "The Case for Higher Social Security Benefits." As these subjects indicate, editorial content is serious and presents the labor point of view. A single department briefly analyzes new books, new films, and new pamphlets.

One color is employed on the cover, which carries a simple black-and-white nameplate and generally plays a striking photograph. Inside layout again utilizes the same color, for art, heads and subheads, and rules. White space is used generously with wide 20-em columns, two to a page. Both drawings and photographs illustrate the articles. The table of contents page bears George Meany's name as editor which may qualify the AFL-CIO president as a magazine journalist, probably honorary.

Various departments of the AFL-CIO issue their own periodicals, such as the *Free Trade Union News*, of the Department of International Affairs; *Economic Trends and Outlook*, of the Education Committee; and *Political Memo from COPE*, of the Committee on Political Education. These often are tabloid in size, hybrids of semi-newspaper format but offering articles in accepted magazine style.

One of the largest union publications, using the criterion of page volume, is *The Electrical Workers Journal*, which runs to 120 pages. This is the monthly magazine of the International Brotherhood of Electrical Workers, with 806,000 members. Incidentally, all membership figures are based on the useful and informative Directory of National and International Labor Unions in the United States, Bulletin No. 1493 of the U.S. Department of Labor, for April, 1966. Apart from a handsome four-color cover, inside *The Journal* uses one-color only, but does vary that color through most of the available tints. No advertising is carried.

In a typical issue, the lead article considers "Nuclear Power—Where Are We Going?", a subject of considerable importance for electrical workers. Then follows a report on a Washington construction conference. The third article breaks the pattern and is introduced by an editor's note which remarks, "As a family magazine, your *Journal*, from time to time, decides to present features not ordinarily in a labor union publication and designed to interest various segments of our readership. Our cultural features have met with warm response."

The striking title page is headed "An Evening At The Ballet" in reverse white on black above a light lavender silhouette of a pas de trois. Then follow several pages in a simple combination of feature and expository style, illustrated with silhouetted photographs of Nijinsky and Pavlova and Nureyev. Certainly a bold departure from the customary single-minded concentration on union issues and policies.

Within a few pages, however, union affairs take over with sober lengthy editorials on the union's pension plan, political action, and membership campaigns. These appear under the byline of Gordon M. Freeman, the International's president, who also is listed as editor. Obviously, official sanction is transmitted directly for the official union publications. After the editorials are a couple of pages, "With the Ladies" for union wives, offering chitchat about children and the home, husband-wife relationships, and "Tea Party Recipes" for sherbet punch and petits fours!

A couple of one-page features cover a blind electrician and the Alhambra in Spain, complete with scenic photograph. After that, the bread-and-butter of ninety pages of local union news and departments on apprenticeships and training, research and education, women's auxiliaries, an "In Memoriam" section. In the midst of the news notes, there appears a "Poem of the Month" and over on the inside back cover may be found a dozen verses, humorous and otherwise, written by various members and their wives. Mostly, however, it's the paycheck coverage of local meetings, personal mentions, and columns of both snap and posed camera shots, showing union members in union activities. Thus, despite the surprising sidetrip into culture, the main road is understandably packed with a solid 83 per cent of union information.

The butcher also is represented, although the candlestick maker will have to be located among the hobby magazines. The monthly publication of the Butcher Workman Educational and Benevolent Association, Inc., affiliated with the Amalgamated Meat Cutters & Butcher Workmen of North America, is (if you're still with us) *The Butcher Workman*, a workmanlike and brisk periodical of 32 all-editorial pages, with one-color art and a Washington newsletter on the same tinted stock which characterizes the business magazine news-letters—but its editorial tone is slanted somewhat differently!

The *Butcher Workman* runs such titles as "Employers Club Workers With Wage Guideposts" and "Trade Unionism in Ireland," along with a blarneying piece on "The Town of Saint Patrick." This in a March issue, which wears the green bravely and plays an Irish labor leader on the cover. Could it be by accident that the editor's name is Patrick E. Gorman (who also is secretary-treasurer of the union association)?

More familiar ground appears in departments devoted to poultry and fish, labor education, fur and leather, retail, and packinghouse. There's a definite off-beat note, however, in two editorials and a verse on Krebiozen, the alleged cancer drug which apparently is a special cause with editor Gorman. Also a family bow is given to stamp and coin collectors, tackle tips for the hunter-fisherman, and some fashions for the seamstress.

Another union monthly which carries advertising is *The Carpenter*, perhaps the oldest labor magazine and the official publication of the United Brotherhood of Carpenters and Joiners of America. Most of its feature material is closely related to the construction industry, with many pages stressing union news. One-fourth of the editorial space carries stories or news items on new construction tools and methods. Advertising in *The Carpenter* will be accepted only if it has "a direct connection with construction." Circulation, chiefly membership, is large as can be expected from a major national union, almost a half-million. It was founded in 1881.

One of the most progressive unions is the International Ladies Garment Workers Union and it is not surprising that its magazine, *Justice*, is among the best. It came into being right after World War I, in 1918, and fifty years after, had achieved a circulation approaching the half-million mark.

A cross between newspaper and magazine, *Steel Labor* deserves mention because of its 1,250,000 circulation and as the monthly representing a major union, the United Steelworkers of America, and its 965,000 members. A tabloid in size, it runs one-color pages and a mixed magazine-newspaper format. Its circulation covers not only its active but also 77,000 retired members. *Steel Labor* won two first prizes in the 1967 annual International Labor Press Association contest—one for editorial excellence and another for the best front page.

To cope with the widespread geographical distribution of its locals, the steelworker publication is efficiently organized. Raymond W. Pasnick, its editor and the U.S.A. director of public relations, describes it, "In gathering and writing news for *Steel Labor* we use six editorial offices throughout the jurisdiction of the Union. We publish four geographical editions in the United States and two in Canada. These cover the northeast United States and Atlantic region; the midwest area, the west coast and the southern states. The Canadian edition is edited from Toronto, Ontario, with a special French-language section produced in Montreal."

Steel Labor carries editorial and feature columns, sports and outdoor departments, as well as the usual articles and editorials. Its varied editorial content also includes a column for stamp and other collectors, a hobby page, fashions, recipes, and advice for family budgets. Lavishly illustrated with line-cut cartoons and photographs, it is designed to appeal to the whole family.

The International Musician, official monthly of the American Federation of Musicians, is, by the very nature of its entertainer members, related to the general cultural scene. In its pages we find regular columns on percussion, trumpet, symphony, opera, chamber music, dance bands, and accordion. Articles deal with contemporary musical affairs and there is the usual news coverage of union activities. Annuals give special attention to jazz, music education, the symphony, and country-western music. Circulation in 1968 was 265,926, mainly membership, and advertising is accepted.

As one might expect, union printers have a monthly magazine, the *Typographical Journal*, official publication of the International Typographical Union of North America. Its circulation is more than one hundred thousand. As is fitting with a communications union, it runs advertising as well as the customary content on union activities. The *Typographical Journal* displays a bright four-color cover. Inside, the table of contents and other special pages show one-color as part of effective layout which offers variety through full-page tint blocks. Editorials emphasize the union viewpoint throughout and are followed by letters from members, and reports on mechanical inventions of printing equipment.

The other major printing union, the International Printing Pressmen and Assistants' Union of North America, is represented by a magazine with suitably fine printing and reproduction, *The American Pressman*. The layout is attractive and white space is used with discrimination. A four-color cover, editorial use of one-color inside, with four-color again appearing in advertising, all add appeal to one of the most effective union magazines. Perhaps it's due in part to an editor who is an editor, rather than titular union president. Educational articles about new printing processes and better press work offer in-service training to the members, a professional service which raises this publication a step above the routine communicator of union messages. There's a substantial volume of advertising from major printing manufacturers, and the ad copy and layout also present a fine appearance.

Union locals in cities as well as state union organizations often produce their own magazines. One of the most attractive is *Lithopinion*, the "graphic arts and public affairs journal" of Local One, Amalgamated Lithographers of America, in New York City. This is, as one might expect, an example of the best in graphic arts in design, in use of color, in reproduction. Editorial material is wide in scope—and in authorship—in the same issue, "Youth Breaks Its Silence" by Robert F. Kennedy and "Hobbies: Doors That Open on Life" by Barry Goldwater!

The romance of railroading, contributing so much to the continental expansion of the United States, has been closely associated with railway unions, brotherhoods as they've been called. In December, 1968, four of the major brotherhoods decided to merge in the United Transportation Union, although the Brotherhood of Locomotive Engineers maintained its independence.

The railroad brotherhoods have their own publications: *The Locomotive Engineer*, produced by the Brotherhood of Locomotive Engineers; the *Yardmasters Journal*, of the Railroad Yardmasters of North America; *The Conductor and Brakeman*, of the Order of Railway Conductors and Brakemen. These three rail periodicals circulate among nearly 70,000 members, keeping them in touch with each other and with their transportation jobs.

AFL-CIO affiliated rail unions maintain magazines for their members. *The Signalman's Journal* appears monthly, circulating 15,000 copies and accepting advertising. *The Trainman News* goes to the 185,463 members of the Brotherhood of Railroad Trainmen. *The Railroad Yardmaster* represents the 4,500 workers of the Railroad Yardmasters of America. The Brotherhood of Railway Carmen of America issues the *Railway Carmen's Journal* to its 121,000 members, while the Railway Patrolmen's International Union has the *News Bulletin* for 2,200 members. More than 55,000 members of the Brotherhood of Locomotive Firemen and Enginemen receive the *Enginemen's Press*.

The Brotherhood of Railway and Steamship Clerks, Freight Handlers, Express and Station Employees, also AFL-CIO, publishes *The Railway Clerk*, a slim 24-page magazine with attractive cover in one-color. Again the editor is identical with the international president, and the actual editorial duties come under the jurisdiction of an assistant editor who also has the title of director of public relations. Editorial material covers current labor disputes, a major merger of two rail lines, news on pension plans and group insurance, personal items, and a joke column. Two primary colors in various hues are used inside for rules and heads, and in photographs, with which *The Railway Clerk* abounds, chiefly group pictures of members, 270,000 strong.

There are three major independent unions embracing more than a million members—the Teamsters, the United Mine Workers, and the Electrical Workers. Each has its own publication—a monthly, a bi-monthly, and a bi-weekly.

The United Electrical, Radio and Machine Workers of America, 165,000 strong, publish the *UE News*, the bi-weekly. The union and its publication should not be confused with *The Electrical Workers Journal*, the monthly magazine of the International Brotherhood of Electrical Workers, the AFL-CIO rival, which circulates among 806,000 members.

150

The *United Mine Workers Journal*, goes to 450,000 members. It is a mixture of magazine and tabloid newspaper format, printed on 16 newsprint pages, of strong union editorials, messages from top union officials, reports on Washington legislation. The cover often varies between striking editorial cartoons and article titles in bold black. The wide two-column pages are typographical, with small body type relieved only by Gothic heads.

The giant International Brotherhood of Teamsters, Chauffeurs, Warehousemen and Helpers of America is represented by its monthly, *The International Teamster*, for its 1,506,769 members. From its cover in blinding orange or dazzling purple to its "Fifty Years Ago" inside back-cover in news-styled reminiscence, this publication is vigorous, lively in design and content.

Turn the front cover and right inside, under a bold drawing in black and white and one-color, is "Labor's Place in History," comment on the current scene in feature-editorial form. Opposite is the color-ruled table of contents page in the best modern style of simplicity and effective use of white space. Then comes another one-page feature, "From the Field," brief union news notes highlighting incidents favorable to public relations and personal mentions. Facing it, a message from a high-ranking union officer, and then page after page on the "State of the Union," articles and news stories on major union events and relationships with government and industry. With a special tint-blocked "kicker" at the top of each page repeating the "State of the Union" tag, this well-edited and designed section runs for a dozen pages.

Following may frequently be found a "Special Report," also carrying special color treatment, and devoted often to highway safety and how to curb accidents—prime concern to the truck-driving members. Then come departments on education, membership drives, a Washington column, and "For Your Information," two pages of mixed anecdote, news briefs, and pointed paragraphs of sharp commentary on the current scene. Under "What's New" are reports on new products and inventions pertinent to trucks and their maintenance. Finally there's the "Laugh Load," a joke feast and one-liner comics.

Fast-paced, briskly edited, with a colorful layout, *The International Teamster* shows that a labor publication can be attractive in appearance and appealing to the reader, while getting the union message across. It's a model which more union magazines might set before their captive audience to keep them reading.

UAW Solidarity is the tabloid paper of the United Automobile, Aerospace, and Agricultural Implement Workers of America, issued since 1957. The name of its dynamic red-headed leader, Walter P. Reuther, appears on its masthead along with those of its director, Joseph Walsh, and six staff members (all members of the American Newspaper Guild, it is noted). With a direct

151

mail circulation of 1,697,783, *UAW Solidarity* has a solid distribution system. Good quality stock, fine offset photos—a credit to both photographer and printer—and effective use of one-color borders and heads make this a happy blending of newspaper and magazine.

UAW also issues a handsome magazine, *New Technology*, which is distributed to the 200,000 skilled tradesmen in the union. A monthly, a full-color cover, effective one-color inside, and modern layout enhance the readable articles.

A new departure in labor periodicals was launched in 1968, a controlled circulation magazine called *American Labor* and distributed to a qualified list of 35,000 labor officials and 15,000 labor relations managers. The publisher is Robert F. Hurleigh, a former president of Mutual Broadcasting System.

Labor has been cramped in the past by its aversion to publicity and by tight finance, but a new day and a new look are appearing in its publications, the best of which would make any publisher proud.

The Colossus of Washington

Largest employer in the United States (and the world), the United States government with 3,002,461 civilian workers on the 1967 payroll is represented, in proxy, by the many magazines issued by the 31 unions to which one million federal employees belong. Of these, there are six AFL-CIO affiliates and nine independent unions, all exclusively federal in membership.

Postal workers are especially well organized, with 10 unions composed of post office employees. Among the AFL-CIO groups, the National Association of Letter Carriers of the U.S.A. has a monthly publication, *The Postal Record*, for its 168,000 members, while the *Rotor* is the monthly magazine of the 6,200 National Federation of Post Office Motor Vehicle Employees.

The United Federation of Postal Clerks publishes *The United Postal Clerk and Postal Transport Journal*, perhaps the longest title extant, which circulates monthly among 139,000 members. It is a 40-page book, with tint-block single color, and a tint-block inside front cover for a miscellany of union and government items under the heading of "Postal Ticker Tape." Otherwise, the inside makeup is a conglomerate mixture of black and white, with a wide variation of headline styles and sizes and body type ranging from six up to 10 point. The editorial matter is composed of editorials and articles, indiscriminately mixed, union reports and news, consumer advice, an outdoor and fishing column, and four pages on women's auxiliaries.

Characteristic of the many local and state union publications is *Press On*, issued by the St. Louis local of the same federation of postal clerks. An eight-page tabloid, it presents personals and union doctrine in a format similar to newspaper style. The chief aim is communication, building and holding the local members, and this it undoubtedly helps to accomplish.

Government workers at other levels also are organized. The AFL-CIO American Federation of State, County and Municipal Employees has a membership of 234,839 distributed among 1,666 local unions. Its monthly is *The Public Employee.*

What Do You Need to Know?

As with most communication careers, the business and labor magazines confront the student with a challenge to know something about everything. With business conducted on a world scale, and involving a myriad of products and services, there's no limit to the coverage of the modern corporate universe. Labor is no less intensive and extensive in its demands for background. Both make increasingly constant use of the most advanced technology, both are interdependent, so that the expert on labor must also be a business specialist— and the reverse.

In this challenge for universal knowledge, however, there are some major needs which may be met by careful college selection of courses. The sound foundation of history, political science, economics, geography should be bulwarked with some science and statistics. Sociology and psychology, if nailed down to reality, can be useful although better dispensed with if taught as esoteric cults. The meat and potatoes of specialization will be found in business and personnel management, industrial and labor history, industrial and labor relations, public and business finance, business and labor law, data systems and processing.

All this, plus, if daylight and midnight oil permit, enough acquaintance with the letters and arts to know and recognize the landmarks, and to pave the way for private reading and learning.

When You Go to Work

Then, when you're ready to go to work, presumably you'll decide which road you want to take, business or labor. This doesn't have to be an irreversible decision, however, and the highways are parallel much of the way. But they do have different settings and make different demands.

Business publishers may like some retail or corporate experience, although it's definitely not essential. In most cases, editorial and advertising staffers start off with their first job on a business publication and develop

153

their knowledge as they do their work. They learn while they earn, in reality.

For the labor publication, the past record and the practice of today throw a clear light on the thinking and the preferences of the union publishers of union periodicals—the staff must be members of the union. While career magazine people are beginning to appear, often via the public relations route, most labor magazines still take their publication staffs from their own membership lists. They place great emphasis on personal belonging to a particular union, and to learning labor loyalty from a job apprenticeship at an hourly wage. The time eventually will come when the labor unions will put a higher premium on professional skills as a communicator, but they still will prize the man who has paid union dues.

The Siamese Twins

Business and labor, labor and business—the Siamese twins which (although they sometimes can't get along with each other) can't get along without each other either in the modern industrial, technological society of today. Each has its problems of communicating within its own ranks, with each other, with government, and with the average citizen. These publications are often special pleaders and to that voice they're entitled, and should speak out. To the degree that special pleading defeats objectivity they can hurt their own cause. To the degree that they serve as effective and reasonably objective spokesmen, they not only attain their goals but also enhance their stature. To the extent that they serve society well, they benefit themselves.

Trade advertisement for *The Wall Street Journal*. Used by permission of *The Wall Street Journal*.

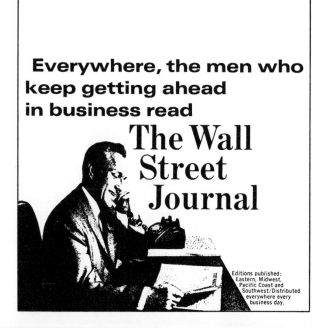

Everywhere, the men who keep getting ahead in business read **The Wall Street Journal**

Editions published: Eastern, Midwest, Pacific Coast and Southwest/Distributed everywhere every business day.

Vol. 10
No. 12
December, 1967

UAW **SOLIDARITY**

VICTORY AT FORD

*160,000 workers and
their families win
the struggle for equity*

Breaking News: As SOLIDARITY went to press, UAW VP Pat Greathouse notified Deere and Co. that the current contract would expire at midnight Fri., Nov. 17 unless a new pact could be worked out beforehand. UAW membership in Deere plants: 20,650.

From Overseas: In Europe, too, the UAW-Chrysler agreement was big news. Wired **Adolphe Graedel,** sec.-treas. of the Int'l Metalworkers Fed.: "Your success in eliminating the differential between the wage of Chrysler workers in Canada and the U.S. is a historic milestone in the battle to wipe out the discriminatory practices of seeking cheap labor across international borders."

West coasters are great fans of columnist **Herb Caen.** They read this opener the other day: "Congressman **Bob Wilson** of San Diego, in a radio interview, staunchly defending Gov. **Reagan** against the vile insinuations of **Drew Pearson:** 'Our governor has never lied and what's more, he never will again'."

In an appeal to the conscience of "white America" to end housing discrimination in the U.S., Sen. **Walter Mondale** (D., Minn.) said "to temporize on the elimination of housing discrimination will be to choose apartheid. Our only real choice is to face squarely and decide now that Americans will live together and not separately."

Over the first nine months of '67, white collar workers in 32 locations voted for UAW while only six said no-thanks-not-just-yet in NLRB elections. At the year's three-quarter mark, some 5,000 technical, office and professional workers had chosen to come the UAW's way—nearly double the number involved in UAW-winning elections for all of '66, according to TOP Dept. Dirs. **Olga Madar** and **Douglas Fraser.**

Following a record 11 fumbles in their game with Minnesota's Vikings, the Detroit

Special Report—
UAW's Skilled Trades Conference

Covers of two UAW publications; by permission of UAW.

This is The General Magazine of Busines

★ Editorial

BUSINESS WEEK—with one of the largest magazine staffs in the world—devotes itself to business news for management. It covers the news that affects business, with unique breadth and depth. It is a source of reliable statistics, authoritative facts, and regular Special Reports on business problems. In addition to news and weekly features, BUSINESS WEEK publishes forecasts, analyses, profiles, and other probing articles on the business world, features designed to be helpful to decision-making management. Here's how BUSINESS WEEK's total business-information compares with other magazines:

BUSINESS AND INDUSTRIAL EDITORIAL CONTENT
(Lines: October-December, 1960-1967)

BUSINESS WEEK	1,979,233
U.S. News & World Report	1,070,104
Fortune	981,849
Newsweek	420,099
Time	354,708

(Source: The Lloyd H. Hall Co. Inc.)

Editorial-coverage comparisons, industry-by-industry and subject-by-subject, are available from your BUSINESS WEEK District Manager.

★ Circulation

BUSINESS WEEK's 580,000 subscribers are concentrated in decision-making positions in industry. 90% are management men. BUSINESS WEEK is not available on newsstands. It is sold only by subscription; only management men are solicited. Subscribers are asked for name, title, company, and type and size of business. BUSINESS WEEK turns down thousands of non-management applications every year. Detailed title figures, and industry breakdown by Standard Industrial Classification, are available from your BUSINESS WEEK District Manager.

SUBSCRIBERS BY TITLE:

	#	%
Top Management & Companies	281,300	48.5
Major Department Heads & Assistants	240,700	41.5
Education, Non-supervisory, Retired, and Others	58,000	10.0
TOTAL	**580,000**	**100.0**

(Based on subscriber-by-subscriber count of March 5, 1966 issue projected to circulation base effective April 6, 1968)

SUBSCRIBERS BY INDUSTRY:

	#	%
Industry	288,260	49.7
Manufacturing & Processing	223,880	38.6
Raw Material & Power Production	22,040	3.8
Transportation & Communications	24,360	4.2
Construction & Installation	17,980	3.1
Finance	86,420	14.9
Wholesale Distribution	39,440	6.8
Retail Distribution	30,160	5.2
Business & Industrial Services	52,200	9.0
Personal Services	5,800	1.0
Government & Education	60,900	10.5
Awaiting Classification	7,540	1.3
Retired	9,280	1.6
TOTAL	**580,000**	**100.0**

(Based on subscriber-by-subscriber count of March 5, 1966 issue projected to circulation base effective April 6, 1968)

U.S. SUBSCRIBERS IN BUSINESS & INDUSTRY BY COMPANY SIZE*:

	#	%
Under 50	162,400	28.0
50-99	40,600	7.0
100-499	92,800	16.0
500-999	34,800	6.0
1,000-9,999	127,600	22.0
10,000 and over	121,800	21.0

U.S. SUBSCRIBERS IN BUSINESS & INDUSTRY BY RANGE OF RESPONSIBILITY*:

	#	%
Administration & Staff	411,800	71.0
Production	121,800	21.0
Engineering	110,200	19.0
Design	69,600	12.0
Research & Development	110,200	19.0
Maintenance & Servicing	104,400	18.0
Marketing, Sales	232,000	40.0
Advertising, Merchandising, Promotion	150,800	26.0
Finance	185,600	32.0
Personnel	191,400	33.0
Purchasing	139,200	24.0

(Percentages add to more than 100% because of multiple responsibilities)
*Based on 1966 subscriber survey projected to circulation rate base effective April 6, 1968.

★ Readership

An average issue of BUSINESS WEEK reaches a total adult male audience of 2,649,000 — over 2,000,000 readers more than its paid circulation. Among them are 1,389,000 professional/managerial readers and 821,000 managers, officials, and proprietors, according to the 1968 Simmons Study. BUSINESS WEEK's specialized editorial and selective circulation provide superior readership among management people. For example, here are the combined results of 57 studies, made by major companies among their own customers and prospects. Each asked: "What publications of all types do you read regularly?"

LEADING GENERAL, GENERAL BUSINESS, AND NEWS PUBLICATIONS READ REGULARLY
(Studies by 57 Companies, 1955-1968)

Publication	Mentions	1-Time B&W Page Rate (Apr., 1968)	Cost Per Mention
1. Time	16,896	$20,600	$1.22
2. Life	16,018	35,900	2.24
3. BUSINESS WEEK	15,056	7,015	.47
4. The Wall Street Journal	11,861	16,730	1.41
5. The Saturday Evening Post	11,341	27,585	2.43
6. Reader's Digest	10,916	46,650	4.27
7. Fortune	9,245	7,310	.79
8. Newsweek	8,752	11,930	1.36
9. U.S. News & World Report	8,243	9,344	1.13
10. Nation's Business	3,170	6,100	1.92

(Total Mailout: 236,620. Total Returns: 67,112. "Cost per mention" is page rate divided by total mentions.)

Ask your BUSINESS WEEK District Manager to show you how BW covers your customers and prospects, according to the 1968 Simmons Study.

★ Results

Dozens of case histories attest to the advertising effectiveness of BUSINESS WEEK. Among them are: *Northern Pacific Railway* — 62% increase in freight movement into the Pasco, Washington area. *Dale Carnegie* — more than 900 quality sales leads. *State of Kentucky*—increase in recognition of 55% in one year, plus quality inquiries. *Fairchild Semiconductor* —total business grew 300%. *Bureau of National Affairs*—deluged by inquiries. These, and other success stories, the direct results of advertising in BUSINESS WEEK, are available from your BUSINESS WEEK District Manager.

★ Leadership

For 31 consecutive years, advertisers and their agencies have invested more pages in BUSINESS WEEK than in any other general, general-business or news magazine.

TOTAL BUSINESS AND INDUSTRIAL ADVERTISING PAGES, 1967

1. BUSINESS WEEK	4,955
2. Fortune	1,854
3. U.S. News & World Report	1,585
4. Time	1,483
5. Newsweek	1,340
6. Forbes	1,078
7. Dun's Review	708
8. The New Yorker	568
9. Business Management	527
10. Nation's Business	487

Source: PIB

★ Cost

As studies of customers and prospects of leading companies show — and the Simmons studies demonstrate — BUSINESS WEEK provides advertisers with the greatest decision-level readership per dollar.

*An Important Reminder
It's never too late to put your message before America's decision-makers. BUSINESS WEEK will accept two pages of advertising each week on the following basis: reservation on Monday; plates on Tuesday; in-the-mail Thursday. Also, 26 times a year, you can reach BUSINESS WEEK's management subscribers on the West Coast — for test marketing or extra advertising support—through BUSINESS WEEK's "Pacific Coast Edition."

You advertise in

Business Week

to inform management
A McGraw-Hill Magazine

9. Professions and Associations

O NCE upon a time a man might grow his own food, make his own tools, build his own house. And his wife would spin and sew, make soap and grind meal, teach the children to read and write, and doctor their aches and pains. But the jack of all trades has disappeared in our modern specialized world. Each man or woman finds what he likes to do best, and then trains to develop special skills. In this differentiated modern world, we have, as a consequence, an almost infinite number of highly diversified professions and occupations.

So we see that the old family doctor has almost disappeared and instead there is the internist, the neurosurgeon, the pediatrician, the obstetrician. The handyman who could tinker with any common household difficulty has turned into the TV repairman, the plumber, the plasterer.

Earning and Joining

Each expert has his own professional or occupational association in which he joins with others of his own kind to exchange trade secrets, to band together for mutual profit and protection, to publicize and lobby for special interest. In a parallel development, the dentist may break out of his ordinary routine to attend the Rotary Club and participate in social and community activity. The railroad conductor joins the Masons and satisfies his need for belonging in a society which is fragmented and compartmentalized.

For each profession, for every occupation, there is at least one trade association or professional society. And, providing variety from daily duties, a host of clubs and fraternal groups offer men and women identity and a sense of social security. Each association, each organization, each club, each group has at least one specialized publication to serve it and cultivate its own peculiar interests.

Professional

Debate persists as to what distinguishes a profession. Often, as men seek to drape a mantle of dignity over their jobs, they assert claims of professional standards and so we have the mortician, the beautician—and the sanitarian who once was known as a street-cleaner! General practice and tradition have tended to recognize the doctor, the lawyer, the clergyman, and the teacher as clearly professional. A few others have associated themselves with these four —the dentist, the scientist, the engineer, the journalist.

Such classifications are bound to give rise to arguments—all distinctions are invidious. How about the veterinary, the nurse, the pharmacist, the "realtor," the civil service officeholder? For that matter, despite Edmund Burke's elevation (or was it Macaulay?) of reporters to the rank of a fourth estate, many still argue as to whether journalism is a profession, a business, a craft, an art, or a disease. The pages ahead will indicate this book's position—and we'll brace ourselves for the onslaught of infuriated and insulted practitioners!

We will consider six major different groups of professional publications. Another, religious, has received special attention in Chapter 5. Industrial publications have their own treatment in Chapter 7.

In this discussion, we'll deal with the magazines of education, government, journalism, law, medicine and dentistry, and science (including engineering) in the customary alphabetical order. The umbrella of science could cover the medical and dental professions but we've given them separate space because of their many publications and because they generally are regarded as applied sciences. We've included pharmacy, nursing, and hospitals with medicine; libraries with education.

Professors, Pupils, and Education

While the college campus and its affiliated publications present a considerable volume of communication enterprises, each level of education from the kindergarten to adult education has its own special magazines.

First in importance because of their concentration in one major educational organization are the 69 publications of the National Education Association, its 33 departments, and its affiliated teaching organizations. They are

156

led by the prestigious *Today's Education*, the official publication of the National Education Association issued monthly except for June, July, and August, the traditional summer "vacation" period when teachers go to school themselves. Mildred S. Fenner is the skilled professional editor who guides this magazine for more than one million teacher-members who account for almost all of its distribution of 1,445,000.

These teachers and a million more in America's thousands of elementary and secondary schools do not include the 600,000 faculty members in more than 2,300 junior colleges and universities. Together they're united in trying to educate 32 million grade school youngsters, 18 million high school teenagers, and $6\frac{1}{2}$ million college students at a national annual cost of about $40 billion. Education is big business in the United States of the later 20th century—although much more than just a business, as any dedicated, underpaid teacher will comment, sometimes bitterly. Big business also is actively becoming a participant in the "learning industry," with Time, Inc., RCA, CBS, IBM, and other communication systems actively engaging in promoting electronic learning for profit.

Pace-setter for all education, the *NEA Journal* was established in 1921 as a professional publication for teachers—its name was changed to *Today's Education*—and that is its personality in layout and content. Articles come from staff and outside contributors (about 200 used yearly) and they are written in a lively, literate style. Subjects range from "The Humaness of Man" to "We Don't Let Nobody Run in Our Halls." In the same issue with a biochemist's psychological analysis is the story of "a demure little moppet whose favorite Christmas carol was 'Old Cumalye, faithful,' Who was Old Cumalye? Jesus' dog, of course." Art accompanies most articles, usually in single color, with makeup design sometimes conservative but generally dynamic modern. See the Appendix for editorial hints to free-lance writers.

Advertising covers teaching aids, books, and travel—and 69 per cent of the readers take vacation trips. A Starch survey shows that 57.4 per cent of the readers of *Today's Education* hold bachelor degrees, 36.2 per cent master's. Public schools employ 93.1 per cent. Cars are owned by 97.7 per cent and their own homes by 68.7 per cent. When it comes to readership, *Today's Education* is way out in front of its commercial competition. "Do you generally read it?" is answered positively by 94 per cent. Asked "if you could read only one magazine about education, which would it be?" two-thirds of the teachers interviewed gave the *Today's Education* as their first, second, or third choice. *The Instructor* was second, with 14.3 per cent and the *Grade Teacher* third with 11.9 per cent.

While concerned certainly with making education a profitable profession

157

for its members, NEA also is devoted to the professional ideals of service to their students. This is the major role of NEA publications. Although *Today's Education* is the leader, other publications edited in its elaborate Washington, D.C., headquarters include: *The Arithmetic Teacher*, 44,000 circulation; *Audiovisual Instruction*, 15,146; *AV Communication Review*, 7,000; *Bulletin of the National Association of Secondary School Principals*, 31,000; *Business Education Forum*, 14,171; *Educational Leadership*, 17,551; *Johper*, 47,576; *Journal of Industrial Arts Education*, 12,700; *Journal of Teacher Education*, 5,357; *The Mathematics Teacher*, 50,000; *Science and Children*, 23,000; and *The Science Teacher*, 23,700. (In case you're curious, *Johper* is the Journal of Health, Physical Education and Recreation.)

Practically all of these, in the familiar calendar for teachers, issue eight or nine times a year, skipping the summer months, and represent member circulation chiefly. Taking *The Science Teacher* as an example, it is distributed among the nearly 16,000 members who compose about 58 per cent of its paid circulation of 23,700. Non-paid or controlled distribution is approximately 6,500. Its editorial policy states,

Science Teacher is the official journal of the National Science Teachers Association, a department of the National Education Association, and an affiliate of the American Association for the Advancement of Science. The magazine serves the administrative and supervisory personnel in science education in the school system, science educators in colleges and universities, and classroom teachers in junior and senior high schools. Biology, chemistry, physics, and the earth and space sciences are covered in articles and special departments. In a year, the editorial content covers major developments; reviews of books, audiovisual aids, and apparatus (10 per cent) of editorial space; classroom ideas (4 per cent); and articles dealing with new equipment or devices (7 per cent). Other special features, special inserts.

Closely affiliated with NEA are the professional teaching organizations of the states—the Montana Education Association, the Illinois Education Association, and 48 others, one for each state. These societies also have their publications, sometimes several to a state, and they have their national advertising representatives, promoting a circulation of 1,895,017 for the State Education Magazines. These magazines, as their publisher representative explains, are "professional publications edited for public school educators at various levels—teaching, supervision, administration. Individually edited to carry articles with application to the educational conditions in the specific states. They promote programs of their sponsoring educational associations which reflect individualized control of Education by State legislatures; carry news about educational events and personalities within the states; general articles of teaching methods and administration problems dealing with curriculums or personnel—with emphasis on conditions within the states; and selective observation of events and general articles designed to be of nation-wide interest." They represent every state except Delaware, Hawaii, and Rhode Island. Most of the circulation is from membership dues although 42,341 is non-paid, controlled distribution.

Illinois Education is a typical example. Running about fifty pages with a four-color photographic cover, it carries an advertising load that varies around 20 to 25 per cent, chiefly textbook and teaching aids. Inside, one color is used on an attractive table of contents and elsewhere throughout the book in titles and tintblocks. Articles concern the impact of the Illinois Education Association on the state legislature, an interview with the N.E.A. executive secretary, an analysis of Illinois teacher salaries, features on personalized instruction, vocational education, and courses in current events. Regular departments include personal news items and teaching tips, association briefs, audio-visual, and current publications notes. *Illinois Education* is handled by two women editors.

More magazines are issued by other levels of the education profession. Chief representative of college and university faculties is the American Association of University Professors and its *Bulletin*, a dignified 100-page publication devoted to academic freedom and the interests of the 22,000 members in 1,075 colleges who receive it. The AAUP in alternate months also circulates *academe*, a four-page newsletter with neat typographical format, to its membership.

Scholarly journals cover the professional interests of every bracket of educational activity. Most of these journals represent scholarly associations and so we see the *American Economic Review* of the American Economic Association or the *American Journal of Physics* of the American Association of Physics Teachers. Circulation of these publications is chiefly among association members who pay for them in their annual dues. Circulations range from the 9,430 of *Psychological Abstracts* (American Psychological Association) to the 60,594 of *Childhood Education* (Assoc. for Childhood Education International).

Commercial printing companies such as George Banta of Neenah-Menasha, Wisconsin, offer editorial services for a fee to these scholarly publications for many of them operate with a part-time editor who may be a professional historian but a rather unprofessional journalist. University presses also print these magazines, with professional university editors sometimes assisting the historian with his editing. In contrast, the many publications of the American Chemical Society are represented by a professional magazine publisher, Reinhold, and such organizations as NEA run large-scale publishing enterprises with professional publishing staffs, as we have noted.

As you might expect from a multi-billion-dollar enterprise, the most important activity supported by American society, education has many specialized publications. Estimates of the Educational Press Association of America place the number at around 2,500, although those of true magazine format and educational content probably do not number more than a fifth of that figure. The SRDS listings under Education and related fields total around 130 different titles. It is not surprising that this major activity has attracted magazines run for profit as well as the professional periodicals.

One of the oldest and strongest of the educational publications for profit is the *Grade Teacher* which claims 275,815 paid distribution and a history dating back to 1883. Published by the Teachers Publishing Corporation, in Darien, Conn., and edited by Paul Abramson, it runs from 180 to 200 pages of features and educational analysis. "Humor in the Classroom" is a lightener among 20 regular departments; another supplies possible solutions for problems encountered by teachers with their youngsters. Layout is open, utilizing white space effectively and one-color rules and titles, plus tint blocks. Advertising rides an open range throughout the book. Refer to the illustrated ad promotion located in this chapter.

Its main competitor on its own level is *The Instructor*, a maxi-size $10\frac{1}{2}$ by 13 inches, with giant display in large body type and out-sized initials, also in one color. This magazine began in 1891 and claims a 269,129 paid circulation, which also is distributed among the main regional areas in proportion to population. Its editorial policy proclaims that it is "edited for teachers, principals and supervisors of the elementary school market—primary grades through junior high. Content: Teacher service, classroom tested aids, suggestions, teaching techniques, poems, plays, audio-visual, science experiments, social studies, health, physical ed., art, music. Each month presents specific plans, devices, practices adapted to months of the school year. Editorial variety (21 depts.)—teacher travel, new products, readers service, reviews (films, filmstrips, books), principal's forum, counselor's service, teaching foreign languages. Special issues: Children's Trade and Library Books. Audio-Visual. Textbook. Science." See the Appendix for editorial tips for free-lancers.

With its home base in Dansville, N.Y., and edited by Elizabeth F. Noon, *The Instructor* leans to art on the light side, done by professionals and by the children whose teachers it serves. Much of the editorial material originates outside the office and about one-third of it is unsolicited. Major articles are written by educational authorities. Special issues cover juvenile books and the school library in November, textbooks in March, and audio-visual in June / July. As with the *Grade Teacher*, the magazine is sent free to school superintendents and principals.

Many of the commercially published education books have a board of educational consultants to add prestige and expert advice.

Such educational periodicals date back to 1811, and Frank Luther Mott states that more than sixty were started in the 1850's. Top circulation today is maintained by the *Scholastic Teacher*, one of the dozen Scholastic Magazines chiefly edited for high school students. *Scholastic Teacher* topped 330,000 paid circulation in 1968, split roughly fifty-fifty between elementary and secondary school teachers. (See Chapter 3 for other Scholastic publications.)

Another major group publisher involved in educational books is McGraw-Hill which produces three paid circulation magazines: *College and University Business*, 24,565 copies, and *Nation's Schools*, 40,119, plus *Business Education World* through its Gregg Publishing Division.

As industry began to get involved in the learning machine and electronic education, in the 1960's, the 3M Education Press of Minnesota Mining and Manufacturing Company brought out *Education Age*. As a regular and feature supplement of *Education Age*, a pull-out center section, printed on special heavy stock, provides visuals from which projection transparencies can be prepared. Naturally the magazine is the promotional child of the Visual Products Division of 3M!

In May of 1968, Gellert Publishing Corporation added *educate* to its list of eight publications with an initial non-paid circulation of 40,000, concentrating on "new instructional systems and technology," for the purchasers of educational "hardware" and school "supervisors." Gellert already publishes in such related fields as industrial photographic methods and business training.

Many other publications in the education field present merchandising (through controlled circulation) which seeks to serve manufacturers of school products and equipment and to bring them to the attention of the people who buy for America's thousands of schools. Thus we have *P/I for Schools* ("*P/I*" stands for product information), with 115,000 controlled circulation, a quarterly produced by the Management Publishing Group, which also distributes *School Management* and *College Management*, both to non-paid lists. The *Educators Guide to Media & Methods* is a similar book, 64,849 circulation of which one-third is paid. Buttenheim Publishing Corporation issues *American School and University Magazine* for some 42,000 administrators, architects, and engineers who get it for free and who are believed to influence this $7 billion-dollar market which involves $7 billion annually for new buildings and $10 billion from Federal aid. Prakken Publications produces the *Education Digest* and *School Shop*, two more non-paid periodicals.

Religious publishers, both church-affiliated and commercial, also are heavily involved in educational publishing operations. Joseph F. Wagner Inc.

has two books—*Catholic Building and Maintenance* and *Catholic Educator*. The Bruce Publishing Company of Milwaukee, Wis., also has two—the *Catholic School Journal* and *Industrial Arts & Vocational Education*. Then there is *Today's Catholic Teacher* with a 94,790 circulation of which 69,735 is paid. Another relationship between religion and education is evidenced in *Faculty Forum*, a bright little news-letter issued by the National Council of Churches, the Methodist and Presbyterian churches, and campus Christian Foundations. Its intended audience is as the title indicates—the university professor.

The Alumni and Fraternity Brothers

Rallying unit for "school spirit" on every campus has been the Greek-letter society which administration today sometimes frowns on—until it wants a homecoming reunion! Dating back to at least 1776, the college fraternity and sorority today has a life span equal to that of the nation, and the more than a hundred national brother and sisterhoods each produce a monthly or quarterly magazine for their more than four million members. These vary in quality as might be expected from their primarily amateur editors. Many are lavish with photographs which, however, too often are "mug" shots or group poses of inferior and static quality, draped around pages of chapter letters of somewhat saccharine substance. Among the better publications are *The Record* of Sigma Alpha Epsilon, the Delta Chi *Quarterly*, *The Rainbow* of Delta Tau Delta, *The Angelos* of Kappa Delta, or *The Trident* of Delta Delta Delta.

A real assist for fraternity magazines (as well as professional and technical publications) has been given down through the years by the George Banta Publishing Company, commercial printer for a large number of Greek-letter organizations as well as publisher in its own right of *Banta's Greek Exchange*, a monthly, and the main reference, *Baird's Manual*.

The first fraternity became the famous Phi Beta Kappa, the honorary which recognizes scholarly achievement. Many other honorary and professional Greek-letter societies have arisen, in almost every academic area and some not so academic—one for real estate students, for example, and some not even on campus. And many of these also have their own publications. Phi Beta Kappa produces the highly respected *The American Scholar* for a circulation of 44,000 paid readers, as well as *The Phi Beta Kappa Key*, a news-letter for the 180,000 members. Tau Beta Pi, the engineering honorary, issues *The Bent* to a circulation of 41,414, both undergraduate and graduate students and many practicing engineers.

Colleges spend a lot of money on fancy alumni magazines, inspired in large part with the hope that it will return to them, bread on the waters, as lavish grants for foundations or athletic stadia. As a means to this end—and

162

maintaining the old college spirit, alumni associations across the land produce publications for the old grad. Prominent among these almost universal products of alumni offices are the Alumni Magazines group of 48, associated for advertising solicitation, with a sworn paid circulation of 1,291,200. As the statement says, "These magazines are edited for the alumni of their respective colleges, giving reports on such matters as enrollment, campus notes, voluminous alumni notes on classmates, and information on athletic activities."

Among the more professional in appearance and content is *California Monthly* of the University of California, with paid articles, often by prominent alumni and faculty members. "Down on the farm," the traditional rival has not only its *Stanford Review* but also *Stanford Today*, a quarterly for alumni, featuring scholarly articles by the university's staff on subjects as diverse as medical transplants, morality and religion, and U.S. policy in Vietnam. Inside, the *Review* displays a bold typographical layout while the colorful cover features campus scenes.

Smaller institutions compete, often with the aid of inserted supplements from Editorial Projects for Education and the American Alumni Council, issuing such periodicals as the *Lawrence Alumnus* or the *Alumnian* of Kansas State College of Pittsburg. Class notes and athletics are a mainstay along with extensive photographic coverage. Often the alumni magazine is supplemented, as is the case with the *Alumnus* of Southern Illinois University, with an *Alumni Newsletter* for alternative months, in simpler, briefer format.

In its own *Alma Mater*, published seven times annually, the American Alumni Council displays an unusual square format with distinctive typography and black photographs on buff laid paper. Time, Inc., in 1965 established, in cooperation with the Council, a national program of awards for alumni magazines, selecting a winner in each of the nine districts of the Council as well as a national winner. The awards in 1968 went to the Harvard *Medical Alumni Bulletin*, Hobart and William Smith *Quarterly*, the Coker College *Alumnae Magazine*, *Baylor Medicine*, Notre Dame *Alumnus*, Missouri *Alumnus*, Loretto *Heights*, Pacific *Today*, and University of California, Santa Barbara, *Alumnus*.

Editors of alumni magazines have many other hats. According to a 1966 survey by the American Alumni Council, half of them also are alumni secretaries or public relations directors, spending only about 50 per cent of their time on their editing responsibilities. Sixty per cent of them have a bachelor's degree (more than 60 per cent in English and / or journalism), while more than a fourth also have received master's degrees. Almost all have had some form of prior journalistic experience.

Six million readers are the audience for alumni publications, whose circulations fall into the following classes: 40,000 circulation, 3.4 per cent; 20,000 to 39,999, 12.5 per cent; 10,000 to 19,999, 28.1 per cent; 7,500 to 9,999, 14.2 per cent; 5,000 to 7,499, 20.1 per cent; 2,500 to 4,999, 14.9 per cent; under 2,499, 5.7 per cent. Alumni magazines are distributed often, in addition to alumni, among faculty, students, their parents, and trustees.

Most of the magazines are $8\frac{1}{2}$ by 11 inches in size with from 16 to 32 pages. Ten-point type is chiefly used for articles and 8-point for the class notes. Offset is favored for production, on coated paper. More than 80 per cent use one color on covers but only 22 per cent inside. Photographs command between 15 and 30 per cent of the space.

Edited and published on campus, too, but vastly different in content and sometimes obviously amateurish, there are the literary and humor magazines of the students which try hard for avant-garde writing and pungent satire and sometimes succeed. Some of these, such as the *Harvard Lampoon*, justly are notorious, long-lived, and even read and quoted off campus. Others appear and vanish as fast as their editors, a sensation for a day. There are some 80 permanent enough to have organized themselves into College Undergraduate Magazines, Inc., for advertising representation and these claim a sworn circulation of 84,000 almost equally divided between paid and non-paid.

Seen as a whole, campus publications are a major enterprise in public relations and in scholarship. With the proliferation of colleges and the boom in education, university magazines will continue a lively contribution to our cultural and educational patterns.

Learning in the Library

Libraries are an indispensable part of education, essential for the teacher and for the student. Almost every school, from kindergarten to graduate, has its own library. And public libraries in every town and city offer continuing education for all ages. In the field of libraries, the American Library Association and its publications command equal attention.

Members of the American Library Association have their own *ALA Bulletin*, founded in 1906, published every month except for a combined July-August issue, and circulating 41,500 copies of which nearly 90 per cent are paid. The *Bulletin* includes articles on trends and recent developments as well as departments, with the ubiquitous Washington report, on "Intellectual Freedom," library technology and equipment. The Association of College and Research Libraries is a division of the American Library Association and its members have their own magazine, *College & Research Libraries*, with an associational subscription arrangement which accounts for nearly all the 14,304 circulation.

A third library association is responsible for *Special Libraries*, produced by the Special Libraries Association for its members who operate libraries for industry, communications agencies, museums, hospitals, trade associations, and government as well as schools. Published 10 times a year, it was founded in 1909 and circulates 9,351 copies, approximately three-fourths among the membership.

Two major library magazines are produced by commercial publishers. They are the *Library Journal*, a bi-weekly except July and August which are monthly, and the *Wilson Library Bulletin*, a monthly except for July and August. The *Library Journal* is published by the R. R. Bowker Company, and is the elder, dating back to 1876, with somewhat larger circulation in 1968 of 59,268. It includes reviews of more than 6,000 books annually and recordings. Advance announcements "provide information on more than 15,000 new books from one to four months in advance of publication." The H. W. Wilson Company produces the *Wilson Library Bulletin*, established in 1914 and carrying a circulation of 37,539. It presents articles on library operation and includes literary features by such critics as Susan Sontag and Dwight Macdonald.

Catholic school libraries are specially served by the *Catholic Library World*, the official publication of the Catholic Library Association circulating 4,400 copies chiefly to the membership.

Big Government and Big Publisher

For many years conservatives gnashed their teeth about the "deplorable trend toward Big Government" and predicted the downfall of the Republic. Government has continued to grow, at every level, and the Republic still stands. And with the extension of governmental operations, there has come a tremendous expansion of specialized publications analyzing and reporting on city hall and the halls of Congress.

Although we've given special consideration because of their importance (and their many specialized magazines) to Education and to Military magazines, they actually form two major branches of governmental operations. In the Business Publications directory of SRDS we find at least 70 listings directly related to government under the categories of construction, fire protection, government administration, police, roads and streets, water supply and sewage disposal. Many others, such as the publications of federal employee unions, are closely and intimately related to government or devote many pages to its coverage. The State Department and foreign service are the direct focus of a half-dozen periodicals such as *The Foreign Service Journal* while practically every news and business magazine devotes leading articles and columns to national and international affairs.

165

When one considers that the Federal government alone employs some 6-and-a-half million civilian and military personnel, it is obvious that government affects every American every day. Let's look a little more closely at the magazines which deal with this colossus.

Starting at the grass roots level (and we're not referring to the famous Hoover remark about growing it in our streets), the American city, town, and village are close to home. Undoubted leader on a national level is *Nation's Cities*, the monthly of the National League of Cities which has a total circulation of 62,500, almost entirely paid. This publication reaches 60,000 municipal officers in 14,000 urban centers of the United States. It's edited for mayors and councilmen, city clerks and city managers, "to report, inform and guide municipal leaders on the vastly changing scene of urban America."

From its cover, with bold Gothic nameplate in lower case, through its equally striking typographical table of contents and dramatic modern makeup with four-color art and titles, *Nation's Cities* carries such featured articles as "Let's Lock Out Car Thieves" and "Modernizing Local Government: A Second Look." Although studded with heavy advertising (construction products, heavy earth-moving equipment, electronic transportation controls), the magazine works to keep reader interest constant with regular departments on American municipal news, and public relations, plus quarterly reports on such subjects as "Improving Your Water Service" from the American Water Works Association.

The *Nation's Cities* has established itself as a reference source due to its carefully researched content. Its promotional department claims that "*The Wall Street Journal, Newsweek,* and *U.S. News & World Report*" all use it as a non-partisan well of facts. Charts and graphs illustrate the articles, and reader services include a "Professional Directory," book reviews, news items.

Another monthly published by a civic organization is the *National Civic Review* of the National Municipal League, which deals primarily with urban situations and solutions. Officers of the League, a "Citizens' Organization for Better Government," include George Gallup, Wilson Wyatt, Charles Edison, Luther Gulick, and similar public leaders who contribute, along with professional workers, to the magazine.

Many universities also operate bureaus of municipal research and a number of these also issue publications.

Two more major magazines with national circulations cover the city as government. They are *American City*, a Buttenheim publication with total circulation of 36,000 of which 27,300 is controlled among municipal administrative personnel, and *Mayor and Manager*, published by Jefferson Publications Inc., with a circulation of 11,300, almost wholly controlled. *American*

166

City began in 1909 and has 12 full-time editors and assistants, several of whom have worked for municipalities. Among its staff there are several civil engineers due to its special stress on information for consulting engineers retained by cities (4,000 such engineers receive the publication).

American City runs an average of 180 pages an issue, filled with a volume of editorial information and some 65 per cent advertising (totaling about $1,000,000 annually, invested by more than 400 advertisers). The "editorial mix" covers the city both horizontally and vertically with 30 per cent devoted to water supply, sewage, and refuse disposal; 25 per cent on street maintenance, traffic control, and parks; 20 per cent for planning, administration, finance; and 25 per cent on lighting, power, purchasing. Layout is conservative, formal and balanced, chiefly black and white.

Mayor and Manager, published in Morton Grove, Illinois, by the Anderson family, reaches out to city officials in towns up to 100,000 population. Of its total circulation, mayors receive 10,000 copies and city managers, 2,100. Content consists of digested data on municipal government, legal matters, equipment, presented conservatively in typographical layouts against wide-open white space.

Most major geographical regions and individual states have organizations of city officials and many of these issue their own magazines for urban government. For instance there is *Colorado Municipalities, Ohio Cities and Villages, Pennsylvanian, Tennessee Town and City, Western City*, and *Municipal South. Municipal South*, issued by the Clark-Smith Publishing Company, has a controlled circulation of 8,800 mayors, city managers, city engineers and department heads, police and fire chiefs, city clerks, treasurers, councilmen, and purchasing agents. It uses one color on cover and a few ads, runs three or four articles on typical cities and their problems, and a half-dozen departments ranging from personal news notes to plugs for suppliers and their products.

City departments also have their own periodicals, again geographically devoted to national, regional, or individual city interests. Purchasing is where your money goes (at least partially in the form of taxes), and so we have the *Government Purchasing Digest*, with 81,800 non-paid distribution, and *Government Product-News*, with 81,050, also non-paid. These also cover county, state, and federal levels as do most of the governmental magazines.

Water and air pollution, sewage disposal, law enforcement, streets, traffic, transportation,—all these and many more modern problems of the city have publications devoted wholly or partially to their handling. They include: *Water and Wastes Engineering, Water & Sewage Works, Traffic Engineering, Traffic Safety, Rural and Urban Roads, Public Works Magazine, Public Safety Systems, Law and Order*, and *I.M.S.A. Signal Magazine*. Such publications are almost evenly divided between paid and controlled circulation policies. Several group publishers are active in publishing governmental books, notably Buttenheim, Reuben H. Donnelley, McGraw-Hill, Lakewood, Jefferson, and Scranton Gillette.

Law enforcement has a comparatively large number of publications. Among the more prominent are the quarterly *National Police Journal* of the Fraternal Order of Police, with its circulation among 60,000 members; and the bi-monthly *The National Sheriff* of the National Sheriff's Association, with more than 21,000 members predominant among its circulation. Two more with large readership are *Law and Order*, published monthly by Copp Publications, and with a circulation of 18,793, of which more than 10,000 is on a controlled basis; and *The Police Chief*, issued monthly by the International Association of Chiefs of Police, with a total circulation of 14,000, of which some 7,000 is associational.

Police books are frequent on the state and local levels also. For example, St. Louis has its *Police Journal*, with a two-man editorial staff producing its 12-page, tabloid-sized monthly filled with "mug" shots of police officers, their babies and their pay, their promotions and their pensions.

Metropolitan

Metropolitan magazines, edited for general readership but specialized toward a specific city, are as old as *The New Yorker* but also as young as *New York*, a late 1968 arrival which is unlikely to become as famous as Harold Ross's brain-child. *The New Yorker* developed into a national journal of satire and comment, fiction and criticism, cartoons and culture, and perhaps reached its peak during its creator's lifetime, aided by the great contributors of the 1930's and 1940's. It has had many imitators, most of which experienced quick and unlamented death.

The metropolitan magazines, while somewhat resembling *The New Yorker* in name and in some superficial content, are spawned by chamber of commerce and mercantile interests chiefly. They vary between paid and partially paid (distribution at hotel counters, airports, etc.) circulations, run high on columns about the jet-set, cafe-society, and the local entertainment scene. *New York* was staffed largely from the deceased "World Journal Tribune." It hopes for a circulation topping 100,000 and started with around 60,000. Its other city cousins have circulations ranging from *The Miamian*'s 10,528 to *Chicago Magazine*'s 88,372.

Most of them are relatively plush in layout and color, feature the beautiful people and the lovely life, and "culture" as it's represented in popular books and popular plays and popular eating and watering places. A few do some critical and serious pieces on local issues. Some estimates of the number of these magazines run as high as 60. They often do run a lot of high-priced ads, for, after all, that is their raison d'etre. Actually many should really be suburban rather than urban in title; their readers live around, not in, "the inner city."

Chicago's *Chicago* is a big 10½ by 13 inches with plenty of color on glossy stock and articles putting the Windy City's best cultural foot forward—on a quarterly basis. There's a piece about repertory theater and a face-lifted artists' section where studios grace remodeled row houses. LaSalle puts forth its claims to financial eminence under a line which crassly states, "It is pretty to see what money will do . . . Money makes the man (and many a woman) . . . Money makes the mare go . . . Money, money, money, the object of every man." This paean is surrounded by impressive ads for banks and brokerage houses, studded with portraits of lofty financiers who say, "The Chicago lawyer has a streak of creative genius" and "Today one can say, and honestly so, anything done in New York can be handled right here in Chicago." Then there are stories about the Board of Trade and a portfolio on "The Girls of Chicago" and a prose poem about millionaires.

The book on *Nashville* offers a color cover on the conductor of its new symphony, formal in white tie and tails; then six citizens' views on Nashville, candid and critical in part while also commending; an "inside story," seemingly misplaced, about the Garrison conspiracy in New Orleans; the cover story on the orchestra; and an entertainment listing—theater, movies, galleries, sports, dining, music, mostly plugs.

In viewing the metropolitans, one should not forget the "out and out" commercial entertainment booklets, such as Nashville's *Tennessee Visitor Guide* which carries a monthly roll of restaurants and hotels, shows and sights, with unabashed little paragraphs of publicity among the ads. These have burgeoned in most hamlets with pretensions to hospitality at a price and, as in the Nashville case, are published and given away by motels and hotels and cafes to their "guests."

While SRDS lists 14 "metropolitans," it also carries Select Metro Magazines, advertising representative for 24 of them with a total circulation of 493,500, 434,280 of which is paid. Three of these are produced by letterpress, the others offset. While none is likely to burgeon into the white swan which *The New Yorker* became, most of them are far from the ugly duckling class.

County

While some political scientists say that county government, like the vermiform appendix, is dead as a dodo except when it kicks up and becomes a nuisance, the counties still gain recognition in such books as *American County Government*, the official monthly publication of the National Association of

Counties with departmental contributors listed as the presidents of the National Association of County Administrators, the National Association of County Treasurers and Finance Officers, the National Association of County Civil Attorneys, the National Association of County Park and Recreation Officials, The National Association of County Planning Directors, the National Association of County Engineers, the National Association of County Recorders and Clerks, the National Association of County Health Officers and—whew!—the Conference of County Information Officers. So you see that the counties are very much alive and intent on staying so.

American County Government has its editorial office in Washington, the proper place today for any governmental group bent on staying active in an era marked, as the managing editor remarks, by "The proliferation of federal financial and technical aids to local governments." Articles concern air pollution on a nationwide *and* county approach, Congress and the counties, county penal systems.

The layouts are open, with generous white space, one-color brighteners, and a considerable similarity in double-page designs. A bright blue cover displays, on a recent issue, a cheerful child's cartoon, a light entry into a serious content. Advertisements come from equipment manufacturers and office supply firms who might do business with a county courthouse. And county business is growing bigger all the time, with *American County Government* predicting $16 billion in 1968. The magazine is growing, too, from 9,000 paid in 1962 to 16,987 in 1968 out of its total of 17,848 county board members, purchasing officers, engineers, and health directors.

Counties are local, also, as the *Illinois County and Township Official* reminds us. This official publication of the Prairie State's two major associations at the county level carried 20 per cent county news, 20 per cent meeting coverage, 25 per cent feature articles, legislative news 20 per cent, attorney general's opinions 10 per cent, and product information 5 per cent, to keep the member-subscribers 100 per cent up-to-date.

Similar books are *Official Michigan* and the *Pennsylvanian* which concentrate on the townships, borough, and municipality for the members of various associations of elected and appointed officials.

State and Federal

In the 50 states, state government finds an advocate, according to SRDS, in *State Government Administration*, a non-paid circulation book for 4,000, of whom 80 per cent are state administrative officers and 15 per cent state legislators. Its monthly distribution does cover the country evenly, but it's planned that way, of course.

At the top-heavy Federal peak of the pyramid, there are plenty of publications for, by, and about all three major branches of government and a thousand bureaus and agencies to boot. No typewriter could survive a listing alone of the endless output of the Government Printing Office, the countless bulletins of the Departments of Agriculture, Commerce, and Labor. The Military have created so many magazines that we deal with them later in a special category. Here we shall consider a few examples, acknowledging that many more exist—which not even the *Congressional Record* records!

Best known publication of the Department of Health, Education and Welfare is *American Education*, issued by the Office of Education. It appears 10 times a year under the editorship of Patricia I. Cahn, aided by 8 assistants and art directors. Originated in 1965, it is handsomely printed, 10 by 16 inches, and its large pages are lavishly illustrated with excellent photographs and art. One-color is used throughout with plenty of white space in layouts designed with informal balance. Covers usually are one-color also although two colors may be used occasionally. Regular departments deal with "Federal Funds," "Education and the Bond Market," and "Research Report."

Late in 1967, *Postal Life* launched itself, through the hands of Kenneth Fulton, its editor for the Post Office Department Office of Public Information. Its purpose was to communicate with the more than 700,000 postal workers of the United States on a bi-monthly basis. Its cover for the second issue showed a small boy tiptoeing high to reach into a rural mailbox atop a stump, while the cover story told of the personal services provided by RFD carriers. And the *Postmasters Gazette*, official organ of the National Association of Postmasters, chimes in with 90 per cent coverage of all U.S. postmasters in "the world's largest business."

Among Agriculture's many monthly magazines, there is the slim and attractive *News for Farmer Cooperatives*, carrying articles on how cooperatives help themselves and are aided by government, with news of individual state societies.

Twenty-five thousand farm and farm-related cooperatives, with a net worth of more than four billion dollars, serve nearly eight million members. No wonder many magazines, including DOA's, exist to inform and report on their work.

Agriculture abroad and U.S. concern with it is the chief content of *Foreign Agricultural Trade of the United States*, a monthly; *Foreign Agriculture*, appearing weekly; and the statistical *World Agriculture Production and Trade*. Domestic agricultural activities are dealt with in the extensive series of the *Poultry and Egg Situation*, the *Vegetable Situation*, and so on through a dozen similar farm crop periodicals issued four or five times a year. *Agricultural Marketing*,

171

another monthly, is less full of figures, more given to school lunch programs, the taste test, and cartoon art to brighten the pages. Technical and research reports are given regularly in the *Journal of Agricultural Research*, a pioneer and leader in its field.

Most of these are offset-produced, illustrated with photographs, black and white, and purposeful. Department of Agriculture began its publications in 1862, its oldest continuous series in 1889. They evidence the government's long effort to supply information to the farmer and his family.

Over in Foggybottom, the State Department goes its monolithic way scarcely ruffled by passing wars or changing administrations. But the career foreign servants, unlike the patronage plum ambassadors, do keep in touch, not only in the official pouch but also through the pages of the *Foreign Service Journal*. This monthly of the American Foreign Service Association of DOS was established in 1924 to carry personal items about personnel and their changes from post to post, articles of scholarly and historical diplomacy, and discreet narratives of embassy experiences. Its paid circulation of 9,000 includes not only the foreign affairs officers of State, USIA, and AID, but also persons interested in foreign affairs.

These affairs also attract the attention of university students of the international scene and thus we find the *Journal of International Affairs* circulated among some 5,000 by Columbia University. The most influential publication of this kind undoubtedly is *Foreign Affairs*, of the Council on Foreign Relations. Since 1922 this thick quarterly with its gray-blue cover and serious analytical articles (from authoritative sources!) has been read by 71,053 concerned citizens and diplomats. While *Atlas* doesn't carry the world on its back, it does try to report, through reprinted articles from foreign publications, what goes on all over the world. Initiated in 1961, *Atlas* appears in formal black-and-white typography and its articles open a window on international opinion outside the United States. After six adless years, it began accepting travel, financial, and other types of advertising in 1967 and its circulation reached 131,504 the next year, with a claimed elite of almost three-fourths in executive or professional positions and nine of ten college-educated.

And whether world government through the United Nations is a threat to Birchers or a hope for the rest of the world, its activities not only are attended by the manifold publications of UNESCO but also the magazine, *Vista*, which goes to members of the United Nations Association. Its pages offer a panorama of the world's people through pictures and personality pieces by such writers as Senator J. William Fulbright and Arthur Larson, features about the role of the Observer States, case histories of UN effort and achievement. Distributed also to libraries, schools, and colleges, it strives to tell the story, as Dorothy Goldberg (wife of the past U.S. Ambassador) writes, of "the quiet work of the UN, not the dramatic crises, that show how valuable an instrument it is in helping people of warring countries overcome their true enemy: starvation, disease, poverty and injustice."

Communicating to Communicators

All the media of communications today mean something quite different to the average reader or viewer than to the communicator who reports, writes, and prints the story or broadcasts it in word and picture. What are publishers and networks planning, what's behind the firing of Turner Appleson, what ad agency got the new account for General Mechanics?

Advertising, book publishing, journalism, motion pictures, photographic, printing, radio-television—these are the seven main headings under which SRDS lists the 150 specialized publications in which the mass media tell their own story. Strangely enough, the magazine industry has no magazine all its own although it receives partial coverage in segmented form.

There are nine bellwethers which lead the flock—*Advertising Age, Broadcasting, Editor & Publisher, Graphic Arts Monthly, Media/scope, Printer's Ink Marketing/Communications, Publishers' Weekly, Reporting, Variety.* By virtue of pioneering and continued leadership, these are bibles for professional communicators, to be read voraciously weekly and monthly, to keep on top of the news—often before it happens!

Let's survey the major media and their magazines, taking them alphabetically and spotlighting influential publications of national significance.

Advertising

While 55 publications are listed by SRDS for advertising and marketing, three stand out preeminently in our judgment for their breadth of coverage and national acceptance—*Advertising Age, Media/scope,* and *Marketing/Communications.*

Advertising Age, a weekly magazine in tabloid newspaper format, carries an endless chain of information about developments and events on the advertising-marketing merry-go-round. Founded in 1930 and published in Chicago by Advertising Publications, it reaches 62,000 paid subscribers—manufacturing executives, wholesalers and distributors, promotional personnel and ad agency men.

While inside ads run in one- and full-color, page one and other editorial matter in *Advertising Age* is in somber black and white, in basic newspaper makeup. Stories run under datelines and generally follow the summary lead, inverted pyramid style. They're written functionally for news value rather than entertainment. Twelve regular departments carry such heads as "Advertising

173

Market Place," "Along the Media Path," "Getting Personal," with special emphasis on personnel changes and promotions. Advertisements are major news in themselves in this book, and attract just as much or more attention.

Media/scope is published monthly by Standard Rate & Data Service for "personnel in advertising agencies and advertiser companies engaged in evaluation and selection of markets and purchase of advertising space and time." It also concerns itself with research and studies which contribute to marketing knowledge. Out of a total circulation of 19,940, 18,213 is controlled for a select group of advertising agency heads and top managers, account execs and media buyers, ad reps and PR directors; also it goes to the decision-makers among national advertisers.

Inside emphatic, graphic, colored covers, *Media/scope* runs stimulating articles in which major media men discuss and argue about their major problems and policies. Regular reporting gives the latest news of important media changes and campaigns; 12 basic departments range from readers' letters to national ad expenditures. Several by-lined columns cover the industrial press, books and broadcast. Charts and graphs are main illustrative items, while advertising plugs printed and electronic channels with colorful advertising.

Printer's Ink Marketing/Communications describes its editorial policies as "specifically tailored to the needs of executives concerned with profitable marketing and the effective use of communications. *Marketing/Communications* examines significant trends and developments—and offers opinions on—markets, media, merchandising, advertising, packaging, new products, sales and promotion, public relations, legislation and other related marketing functions."

Published monthly by Decker Communications, Inc., its circulation of 82,674 goes to manufacturing, advertising agency, and marketing executives as well as the top personnel in communications media. It was established in 1967 and represents the merger of the esteemed *Printer's Ink*, born in 1882, and two other books.

Actually, *Printer's Ink* has taken a secondary spot in the book's title, much subdued on the cover and not even appearing in the logotype on the table of contents or the page folios. Almost half the cover is taken up with a full-page color shot tied in with the featured article. The other, slightly-less-than half, is white space with a couple of lines of title, date, and price, $1.

Five personal columns dominate the regular departments which include a "Marketing Trendletter," "Which Ad Pulled Best," and "News Products and Packaging." Magazine format, liberal use of white space, one-color rules and boxes give a modern feel to this magazine which naturally carries a heavy load of media advertising.

174

Widely read also are the advertising-marketing magazines of the American Marketing Association, the *Journal of Marketing* and the *Journal of Marketing Research*, and also *Ideafile, Marketing Forum, Media Decisions*, and *Spot*. Four other publications come from Advertising Publications, Inc.: *Advertising and Sales Promotion, Business Insurance, Industrial Marketing*, and *Marketing Insights*, published weekly for college students. Then there are several local or regional periodicals such as *MAC/Western Advertising, Southwest Advertising & Marketing, Southern Markets/Media, Southern Advertising and Publishing, SAM* (Serving Advertising in the Midwest), *New England Advertising Week*, and, of course, *Madison Avenue*.

Specialized forms of advertising have their own publications. Direct mail is covered by *D/A* and the *Reporter of Direct Mail Advertising*. Outdoor signs are the focus of *Creative Signs & Displays, Sign and Display Industry*, and *Signs of the Times*. When premiums are used to stimulate sales, such periodicals as *Incentive, Premium Practice, Premium Merchandising, Premium and Incentive Product News* are present. Even that does not exhaust the list! *The Public Relations Journal* spurs on those self-starters, the PR men. *TradeShow* tells how to put your product across at fairs and exhibitions. And *Linage*, the quarterly of Alpha Delta Sigma, is for college students of advertising. Surely the sun never sets on the adman's appeals!

Book Publishing

While millions of books pour off the presses, especially in this day of paperbacks, only a few magazines devote themselves primarily to book publishing. They are led by *Publishers' Weekly*, replete with book news and book ads, founded in 1872 and published by the R. R. Bowker Company, a subsidiary of Xerox.

Publishers' Weekly's circulation of 25,000 is distributed among libraries which get nearly half the copies, and book sellers and book publishers who divide the remaining half almost evenly. The chief concession to its literary concern is the graphic ivy-entwined PW logo enthroned in a circle on cover and major divisional pages. Otherwise the book ad occupying premium cover position just below the nameplate and the contents all testify to the accuracy of the sub-title, "The Book Industry Journal" with emphasis on industry. Book ads of course are big; so are trade items on publishing houses, editors, authors. A couple of articles appear—for example a book excerpt on legal rulings on what constitutes hard (and soft-cover) pornography. A major department is "Forecasts," previews of new books in a nutshell, a guide to professional book buyers. "Weekly Record" lists new domestic and foreign productions.

175

Several other magazines concern book marketing. The North American Publishing Co. describes *Bestsellers* as "the only merchandising publication of the periodical and paperback industry. It tells retailers and wholesalers of magazines, paperbacks, comics, children's books and other mass-market lines what's new and best each month . . . *Bestsellers* reaches most publishers, every national distributor, all 700 local wholesalers and the 46,000 retailers (who account for 85 per cent of total industry volume." Its circulation of 42,288, 93 per cent paid, also has the same percentage of retailer readers, all gained since its origin in 1946. A similar periodical is the *Book Buyer's Guide*, established much earlier, in 1898, but with a considerably smaller circulation at 6,620.

Book Production Industry, a Penton Publication, is a monthly with 7,417 controlled circulation which really bridges the closely related activities of book publishing and printing. Edited for management personnel in book production, design, and marketing and for manufacturers, printers, and binders of books, it reports on new equipment and procedures. As we shall see later in this chapter under library periodicals, most of these naturally are involved in publishing news and advance notices of new books.

Journalism

Journalism for many years has meant newspapers, daily or weekly, to most people, and professional periodicals for the newspaperman will be given prime attention at this point.

No magazine in the newspaper field compares with *Editor & Publisher*, either in command of the readers' attention or in scope of its coverage. When this is said, it must also be added that it is a magazine for management; while it contains news for the working reporter or deskman, its editorials and stories speak for the publisher. The editorial policy acknowledges this; it provides for "Spot news and features . . . directed to newspaper publishers, general and business managers, editorial and news executives, advertising, circulation promotion managers."

Representing the merged fortunes of several defunct periodicals, *Editor & Publisher* survives today largely because of the energies of James Wright Brown and his family. Circulation is 25,270.

Editor & Publisher has outlived four other periodicals which it swallowed over the years—the *Journalist* which originated in 1884; *Newspaperdom*, begun in 1892; the *Fourth Estate*, 1894; and *Advertising*, 1925. *Editor & Publisher* itself was founded in 1901 by J. B. Shale, who owned the Publishers Press, a wire service. The present dynasty came on the scene when James Wright Brown became general manager of the *Fourth Estate* in 1911, the next year buying control of *E & P*. His editorial insight gave him influence among newspaper owners throughout an active life. His editor over many years, Marlen Pew, exerted additional leadership in newspaper circles.

Special issues give particular emphasis to newspaper highlights and problems—the annual convention issue for the American Newspaper Publishers Association, ROP-color, mechanical production, syndicates. Two mammoth annuals, the "International Yearbook" and the "Market Guide," provide essential directory and reference sources.

Editor & Publisher adheres to a steady format, changing less than perceptibly over the years, black and white pages of four newspaper-slim columns, with occasional formal photographs of industry figures. A half-dozen articles of timely concern and a dozen departments blanket the field of seemly printable newspaper news, praising and seldom critical. The departments include: the "Readers' Column" of semi-humor, "Personal Mention," and "Shop Talk at Thirty," the editorialized voice of the publisher, speaking for himself and presumptuously all publishers! House ads for newspapers and equipment manufacturers complete the book.

As the Civil War came to an end, the weekly newspaper began spreading westward into new territories as the frontier was pushed back. And in 1865 *Publishers' Auxiliary* was founded. For many years operated by the Western Newspaper Union, the long-time giant supplier of "readyprint" and "boilerplate" to country weeklies, today *Publishers' Auxiliary* is published by the National Newspaper Association. The National Newspaper Association was the name adopted in 1965 by the National Editorial Association, composed of weekly and small daily newspaper publishers and editors. More a newspaper than magazine, bi-weekly issues of *Publishers' Auxiliary* go to a circulation of 15,800, 87 per cent controlled "to every weekly and daily newspaper in the U.S., addressed by name to the chief executive." National Newspaper Association also publishes the *National Publisher*, also a bi-weekly in tabloid newspaper format circulating to 7,685 publishers and editors of small dailies and weeklies, mostly on a paid basis.

The American Press carries two sub-titles, "the monthly feature magazine for newspaper management" and "offset newspaper publishing." Once the association periodical for the National Editorial Association, it now is owned and published by Michael & Ginsberg Publishing Co. as a controlled circulation journal with 13,253 copies for publishers and production managers of urban and suburban dailies and weeklies and shoppers. Dating its birth in 1882 and formerly chiefly supplying news and features about weeklies and weekly publishers, today its pages are occupied mainly with production and equipment how-to.

Edited on the campus of Southern Illinois University, *Grassroots Editor* is a bi-monthly devoted chiefly to the weekly and small daily field from the standpoint of social concern. Founded by Howard R. Long as secretary of the International Conference of Weekly Newspaper Editors, its articles examine various aspects of editing and publishing a weekly newspaper in an era of mass communications.

Individual newspapers or newspaper chains also produce magazines about newspapers. *Seminar* is a quarterly review, published by the Copley Newspapers "for newspapermen," distributed both on a paid and controlled basis. Its dignified blue-and-white typographical cover contains a dozen articles, basically serious, about editorial, economic, and social problems of the press. Chiefly illustrated in black and white, occasionally it blossoms into full-color as in a special portfolio on "The Newspaper in American Art."

The Gannett newspapers and broadcasting stations issue *The Gannetteer*, an elaborate internal magazine for the 6,500 Gannett employees, carrying a mixture of general stories on communications and specific accounts of personal and feature interest. Lavishly illustrated in black-and-white photography, *The Gannetteer* also has some controlled circulation to other communicators, libraries, and journalism schools.

Motion Pictures & Photography

While film fan books of the entertainment and juvenile variety are considered in chapters 3 and 4, this is the place and now is the time to look at the professional publications of the movie-maker and cinematographer. There are about 20 of these, if you consider both Hollywood mogul and the pop art semi-pro as readers (which may be the neatest trick of the decade). Publications in this group are of two main kinds—there are those for the entertainment industry, and also the periodicals for educational, business, and government makers and users. Content is addressed to a wide range of film talent: directors and producers, distributors, exhibitors, photographers, sound engineers, and other technicians.

Film makers for the box office are largely supplied their trade information by tabloid daily and weekly newspapers, rather than magazines. Prominent names are *Variety*, the *Hollywood Reporter*, the *Motion Picture Daily*, all dailies and with circulations from 3,400 to 11,000 each. All are big with advertising and publicity. *Variety* especially is known for an invented language all its own. Among the weeklies, there are *Boxoffice*, *Motion Picture Exhibitor*, and *Motion Picture Herald*. The *Daily* and *Herald* are Quigley publications, as are several annuals also dealing with the film industry. *Boxoffice* ranks highest in circulation with 16,360, and is edited chiefly for theater owners and personnel, as is *Greater Amusements and International Projectionist* which also addresses itself to distributors.

Movie production or use by business companies, educational, or other circles forms the focus of such magazines as *Audio-Visual Communications, Business Screen, Industrial Photography*.

Technicians, professional film photographers, and research scientists are the audience sought by such magazines as the *Journal of the Society of Motion Picture and Television Engineers; American Cinematographer*, the association publication of the American Society of Cinematographers; *Photographic Applications in Science and Technology*, and *The Rangefinder*.

The advanced amateur or professional photographer is served by *Modern Photography*, another Billboard publication, which goes to 281,490. In its analysis of its audience, *Modern Photography* claims that it "reaches more professional photographers than any professional photographic magazine." Of its readers, it says that 64 per cent are advanced amateurs or professional, with 58 per cent college graduates whose average annual income is more than $13,000, and with 59 per cent doing their own darkroom work.

At the retail dealers' level, there are *Photo Dealer, Photographic Business & Product News, Photographic Trade News, Photo Marketing*, and *Photo Weekly*, five periodicals with a total circulation of 55,800, selling cameras, films, and processing to the millions of Americans who snap pictures as a record of family fun and for personal enjoyment.

Printing—the Graphic Art

Singling out printing as *the* graphic art is a personally preferential bow to its ancient and distinguished history as a communicative pioneer. Going back to Chinese wood block printing of characters that became an art themselves through calligraphy, remembering the papyrus of Egyptian scribes, we call to mind also the astonishing impact of Gutenberg's press on a medieval, feudal world and what relatively inexpensive books could do for literacy where heretofore the cloistered monk had dedicated the glory of his hand-illuminated manuscripts to God.

Among some thirty printing magazines, half-a-dozen stand out, for circulation influence and (or) their own quality of content. As one might expect, the best printing magazines travel first-class when it comes to printing. Fine color, fine reproduction, quality stock, artistic layout, are all characteristics of these books.

The connoisseur will be partial particularly to *Print* which subtitles itself "America's Graphic Design Magazine" and lives up to its goals. Issued bi-monthly, to a circulation of 12,189, from its sans serif body type to its generous

179

use of white space, the articles and abundant photographic art evidence a sincere effort to establish an example for its professional readers. As with all these graphic art magazines, the advertising is a rainbow of bright color splashed onto premium stock in frequent fold-outs and special inserts. In fact, in several such magazines, the gorgeous advertising puts the tamer editorial distinctly into second place.

Printing Magazine/National Lithographer also will command the admiration of the graphic arts elite. Perhaps partly because of its devotion to excellence in printing, *PMNL* has a relatively small circulation (19,127) but one which is paid and concentrated among the executives and superintendents of commercial printing plants especially in the East. It traces its history back to 1894, certainly one of the older American printing publications. *PMNL*, as it calls itself, is a Walden-Mott publication, product of a company which specializes in periodicals of printing. A marriage of one color with effective typography gives *PMNL* a series of editorial layouts which strive to hold their own among the elaborate ads. An inside cover introduces "the lithographer's partner since the stone age," *PMNL*'s way of presenting its special lithography section.

"Birds of a feather" is an adage with special application to the publishers of specialized publications and nowhere more so than with printing periodicals. Penton, Maclean-Hunter, North American, Peacock, Ojibway, and Gellert are all major names in printing, processing, packaging, and reproduction, responsible for multiple titles.

Printing Impressions is from North American and distributes 64,000 copies to the owners and executives of commercial printing and packaging firms. It claims the number one position for dollars of advertising revenue, and it certainly is in page size, with $9\frac{1}{2}$ by 15 big inches of space for its giant spreads. With coverage chiefly through columns and departments, editorial is surrounded and seemingly secondary to an overpowering parade of ads. This publication is all-business; save for striking color covers, and some advertising inserts, design and layout are subordinated to information. One unusual feature is its editor's page, a four-language commentary printed in parallel columns of English, Spanish, German, and French.

"Edited specifically for production management men in the printing industry," *Printing Production* is one of Penton's three graphic arts periodicals. Two major editions are issued, one for graphic arts and the other for newspaper production managers. Their combined circulation, all controlled, is 20,000. New developments in production methods and equipment command 80 per cent of the editorial content. Half-a-dozen articles in each issue, segregated from advertising, and more than a dozen departments give emphasis to the constantly changing technology of the printing industry, while advertising presents in different form the innovations of equipment and supplies.

Graphic Arts Monthly, with a controlled circulation of 58,300, holds a major position among the printing publications. Its three full-time editors and 20 departmental editors contribute news and information along with an annual run of more than 2,000 pages of colorful advertising. Digest-sized, the book is thick with ads packing the 200-plus pages per issue. Expert comment and technical advice are so intermixed with ads that the reader must persevere to seek out and follow the editorial matter. It stresses seven special issues covering the conventions of associations in printing and allied fields.

As might be expected, graphic arts is a popular term among the printing books and several publications incorporate it as part of their names. These include *Graphic Arts Product News* with its controlled circulation of 48,900 and *Graphic Arts Supplier News*, with dealers, and salesmen forming a major portion of its non-paid circulation of 5,167. Other leading publications are *Inland Printer/American Lithographer*, 54,000 circulation, dating back to 1883; *Reproduction Methods for Business and Industry*, circulating 45,300 copies; and *Reproductions Review*, with a circulation of 38,500.

Radio-Television

Electronic journalism with the transistor and the home viewer has captivated and captured much of the mass audience from the print media but radio and TV still depend on specialized publications to tell their story to specialized audiences. Of all the broadcasting books, one, fittingly named *Broadcasting*, has a commanding hold on the reader. Calling itself the "Business weekly of Television and Radio," *Broadcasting* was founded in 1931, five years after organization of the first network and three years before the Federal Communications Commission was established as the guardian of the airwaves.

Broadcasting is published and edited by Sol Taishoff who has made it the printed voice of the electronic media. *Broadcasting* is published weekly and its paid circulation of 29,700 testifies to its following among station and network owners and managers along with advertisers and agencies which use the air.

Broadcasting's continuing story is the running account of radio-TV stations and networks, business operations and problems, plus what it seems to consider a constant battle with government regulation, represented by the Federal Communications Commission.

Overlooking the fact that the FCC was formed at the frantic appeal of station owners to save them from their self-created chaos, Taishoff and his

181

publications valiantly try to slay the dragon! Although government licensing and regulation affect much that radio-TV does, *Broadcasting*'s editorials appear obsessed with it as an enemy. But the editorial coverage, through articles and departments, does give a complete view of every activity in the broadcasting world—advertising and its array of sponsors and commercials, equipment, promotion, personnel, programming. It has no competitor when it comes to total reporting of its chosen field.

In layout and format, *Broadcasting* is strictly business. From the cover, with only its black logotype above a full-page ad in red for some station, through the tight, solid three-columns of news reports and articles, only one-color brightens the black and white pages, with illustrations restricted to small "mug" shots. News story headlines and summary leads stress current developments while articles and departments interpret and analyze events. This detailed reporting is focused on news happenings although socially conscious criticism and appraisal either of programs or operations is scarce.

"Broadcasting Yearbook" has rightfully taken its place as the reference manual of fact and figure for all radio-TV and is an essential source. Other useful aids are the "Television Almanac" and "Television Factbook."

The bi-weekly *Television Age*, splits its circulation of 12,300 almost equally between paid and non-paid.

"Visual graphics" are a constant companion of the TV screen and, as one would expect, several publications give them special attention. Among them are *Art Direction, CA* (for Communications Art), *Graphic Arts Buyer, Graphics: USA,* and *Industrial Art Methods,* five periodicals with a circulation total of more than 80,000.

Radio-TV periodicals also focus attention on the electronic technician and engineer. Two run almost neck and neck in controlled circulation. *Broadcast Management/Engineering* with 23,033, and *Broadcast Engineering,* 22,804, both aimed chiefly at station and network personnel. A third publication, *Electronic Technician/Dealer,* reaches a paid circulation of 83,359 dealers and "repairmen" (whom the industry prefers to call "servicemen"). This is an Ojibway book.

Ziff-Davis is responsible in an allied, companion area for *Electronics World,* including military, government, and communication company engineers as well as those in industry, and circulating 173,279 paid copies. The *PF Reporter* is another major source, published by the Howard W. Sams & Co., electronic publishing specialists, who have built it up to a paid circulation of 68,885. *Radio-Electronics,* produced by Gernsback Publications, is a rugged competitor with a press run of 157,962. All of these books are monthlies.

The *Radio & Television Weekly* is indeed in newspaper format and seeks to report trends and developments for manufacturers, distributors, and retailers. Although founded in 1916, in the early days of radio, its circulation is relatively small at 6,087. *Electronic Distributing & Marketing* circulates 17,714 copies as an imposing competitor.

Every electronic interest conceivable is the special interest of some specialized publication. Cable TV or CATV has *TV Communications* and *Cablecasting & Educational Television*. The Society of Broadcast Engineers publishes its own *Broadcast Journal*. "Ham" enthusiasts can follow *CB Magazine, CQ, 73 Magazine, S9 | The Citizens Band Journal*, and *QST*, of the American Radio Relay League. These alphabetical, numerical books have an amazing following with a total circulation of more than 400,000 amateurs, hobbyists, and users of Citizens Band 2-way radio. That accounts for the CB. "CQ" originally meant "call quarters," and today is a general air hello announcing that one operator, often amateur, wants to talk. "QST" announces a general message to anyone concerned, while "S9" reports "you're coming in, loud and clear." "73's" means regards and is a courtesy sign-off. Do you read me S9?

Popularized books such as *Electronics Illustrated* and *Popular Electronics* have attracted part-time fans as well as the serious professional. *Electronics Illustrated* is published by Fawcett and goes to 306,728 how-to enthusiasts. *Popular Electronics* has Ziff-Davis as its publisher and a circulation of 389,334.

Sleepless nights spent in air conversations, rescues half around the world as a result of "ham" relays, police calls, directions from sawmill to logging truck, these and many more everyday examples testify to the enthusiasm and practical value of these magazines and their expert and fanatic followers.

Specialized Magazines About Magazines

While there is no publication devoted to trade coverage exclusively of *all* magazines, there are several which serve certain types of editors or writers for magazines. New and hopeful free-lance writers are born every day and their aspiring spirits are fed with hints and tips by three publications: *Writer's Digest, Author & Journalist*, and *The Writer*. Of these, the oldest is *The Writer*, founded in 1887 and still serving a circulation of 42,221 with market information and articles about writing techniques. *Writer's Digest* was established in 1919, circulates 77,802 copies monthly, and with its affiliated publication, the annual "Writer's Market," has the largest following. *Author & Journalist*, originated in 1916 and publishing 10,000 copies, is issued by the Farrar Publishing Company.

Technical writers, preparing manuals and publications for industry, individual companies, the military services, and government agencies, are a development of today's technological age. They had a magazine of their own, the quarterly *Technical Communications* until its decease in 1968.

Company editors and their staff members generally belong to the International Council of Industrial Editors or the American Association of Industrial Editors, sometimes to both. Each organization has its own association magazine. The ICIE publishes the monthly *Reporting* which chiefly circulates among its 6,500 members. Edited by Lawrence Ragan, it has adopted a literally colorful layout with pages in solid tint blocks of avocado green or shocking pink within chromatic covers bearing the lower case logotype. Members write many of the articles, dealing with their varied approaches to company communications, while departments comment on photographic illustrations, copy-editing techniques, and provide personals about members.

Similar are the subjects of the *editor's notebook* which goes to the 1,200 members of the AAIE every two months. Emphatically printed in bold black and white, the cover and interior pages are effective examples of typographical layout, with varied type faces, title positions, and screen effects. Again, the members and their publications receive the spotlight and, as an association periodical, a special "editor's newsletter" on colored stock furnishes commentary and news notes.

From the Campus

Journalism schools and their students provide quarterly reviews and association journals devoted to the social, technical, and economic issues of the day, as well as news notes about journalists and their activities. Of the publications of comment and criticism, one with circulation chiefly among the professors of journalism is their serious *Journalism Quarterly*, "devoted to research" and published by the Association for Education in Journalism though founded originally in 1923 by the American Association of Schools and Departments of Journalism, still listed as a cooperative sponsor. Its articles deal with quantitative studies, historical and sociological analysis, and regular departments report on research, journalism education, new books, and carry a running bibliography. A similar, slimmer quarterly, *Journalism Educator*, is published by the American Society of Journalism School Administrators for its members.

Since the prestigious Nieman Fellowship program was initiated at Harvard in 1936, a dozen able newspapermen a year have followed individual programs of postgraduate study. A fruit of their inquiry has been the quarterly *Nieman Reports*, articles analyzing newspapers and mass communications in today's society, contributed by present or former Fellows. Founded in 1947, the quarterly reflects the reputation achieved by the recipients.

Two national fraternities, Theta Sigma Phi for women and Sigma Delta

Chi for men, were founded on college campuses in the first decade of this century and today have become even better known for the activities of their 21,000 alumna and 18,000 alumni. Both publish magazines. Sigma Delta Chi's *The Quill* was established in 1912 and circulates 19,510 copies, four out of every five going to its own members. Features about newspapers and newspapermen, articles about press battles for freedom, these are its stock in trade, generally written by members for the members. The usual news items appear, and accounts of chapter activities.

Matrix is the Theta Sigma Phi bi-monthly magazine for its members and it concentrates on their personal achievements and, naturally, on the accomplishments of women journalists.

Several individual journalism schools publish quarterly reviews, analyzing the role and performance of the communications media. Among the better known journals of this type are the *Montana Journalism Review* and the *Columbia Journalism Review*. Contributors are drawn mainly from the ranks of each school's staff, students, and graduates, and their articles compare favorably with the content of other journalistic quarterlies.

A second form of magazine, also issued by journalism schools or affiliated associations, is for the secondary school student, the high school journalist who, with his adviser's constant help, edits a school paper or yearbook. The magazines offer more advice, suggestions, and examples of model performance. They include the quarterly *Quill and Scroll*, sponsored by the Quill and Scroll Foundation and intended for high school members of the honor society. Others are the *School Press Review*, published by the Columbia Scholastic Press Association monthly during the school year, and the *Scholastic Editor*, the monthly issued by the National Scholastic Press Association. *Photolith* is intended for yearbook staffs, and is produced monthly by the National School Yearbook Association.

While journalists sometimes accuse themselves of being poor public relations performers in their own interest, this survey of their own specialized magazines should prove that they have not totally neglected their own profession, craft, art, business or whatever you want to term it. Themselves, they sometimes call it worse!

At The Bar

Lawyers must prefer to communicate by talking, for their profession has relatively few publications—at least compared with doctors or teachers! They do have one major organization, the American Bar Association, and its monthly *Journal* circulates 134,066 copies, almost all among the members.

Somewhat surprisingly, the *American Bar Association Journal* was not published until 1915 although courts accompanied the colonists to the New World. A dignified if static one-color cover presents photographs of distinguished legal landmarks and a list of leading articles. Eight or nine serious articles follow each other in black-and-white layout, duly foot-noted and illustrated only by equally serious portrait photographs. A variety of departments deal with Supreme Court decisions and other new opinions, legislative developments, as well as the usual reports on association matters. While three editors are listed on the masthead, a formidable system provides an 11-man board of editors plus an advisory board representing each of the 50 states. A relatively small advertising section primarily involves legal reference books.

Several of the 21 "sections" of the A.B.A. have their own periodicals, and the A.B.A. has joined with the American Law Institute in a Joint Committee on Continuing Legal Education to publish the *Practical Lawyer* eight times a year for 16,180 subscribers. Legal education also is one of the more prolific sources of legal journals. Practically every law school has its law review, edited by students and faculty, and presenting their research and that of contributors. Such publications are chiefly quarterlies.

Each state has its own bar association which, in turn, issues a publication. Thus there is the *Illinois Bar Journal*, appearing monthly and printing, within a colorful cover, a dozen features and departments, plus reports and news about Illinois cases and bar activities.

The courts, as a forum for law, are represented also in such periodicals as *Judicature*, the 10-monthly journal of the American Judicature Society, a society of more than 30,000 lawyers and judges in the United States, Canada, and some 40 other nations "to promote the efficient administration of justice." The *New York Law Journal* is the official publication of the First and Second Judicial Departments and, like many metropolitan legal papers, is a daily newspaper, giving court decisions, bar calendars, personal notes, and covering events of special interest to members of the bar.

One of the few commercially-published law periodicals is *Case and Comment*, issued by The Lawyers Cooperative Publishing Company every other month on a controlled circulation basis to 141,678 lawyers and judges. Digest-sized and founded in 1894, *Case and Comment* carries articles on unusual cases, trial and office procedures, the education and economics of the legal profession. It also indulges in cartoons and humorous stories about the law and its practice!

Legal Newspapers

Specialized legal newspapers are published in most large cities around the country, giving court calendars and rulings. These, in many cases, are not much more than printed dockets or bulletin boards which, however, are necessary for practicing lawyers. They also carry legal advertising. There are at least 40 such papers, most of them issued five times a week. The *Law Journal*, published in New York City, has the largest circulation with 9,200.

Your Health!

What do you prize most? Health and happiness will be frequent answers —and in that order! Health makes happy humans. Seven professions and related institutions join in a search to give and restore health: medicine and the physician, dentistry, nursing and the hospital, the drugstore and the pharmacist.

Probably no other professional area has placed such emphasis upon publications; they serve as daily postgraduate training for those who seek to keep us in good health. At least 325 different periodicals dealing with health are listed in SRDS directories: 208 medical (the largest single listing by far), 31 dental, 30 pharmaceutical, 20 hospital, 15 optical, 14 nursing, and 7 health.

Medical

The major medical organization both in size and in publications is the American Medical Association. Thirteen different specialized publications are issued by the AMA, serving the general practitioner, the specialist, and the layman. They all trace their beginnings back to the May day at Philadelphia in 1847 when 250 doctors gathered together to form one of the most influential associations of our time. Today its members number more than 206,000 physicians. Its budget runs around $23 million annually and, note well, 44.8 per cent of that comes from advertising in AMA publications! Two of its main seven divisions are closely concerned with publications. The Communications Division is responsible for editorial handling of *The AMA News* and *Today's Health* as well as news departments, contact with communications media, program and speaker activities, exhibits, and community relations. The Scientific Publications Division prepares editorial material for the *Journal of the AMA* and 10 other publications: *American Journal of Diseases of Children*, *Archives of Dermatology*, *Archives of Environmental Health*, *Archives of General Psychiatry*, *Archives of Internal Medicine*, *Archives of Neurology*, *Archives of Opthalmology*, *Archives of Otolaryngology*, *Archives of Pathology*, and *Archives of Surgery*.

Following three years of planning, the *Journal of the American Medical Association*, known as *JAMA*, was born in 1883 with Dr. S. Davis as its first editor. Today it claims the widest circulation of any medical magazine in the world. Published weekly, it runs articles, preferably not over 6,000 words in

187

length, reports and news from medical and scientific councils, abstracts and reviews. Subscriptions both to *JAMA* and the appropriate specialty periodical are covered by the individual membership dues. Each thick issue, numbering 200 or more pages, goes to a total circulation of 210,076.

The familiar red and black logotype surmounting a double-columned table of contents has identified the *JAMA* cover for years although an occasional special issue may flourish a full-color illustration such as a classical medical scene. Inside, lavish pages of advertising, replete with graphic full-color art, exhibit with maximum realism all the ills to which man is subject. The articles succeed each other, in black and white double columns with black and white photographs. These are numbered concurrently from issue to issue; all pages are also numbered separately for each issue. Regular departments such as medical news, letters and reviews, questions and answers, appear among the ads in three-column width.

The ten specialized publications of the AMA have similar cover designs, a rectangular nameplate with white lettering against a one-color tint block above a white page which carries article titles or simply the announcement of a major medical meeting. At the bottom, in the same one-color, is the single line, "American Medical Association Publication." Inside is a sequence of professional articles in double columns, occasionally illustrated by black-and-white photographs. Fore and aft appears the advertising of ethical pharmaceuticals. Four of these periodicals serve also as official publications of specialized medical associations. Total circulation for all ten is approximately 210,000, the largest being the *Archives of Internal Medicine* which goes to 59,481.

A weekly newspaper in tabloid size, *The AMA News* was established in 1958 and circulates on a controlled basis, it is claimed, to more physicians, more than 334,500, than any other medical publication. It is "edited for the physician in his role as a consumer—to bring him news of political, social and economic developments affecting the practice of medicine and his personal life." It carries information about practice management, medical-legal problems, insurance and investments, home and office equipment, travel and recreation.

Originally founded in 1923 as *Hygeia, Today's Health* is published by AMA for the American family. Every month its bright-colored cover adorns reception rooms and homes, with 700,000 paid copies carrying a message of health. Typical articles discuss "Making a Success of Marriage," "The Housewife and Her Hands," "What a Baby's Cries Mean." It explores "the world of medicine, translating many of the exciting discoveries into language the non-medical person can thoroughly understand." Dramatic four-color lay-

188

outs, plenty of art, and feature style in writing dress the pages with attractive appeal. Departments range widely from recipes to cosmetics, from dieting to "Growing Pains."

AMA is not alone in medical publishing. Many other medical associations either produce their own magazines or have worked out harmonious agreements with a commercial publisher. Among the organizations which edit their own are: the American Society of Abdominal Surgeons which, with five other related associations, publishes *Abdominal Surgery*, a handsome monthly; the American College of Physicians, whose *Annals of Internal Medicine* is a giant which runs to as many as 360 pages of detailed analytical reports presented in simple, clear type and, also, blocks of solid full-page advertising. Its circulation is 43,150. *Circulation* (of another kind) is the official journal of the American Heart Association. Its cover bears the association's familiar heart in red with flaming torch and its title, also in bright scarlet. The same organization not only issues large *Circulation* supplements but also publishes other periodicals such as *Circulation Research*.

Group publishers have become centers of medical publication in their own right or under the sponsorship of major medical associations. These publishers are another good illustration of how specialization proliferates—one medical publication leads to another and soon a cluster exists, where meticulous accuracy is stressed and reputation grows in consequence.

The great name among multiple medical publishers is The Williams & Wilkins Company in Baltimore which, with considerable aid from the close presence of The Johns Hopkins University, first moved into the field with the publication of *The Journal of Pharmacology and Experimental Therapeutics* in 1909—although the firm traces its origin back to 1890. William & Wilkins, whose romantic history we write in Chapter 11, produces 32 medical publications, as well as serving as publisher or printer for many other specialized fields. Among its chief medical journals, the names stand out, for prestige and longevity, of the *Journal of Nervous and Mental Disease*, founded in 1874, and the *Journal of Bacteriology* (official publication of The American Society for Microbiology), which began in 1916. Considerable circulations belong to *Current Medical Digest*, established in 1934 and going by controlled distribution to 146,000, and the *Technical Bulletin of the Registry of Medical Technologists* (official journal of the Registry of Medical Technologists of the American Society of Clinical Pathologists) with a paid circulation of 46,466. Much of W & W publishing consists of publications with relatively small circulations of two or three thousand but of large importance to the specialists who depend on them. W & W publications are distinguished also for handsome format, excellence in printing, and simple, effective design.

189

The book publishing house of J. B. Lippincott in Philadelphia has a major medical publications division with 11 properties. Two have circulations in the neighborhood of 15,000 each. They are *Annals of Surgery*, founded in 1885 and the official publication of four surgical associations, and *Anesthesiology*, published for the American Society of Anesthesiologists.

Nine medical periodicals are published by the C. V. Mosby Company of St. Louis. *The American Journal of Obstetrics and Gynecology*, founded in 1920 and the official publication of 35 medical societies, leads the Mosby group with a paid circulation of 17,152. Another Mosby bellwether is the *Journal of Pediatrics* with more than 13,000 paid circulation.

A major enterprise and service is provided by the Medical Digest Group, composed of 10 digest magazines edited for specialists in as many varied fields of medicine. Their publication headquarters at Northfield, Ill., handles combined advertising. "Each year more than 5,000 articles dealing with subjects of interest to each specialty are digested from the world's medical literature. More than 1,000 journals are reviewed each month." Total circulation for the group is more than 200,000, with *Medical Digest* at the head of the list, circulating among more than 62,000 general practitioners.

Other leading medical group publishers include the Hoeber Medical Division of the book firm of Harper & Row, with six titles; and the Yorke Medical Group of Reuben H. Donnelley Corporation, publishing three medical books. Hoeber's publications have a total circulation of approximately 40,000. Their oldest book is the *American Journal of Pathology*, initiated in 1924; their circulation leader is *Obstetrics and Gynecology*, totaling 16,453. The Yorke publications and their circulations are: the *American Journal of Cardiology*, 10,853; the *American Journal of Medicine*, 23,348; and the *American Journal of Surgery*, 11,908, and dating back to 1891. Litton Publications is another leading medical publishing firm.

Medical bulletins in three large geographical categories have associated together for advertising and some shared editorial matter. The Medical Society Magazine Group is composed of 157 magazines representing 126 official county medical society publications and 31 official state, county, or city general practice periodicals. A total circulation of 186,952 is involved, with the monthly publications office at the Academy of Medicine, in Phoenix, Arizona.

Then there is the State Journal Group, representing the official monthly publications of 34 state medical societies and a circulation of 148,994. State Journals West is a similar group, formed from the four official medical associations of 11 Western states and Hawaii, representing a circulation of 40,573.

There are a number of outstanding medical magazines, published independently by medical associations or as individual enterprises by commercial publishers. Among them are such distinguished journals as the *American*

Journal of Public Health, 25,207 circulation, founded in 1911 as the official monthly publication of the American Public Health Association; the *Annals of Internal Medicine,* 43,150 circulation, the official publication since 1927 of the American College of Physicians; and *The John Hopkins Medical Journal,* 10,322 circulation, established in 1889 by that famous medical school chiefly for its own alumni. The American College of Surgeons has edited and published (through the Franklin H. Martin Memorial Foundation) *Surgery, Gynecology and Obstetrics* since 1905 for a paid circulation of 23,335 eminent surgeons.

Perhaps the oldest, still surviving medical publication in the United States is the *New England Journal of Medicine,* founded in 1812, the same year as our first national war. It is the official magazine of the Massachusetts Medical Society and, despite its name but as a witness to its standing, distributed to a circulation of 108,232 throughout the United States and Canada, with more than 8,000 copies going outside North America.

An import from England, also because of its prestige, is the North American edition of *The Lancet,* published weekly by Little, Brown and Company, the book firm, and going to 17,512 American physicians. It was established in 1823. The major multiple magazine organization of McGraw-Hill publishes *Postgraduate Medicine,* with a paid circulation of 49,567, as a monthly of complete original articles.

Many another serious medical magazine appears, often from professional organizations or medical schools, too many of them for individual mention. Typical of their extensive information programs is the activity of the American College of Radiology, founded in 1923. Its public service includes films, radio-TV programs, exhibits, and a considerable output of booklets and publications such as a monthly newsletter and *Your Radiologist,* a quarterly. We have special interest in this publication and the program for one of our students, Rona Talcott, became assistant editor of *Your Radiologist* as her first position after graduation, a testimony to the fact that personal intelligence and specialized college training in specialized publications can create an entree into the intricate atmosphere of medical publication.

Controlled circulation as a vehicle for profitable advertising revenue is the road followed by many medical publications from commercial publishers. Many of these magazines exhibit extremely glossy editorial layouts, fantastically elegant advertising, and a number of articles on applied or semi-medical topics. Most of them have medical advisory boards and editors. Prominent among these publications are: *Medical World News,* a McGraw-Hill subsidiary with weekly circulation of 244,078; *MD Medical Newsmagazine,* reaching 176,593 and even offering fiction and film puffs; *Medical Economics,* a Chapman-Reinhold subsidiary founded in 1923 and printing bi-weekly

191

187,955 copies. *Hospital Physician*, circulation 70,108, is another Medical Economics book, as is also *Medical-Surgical Review*, a 265,695 quarterly.

More of the controlled circulation medicals include: *Medical Opinion & Review*, 167,046; *Medical Tribune*, a twice-weekly newspaper with a press run of 173,412; *Modern Medicine*, a bi-weekly reaching 212,697; *Physician's Management*, 166,000, and *Patient Care*, 102,134.

Patient Care has acted ingeniously to speed up reading through imaginative editing and layout devices. They explain their time-saving idea: "If you curl the magazine slightly, you can spot the start of each editorial feature by the lineup of color cards in the upper corner. You can get the most out of each article in the least time by first reading the Express Stops—printed in color and in italics." The color cards are triangular tint blocks in the upper corners of the significant right-hand pages. The cover itself carries the logotype *Patient Care* in a similar triangle and also the line, "Express-Stop reading time for this issue: 5 minutes."

Just these publications named—and there are many others—add up to a total controlled circulation of around 1,800,000. That's a lot of advertising dollars and printed paper! No wonder that medical publications are number one in advertising page volume of all specialized publications!

Hospitals are monumental institutions in today's society, due to Medicare and skyrocketing costs, and many a staff doctor, resident, or intern spends his days or nights under their roofs, learning, teaching, caring for patients. Millions spent on hospital equipment and supplies are a giant market. Therefore it's not surprising to find controlled circulation publications such as *Hospital Medicine*, 185,531; *Hospital Practice*, 188,632; and *Hospital Tribune*, 116,793.

Medical magazines, whether published under the auspices of a medical association or by a commercial house, have several characteristics in common —doctor-editors, medical advisory boards, well-written articles, some remarkable color photography and reproduction, excellent printing, and a mass of elaborate advertising.

One can not leave this colossus of profitable publishing without noting that even the beginners, the medical students, have their own specialized periodical. It is *The New Physician*, circulating 61,227 copies and including medical educators among its readers. Finally, believe it or not, there is *Rx Golf and Travel*. We quote the inimitable editorial statement—"edited for doctors of medicine and osteopathy under the age of 70 years and who are engaged in active practice of medicine or osteopathy. The articles are designed to entertain and serve the doctors in the areas of their leisure and recreational interest." *Rx Golf* (perhaps by a slip we first typed "Golf" with a final "d") goes to a non-paying circulation of 196,486. Alas, the poor paying patient!

Hospital

Administrators are the prime audience for most of the 20 publications chiefly concerned with hospitals. Their professional duties and their purchasing power are the twin subjects of the articles, departments, and advertising. Two publications stand out—McGraw-Hill's *Modern Hospital* and *Hospitals*, of the American Hospital Association.

Modern Hospital, established in 1913, has a monthly circulation of 30,037, one-third paid. Its monthly news and articles cover patient care; special departments such as operating rooms, personnel, finance, construction, feeding, and maintenance. Basically a distinction is made between professional and non-professional department heads, the first dealing chiefly with medical and nursing services and the latter with housekeeping. The issues are large, elaborate in content, and have received 10 professional awards in seven years. It has a sister publication, McGraw-Hill's *Modern Nursing Home*, published bi-monthly for a controlled circulation of 20,530.

Hospitals has been published twice a month since 1936 and three-fourths of its 35,093 circulation is paid. Executive personnel in both members and non-member hospitals receive its copies. The publishing policy calls for a fifty-fifty split between editorial and advertising, which means about 2,000 pages of each annually. It publishes six special issues on planning and construction (a $2 billion expenditure in 1968), administration, purchasing, the association's convention, and small hospitals (those with less than 100 beds—but which still spend $1.7 million daily for supplies, equipment, and services!).

This association magazine has personal interest to the writer. Arnold Rivin, one of our first graduates to enter the specialized publications field, initially served as Washington correspondent for *Hospitals* and then became its editor.

A gigantic debut of a new magazine, certainly related to hospitals, is planned by *Redbook* for new mothers in 5,000 maternity wards. Starting with an initial circulation of three million copies, *Young Mother* will be distributed by Gift-Pax along with other free presents. The new publication's own birthday was scheduled for early 1969.

Front-runners among hospital publications today include: *American Hospital Professional*, with a controlled circulation of 42,487; *Hospital/Nursing Home Product News*, 60,303 non-paid; *Hospital Management*, 32,494, of which more than 36 per cent is paid; *Hospital Topics*, 35,711, with approximately 25 per cent paid; and *Nursing Homes*, the official publication of the American Nursing Home Association, with a controlled circulation of 17,559. All of these are monthlies, and all share the same qualities of good format and elaborate advertising which mark the medicals.

Nursing

Ever since Florence Nightingale, nursing has been a sympathetic calling, sometimes glamorized but always appreciated by patients grateful for a smile and tender hand—especially in the antiseptic hospital routine, anything human is a saving grace. Hospital magazines remind us that nursing also is a profession, based on hard training and arduous duty.

Oldest and largest of the nursing publications is the *American Journal of Nursing*, founded in 1900, the official publication of the American Nurses' Association. With its paid monthly circulation of 259,621, it reaches more than 50,000 staff and almost as many student nurses as well as more than 30,000 supervisors and head nurses. Half its editorial content is devoted to nursing care, with considerable space also given to nursing news, association news, public health nursing, and nursing education. Another periodical, also published by the American Journal of Nursing Company, is *Nursing Outlook*, the official monthly of the National League for Nursing. Designed especially for nursing administrators and educators, it stresses public health and supervisory responsibilities and goes to a paid circulation of 30,215.

RN is published monthly by a subsidiary of Chapman-Reinhold, the parent company of so many chemical publications and several medical titles. As its initial title indicates, it's edited for the registered nurse. Half its editorial content deals with the clinical and the rest is divided among professional and personal subjects. Established in 1937, *RN* reaches, the publishers state, almost 200,000 registered nurses on a paid basis and more than 23,000 senior students on a controlled circulation count. "Two-thirds of our readership is unduplicated by any other nursing publication," according to the publishers.

Reading the nursing publications we are reminded that it also is a profession with specialties. There are publications for operating room nurses (*AORN Journal*), practical and vocational nurses (the *Bedside Nurse* and the *Journal of Practical Nursing*), for nurses of the elderly (*Geriatric Nursing*), for nurses of the mentally ill (*Perspectives in Psychiatric Care*), for nurses practicing anesthesia (*Journal of the American Association of Nurse Anesthetists*), for nurses in industry (*American Association of Industrial Nurses Journal*). Several of these are, as the titles indicate, association periodicals; most of them circulate on a paid basis.

States have their own nursing associations and they also have their own magazines. In California, it's the *Bulletin of the California Nurses' Association*; then there's the *New York State Nurse* at the other side of the continent. And all across the three thousand miles between, nurses at bedside and by operating table reach out their skilled helping hands.

194

Dental

Regardless of jokes about the dentist's drill, we know where to turn when we get a toothache—no appointment can be too soon!

The American Dental Association, professional society for the nation's 106,000 dentists, also is the major publisher of dental publications with four periodicals, led by *The Journal of the American Dental Association*. From its origin in 1913, *JADA* has been a monthly resource and continuing library furnishing original articles, news, and reviews.

On a recent holiday issue, St. Appolonia, the patron saint of dentistry, appeared on the cover in bright illuminated colors against the indigo blue background, topped by a bold sans serif nameplate superimposed in black on a white block. Inside, on buff-colored stock is a special four-page section of "Bulletins & Highlights" of association and Washington news. The table of contents not only lists the articles but also summarizes their contents in one brief sentence, simplifying selection for the reader. Editorial matter leads off with a comprehensive news section followed by the articles in simple black-and-white, double-columned layout. Advertising features equipment and supplies; it is prodigal in the use of color, special stock, and inserts. Circulation, basically association and paid, is 103,369.

The Association's other periodicals are the *Journal of Dental Research*, chiefly for dental educators; the *Journal of Oral Surgery*, and *Dental Abstracts*. Professional associations also sponsor other dental publications such as the *American Journal of Orthodontics*, published by the C. V. Mosby Company (the medical publishers), who also produce the *Journal of Prosthetic Dentistry and Oral Surgery*, *Oral Medicine*, and *Oral Pathology*.

Another multiple publisher is Oral Hygiene Publications with *Dental Digest*, established in 1894, stressing clinical dentistry; *Dental Economics*, founded as *Oral Hygiene* in 1911; and *Proofs, The Dental Trade Journal*. *Dental Economics* deals with practice management and financing, has a controlled circulation of 102,099. One of its two chief competitors is *Dental Management*, with a non-paid distribution of 100,316.

Dental publishers seem to run to three's. Dental Survey Publications (a Cowles Communications, Inc., subsidiary) produces *Dental Survey*, the other main competitor in management, which was founded in 1925 and has a controlled circulation of 95,900. It also provides technical and clinical information while its competition concentrates on practice administration. *Dental Survey's* siblings are *Dental Industry News*, a dealer-marketing magazine, and *Dental Laboratory Review*, for commercial fabricators of dentures.

Dental Products Report, a merchandising publication, was launched in

195

1967 with a "guaranteed non-paid circulation of 100,000." Other noteworthy dental periodicals include *The Dental Students Magazine*, the *Journal of the American Dental Hygienists' Association*, the *Journal of Dental Education*, *The Journal of Dentistry for Children*, the *Journal of Periodontology*, and the *NACDL Journal*, for dental laboratories and technicians. A number of state dental associations also publish regularly.

Professional societies sponsor two-thirds of the 31 dental periodicals listed in SRDS. Their content emphasizes the professional article in simple, effective layout, an advisory board and editor-in-chief with dental qualifications. The commercial publications naturally run to heavy advertising (which makes non-paid circulation profitable) and editorial stress on equipment and management.

Eye Care

The eyes have it, if most of us vote on our most prized personal possession. The optometrist and optician keep their eyes on a dozen professional publications as postgraduate texts that come in the mail.

Professional associations are mainly responsible for these publications, as in other medical areas. The American Optometric Association sends its *Journal*, founded in 1928, to 15,194 member doctors, with a monthly budget of at least 50 editorial pages devoted to educational and professional material. The American Academy of Optometry edits the *American Journal of Optometry and Archives of American Academy of Optometry*, established in 1924 (a suitable entry for marathon magazine nomenclature), to a primarily paid circulation of 5,192, about one-third members.

Oldest publication in the field is the deserved claim of the *Optical Journal and Review of Optometry*, issued twice a month, by the major publishing house of Chilton. Dating back to 1891, this periodical claims exclusive vertical coverage in all divisions of the opthalmic optic field—optometrists, dispensing opticians, optical manufacturers, supply houses, and laboratories. And it also boasts a remarkable renewal rate of nearly 85 per cent for its 9,935 circulation. Other commercial publications include *Optometric World*, pledged to promote professional ethical standards with articles by professional optometrists and news of their associations; *Optometric Weekly*, founded in 1910, with paid circulation of 13,270 optometrists and opticians; and *Optometric Management* which deals with practical rather than clinical areas and has 21,078 controlled circulation.

Opticians are served by two publications chiefly. They are *Guild Guide*, official publication of the Guild of Prescription Opticians of America, and *Dispensing Optician*, stressing the mercantile aspects of serving the retail optical business. Each has a controlled circulation of around four thousand.

196

Pharmaceutical

This polysyllabic designation for drugs and the druggist's business is probably a good reminder that pharmacy is a serious profession and not just a corner department store. Publications are published, however, for both interests which sometimes join under the same roof.

The diversity of pharmacy doesn't end here, however, for as a profession it involves an extended educational background, meticulous prescription compounding, and lifetime attention to new developments. As a business, there is the manufacture and marketing of pharmaceuticals, and wholesale and retail selling. Specialized publications deal with all these phases, sometimes with single-minded concentration on one, more often with editorial attention to several.

Leader of the professional association magazines is the monthly *Journal* of the *American Pharmaceutical Association*, reaching 49,332, chiefly APhA members. Established in 1912, the *Journal* devotes a high 60 to 70 per cent of its editorial space to articles which may be papers from APhA meetings or original treatises on important drug developments. Regular departments, under standing all-cap heads with bendayed symbolic sketches, cover government agencies, legal information, news of pharmaceutical meetings, and a half-dozen other recurring topics. Color is added for titles and rules.

An attractive feature is the dedication of a single issue to a subject of major interest. The golden anniversary issue drew a parallel between the history of pharmacy and the Civil War. Another special issue dealt with drug abuse in society. Although occasional photographs and sketches lighten the layouts, they are largely typographical in tone with a tendency to grayness.

Pharmaceutical research, regulation, education, and production are the core of editorial attention by another APhA periodical, the *Journal of Pharmaceutical Sciences*, addressed to scientists and technologists and reaching 14,000 of them with its paid circulation.

Independent magazines which focus on manufacture and marketing include *Chain Store Age* in its "Drug Executives and Drug Store Managers" editions, *Drug & Cosmetic Industry*, *Drug Trade News*, and *Wholesale Drugs*, all primarily with paid circulation.

When we consider the retail drugstore, we encounter the results of the modern trend to economic concentration and the diminishing of the independent outlet. Also, although some druggists still operate exclusively on a prescription basis, most pharmacists are surrounded by non-professionals selling soap, toys, magazines, sporting goods, and you name it. The drugstore manager must understand turn-over, salesmanship, displays, food service, and

197

perhaps pharmacy! Fortunately he can turn to his specialized publications for aid in the roles he must play.

The *NARD Journal*, founded in 1902 as the official publication of the National Association of Retail Druggists, appears twice a month and goes to a paid circulation of 32,815, almost entirely membership. Ninety per cent of the nation's retail pharmacists practice in NARD stores. This publication also has the largest circulation of all drug trade periodicals distributed exclusively to retail drug store owners. Its readership, according to a Nielsen survey, is 92 per cent for both advertising and editorial material.

Each *NARD Journal* issue contains much association news, reports on legislative activity, and one topic of special interest. Features have focused, for example, on poison prevention, sickroom needs, pharmacy education, vacation promotions. Red and black are standard for the cover, but inside editorial items are seldom displayed with color aids. Four-color appears on inside and back cover ads and, from time to time, in other positions. Layout is lightened by some cartoons but photos tend to the line-up variety. Simple and direct writing does give an assist.

Commercial books find the Hearst Corporation's *American Druggist*, dating back to 1871, in first place in circulation, 67,236, almost all controlled. Two-thirds goes to independent retail drugstores with prescription departments, the rest mainly to chain units. Content features news in "Teleflashes" about the drug industry, new pharmaceuticals, and marketing trends as well as articles on such topics as "The Ocean; New Source of Drugs." Cluttered and crowded layout suggests that *American Druggist* is modeled more on newspaper than magazine format. Ads abound, many in color, but color appears on editorial pages infrequently, and then as one-color tint blocks.

Attractive format and quality editorial matter does appear in the *American Professional Pharmacist*. A Romaine Pierson publication, it stems from a house also responsible for three medical journals. *American Professional Pharmacist* was founded in 1935 and reaches 41,256 in a controlled circulation directed to "high-volume retail pharmacies, hospital, and nursing home pharmacies." Both its editorial and advertising content is restricted to prescriptions and health-related products. Layout shows imagination, with red, blue, and green titles over pages effectively designed to display twin columns of type liberally set against liberal white space, with color subheads and artistic photographs, large and often bleeding on one or more margins.

A variety of other magazines also testify that the variety store of yesterday has become the drugstore of today. Several books such as *Better Buys* and *Buying Guide* are available to aid the manager when he's purchasing. Other publications concentrate on hospital needs—the *American Journal of Hospital*

Pharmacy or *Hospital Formulary Management*. The bi-weekly *Drug Topics* is available to almost all retail drug outlets with its distribution of 67,000 non-paid copies. Its main competitor, *PM, The Pharmacist's Management Journal*, has a similar circulation, both in audience and size.

Regional associations, primarily professional in character, are represented in the State Pharmaceutical Group, the monthly official publications of 15 states and the District of Columbia, all edited by the State Pharmaceutical Editorial Association in Mahway, New Jersey, and totaling 35,266 in paid circulation. The Affiliated Regional Drug Publications is an advertising operation for nine association and commercial monthlies with a total circulation of 71,671, three-fourths on a controlled basis.

Despite advancing professional standards in pharmaceutical education, the drugstore of today in many cases has become a merchandiser of everything under the sun, including proprietary products also found on the counters of discount stores and filling stations. Perhaps appropriate is the SRDS note in an early 1968 directory: " *Drug News Weekly*—Note: No longer published as a separate publication. Will be incorporated into *Supermarket News.* " Fortunately, a number of pharmaceutical magazines still exist.

Health

If "the groundwork of all happiness is health," as a poet has said, then the specialized magazines devoted to health should also provide happiness. As we've seen, the American Medical Association attempts to help in *Today's Health* and the American Association of Health, Physical Education, and Recreation through *Johper*. In *Life and Health*, its editors seek "to aid both young and old in acquiring basic information that will contribute to the health welfare of the family." Edited by a physician, it features articles written by medical authorities and, with a long life of its own since 1885, now circulates monthly to 123,565, with 93 per cent paid.

Less orthodox but no less dedicated, four periodicals advocate "natural foods" as the way to health. *Prevention*, published at Organic Park in Emmaus, Pennsylvania, is edited "for the health-conscious who believe good health may be maintained through the use of natural foods, vitamins and supplements and through the use of exercise." Since its founding in 1950, it has built a circulation of 498,333, 98 per cent paid.

Similar beliefs are presented in the pages of *Better Nutrition*, with controlled circulation of 153,550; and *Let's Live*, distributed to 31,230 paying readers. Departments also provide recipes and natural gardening tips, suggest beauty aids, travel ideas, and exercise hints.

The *Herald of Health* not only recommends natural foods but calls also

199

for the discontinuance of "poison pesticides and food additives." It suggests "the value of schools of thought on healing" and, established in 1896, today reaches a paid circulation of 5,600.

So, down through the years, the professions and the publications promote the philosophy that "Health is the vital principle of bliss."

Military Power

Military publications today, in number and circulation, reflect that power-house, the Pentagon which gets more than $75 billion in the U.S. budget each year. "The total influence—economic, political, and even spiritual—is felt in every city, every state house, every office of Federal Government," President Eisenhower said in his farewell message to the American people before leaving the White House. And just in case it's not felt sufficiently, military associations, supposedly independent, issue magazines with large circulations, while no-body knows exactly how many "official" or "authorized" publications are poured out of units all the way down to regimental size, by bases, reserve organizations, by veterans organizations, and women's auxiliaries. A partial list, based on SRDS, gives a circulation of 3,500,000 for the specialized publications serving the Armed Forces.

Things have changed since Admiral Ernest J. King, the Chief of Naval Operations in 1942, said "Don't tell them anything. When it's over, tell them who won."

Now the Armed Forces all have their own publications, on a service-wide basis as well as for individual units and bases. The major service magazines are the *Army Digest*; *All Hands* (Navy); *The Airman*; and for the Marine Corps, the *Leatherneck* for enlisted men and the *Marine Corps Gazette* for officers.

Without doubt the best known Service publication for overseas personnel is *Stars and Stripes*. Dating back to World War I, it was founded in 1918 as a newspaper printed in Paris. One of the best known members of a famous staff was Harold Ross, later to establish *The New Yorker*. Others included Grantland Rice, the sports writer, and Alexander Woollcott, rotund critic of the theatre. It was re-created in World War II, first as a weekly and then a daily. As American troops took territory, it accompanied them—to Algiers, Rome, Normandy, and Germany, while the Pacific edition finally appeared in Tokyo.

The second time around, cartoonists became better known, with Bill Mauldin, George Baker's "Sad Sack," Milt Caniff's "Male Call," and Leonard Sansone's "Wolf" getting GI laughs often at the expense of the brass.

200

Stars and Stripes hardly had time to cool off after VE and VJ days for an occupation paper continued. Today there's a European edition, published in Darmstadt, Germany, in 150,000 copies daily; and a Pacific edition from Tokyo with 205,000. Of these, 106,400 copies were earmarked for the troops in Vietnam.

Yank, a magazine which reached 2,500,000 circulation in World War II, with 22 rotogravure editions all over the world, received an honorable discharge on 31 December, 1945, signed by General Dwight D. Eisenhower. However, the Department of Defense still publishes *Yank* once a year to hold the copyright.

There's not only a major military lobbying effort in Congress spending $4,810,458 in 1967 and employing 338 lobbyists, but also a major communications program to influence industry and taxpayer. At the center of this program are The Association of the U.S. Army with 104,000 members; the Navy League, with 41,000; the Air Force Association, 90,000; and the Marine Corps League and Marine Corps Association, 46,000. All of these are the primary sponsors of important military service magazines.

These are the official association publications: *Army*, published by the Association of the U.S. Army; *Navy*, from the Navy League; *The Leatherneck*, by the Leatherneck Association and the *Marine Corps Gazette* of the Marine Corps Association; and *Air Force/Space Digest*, of the Air Force Association.

One other also must be named because of its commanding influence— *Armed Forces Journal*, edited for the career officer corps, regular and reserved, active and retired, and "read every week by senior members of the House and Senate Armed Services and Appropriations Committees," according to its own promotion. *Armed Forces Journal*, a weekly, has a seemingly small circulation of 25,358, 80 per cent paid, but it goes to 1,530 generals or admirals, 210 Department of Defense executives, 157 members of Congress. It's been a moving force for some time, founded in 1863 during the midst of the Civil War.

A major private publisher of Armed Forces books is the Army Times Publishing Company, located in Washington, D.C., and publishing not only the *Army Times* but also the *Air Force Times*, the *Navy Times*, and the *Federal Times*, with total circulations of more than half-a-million, 97 per cent paid and distributed every Wednesday in tabloid newspaper format in four major editions, worldwide, United States, European, and Pacific, and published in the United States, Tokyo, and Frankfurt. There also are "Family" and rotogravure supplements.

Editorial policy, as described for the *Army Times* (applies with marked similarity to the *Navy* and *Air Force Times*), states, "*Army Times* tries to serve as an unofficial source of information emanating from government agencies which affects Army people and their families specifically, and service people generally. It regularly reports, through official and unofficial channels, the activities of our troops and their families at home and abroad. Its news columns are aimed at the *career soldier*, both officer and enlisted, but it also offers feature material which, hopefully, appeals to a diverse readership: business pages, developments in defense industry, book reviews, women's sections, sports, editorial comment and cartoons, as well as periodical special sections."

At this time, we might examine Service policy for publications.

"Command" or internal publications range from small mimeographed news sheets to major periodicals, serving a 100-man unit or a major military installation of 100,000 men. They also are known as "Station newspapers," serve a particular unit, and their readers are the members of that unit. In format, they actually may be either newspapers or magazines—more often, the latter. In either case, they're highly specialized.

They also can be divided into "authorized" or "official," or civilian and commercial enterprises. The "authorized" publications are, in most cases, prepared and distributed by uniformed service personnel. But they are not officially considered "official" and may not designate themselves as such in their mastheads which must carry a statement that "views or opinions expressed are not necessarily those of the Service involved."

"Official" publications are required to carry in their mastheads a statement that opinions expressed "by the publishers and writers are their own and not to be considered an official expression of the Department of the Army." They also are written and edited by uniformed personnel, of course. Despite supposed distinctions, many readers still regard both "authorized" and "official" as authoritative—and that's generally correct. Both may be printed on government equipment or by private contractors.

The military personnel who form the staffs of "authorized" and "official" publications bear different designations in the various Services. In the Navy and Coast Guard, they often are termed Journalist. In the Army, Air Force, and Marine Corps, they are given a Military Occupational Specialty (MOS) of Journalist, Clerk-typist, or Correspondent. In some instances, the publication may have civilian employees also. All such staff members are under the immediate supervision of an officer who may be designated Public Affairs Officer, Public Information Officer, or Officer-in-charge.

No "authorized" or "official" publication may carry any advertisement from a private individual or corporation, or contain material which implies in any manner that the government endorses or favors any specific commercial product or service.

"Civilian" or "unofficial" publications are those issued primarily for military readers, with the cost of production and distribution borne entirely by the civilian publisher. They are designed as profit-making enterprises with advertising a major source of revenue. Military personnel on active duty are not permitted to serve on their staffs nor be named in the mastheads. These publications also can not use any emblem or statement which would infer that they are "authorized" or "official."

Much of their editorial content, however, is supplied by military organizations, with copy and photographs furnished by Public Information Offices following the principle of general release to any civilian medium requesting the material. Content of such publications is not subject to military control, but appropriated funds may not be used to pay for any publication costs.

Non-appropriated funds can be used, however, to buy copies for distribution to military personnel. Distribution at any military installation is normally limited to one civilian enterprise in the newspaper, magazine, and comic book categories. Authorized and official publications may not be distributed as supplements or inserts in any civilian or unofficial publications, nor may civilian publications be distributed as part of an authorized or official publication.

With these ground rules, which apply similarly in all the Services, we can look more closely at the publications themselves, leading off with the United States Army's *Army Digest*, official magazine of the Department of the Army and published "to provide timely and authoritative information on policies, plans, operations, and technical developments . . . to the Active Army, Army National Guard, and Army Reserve." *Army Digest* was founded in 1946 and has a controlled circulation of 265,184. Its staff consists of officers, non-coms, and enlisted men, and it is distributed to all personnel.

A monthly, an *Army Digest* special issue has a full-color, wrap-around cover, with inside covers forming monochromatic double-page spreads. Covers, inside and out, exhibit top photographic action shots by Army personnel. Features show the Army in action across the world, with maximum use again of fine photography. Dramatic layouts utilize bleed pictures and bold black captions against generous white space. Tint-blocked pages offer departments: "What's New for You and the Army," "Army Trends," and "Legal Eagle," with typescript set in full-page width for a feeling of immediacy. Combat art by military artists gives full-color reality and impact.

Aviation Digest is another Army official monthly published under supervision of the Commandant of the Army Aviation School at Fort Rucker, Alabama. This periodical also offers high quality layout, expert photography, and skillful use of one-color in various hues for photographs and typographical display. Articles run to such subjects as "Jungle Survival . . . or, How I Learned to Stop Worrying and Love the Jungle." Research and technical

203

material is supplied, health hints, and a letters department. The staff consists of officers and men, with contributions coming largely from Army aviators. Circulation is 60,000.

Association magazines likewise are high-powered. *Army*, is the official periodical of the Association of the U.S. Army. A typical cover shows the black silhouettes of four infantrymen against a cloudy cream-and-gray sky, moving out on a search-and-destroy mission in South Vietnam. Above, in blazing red capitals, *ARMY*. One-color in every hue is used for art, rules, and titles in every article—with priority given to the "brass" in by-lines or subject matter. A recent issue had four generals as contributors and four of nine main features dealt with officer activities. A layout innovation is noteworthy—between each main article is a full-page or spread advertisement for Beech Military Aircraft, Honeywell Aerospace & Defense Group, or some such military contractor. *Army*'s circulation is 111,210, all paid and more than 90 per cent association.

Army Aviation reminds us again that the Air Force does not wholly rule the air. It is the official publication of the Army Aviation Association of America. The material is 10 per cent staff-written, 90 per cent from Army personnel. Circulation, almost wholly paid is 11,431, 92.2 per cent military. *The National Guardsman* is the official publication of the National Guard Association of the United States and its circulation of 74,351 is 100 per cent military.

"All hands" in U.S. Navy lingo means "an evolution in which the entire ship's company takes part" and so it forms a perfect name for the official Navy monthly which is distributed throughout the Fleet. As the publication of the Bureau of Navy Personnel, *All Hands* is edited "for the information and interest of the naval service as a whole." Originally published in 1914 as *BuPers Newsletter* but changing its name in 1922, its contents are designed more for the enlisted man than the officer, with stories about daily routine and shipboard life such as "Rescue at Sea: A Navy Routine" and "A Report on Judo: Black Belt Navy." With a circulation distributed by airmail and averaging about 85,000 copies, the cover carries a box saying "intended for 10 readers . . . pass this copy along."

Stories are provided by a small staff and personnel of the Public Affairs Offices of Navy ships and shore bases. Many photographs accompany most features, while cartoons decorate "The Bulletin Board," a regular department of information on new service opportunities and various duty stations. Other departments include letters, "Today's Navy," and "Servicescope—News About Other Services." Balanced layouts present the articles in fairly attractive form. No advertising is carried and distribution is free.

Competing with *All Hands* is *Our Navy*, a private publication dating back to 1897. *Our Navy* has a paid circulation of 8,635. Its strength impaired when the Navy came out with *All Hands* in improved magazine format, *Our Navy* still holds loyal readers.

Navy, the Navy League's association book for its membership, carries articles chiefly on the fighting service but runs an occasional piece on the merchant marine and oceanography. Regular departments provide news of the Naval Sea Cadet Corps, the Marines, and U.S. Coast Guard. Its circulation is 46,726, 92 per cent paid and almost 88 per cent to members. Other publications include the American Society of Naval Engineers' *Naval Engineers Journal*, founded in 1888, and *Shipmate*, produced by the Alumni Association of the United States Naval Academy in Annapolis.

A distinguished magazine in any company is the *United States Naval Institute Proceedings*, established in 1874, which covers professional naval subjects and strategy, geopolitics, and naval history. Printed on fine quality stock and with excellent color reproductions of paintings showing famous sea battles, this monthly is edited for members of the U.S. Naval Institute, chiefly officers of the Navy, Coast Guard, and Marine Corps. They receive 84 per cent of its 65,000 circulation.

The Marine Corps, priding itself as an elite force, of course has its own publications. The official publication of the Marine Corps Association, the *Marine Corps Gazette* reports on Marine news and military policy. Most of its material is contributed by and for Marine officers, regular, retired, and reserve. Established in 1916, its circulation is 20,053. Larger, for it goes to enlisted personnel as well as officers, *The Leatherneck* immortalizes a famous Service nickname and the tradition of "Semper Fidelis." Published by the Leatherneck Association since 1917, it lists the Corps Headquarters as its headquarters, and goes to 200,345 Marines from "boot" to grizzled veteran, with 94 per cent paid.

Articles in *The Leatherneck* range from historical pieces on the capture of Okinawa in World War II to a feature about the thousand Marines serving as security guards for U.S. Embassies throughout the world. Regular departments are wide-ranging in scope, from cartoon to combat paintings by Marine artists, from "Mail Call" girls who want to correspond with Marines to a monthly pin-up to medals presented for valor. Traditionally the staff is composed of Marine sergeants with the editor-publisher an officer. Much material comes from the two correspondents and four photographers permanently assigned to each Marine division, with more on duty during combat. "Writing for Marines about Marines is not an easy job. They know themselves very well and if they don't recognize themselves in what they read, we hear about it in no uncertain terms," comments its managing editor.

Layout is lavish with action photographs, bold black Gothic titles, use of one-color for standing heads. Four-color is used for the center-spread painting and occasional photographs. Advertising ranges from Marine desk sets to Marine rings to "survival" knives. *Leatherneck* lives up to its name throughout; as one former Marine comments, "It's the word."

The fourth and newest branch, the Air Force, suiting its fast growth and size, has many publications, headed by *The Airman*, official magazine of the U.S. Air Force, reaching a circulation of 250,000 copies. Excellent full-color and monochromatic photographs taken by USAF non-coms adorn the front, back, and inside covers in dramatic style, while similar art decorates every article. Writers are Air Force officers and men and they contribute features on "Thrust of the Screaming Eagles" or "Forgotten Ace of World War I." Regular departments provide cartoon humor; "Pentagon Personal," inside info on potential duty assignments; and "Air Force Report," news shorts. Layout is lively and well-conceived.

The Talon is the official monthly, edited by and for the cadets at the U.S. Air Force Academy. Its content includes fiction and articles, sports and humor, all with an Air Force and Academy background. Circulation, all paid, is 5,500.

A private, commercial publication, *Air Force/Space Digest*, claims that it wins more editorial awards than any other aerospace publication. As an association publication, its circulation of 100,326 is 97 per cent paid, with 46 per cent going to USAF personnel and 14 per cent to the aerospace industry. Its editorial policy declares it is "for management personnel with policy / planning responsibilities in aerospace industry, the USAF, and aerospace government agencies." Its advertising testifies that it "covers in depth the world's largest market—$10 billions in procurement, and research and development for the fiscal year 1968."

Competing publications include *American Aviation*, with a circulation of 100,000, 82 per cent to manufacturers and contractors, 18 per cent to United States military, NASA, and other government agencies. Then there are *Aviation Week*, *Space/Aeronautics*, *Space Age News*, *Vertical World*, and *Vertiflite*, all circulating substantially among military personnel as well as the aviation manufacturing industry.

With defense the biggest business in the world, many other commercial publications serve defense industries and the military establishment . . . and attract a huge volume of advertising. Of the 435 Congressional districts, 363 have one or more major defense plants or military installations. And of the 38 major defense contractors from 1961 to 1967, 15 of them derive more than half their business from defense contracts . . . who also employ a large number of retired military officers. No wonder this array is served by such periodicals as those already named and more. For example, there is *Armed Forces Man-*

206

agement, one of four aviation publications of American Aviation Publications —which, as we mentioned in Chapter 1, has 33 correspondents accredited by the Congressional Press Galleries.

Armed Forces Management carried 782 pages of advertising from defense manufacturers in 1967 and claims first position in its field. Its circulation of 36,757, chiefly controlled, is 94 per cent to top military in administration and research, and other U.S. government leaders; 7 per cent to defense suppliers. Similar periodicals are: *Data-Magazine of Military RDT & E Management, The Military Market Magazine, The Review* of the Defense Supply Association.

Private publishers also supply super-specialized periodicals on technical military subjects. *Signal* deals with military communications and electronics. *Ordnance* covers weapons and armaments. *Naval Engineers Journal* and the *Military Engineer* carry self-descriptive titles. *The Officer* is the official publication of the Reserve Officers Association of the United States and has a paid circulation of 58,000. Post exchanges have three publications dedicated to them, testimony to the magical PX: *The Club Executive,* for the 2,500 operators and buyers of the 2,500 military clubs; *Post Exchange and Commissary Magazine,* ditto; and *Exchange & Commissary News,* likewise—these are all controlled circulation.

Families are not forgotten, for the military may marry. *Overseas Family* is a weekly in tabloid format, published by Marion von Rospach, the controversial and enterprising publisher also of the *Overseas Weekly.* Both are published in Frankfurt (the *Weekly* also in Hong Kong) and are popular among enlisted personnel though frowned on by many officers. *Overseas Family* offers columns on cooking, housing, child care for the military housewife and is described as "basically a local community newspaper." It has special travel and entertainment supplements. Total paid circulation is 18,510 for the European edition. Its better known brother, sometimes called the "Over-sexed Weekly" due to its sensational exposes and pin-ups, is banned from many military installations. Offering both European and Pacific editions, it has a circulation of 28,472.

Published since 1955 for wives of Armed Forces and Foreign Service personnel, *U.S. Lady* acts as a monthly guide on overseas living, travel, and caring for children. Features play up personal experiences, both the humorous and the practical. Departments give hints on how to stretch the dollar, how to live a fuller and easier life abroad. Circulation is around 30,000.

There also are the American Armed Forces Newspapers, published by the W. B. Bradbury Company for military personnel and comprising 150 different papers with a total, non-paid circulation of 1,454,026. Bradbury also publishes American Armed Forces Features, distributed as color comics sections with the newspapers and totaling a non-paid circulation of 803,526. Advertising of course picks up the tab.

Finally there is *The Retired Officer*—and the veterans' magazines! *The Retired Officer* is for commissioned personnel and their families of all the Armed Forces. It reports on legislation and governmental action affecting retirement rights and benefits; runs articles of a historic and cultural nature. And, "since most readers are either in or planning a second management career, coverage of business and career opportunities is an important editorial feature." Its total circulation is 96,522, 97 per cent paid.

GI bills, veterans' benefits, and pensions have rewarded those who fought the nation's wars, probably in large part because veterans' organizations have fought for their interests. The oldest organization is The Veterans of Foreign Wars, founded in 1899. It has a membership of 1,290,162 and its magazine is *V.F.W.* This monthly, established in 1914, circulates to all members and has an eight-man staff including a Washington correspondent.

In a recent issue, the cover featured the nameplate in large white initials against a purple background and below, in full color, the Purple Heart medal surrounded by caps of the four major services. The lead article featured military cemeteries and pilgrimages by loved ones. It was followed by a story on "Snowmobiling" and "How to Play Russian Roulette and Win," a how-to buy a good used car. Regular departments, often written by national V.F.W. officers, include "Along the Red Front," a warning against Communism; "National Security," "Capitol Digest," and "The Best of Yank," excerpts from the World War II service publication. Layout, embodying a wide variety of one-color, utilizes formal and informal balance. Photographs illustrate all articles. Advertising is of the mail-order variety.

The American Legion is that association's monthly, circulated mainly to the membership of 2,500,000. It was established in 1919, the same year the organization was founded, right after World War I. Its editors spell out their policy to publish "a general-interest consumer magazine," with major articles on world events, subjects of broad consumer interest, and "milestones of history." Departments include a Washington letter, outdoor life, and humor pages while a center section stresses American Legion news and information on veterans' affairs. A regular feature presents opposite views on major issues by Congressmen. Large action photographs and effective pen-and-ink sketches embellish modern asymmetrical layouts, aided by attractive use of one-color for bylines, initials, rules and art. Several national display ads appear, along with mail-order items.

The third veterans' magazine is *The DAV* of the Disabled American Veterans. A monthly, it goes as paid circulation to the 240,000 members and also has a non-paid distribution of 15,000. *DAV Magazine* was established in 1960, succeeding an organization newspaper which had its origin with the organization in 1920.

Science Tells Its Story

In our universe which science has done so much to explore and explain, the problem of communication is still one of its great problems. The scientist with his prolonged, detailed training is a million light years away from the average man—not only in his work but also in communicating what that work *means*. This is partly due to the intricacies of science, partly the responsibility of the scientist due to his reluctance or inability to communicate intelligibly, largely because the ordinary man can't or won't try to learn and understand.

Scientific magazines and magazines about science have reached out to help bridge the gulf. Two in particular have served as important links among the sciences (which, due to specialization, have become further apart in understanding each other while, at the same time, their hypotheses and empirical findings bind them closer together) and also with mankind. A great challenge still confronts the scientist and the communicator—to translate and interpret science to the layman and to government leaders so that they can act rationally and wisely. Specialized science publications must step up their efforts to create clear communication so that science may lift man to a better life rather than be used to destroy all life.

The two most successful communicators have been *Science* and *Scientific American*. *Science* is the official publication of the American Association for Advancement of Science, the scientific society for 115,512 scientists from every discipline. The association itself was founded in 1848 with four main objectives: "To further the work of scientists, to facilitate cooperation among them, to improve the effectiveness of science in the promotion of human welfare, and to increase public understanding and appreciation of the importance and promise of the methods of science in human progress."

Particularly in keeping with its fourth aim, in 1880 A.A.A.S. founded *Science* as "a journal for the scientific community." Circulation is 139,357. Its editorial policy seeks "to publish information rapidly while maintaining the reviewing procedures customary among scientific societies. It contains articles on new developments in the various disciplines; reports of current research work in university, government, and industrial laboratories; appraisals of scientific books; summaries of research results presented at selected scientific meetings; and news on the interactions between science and public policy. It also provides a forum for discussion of issues, both scientific and political,

209

related to the advancement of science, including presentation of minority or conflicting views upon which scientists are not entirely agreed."

To see how it practices this editorial policy, let's examine some recent issues. The logotype, *Science*, extends in red Stymie capitals above the association's name at the top of the cover. Below it, a single large black-and-white picture, bleed at the bottom, may demonstrate the marvels of electron microscopic photography with the portrait of a deep seashell's spines or the supramolecular structure of semicrystalline polymers. Lead articles have concerned "Ultraviolet Spectra of Stars" or "Federal Science Policy." Considerable space is given to the reports which are apt to be more abstruse. Sample report titles: "Creatine Kinase and Adolase in Serum: Abnormality Common to Acute Psychoses" or "Extra-terrestrial Life Detection Based on Oxygen Isotope Exchange Reactions." Departments include an editorial, letters, news and comment, reviews, and meeting coverage. Simple and unrelieved black-and-white layout in three columns, with small heads and black-and-white illustrations, is dignified to the point of grayness. Limited advertising primarily involves scientific instruments and equipment.

Certainly this is reporting of current developments and research. The forum is definitely provided and used in the letters section regularly. This weekly has a total paid circulation of 137,000, of which 83 per cent is association membership.

Scientific American was founded in 1845 as a weekly by Rufus Porter, an inventor and painter, who had the misfortune to have his offices burned after a couple of months of publishing. Financially stricken, Porter sold the magazine to Orson D. Munn and Alfred E. Beach for $800 and it reported scientific news and aided serious inventors. By the second decade of the 20th century, the magazine became a monthly concerning itself chiefly with industrial research. In 1947 circulation had dropped more than half and the Munn family sold it to a couple of former *Life* science editors, Gerard Piel and Dennis Flanagan, and Donald H. Miller Jr. The new owners decided to make it an interscience medium in which scientists could communicate with each other and with lay readers. They succeeded and *Scientific American* rose steadily in prestige and in circulation to 420,748.

Magnificent four-color photographs adorn the cover of *Scientific American* below a 48-point all-cap logotype, black against the white margins. Editorial content is extensive, running as high as 150 pages in the larger issues, and the authors of the articles are impressive in positions and degrees held, with many Nobel prize-winners represented. There are two main divisions, articles and departments. The articles carry such titles as "The Sexual Life of Mosquito" and "Oxygen in Steelmaking." As one of my students commented,

210

"Surprisingly, the magazine is very readable even if one is not too scientifically orientated. Most of the articles can be understood with a basic background in science. The style is really refreshing. For some reason, one expects the articles to be formal and text-bookishly dull. Actually they are informal and personal, often giving the history of the subject, how the hypothesis was formed, developed, and proven."

"Science and the Citizen" is one of the leading departments; others include "Mathematical Games" and "The Amateur Scientist." Most of the material in both departments and articles reports on applied rather than theoretical science. Layouts are clear, simple, and illustrations, appearing with every major story, are examples of masterful photography or take the form of effective charts. Advertisements feature computers, photo-copiers, measuring instruments as well as such consumer products or services as automobiles, airlines, telephones.

There is a third publication, useful to the layman especially for its clear presentation, which deserves attention also for its origin and purpose. *Science News* originates from Science Service, Inc., established by E. W. Scripps, who built the Scripps-Howard communications empire. The publication was founded in 1922 as a weekly and has a paid circulation of 82,500. *Science News* is edited for professional scientists, science teachers and students, as well as the lay reader. Each issue reports on current science happenings.

Science News runs to a very simple format, a one-color cover with 20 pages inside of plain black-and-white news magazine layout. The cover carries the name in over-fancy capitals superimposed upon a stylized one-color branch, above a large and generally static photograph in black and white. Overlines above story titles carry an identifying label—"paleontology" and the like. Most stories are short, written in a rather dry news style, although occasionally some trace of feature life may be observed. Brief notes are offered on books and films of the week.

The scientist (and to some degree, other readers) is served by two other general science publications, *Scientific Research* and the *American Scientist*. *Scientific Research*, published by McGraw-Hill and founded in 1965, is subtitled a "news magazine for scientists." It has a controlled circulation of 55,518, distributed bi-weekly to institutions and universities, and to medical, hospital, industrial, and governmental research laboratories. The circulation ratio is 36 per cent to physicists, 33 per cent to chemists, 30 per cent to life biological scientists. The editorial policy calls for four or five pages of concise science news, features from Washington "and other points where science policy is made, and timely technical articles which review progress in research." Reports also cover major scientific meetings and new products for research.

211

In format much resembling general news magazines, the cover is in deep black, with a full-color photograph of some scientific news event, topped by logotype in red sans-serif capitals. The organization of editorial matter seems somewhat haphazard, perhaps due to the interjection of advertisements throughout the book, between articles and their individual pages. This undoubtedly is largely due to a desire to provide maximum returns for the advertisers who make the controlled circulation possible. (There may be a question of whether it is self-defeating when it comes to readership.) Layout utilizes three columns with drawings and photographs presented in black and white, one-color, or full-color. Article style is concise and to the point, befitting a news magazine.

The American Scientist is the quarterly publication of Sigma Xi, the scientific research society. It summarizes what it considers significant new research and reviews new books. Initiated in 1911, its paid circulation is 122,981.

Professional associations for individual sciences and commercial publishers are responsible for other scientific or applied science publications. Sometimes they combine forces, as in the case of the American Chemical Society and the Reinhold Publishing Corporation, a subsidiary of Chapman-Reinhold which, as we have seen, also publishes medical and nursing titles. Litton Publications, Inc., acquired all the Reinhold and Chapman-Reinhold properties in 1968. A more detailed account of this major group publisher is presented in chapter 11 but we will review the leading publications here.

Reinhold's own properties total three monthlies in other fields and two chemical annual catalogs. It provides advertising sales management for 16 publications of the American Chemical Society, an arrangement dating back to 1923 and performed to mutual benefit and satisfaction since. The earliest ACS periodical, *Journal of the American Chemical Society*, dates back to 1879. A 17th ACS publication, the *Journal of Chemical Education*, is published by its Division of Chemical Education. There also are two more for a total of 19 A.C.S. publications. Circulation for all 17 totals approximately 400,000. Two others are published by cooperative sections of the organization.

Chemical publications of all publishers number more than 45. Not counting the ACS periodicals, those listed in the "Chemical and Chemical Processes" category alone ranked eleventh in advertising page volume among the 159 classifications listed in the SRDS Business Publications directory, according to a SRDS survey published in 1967. Several other professional chemical and chemical engineering associations publish periodicals, and a number of commercial publishers have major properties in this field and in the related area of industrial applications. Important journals include *Chemical Engineering Pro-*

212

gress, of the American Institute of Chemical Engineers, and McGraw-Hill's *Chemical Engineering* and *Chemical Week*.

All of these and the ACS *Chemical & Engineering News* are in head-on competition for advertising and circulation. *Chemical & Engineering News*, a weekly established in 1923, has the largest circulation, 130,875 paid. (Of course it has a built-in start with 113,613 ACS members as subscribers.) It also claims the largest circulation in industry, management, and engineering-scientific circles, and the largest editorial staff with 45. From 1965 to 1967, it won six awards for editorial excellence.

Chemical Engineering, of McGraw-Hill, dates back to 1902 and its circulation is 67,199 paid. It claims a clear first in total advertising pages (in 1967), and that it is read by more buyers of more products than any other publication in chemical processing industry. It is a bi-weekly. *Chemical Week*, also of McGraw-Hill, was established in 1914 and has a paid circulation of 59,938. It states, "In over 100 studies among customers and prospects of chemical process industry advertisers, *Chemical Week* has been a constant front-runner . . . almost universally 1st among chemicals buyers, 2nd in equipment surveys and 1st among buyers of engineering / construction and other services." Its contents are produced by a 36-man staff.

The AICE entry, *Chemical Engineering Progress*, founded in 1947, is a monthly with a circulation of 31,783 paid, of which 87 per cent is membership. Its promotion declares "We don't have the most . . . only the best!" A fourth publication is *Chemical Processing*, established in 1938 and published in 13 issues annually by Putman Publishing Company, which declares that it "serves supervisory-management men responsible for 'running the plants'—contrasting sharply with publications containing technical education of chemists, engineers, etc." Its controlled circulation is 75,071.

All the publications testify to one fact, the size and importance of chemistry in modern life and industry. During 1968, the chemical process industry was scheduled to spend $10 billion on plants and equipment (over one-third of all money spent by manufacturing) and $70 billion on raw materials, energy and contract services—better than one-fourth of that spent by all U.S. manufacturing, according to an estimate by *Chemical Engineering*.

Physics is another science which has its own publications, published by the scientists themselves. Following the example set by the American Chemical Society and impelled by financial pressures of the Depression, three scientific organizations, the American Physical Society, Optical Society, and Acoustical Society agreed to establish the American Institute of Physics in 1931 (joined promptly by the Society of Rheology) as detailed in chapter 11. A major publishing program resulted.

213

In 1968 the AIP published 16 journals and 3 society bulletins. It also produced 13 translation journals of Russian scientific societies. Its advertising department, representing 10 journals, scheduled an estimated 2,750 pages for 1967. The 19 publications published nearly 60,000 text pages the same year, straining printing resources which have extended as far as Ireland!

Of the 10 publications for which AIP acts as advertising representative the oldest is the *Journal of the Optical Society of America,* founded in 1917. Circulations range from the 4,055 of *Vacuum Science and Technology* to the top figure of 54,332 for *Physics Today,* which is underwritten by membership support from all the present seven sustaining societies of AIP. Physical and related fields covered by the magazines, most of them monthly, range from acoustics to optics to spectroscopy and include scientific instrumentation.

Physics Today evolved from a technical archive into a general physics publication, providing expression and communication for physicists of all varieties. Founded in 1948, its circulation today is 90 per cent associational. With a ratio of editorial to advertising of about 47 to 53 per cent, *Physics Today* is a 150-page monthly featuring a half-dozen articles and an equal number of departments. Representative articles have carried such titles as " Gravitational Waves" and "Energy Bands in Solids." Departments include "State and Society," reporting non-technical news of government grants and Congressional actions; "Phimsy," humor and whimsy; guest editorials, and meeting reports.

Symbolic and graphic art in color adorns the cover under the all-cap logotype superimposed on a white border. One- and four-color drawings and photographs illustrate the articles which are displayed with informal balance embodying plenty of white space. Advertisements even appear between the lead articles which permits continuity rather than jumps, but which interferes also with editorial impact.

With the multiplicity and diversity of modern science and its infinite, continual splitting into more and more advanced esoteric specialties, publications proliferate infinitely also. We can name a few representative titles as a sampling. The American Institute of Biological Science publishes *BioScience.* *Geotimes* is for geologists, geophysicists, and other earth scientists. *Lipids* is a bi-monthly issued by the American Oil Chemists Society. There's the *Journal of the American Veterinary Medical Association.*

BioScience has an imaginative layout in its table of contents which other magazines might emulate. Using one-color for titles and headings, the table of contents extends over two pages and unites an editorial 28-picas wide in a design which also gives several sentences of description to each major article. After the articles come research reports, a special feature about a topic of general social concern as well as scientific interest, departments of news on new books, products, and a question-answer section on instruments. *Bio-Science*'s cover also is outstanding; a pastel watercolor of bamboo with delicate Oriental touch or photograph of starfish in a tide pool, all tints of green and blue. The magazine was founded in 1951 and has an all-membership circulation of 25,000 life scientists employed in higher education, government, and industry.

All science employs empirical research and today's industry is dedicated as never before to research and development, carried out in laboratories ranging across the continent. This fast-multiplying activity of applied science and technology has been accompanied by many publications, with effective examples found in such titles as *Research/Development*, from F. D. Thompson Publications; *Industrial Research* of the company with the same name; and *Laboratory Management* of United Business Publications. These periodicals, all monthly, have circulations ranging from the 24,781 of *Laboratory Management* to the 150,283 of *Research/Development*. All were established in the 1950's or '60's and are chiefly controlled circulation. Their covers use color attractively; layout is professional, editorial matter is expert, and advertising is heavy. This is technology at work in publishing too.

Engineering

Applied science is another name for engineering which is a whole world in itself of specialized publishing, with many different continents such as civil engineering, chemical (which we've touched on under chemical periodicals), electrical, mechanical, petroleum, —plus a few self-elected upgraders such as building engineer for janitor! SRDS' Business Publication directory lists four classifications in which engineering forms part of the name: Engineering & Construction, 88 titles; Electronic Engineering, 38; Product Design Engineering, 11; and Ocean Science and Engineering, 1. All publications thus listed had a total advertising page volume in 1966 of more than 112,000 which would put engineering publication at the top, even ahead of medical. However, scrutiny reveals more than 50 of the periodicals named under Engineering & Construction as being addressed chiefly if not exclusively to contractors and builders rather than trained engineers.

On the other hand, we have seen that the Science classification includes at least four periodicals primarily devoted to engineering, and that the Chemical & Chemical Process Industries category names a dozen more. There also are at least 16 publications serving oil, gas, and petroleum engineers. Therefore a corrected total indicates around 115 different titles related primarily or in large part to engineering. So it is safe to conclude that, next to medicine,

215

publications for engineers rank second in number, and that their advertising volume may even put them in first place on that basis. Without doubt, engineering publications are of major importance.

Major publishers of engineering periodicals include several of the biggest names in specialized publications: Cahners, Chilton, Conover-Mast, Reuben H. Donnelley, McGraw-Hill, Penton, Simmon-Boardman. Then there are publishers, less known except to their own special clientele, who concentrate chiefly or exclusively on some engineering specialty: Horizon-House Microwave, Inc., in electronics; Industrial Publishing Company, in hydraulics, pneumatics, and power transmission; Technical Publishing Company, in plant and power engineering; United Technical Publications, also in electronics.

Several professional associations (besides those in chemistry and chemical engineering) issue engineering books. They include the American Institute of Mining, Metallurgical, and Petroleum Engineers, Inc., and the American Society of Mechanical Engineers. Under the generic title of *Transactions of the ASME*, the American Society of Mechanical Engineers publishes six quarterly journals in applied mechanics, basic engineering, power engineering, heat transfer, industrial engineering, and lubrication technology. Established in 1959, they have a total paid circulation of close to 30,000. The monthly *Mechanical Engineering* of the association dates back to 1907 and has a paid circulation of 50,105, 90 per cent membership, with additional unpaid distribution of 14,132 copies.

There is a complex of petroleum engineering publishers: Gulf Publishing Company, Oildom Publishing Company, Moore Publishing Company; Petroleum Publishing Company—with a total of 20 periodicals among them. Yes, engineering is big business and so are engineering publications.

One of the biggest is *The Oil and Gas Journal*, a weekly with a giant volume of advertising. Its weekly yellow and black nameplate has been familiar since the publication was established in 1902. Operated by the Petroleum Publishing Company, it has a paid circulation of 47,311.

There are more noteworthy names. McGraw-Hill's *Engineering News-Record*, a weekly established in 1874, with a circulation today of 97,205, is a landmark in that great multiple publishing house which has a good dozen engineering properties. You may recall our interview with some of these top engineering editors in Chapter 7, including A. J. Fox of *Engineering News-Record* and Harold J. McKeever, of Reuben H. Donnelley's *Roads and Streets*, founded in 1906 and distributing 56,294 copies now.

Product and design engineering means direct competition among Cahners' *Design News*, 97,290 controlled circulation; Chilton's *Product Design & De-*

216

velopment, 87,713 controlled; and the McGraw-Hill *Product Engineering*, 85,352, 96 per cent controlled. The last-named was established in 1930, the other two in 1946. *Materials Engineering*, belonging to Litton Publications through its subsidiary Chapman-Reinhold, was established in 1929 and has a 58,745 circulation.

Say "electronics" and you've given part of the title for magazines produced seemingly by every major publisher: Cahners, Chilton, Conover-Mast, Fairchild, McGraw-Hill, as well as a number of smaller houses such as Mactier, and United Technical while more popularized versions are issued by Ziff-Davis and Fawcett.

Publishers are busy commercially today with what once would have been considered "way-out." There's *Ocean Industry*, *Oceanology International*, *Ocean Product News*, *UnderSea Technology*. Also *Aerospace Technology*, *Astronautics & Aeronautics*, *Aviation Week & Space Technology*, *Space/Aeronautics*, and *Space Age News*. These are published by some of the largest multiple houses; they're not science fiction any more—not when they involve millions in advertising and several hundred thousand in circulation!

Whether science or applied science, printing presses are kept whirling in the twentieth century with publications advancing man's knowledge of his physical universe—and confronting him with the question of how he can control that knowledge!

The Work Week

SRDS's listings show building, bottling, brewing, bricks, brushes and *The American Builder*, *National Bottlers' Gazette*, *Bar Management*, *Brick and Clay Record*, *Broom Corn News*. Or maybe you are looking at the "L's", and landscape and *Landscape Architecture*, laundry and *Rental Laundry Management*, leather and *The Leather Manufacturer*, lighting and *Lighting*, linens and *Linens and Domestics*, luggage and *Luggage and Leather Goods*, lumber and *Lumber Merchant*.

All this multitude of occupational publications cover the product from commodity to consumer. Along the assembly line, the worker, the trucker, the storekeeper, the clerk each has his or her own publication, and you can continue the chain until you reach the disposal unit repairman, the garbage collector, the sewerage "engineer," and the air or water pollution expert.

Among the scores of occupations, we can pick out several for a look at their magazines. Let's take the grocery business and the grocer. There are about 30 publications for the retail grocer—or should we say "supermarket manager," as well as an individual periodical for almost every state. Several publications contend for top circulation—and one group publisher, Shamie Publications produces three regional food tabloids.

Progressive Grocer, founded in 1922, is published by the Butterick Division of American Can Company. Its controlled monthly circulation of 74,049 goes to grocery executives, managers, and owners "to provide practical 'how-to' information which will enable them to conduct their business more efficiently and profitably." *Supermarket News*, a Fairchild Publication, was established in 1952, and has a paid circulation of 61,300. Both claim to be first in readership. *Supermarket News* is a tabloid weekly newspaper in standard newspaper format, running a news summary and index to such main departments as promotion, operations, general merchandise, health and beauty, perishables. It claims first position in advertising pages for 1967.

Two other leading publications are *Food Topics* and *Chain Store Age* supermarket edition. *Food Topics*, a Conover-Mast monthly, began in 1946 and carries 70,973 controlled circulation. It singles out the retail store and its operator for primary attention. Winner of several national awards for editorial excellence, it features a profile article stressing "the unique difference of one organization," as well as half-a-dozen news and merchandising departments. *Chain Store Age* is a Lebhar-Friedman Publication with multiple editions for not only the supermarket but also drug and variety stores, each also subdivided into separate "guides" and "manuals." Established in 1925, it has a paid monthly circulation of 47,750, divided into Supermarket Executives and Supermarket Store Managers editions.

The *Nargus Bulletin* is the official publication of the National Association of Retail Grocers. As such, it has a special built-in readership appeal. Started in 1914, the *Nargus Bulletin* is a monthly edited for owners of supermarkets and multi-unit stores with the objective of providing information helpful to successful management. Its circulation is 41,535, 76 per cent paid. From its red-and-white striped cover to its glossy stock and four-colored ads, *Nargus Bulletin* offers the sheen and polish that we customarily find in trade publications. It provides special issues on such topics as promotion, and such regular departments as retailing, modern stores, Washington News, association meetings. With women responsible for buying and using groceries in the home, it's worth noting that Marie Kiefer is the editor of *Nargus Bulletin*.

Shamie Publications has three grocery tabloid papers: *Food Mart News*, for the Chicago area; *Grocers' Beacon*, serving Ohio; and *Grocers' Spotlight*, in Michigan. Two were established in the 1930's, the other in 1948; their total circulation, all controlled, is 47,568. These five-column tabloids run one-color, varying the hue monthly, on the front page. Inside, tint blocks in various shades of gray, and art sketches give more life to standing departmental heads. News reporting is the big job of these papers and they do it. The *Grocers' Spotlight* uses an unusual technique in what the editors call the "second front page," playing major stories with special emphasis.

One other magazine will be considered as an example of a company external going to town in the grocery business. It is *The Quality Grocer*, published by the Quality Bakers of America Cooperative, chiefly of course to promote their bakery products. It keeps self-promotion at a minimum, however, giving a majority of space to display tips, special merchandising ideas for store departments such as produce or dairy, and a variety of useful suggestions for better grocery management. Issued in digest-size on quality stock, this little but attractive monthly, born in 1924, goes to 29,176 grocers who receive it free—it's fully paid for by member bakers of the cooperative. To receive the magazine you have to be a food store customer of a Quality Baker. One-color is used on the cover and throughout the magazine for titles and rules.

Following this survey of a retail business, it may be worthwhile to consider an occupation which depends on personal selling—insurance. There are 41 insurance publications listed in SRDS, with different magazines issued for each major variety of insurance—life, health, fire, casualty—plus some on a state or regional basis. There are several multiple publishers in the field; two of the best known are Alfred M. Best Co, Inc., with half-a-dozen titles totaling approximately 89,000 in paid circulation, and National Underwriter Company, publishing three books, two paid and one chiefly controlled, with a circulation of 47,826.

Naturally there are associations for underwriting agencies and insurance agents. The official publication of the National Association of Insurance Agents is the monthly *American Agency Bulletin*, dating back to 1903, edited chiefly for independent agency owners. Its paid circulation of 36,741 is almost 100 per cent membership. The National Association of Life Underwriters publishes *Life Association News*, founded in 1906 and with a circulation of 96,000, 99 per cent paid and membership.

A representative magazine for the insurance agent is the Commerce Publishing Company's *Life Insurance Selling*, carrying articles on "Eight Successful Agents Describe Their Approaches," and "Selling in the Professional Market." On the cover, logotype stands out clearly in white against a solid color background and below it, article titles in black, giving a spacious, clean appearance. Layout is in three-columns and depends almost entirely on headlines, boldface, and an occasional small portrait photograph. You can call it dignified; it also is gray and static. Articles are broken up by ads, more striking in design and employing color. A dozen departments run the gamut of life

219

insurance tips, advice, and information. A no-nonsense, strictly business publication, founded in 1926 and with 34,543 paid circulation. Commerce also has *The Local Agent*, for fire and casualty business handled by general insurance agents or brokers. Established in 1929, it has a paid circulation of 19,121, features 9 or 10 articles monthly and a dozen informative departments.

Even individual agents issue publications. For example, Joe Mondino of Centralia, Ill., who gets out each month for his own customers and future prospects a little eight-page compilation of suggestions, called *The Notebook of Joe J. Mondino*. It's helped make him a life member of the Million-Dollar Roundtable!

The typewriter's invention put women in the office and the office wouldn't run without them today. While not all women workers are secretaries, the stereotyped jokes are about the girl from the stenographic pool and certainly business couldn't get along without her. There are 30 million working American women today, with their numbers growing four times as fast as the male work force. So let's shift our occupational scrutiny to women in general and secretaries in particular. Fittingly, you find their magazines listed under the SRDS classification of "Office Methods and Management!"

There is one vital commercial publication for the feminine secretary and two association magazines. McGraw-Hill has its fingers in this pie also with *Today's Secretary*, a slim book of some 60 pages for "Successful Secretaries" founded back in 1899 and going strong today with a paid circulation of 154,462. Feature articles pick out secretaries in special jobs and profile them, like the piece about Nettie Moscowitz, secretary to Mrs. Lee Wurlitzer who runs the famous musical instrument business. Or the article "Top Secret" about the industrial espionage wind which whirls around the secretary today. Then there are the useful bread-and-butter departments under "Skill Building"—typing and transcribing tests, rapid reading and vocabulary boosters, all in pages of shorthand. Fashion and beauty tips, of course, and four tan tint-blocked pages of top news items about equal civil rights for women, Social Security benefits, and new office machines. All wrapped up in a striking white-on-black cover with *Today's Secretary* reading, in block letters, from bottom to top.

The Secretary is the official 10-times a year magazine of The National Secretaries Association, edited for the career secretary—or rather the 27,841 of them who subscribe. The association's goal is "to elevate the standards of the secretarial profession and keep the secretary informed in her growing role as an extension of management." Supporting that aim are articles on office management, human relations, office design and equipment, with a continuing stress on continuing education. Departments cover "The Secretary's Library" and "Secretarial Second Savers" plus four or five other subjects of personal and business interest.

The National Federation of Business and Professional Women's Clubs, representing 178,000 members, publishes *National Business Woman* which reaches all of them as part of their dues. Its articles deal with executive training for women, a "Salute to Women in Congress," and lots of news about club achievements and national conventions. Monochromatic art and heads give color to layouts of somewhat uneven quality. The cover generally displays a photograph—of a woman at work of course! Needless to say, all of these publications are written and edited by women.

Belonging

As soon as a group has five members, it elects officers. Just as soon as it has 20 members, it starts a publication. No man living can do more than estimate how many periodicals fall in this category, but five or six hundred isn't a hazardous guess. Organization publications especially emphasize their social and fraternal benefits, their philanthropic activities. Some of the larger organizations have full-time publication staffs of as many as ten. Many of the smaller or more specialized hire one of their members as editor on a full-time or part-time basis and get the rest of the work done by a commercial printer.

There are fraternal organizations, service and civic clubs, professional associations (as we've seen in this and other chapters), welfare societies. To start off, consider the men's civic, service, or lunch clubs, whatever you call them.

The Rotarian of Rotary International is the oldest, going back to 1911 (the organization itself was created six years earlier). *The Lion* is the largest in circulation with 623,406. Two others are *Kiwanis Magazine* and *The Optimist Magazine*. And you might include the United States Junior Chamber of Commerce *Future*.

Although often believed one of the original models for Sinclair Lewis' bludgeoning satire of Babbitry, Rotary International, founded in 1905 and numbering more than 600,000 members, has also led the way among publications for men's service and luncheon organizations. *The Rotarian*, edited by Karl Krueger, has a paid circulation of 427,015, of which 90 per cent is membership. Approximately 20,000 is unpaid distribution for promotional purposes. Chief purpose of *The Rotarian* naturally is to report Rotary's activities, and also to advance its goals of international understanding and better human and community relationships. This is translated often into accounts of Rotary's meetings on a local, district, and national level.

There's a considerable amount of advertising for men's clothing, business machines, travel and vacations, but liquor and patent medicine ads are verboten. Standing reverse heads cover regular departments with "the Clubs in Action," "these Rotarians!!!," "Sale by Mail," "Where to Stay and Dine." Color is sparingly used, except for spot one-color but black-and-white photographs are a common accompaniment for articles. Writing rarely rises above the commonplace although inspirational appeals, leavened by pragmatism, are frequent.

The Rotarian's promotional advertising draws a realistic portrait of the Rotarian—average income more than $18,000, 87 per cent owners of single-family homes, 73 per cent stockholders, 39 per cent country club members, 54 per cent two-car owners. The affluent American.

Differences among such service clubs seem more a matter of age or local status—one might say, when you've seen one you've seen them all. But different organizations exist and so do different magazines. The Kiwanis International, founded in 1915, has *The Kiwanis Magazine* for its 270,000 members for whom it claims the highest median income and the highest percentage of readers who are managers or officials plus the most on several other living standards. *The Kiwanis Magazine*, established in 1917 and with a paid associational circulation of 277,481, seems more professional in layout and article content, demonstrating skill in employing art and in the diversity and breadth of subjects. Less space is devoted to Kiwanis (although regular departments do that also) and more to reading interest appeal.

Lions International started in 1917 and founded *The Lion* the next year. Organization membership is 817,275. Dramatic use of color and art dresses up *The Lion* and gives it more impact. Articles range widely from Australian aborigines to "it starts with a bird" (parrot fever). Departments of "Service" covering Lion goals of community beautification and aiding the blind, appear regularly as do, of course, reports on club meetings and members. Contributing to the success of *The Lion* is associate editor Glenn Loyd, another of our graduates and an ardent exponent of association publication. It's worth noting that state magazines also are published, with *Illinois Lions* appearing nine times a year.

The Optimist is the monthly produced by Optimist International which was founded in 1919 and has a membership of 88,241. It is a digest-sized magazine, dedicated as is its sponsor to the "sunny side"; established in 1921, it has a circulation of 100,000. The many snapshots undoubtedly attract readers as do all the stories about Optimist clubs. This does not attempt to compete with general magazines; it's unabashedly for Optimists and, as their own, it may well be on the right path.

While less a lunch and service club than a younger chamber of commerce group, the United States Junior Chamber of Commerce has features that closely exemplify both, not the least of which is its pocket-sized *Future*. From its bright colored cover to the "JCI World" section introduced by a second cover in color, *Future* uses its some 60 pages almost exclusively for features and short items about the Jaycees. *Future* was founded in 1938 and serves a circulation of 279,062, almost 100 per cent membership.

Claiming lineage as ancient as Solomon's Temple and certainly with roots in the 14th century, the Masons proudly point to George Washington as a Grand Master and paved the way for many other fraternal orders to come. With a mystic ritual and ceremonies full of symbolism Masonry led to the creation of a menagerie of Elks, Moose, Eagles, all men's societies to express man's social, spiritual, and fraternal nature. The Odd Fellows trace their origin back to 1819; the Knights of Columbus to 1892. Women's auxiliaries, junior societies, and offshoot groups abound. Publications serve the membership of all these bodies, nationally and in many of the states.

Two of these orders have publications with circulations of more than a million, *The Elks Magazine*, 1,443,749 (90 per cent associational; total membership 1,400,000), and *Columbia*, 1,056,279 (91 per cent associational; total membership 1,179,218). These periodicals, founded in 1922 and 1893 respectively, and those of other organizations have considerable resemblance—a few feature articles of general interest and a substantial number of departments devoted to organizational activities, meetings, and members. *The Elks Magazine* uses one-color generously in illustrations, full four-color for the cover; also a common characteristic is their monthly frequency and 8½ by 11 inch size. As witnessed here, circulations are almost entirely among members and paid for by annual fees.

Official magazines of other large national fraternal groups include: *The Eagle Magazine*, founded in 1913, 683,322 circulation; *Moose Magazine*, established in 1910, 865,036 circulation; *Woodmen of the World Magazine*, first published in 1891, 428,264 circulation.

In many American cities, athletic, country and yacht clubs play a considerable social role in upper-income circles and, of course, they also have their publications. Twenty club magazines of this type with a total circulation of 75,760 have a common advertising representative. Their editorial content carries photographs and news stories of social and sports activities of the members and their families. Sports gets a lot of play—golf, tennis, yachting, any athletic games. Circulations range from the *BAC Magazine*'s 2,000 of the Buffalo Athletic Club to the 8,400 of New York Athletic Club's *Winged Foot*.

Women have created many social and civic societies in today's America. Probably the largest such association is the General Federation of Women's Club's formed in 1890, with the mammoth membership of 11,000,000. Its magazine is *Clubwoman*, established in 1917, and circulating 23,371 copies. Articles promote the Federation's community and civic goals—ending pollution, conservation, aid to youth, literacy, and departments cover the usual run of club news and activities.

Hadassah is the women's Zionist organization with 317,492 members and its publication, bearing the same name, is edited for American Jewish families. Editorial material concerns Israel, and American and world Jewish life. Departments include the "Diary of a Jewish Housewife," travel, book and record reviews. The magazine was established in 1925 and has 332,966 circulation, 95 per cent paid associational.

The Association of Junior Leagues of America publishes the *Junior League Magazine* for its 99,611 members. For women with "social" (some say "society") interests, the features cover Junior League activities and community service projects in the arts, health and welfare. It was founded in 1915.

Social Welfare Organizations

The national social welfare organizations often have publications on the state and local level as well as national periodicals. Most of them are distributed free to supporters and members. The American Red Cross, organized in 1881 by Clara Barton, publishes the *American Red Cross Journal*. It was established in 1925 and circulates to 160,000 members and institutions. The National Safety Council, formed in 1913, issues the *National Safety News* which has a circulation of 42,065. Blue Cross and Blue Shield both have newsletters issued by city or state groups.

The American Cancer Society publishes both national and state magazines. *ACS Cancer News* is a quarterly intended for volunteer workers and interested contributors. It's a slim magazine of news briefs and features, bright with one color, perhaps to relieve its tragic content. *Ca* also is issued as a bimonthly in pocket-digest-size for clinicians, and is semi-medical in content.

The college student is the reader sought by *The Inter-Collegian*, a modern-looking quarterly published by the National Student Councils of the YMCA and YWCA. Dealing with serious, campus-problem subjects such as student freedom, the draft, and educational reforms, the *Inter-Collegian* displays its editorial wares with effective one-color art and dramatized layout.

Common Bonds of Communication

As professional training has become essential with increased knowledge to qualify for a profession, and as occupational employment has emphasized

224

Media/scope cover; courtesy of *Media/scope*. Copyright, 1968, by *Media/scope*.

Promotional booklet for the *NEA Journal*. Used by permission of the National Education Association, the *NEA Journal*, and Daniel Starch and Staff.

Pacific Stars and Stripes sports editor Lee J. Kavetski (wearing sun glasses) studies the day's copy which will go into the daily *Stars and Stripes* sports pages. Other sports staff members (from left to right) are Mike Berger, George Crowe and Kent Nixon. (By John Durbin.)

In its May/June 1968 issue GRADE TEACHER talks about

Promotional booklet for teacher-readers and advertisers in *Grade Teacher*; by permission of Teachers Publishing Corporation.

the importance of keeping up with know-how and new developments, the professional and occupational publications of America have proliferated into a multitude of infinite variety and consequence. With the growing complexity and geographical extent of American society, associations and organizations have sprung up to serve every interest. Today's tremendous total of specialized publications is a tribute to the need for common bonds, for sharing mutual skills and for mutual benefits.

10. Down on the Farm

W HERE are the farms of yesteryear, the barefoot boy sauntering along a dusty back road, the little red schoolhouse? Gone with the ever-spreading concrete highways reaching their tentacles through more and more green fields. Vanished with the upward thrust of the skyscraper and the outward push of the suburb.

The plowman won't plod his weary way homeward today for he'll more likely be riding a giant tractor. And when he settles back to relax after supper, he can choose from a multitude of farm magazines. There are more than 200 of them with a circulation of around 19,500,000 for the 12,300,000 men and women, boys and girls, living on farms today. Probably no other activity is more surrounded by printed advice, suggestions, and entertainment.

Once upon a time the American farmer was the average American; today he's the hired man of a big corporation. Today there are 3,250,000 farms, a decline of more than 20 per cent in the 1960's alone. Twenty years ago the average farm was 175 acres; it has since doubled in size. Agriculture is the No. 1 U.S. industry, with assets of $275 billion, and big companies have supplanted the family farm. In turn, farm magazines have become more technical and more specialized.

Early Farm Magazines

Early in the history of American magazines, there appeared publications for the farmer and his family. Perhaps the earliest of these was the *Christian's Scholar's and Farmer's Magazine* in 1789, with serious articles on rhetoric,

226

theology—and farming, among a multitude of semi-intellectual subjects. In 1810 came the *Agricultural Museum* and, after the 1830's, a bumper crop including the *Genesee Farmer*, 1831; the *Prairie Farmer*, 1840; *Southern Planter*, 1840; *Ohio Farmer*, 1848; and *Farm Journal*, 1877. All the last four are still published today and so farming journals are among the most long-lived of magazines.

As may be seen, regional publications were among the earliest, and they flourish vigorously today, due to geographical differences in the weather and temperature which, of course, affect farming. By 1860 more than 40 agricultural magazines had sprung into life, and they continued to grow as the nation expanded westward. Today there is at least one special farming magazine for 39 of the 50 states.

Not only are there regional and state periodicals for the farmer, but also specialized publications for every farming occupation as well as for the farm family. This writer would recognize 11 varied groups as follows: dairy and dairy breeds, diversified farming, family, farm education, farm organizations and cooperatives, field crops, fruits, nuts and vegetables, land use and conservation, livestock and breed, and poultry.

In addition, the farmer is the sought-after reader by many farm supply and equipment companies through their externals which constantly cajole and persuade him to use their products. Another major source of farm periodicals and bulletins is government. The federal Department of Agriculture operates through both direct channels and the well-known state extension service of county agents. Probably no other human activity has been accompanied by more advice and suggestions.

The Leaders

There are only two independent general farm magazines which can claim a national circulation. They are *Farm Journal* and *Successful Farming*. *Farm Journal*, published in Philadelphia, and more than 90 years old, has a circulation of 3,056,563 in 23 different state and regional editions. *Successful Farming* is a Meredith publication, with 1,329,299 circulation, begun in Des Moines, Iowa, in 1902.

Two others are above the million-circulation total. The American Farm Bureau Federation's *Nation's Agriculture*, has a built-in circulation of 1,786,650, almost wholly to the organization's members. The other is a regional, *The Progressive Farmer*, serving the South intensively and almost exclusively.

Six rural electric cooperative publications, with a total circulation of 955,000, are represented for advertising purposes by Allied Rural Electric

Consumer Publications as a group. They are *Rural Electric News* (Illinois), *Rural* (Louisiana), *EPA News* (Mississippi), *Rural Electric Missourian* (Missouri), *Rural News* (Oklahoma), and *Texas Co-op* (Texas). The Reuben H. Donnelley commercial industrial, Electricity on the Farm, also concerns this modernization of agriculture, and reaches 705,143 readers.

Farm cooperatives are an important fact of life in modern agriculture, extending the farmer's business interests not only into rural electric power but also into oil refining and gas stations, feed, farm equipment, groceries, grain elevators, and many other ventures. It's to be expected, therefore, that farm cooperative publications flourish. *The Cooperative Consumer*, and the *Cooperative Farmer*, 182,467, are just two examples of periodicals circulating among these farmer members of cooperatives.

When one considers circulation size, there are other farm publications which require mention. They include *Capper's Weekly*, 455,422, from a famous old Kansas agricultural publisher strong in the Midwest. *Capper's Weekly* is a diversified and farm family magazine. Another revered name in agricultural publishing is Wallace, and *Wallaces Farmer*, 220,590 circulation, still represents the family which furnished two secretaries of agriculture and a vice-president. *Wallaces Farmer* is one of the *Prairie Farmer* publications, the two others being the *Prairie Farmer* itself and the *Wisconsin Agriculturist*. Then there is *Farmer-Stockman*, 411,022, concentrating on the livestock rancher and feeder, as does the *National Live Stock Producer*, 327,857. The dairy farmer has *Hoard's Dairyman*, 345,711 circulation.

Size alone, however, is not the exclusive criterion for influence and impact. Many farming publications, devoted to a single state or breed, command respect and offer saturation readership. Their strength is that they can address themselves to a single geographical area or farming specialty with undiluted emphasis.

First Place for the Farm Journal

Founded in Philadelphia by Wilmer Atkinson, the *Farm Journal* had a 200,000 circulation as long ago as the 1880's. Its low selling price, 25 cents a year, and home-grown advice made it welcome in the farm home. Today that subscription price has risen to $1—a remarkable bargain for the leading monthly in its field, and indicative of the pricing policy that has made most farm magazines the most stable buy to be found in an inflated world.

Not only is *Farm Journal* a good buy, it's also almost as timely as the daily paper. Despite its alphabetical range of 26 editions, identified from A to Z, and many split-runs for advertising, its readers get the magazine within four days of its editorial deadline. For an example of the speed and force with

228

which *Farm Journal* operates, on Aug. 8, 1966, Secretary of Agriculture Orville Freeman announced that wheat allotments would increase 15 per cent. Six staffers were put "to work on the story. Four field editors queried farmers all the way from Spokane, Wash., through the Great Plains and Corn Belt to eastern Ohio. Our farm policy editor dug into just what the Secretary's offer is. Our crops editor dealt with crop-production aspects . . . we were able to get this story to some readers by Aug. 20, and to all three million of them the week of Aug. 21."

Two other farm publications of prestige and influence have been absorbed by *Farm Journal*. In 1939, *Farmer's Wife* was acquired and if you turn to the middle of *Farm Journal* today, you'll find there a colorful cover for *Farmer's Wife* and following it, a magazine within a magazine. Once a separate publication with a circulation of more than a million in its own right, today it still offers feminine reading for the woman on the farm.

Once printed in Albany, N.Y., the *Country Gentleman* moved when the Curtis Publishing Company added it to its Philadelphia magazine family. But when Curtis found itself financially hard-pressed in mid-20th century, despite the high circulation which made *Country Gentleman* a major competitor of *Farm Journal*, it sold the magazine to its chief rival.

Today the *Farm Journal* has a clear circulation lead and maintains its editorial policy of "service to families who own, rent, or operate farm land or to those doing business with farmers." While its editorial layouts are not lavish with color (although a few four-color pages do appear), its contents range widely and thoroughly over many subjects of maximum farm interest. Looking at a few sample copies we see regular departments covering "Farmcast," specific advice to farmers about what to grow, when and how to buy or sell; a Washington report on what the government, that agricultural Santa Claus, has up its sleeve; "Farm Business," a feature on how to manage most profitably; "Today in the Central States," news items varying by edition; machinery and weather news: jokes and cartoons, and the editorial page.

Articles are mixed up thoroughly with the ads, only a few straight editorial pages running without a break. Mostly staff-written, they deal with co-ops, milk marketing, handling of surpluses, grain dryers, protein supplements—the bread and butter information of vital concern to the working farmer. There are many columns of "news," much of it in the form of reports on applied scientific and technical information on recent research developments—*Farm Journal* terms itself a "news magazine."

Behind the second cover in full-color adorning "The Farmer's Wife" are the features which carry out its motto of "A good life as well as a good living." You may read about a supper-time barbecue, recipes for cheese-spinach salad or fudge ripple bars, or a couple of pages on green and golden squash. There'll be a page or more on fashions and patterns, poetry and letters, and girl talk from the woman editor. The 30-odd pages will never throw a scare into the regular magazines for women, but they do offer a distaff balance for the masculine farming know-how.

Jam-packed with ads, the *Farm Journal* also gives special attention through special editions to farming specialties. In special sections bound into the regular magazine, and rotated on a quarterly basis, there are beef, dairy, and hog extras. Also the advertiser may feature two different products in alternate copies of the magazine, "so that each ad will be distributed uniformly to half the total circulation."

As it nears its hundredth birthday, *Farm Journal* is vigorous and strong, a pioneer and pace-setter still.

How to Succeed with Successful Farming

In the highly competitive world of agricultural publications, only one offers a national challenge. Meredith's *Successful Farming* is that rival and it has operated from a strategic base in the center of Iowa's rich corn country ever since 1902. A wedding gift from his grandfather, the "Farmer's Tribune" came to E. T. Meredith when he reached 19. He had worked on the paper already and was to work even harder. But he had ideas for a magazine and seven years later, with his wife's help, he got it going under the name *Successful Farming*.

Today's it's still vitally concerned with successful farming by top farmers who make money by first-class farm management. That's the editorial policy and goal of editor Dick Hanson, born and raised in the little country town of Algona in northwest Iowa. Editor of *Successful Farming* since 1949, Hanson looks and acts younger than he is, for he's enthusiastic about his job and he talks about it with a contagious combination of confidence and eagerness.

"We're a trade paper for farmers—that's our philosophy," said Hanson, leaning forward over his desk. "Our number one question is this—does the article give the farmer and his wife *management* help in his or her business. All our editing has that aim, to help solve the management problems of families that make farming their business.

"We're not just a service magazine for farmers; we're a service-oriented management guide for a select group of businessmen—the best farmers in the country."

Hanson's not only enthusiastic, he knows what he's talking about. He's from Ames as it's familiarly known, a graduate of what is now Iowa State

230

University with his degree in agricultural journalism. His first job with *Successful Farming* was as agricultural engineering editor. Since then, before getting the top rung, he's worked as crops and soils editor, farm management editor, livestock editor.

"We emphasize five main subjects in our articles," and he ticked them off for me on his fingers. "The top money crops grown in the top half of the United States—corn, wheat, soybeans, forage crops, sorghums and range grasses. Second, the principal livestock classes, hogs, feeder cattle, beef cow herds, and dairy. Machinery and building needs of crop and livestock farmers. The increasingly important money problems of big capital and credit-using readers. The always important women on the farm, active partners with their husbands."

I asked about that audience of farm men and women, and how much they knew about it.

"Quite a lot. We make a lot of reader studies and we get good cooperation from them. Perhaps our dollar-bill gimmick has something to do with it——"

"What do you mean—dollar-bill gimmick?"

"When we send out a reader questionnaire, we enclose a crisp, new dollar bill for their time and trouble. That helps to get a surprisingly high response—and we get to know, really know, our readers.

"Personal face-to-face contact, however, is what we depend on most. We require our editors to go out constantly, talking with farmers. One of our main criteria for hiring a man is, does he have the personality to go out and talk farm language convincingly.

"Certain things we know. We qualify each subscriber. That means circulation field men, who're responsible for about half our subscriptions. The other half come by mail. Each subscriber must either own and operate a farm, live on a farm as tenant, or be in a farm-related business. Our circulation is concentrated in the upper Midwest, New York, and Pennsylvania."

The ABC report certainly testifies to that—77.3 per cent of *SF*'s circulation is in the 12 Midwestern states. Refer to the maps reproduced in this chapter.

"And we know our audience comes from the larger farms. Incidentally we know that the number of incorporated farms has increased so far as family corporations are concerned, but that the number of corporate farms has not."

I asked about their editorial policy and articles. How did they attract and hold this select farm audience?

"We give management advice and counsel rather than trying to be a farm home paper," Dick Hanson said, stretching his arms high. He looks like a husky farmer himself, blond, rugged, unassuming but quietly confident. "Our

231

anticipation for the future is even more of the same—an increase in pages dealing with money management and a decrease in such elemental basics as how-to-do-it.

"We believe *Successful Farming* can give management advice better than the county agent or a professional farm management service. *Successful Farming* is inexpensive. It's widely read. It's reliable. It brings new help every month. It's timely. It presents the latest developments. It covers all major phases of the farming enterprise. Where else can a farmer get that kind of management service?"

But where and how does *Successful Farming* find the staff to supply such service?

"That's a good question and the answers aren't easy. They've got to be good, trained men to meet the needs of our readers—think of it, more than a million farm families who account for two-thirds of American agricultural production!

"We recruit new staff from the ag journalism schools and they start at from $8,500 to $9,500. Experienced personnel we often get from the extension services. They all *must* have a farming background. We've got 11 editors. Knowing how to write well is a must, and skill in editing. Layout and photographic work is handled through the central art department. Our content is moving to specialized articles for specialized farmers. We don't expect 100 per cent readership on each article. Politically and in regard to farm organizations, we don't take sides—we aim to present all important viewpoints, with plenty of space for reader reaction."

A look at *Successful Farming* underwrites Hanson's statements. Inside the vivid four-color cover, blue sky and red A-frame hog house, green fields, and six hungry piglets. After pages for Washington news, money, machinery, and weather, comes the "Price Outlook and What's New" for dairy, crops, beef, hogs, and sheep. There are special articles under each of those main headings, too, plus machinery. Opposite a green and blue photograph of a mechanical dinosaur spewing out sorghum is the story titled "Let's take another look at the high-yielding grass forages." Next, under pictures of black and russet calves and bulls, is a report on "Beef Crossbreeding: they make it work" and it goes into detail on Angus × Hereford and Shorthorn × Angus × Hereford and relative daily gain.

"*Successful Farming*'s editorial purpose," Hanson emphasized, "is to serve the management needs of families that make farming their business . . . and to provide this service in the form of timely decision-making guidance for the total farm operation. The basic objective of this editorial philosophy is to move readers to action."

There are special editions on hog, beef, and dairy and, in addition to the regular magazine, the Successful Farming Books, such as "Soils and Crops," 112 all-editorial, no-advertising pages, many in full-color, in the 11th edition. Ten per cent of this book content is new material, 90 per cent revised and updated from the magazine. The books are sold only through the circulation salesmen.

Successful Farming has its eyes on the future and future farmer. It seeks to build future circulation through the Vo-Ag program in high schools, supplies a special Vo-Ag kit with teaching guides and wall charts for school use, and offers a special circulation rate for classrooms. Meredith also furnishes financial aid for agricultural education through national 4-H scholarships.

Regional Rulers

Supreme among the regional publications of agriculture for its long history and circulation size is *The Progressive Farmer*, born in 1886, which has 1,254,928 subscribers in the South. Outside Dixie (and the Southwestern states) there is only a scattering of less than 60,000 subscribers, divided among the border states, Colorado and New Mexico. Alaska has 38, certainly homesick Confederates!

The Progressive Farmer is the story of one man's life, Clarence Poe, a North Carolinian who started writing for the little farm paper when he was 14, joined its staff at 16, became the owner at 22, and was still serving as editor 60 years later. In a sentimental and thoroughly Southern story, "My First 80 Years," Poe describes how he grew with the magazine from less than 5,000 readers to its million-plus stature, fighting crop and livestock pests, working to lift the Southern farm out of the morass of its minimal earning power of $500 a year.

For Poe it was a crusade against poverty and ignorance, eroded land and human lives. While his main battle was for first-class farming, he was in the forefront of every vital social cause—child labor in the cotton mills, chain gangs on the county roads, backward country schools, hookworm, and quack peddlers.

The Progressive Farmer has an attractive dress, from its colorful cover to its special inside, second cover, titled "Southern Farm Living," which precedes a dozen pages of fashions, recipes, and teen-age features. Extra large in $10\frac{1}{2}''$ by $13''$, the pages give room for maximum display. As with many farm publications, articles are mixed with ads except on a few rare pages, thus distracting from maximum editorial effect but undoubtedly pleasing the advertisers. Content ranges over livestock, field crops, and equipment, with many short items and half-a-dozen regular agricultural departments.

Concentrating its 455,442 circulation in the central United States, *Capper's*

233

Weekly provides general reading for the farm family as well as helpful advice for the farmer. With its headquarters in Topeka, Kansas, the bulk of its readership is in Kansas and the adjacent states of Iowa, Nebraska, Oklahoma, Missouri, and Colorado. It represents the remaining magazine member of Capper Publications, Inc., a mid-century communications stronghold of newspapers, periodicals, and radio-TV. By the early 1960's, Capper divested itself of its other magazine interests, including *Capper's Farmer* and sold its holdings in several state farm publications.

Home State Farm Publications acquired considerable Capper property in 1961—the *Kansas Farmer*, the *Missouri Ruralist*, the *Michigan Farmer*, the *Pennsylvania Farmer*, and the *Ohio Farmer*. Home State itself was purchased by Harcourt, Brace & World in 1967 and renamed The Harvest Publishing Company with its main offices in Cleveland. Their circulations range around the 112–20 thousand mark, with the *Kansas Farmer*, the only member below that figure, at 97,125. While the central office handles advertising and printing, state editors dig up and write many of the articles and, as their promotion states, these state farm publications stress "local" coverage.

The Oklahoma Publishing Company operates the three state farm publications which serve the adjoining areas of Oklahoma, Texas, and Kansas. First of the trio was the *Oklahoma Farmer-Stockman* which traces its origin back to half-a-dozen other pioneer farming journals, starting in 1893, and absorbed and merged along the way. The surviving *Farmer-Stockman* itself was established under that name in 1911 and grew under the editorship of Carl C. Williams. Expansion into Texas and Kansas followed in 1943 and 1961—each periodical carries the name of its state and *Farmer-Stockman*. Circulation for the three is more than 400,000. The parent company also operates, under the direction of E. K. Gaylord, president, and Edward L. Gaylord, executive vice president, the Daily Oklahoman, the Sunday Oklahoman, and the Oklahoma City Times as daily newspapers, and radio-TV stations in Oklahoma City, Tampa-St. Petersburg, Florida, Fort Worth-Dallas and Houston, Texas, and Milwaukee, Wisconsin, as well as printing plants, an express service, a packaging material company, and an oil-gas firm.

The *Prairie Farmer* (for Illinois and Indiana) is probably the best known of the three publications in its group, aided undoubtedly by its long relation to WLS, the one-time voice of the *Prairie Farmer* in Chicago! However, *Wallaces Farmer*, in Iowa, carrying a respected agricultural name, undoubtedly contends for the honor. These two and *The Farmer* (for Minnesota and the Dakotas), the *Wisconsin Agriculturalist*, and the *Nebraska Farmer* all taken together offer a total circulation of well over a million, ranging from the 100-plus thousands of the *Nebraska Farmer* to the hefty 358,000 of the *Prairie*

234

Farmer. They are all represented for advertising purposes by the Midwest Farm Paper Unit, in Chicago.

Special Breeds and Special Crops

Today's farmer is not only a big businessman but he's also a specialist served by specialized publications of infinite variety. The revolution of modern farming into a specialized business is underlined by the fact that Standard Rate & Data Service lists 110 farm-related publications in its Business Publication directory covering 12 such classifications as dairy, farm supplies, feed, fertilizer, poultry, and tobacco. Representative of the larger periodicals for specialized agricultural are *Hoard's Dairyman*, the *National Live Stock Producer*, and the *Poultry Tribune.*

Hoard's Dairyman is published in Fort Atkinson, the heart of Wisconsin's dairyland, and reaches 345,711 dairymen. Also intimately involved in dairying are the dairy breed magazines devoted to the Ayrshire, the Brown Swiss, the Guernsey and Jersey, and even the milch goat!

The *National Live Stock Producer* has cattle, not cows, as its bailiwick and 327,857 ranchers and feeders buy it regularly. This magazine also tips its hat to the stockman's wife with a couple of special pages in color on recipes, dress patterns, and feminine features. Once more, many different breeds and states make their individual readership appeals—SRDS lists eight breed magazines and 32 state or regional livestock publications.

The *Poultry Tribune* is a product of the Watt Publishing Company of Mount Morris, Ill., and testimonial to the tendency of concentrating a particular kind of specialized publishing in a single house. Or would you call it putting all your eggs in one basket?

In any case, it's natural that where specialists are needed and gathered, that's where they will be able to produce more periodicals for closely-related interests. We've seen how this is true for geographical regions. Watt demonstrates it's also profitable for periodicals written for farmers who are specialists. Celebrating its fiftieth anniversary in 1967, Watt lists seven different magazines (including one in Spanish), all about chickens and eggs, and with a total circulation of more than 270,000.

Large-scale specialized farming "has increased the need for specialized farm publications," according to Richard T. Meister, editorial director of the Meister Publishing Company, in Willoughby, Ohio. The Meister company publishes five special farming magazines and two annuals, circulating several in foreign countries as well as the United States. One of its main books, *American Fruit Grower*, was founded in 1880 and is distributed in 66 nations.

Another with many overseas readers is *American Vegetable Grower*. Home base for a third is Memphis, Tenn., where *Cotton* is published, with the international edition circulating in 88 countries.

Specialized farm publications will increase in number, in the opinion of Meister, who adds:

> The specialized farmer today needs technical information on which he can base decisions. Our publications, being specialized in nature, as opposed to general farm publications, offer the specialized grower the information he needs.
>
> There are important editorial reasons why the specialized farmer finds his specialized farm magazine the most useful to him of all the publications he reads. We are just at the beginning of chemicalization and mechanization in agriculture and his specialized farm publication keeps him up to date on the ever advance technology of raising yields and lowering costs.
>
> Also, the specialized producer with large capital outlays invested in a crop can no longer rely on someone else to promote and market his crops or to protect his interests in federal and state legislation. He needs his vertical publication to alert him when there is trouble ahead, to be a strong voice protecting his unique interests in marketing or legislation. We are happy to be a part of this new look in agricultural publishing.

Multiple publishers also include Vance Publishing Company which purchased Corn Belt Publishers, Inc., in 1966 and merged the *Drovers Telegram*, the *Livestock Reporter*, the *Stockman's Journal*, and *Drovers Journal* into one publication which retained the name of *Drovers Journal*, now published in two editions. Vance also publishes *The Packer*, established in 1893, which circulates nearly 17,000 copies to commercial fruit and vegetable growers, packers, and shippers. The *Drovers Journal* appears as a daily newspaper, five times a week.

Then there is the Northwest Farm Paper Unit, with five different *Farmers* for Idaho, Oregon, Utah, Washington, and Montana; and Southern Farm Publications, at Nashville, Tenn., serving nine southern states.

Many publications issued by farm supply, service, and equipment corporations find both free and paid circulation among farmers and the many dealers in agricultural materials. In addition to the more than a hundred periodicals listed in Standard Rate & Data Service's "Business Publications," there are scores of internals and externals distributed by manufacturers and processors.

Efficiency and economy in editorial, advertising, and printing are good reasons for this kind of concentration, and modern agriculture is served by modern magazine methods.

236

Farm Newspapers

One of the more aggressive and relatively new farm organizations is the National Farmers Union which publishes a tabloid newspaper, the *National Union Farmer*, as a monthly, skipping July and August, from its headquarters in Denver, Colorado. This is an 8-page sheet on low-priced newsprint and is given life chiefly, so far as layout is concerned, by bright red heads.

Two more general specialized farm papers appear. They are the *Daily Market Record* in Minneapolis, 2,600 circulation; and the *Oklahoma Livestock News*, published three times a week for 2,500 readers. In the livestock field, there is also the *Drovers Journal* which we have mentioned. Two related dailies appear in the produce business: New York's *Fruit & Vegetable Reporter* and the *Producer's Prices-Current* in Jersey City—each with circulations between 2,500 and 3,000.

The Future Farmer and His Girl

No occupation has been subsidized more lavishly by federal and state governments than farming, and government investment in farm education has paid off in millions of husky young farm boys wearing the navy blue jacket emblazoned with the golden emblem of the Future Farmers of America.

With headquarters in the U.S. Office of Education in Washington, the Future Farmers of America had a 1966 membership of 454,516, with branches in practically every high school. Its companion group, the Future Homemakers of America, though founded 17 years later in 1945, outnumbers it with 600,000 members.

Operating through the Extension Service of the U.S. Department of Agriculture, the 4-H Clubs, with 2,221,000 enrolled, is the giant of the youth organizations. Its *National 4-H News* has a circulation of 120,446, chiefly members, and carries monthly articles on youthful agricultural activities, reports on club activities, and personals.

The *National Future Farmer* is a colorful, handsome monthly, with rounded content of jokes and sports as well as farming features and club news. It reaches 438,549 young men in farming, average age 17 but ranging from 14 to 21, most FFA members and studying vocational agriculture in high school. The editorial profile says, " Feature articles aim to show farm youth there is a future in farming. . . . Approximately 50 per cent of the editorial content is devoted to FFA related articles, 25 per cent to technical agriculture, and 25 per cent to sports, fiction, cartoons, jokes, outdoor articles, and general interest reading for the 17-year-old."

237

Future Homemakers of America distributes *Teen Times* to each of its chapters on a ratio of one copy for every 10 members. Its current circulation, according to its editor, Mrs. Millis A. Stolbach, is approximately 66,000. Bright in layout and color, it is effectively edited to appeal to its young, enthusiastic readers.

How You Going to Keep 'Em Down on the Farm!

With the farm exodus, keeping 'em down on the farm may be a modern conundrum, but the best of the farm magazines certainly do their chores in a lively fashion. Expert advice is based on laboratory and field research, many-hued layouts offer attractive and helpful reading to today's farmer and farm wife. No matter what the agricultural specialty, there'll be a publication to meet the special need. Farm youngsters have their own periodicals; so do the many million members of farm organizations. No field of human endeavour in 20th century America receives more concentrated and sustained attention from specialized publications.

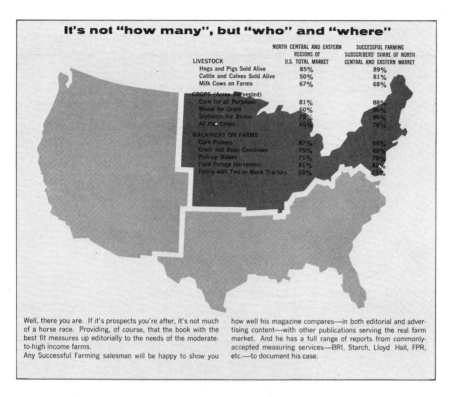

Farm management means selective farmers and selective advertisers—an advertisement for *Successful Farming*. Used by courtesy of Meredith Corporation.

The Publications of The Harvest Publishing Company
CLEVELAND, OHIO

Harcourt, Brace & World, Inc.
NEW YORK/CHICAGO/SAN FRANCISCO/ATLANTA/DALLAS

Financing the farm publication depends on advertising—the goal of this promotional page from a booklet of the Harvest Publishing Company, a subsidiary of Harcourt, Brace and World, Inc. Used by permission of the Harvest Publishing Company.

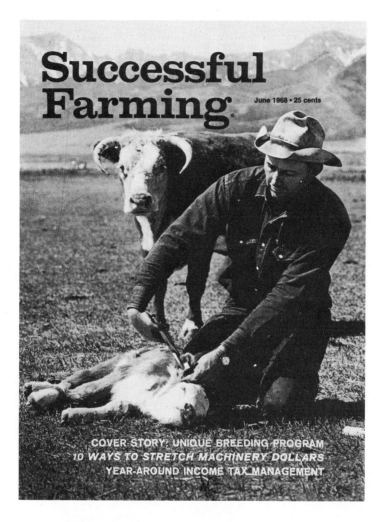

Successful Farming

June 1968 • 25 cents

COVER STORY: UNIQUE BREEDING PROGRAM
10 WAYS TO STRETCH MACHINERY DOLLARS
YEAR-AROUND INCOME TAX MANAGEMENT

Successful Farming cover; courtesy of Meredith Corporation. Copyright, June 1968, all rights reserved.

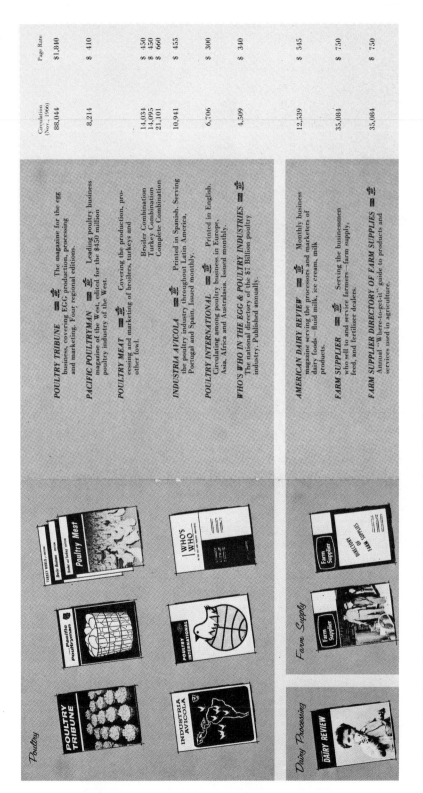

	Circulation (Nov., 1966)	Page Rate
POULTRY TRIBUNE The magazine for the egg business, covering EGG production, processing and marketing. Four regional editions.	88,044	$1,840
PACIFIC POULTRYMAN Leading poultry business magazine of the West, edited for the $450 million poultry industry of the West.	8,214	$ 410
POULTRY MEAT Covering the production, processing and marketing of broilers, turkeys and other fowl. Broiler Combination / Turkey Combination / Complete Combination	14,034 / 14,095 / 21,101	$ 450 / $ 450 / $ 660
INDUSTRIA AVICOLA Printed in Spanish. Serving the poultry industry throughout Latin America, Portugal and Spain. Issued monthly.	10,941	$ 455
POULTRY INTERNATIONAL Printed in English. Circulating among poultry business in Europe, Asia, Africa and Australasia. Issued monthly.	6,706	$ 300
WHO'S WHO IN THE EGG & POULTRY INDUSTRIES The national directory of the $7 Billion poultry industry. Published annually.	4,509	$ 340
AMERICAN DAIRY REVIEW Monthly business magazine serving the processors and marketers of dairy foods—fluid milk, ice cream, milk products.	12,539	$ 545
FARM SUPPLIER Serving the businessmen who sell to and service farmers—farm supply, feed, and fertilizer dealers.	35,084	$ 750
FARM SUPPLIER DIRECTORY OF FARM SUPPLIES Annual "Where-to-get-it" guide to products and services used in agriculture.	35,084	$ 750

Poultry

Dairy Processing

Farm Supply

Promotional booklet for farm advertisers; courtesy of Watt Publishing Company.

11. Land of the Giants

WHEN you consider the time, effort, and knowledge that go into the publishing of a single specialized publication, it is hard to calculate the truly Herculean labors involved in those giants of publishing, the multiple houses, whose properties range from 2 to 51 titles. Yet there are more than 300 of them and, as specialized publishing grows constantly in importance, the trend toward merger promises more of these giant group publishers.

There's logic in this magazine growth and concentration. The skill and information-gathering necessary to produce one engineering book can be extended to a second periodical in a related engineering field. It's Ford's law that multiplying properties accompany diminishing costs; or, if that's too rosy, that increased production means less unit cost—whether for a single magazine or a whole family of them!

Along with the expanding universe of specialized publications, there has been a corresponding development of specialized agencies to aid and serve them—associations of publishers with mutual goals and common concerns, service organizations which audit circulations with strict accounting and thus keep competition honest and advertisers happy.

In this chapter we shall consider first the multiple publishers—not all of them, but those we have chosen as outstanding or representative of a particular field of publishing. Demonstrating the close interplay of modern social institutions, several of the largest multiple publishers are principal scientific societies. Then we will take a look at the publishers' associations, AAIE, ABP, ICIE, MPA, and the vital circulation-auditing organizations, ABC, BPA,

OCC, VAC, and try to keep afloat in the alphabet soup. To do this, we ourselves propose to proceed alphabetically, starting with A!

Here's a list of the publishers and associations in the order we've considered them:

Publishers

American Aviation Publications
American Chemical Society
American Institute of Physics
American Medical Association
Bill Publications
Cahners Publishing Company (Conover-Mast)
Chilton Company
Condé Nast Publications, Inc. (Street & Smith)
Davis Publications, Inc.
Dell Publishing Company
Reuben H. Donnelley Corporation (Dun & Bradstreet, Inc.)
Fairchild Publications, Inc.
Fawcett Publications, Inc.
Haire Publishing Company
Harcourt, Brace & World, Inc. (Harvest, Ojibway)
Hearst Corporation
Johnson Publications Company, Inc.
Macfadden-Bartell Corporation
McGraw-Hill, Inc.
Magazines for Industry, Inc.
Marvel Comic Group
Meister Publishing Company
Meredith Corporation
Miller Publishing Company
Peacock Business Press
Penton Publishing Company
Petersen Publishing Company
Prairie Farmer Publishing Company
Reinhold Publishing Corporation
Simmons-Boardman Publishing Corporation
Standard Rate & Data Service
Watt Publishing Company
Williams & Wilkins Company
Ziff-Davis Publishing Company

240

Associations

American Business Press, Inc.
Magazine Publishers Association
American Society of Magazine Editors
International Council of Industrial Editors
American Association of Industrial Editors
Comics Magazine Association of America
Associated Church Press
Other Religious Associations
More Magazine Associations
Audit Associations

Multiple Publishers

American Aviation Publications

In 1937, the same year that the China Clipper began transoceanic air passenger travel, American Aviation Publications began with Wayne W. Parrish, who introduced *American Aviation* as a bi-monthly. It's been converted into a monthly and is still flying high with a circulation of 100,000, 43 percent controlled. In 1939 it was joined by *Aviation Daily*, an industry newsletter, also flourishing today. In 1968, *Aerospace Technology*, another American Aviation book, was merged with *American Aviation*.

American Aviation Publications operates the largest staff of specialized correspondents in Washington, D.C., to gather news and information for its 12 publications, nine in aviation, and 3 directories. Total circulation, a mixture of paid and controlled, is 145,600. This is the house which sets the pace in space.

President: Wayne W. Parrish, 1001 Vermont Ave., N.W., Washington, D.C.20005.

American Chemical Society

With 110,000 members, many in the huge chemical industry, the American Chemical Society, founded in 1876, is deeply involved in publishing. In 1923, it arranged with the Chemical Catalog Company, which had just published the "Condensed Chemical Dictionary," to issue the first American Chemical Society monograph, of which 145 have since been published. In the same year, the Society also appointed the company to act as advertising sales manager for all ACS periodicals, an arrangement successfully followed ever since. In the intervening years, the Chemical Catalog Company became Reinhold Publishing Corporation (see under that name), which today handles advertising

241

for 16 ACS publications. The earliest, the *Journal of the American Chemical Society*, was established in 1879. Three more periodicals are published separately by cooperative ACS sections. Total circulation, more than 400,000.

Director of Applied Publications: Dr. Richard L. Kenyon, 430 Park Ave., New York 10022.

American Institute of Physics

Four scientific societies in physics, optics, acoustics, and rheology united as the American Institute of Physics in 1931, and a year later, a fifth group, the physics teachers, joined. One of the prime purposes was to aid existing physics publications and to add new ones as needed. So *The Physical Review* was sponsored and its editor, J. T. Tate, was named adviser on publications. A second publication, *Reviews of Modern Physics*, was also adopted and Madeline M. Mitchell, who had been on its staff, was appointed publications manager. The Institute would publish all journals of all the societies through a central editorial office, utilizing a uniform size and format and a single printer. In 1932 it was decided that *The Review of Scientific Instruments* should serve as the advertising organ of the Institute, with all advertising from all physics publications concentrated in it. By World War II, both the Institute and its publications were thriving and today 19 periodicals, with total circulation of more than 120,000, and 13 Russian translation journals are published to serve the 46,000 Institute members and other physicists.

Director: H. William Koch, 335 E. 45 St., New York 10017.

American Medical Association

Medical publications, as with other specialized periodicals, are the means by which professionals keep up to date. It's logical that the largest medical association, formed in 1847, when there were only 29 United States, should also be the major medical publisher. The very first of its 13 periodicals was given birth (did an obstetrician assist?) in 1883 when editor Dr. Nathan S. Davis delivered the *Journal of the American Medical Association*. Ten publications are monthly specialty journals, then there's a weekly medical newspaper, a consumer health magazine, and eight medical directories and reference books, plus many manuals, annuals, and booklets. Total circulation, 1,450,200.

Director, Management Services Division: Russell H. Clark, 535 N. Dearborn St., Chicago, Ill. 60610.

Bill Publications

Bills and publishing have been synonymous since the early days of printing—no, not that kind of pay-me reminders, but the Bill family. A Bill was partner in the first English newspaper. Another Bill, as court printer to

King James, produced the King James version of the Bible. The American firm began in 1891 when Edward Lyman Bill gained control of *Music Trade Review*. After his death, Col. Bill's widow ran the company for years until his sons, Ray and Ed, took over in 1916 and operated the business until 1957. Many firsts in specialized publishing were initiated by Bill—in the rubber and tire field, magazines for premiums and incentives, marketing and recording, in food wholesaling. *Sales Management*, founded in 1918, was a pioneer in total selling and through its bi-weekly and special issues influences all business in marketing information. Other Bill firsts, still being published, are *Modern Tire Dealer* and *Modern Floor* while *Rubber World*, which they acquired, was also an original. Through the years, Bill has also produced *The Antiquarian* and *Tide*. Today the nine Bill Publications are distributed to a circulation of approximately 265,000 and it operates, through its book division, direct-mail sales of maps, sales aids, and books.

Director of Special Projects: Harlan Lang, 630 Third Ave., New York 10017.

Cahners Publishing Company (Conover-Mast, subsidiary)

To comprehend the complicated structure of Cahners (and several other giant multiples), you need the unscrambling talents of a cryptographer even when you have management's help. Cahners, which began as recently as 1946 with *Modern Materials Handling*, is 40 per cent owned by International Publishing Corporation Ltd. of Great Britain, the largest publishing organization in the world, and operates as its American partner. International Publishing Corporation took a major part in 1967 in forming International Business Press Associates, composed of more than 200 industrial publications in which it has an interest.

In 1968, Cahners merged into its corporate structure the major multiple Conover-Mast Publications, thus involving itself in publishing 10 more periodicals, 5 directories and convention publications. Because of a conflict of interest with *EDN*, one of its own magazines, Cahners then sold *Electro-Technology* to Industrial Research, Inc. Conover-Mast will continue to operate independently as a Cahners division. Conover-Mast, which grossed more than $19 million in 1967 is under the direction of Bud Mast Jr., chairman, and Harvey Conover Jr., both sons of the founders. Cahners already controls as subsidiaries: Industrial publications, Inc., Medalist Publications, Inc., Watson Publications, Inc., and Rogers Publishing Company. The first three have their offices in Chicago, Rogers in Denver. The over-all results create a $47 million consolidated company, second only to McGraw-Hill in size. Cahners now operates 36 regularly issued, controlled circulation publications and directories, just eight behind McGraw-Hill.

243

Norman L. Cahners intends to acquire "additional companies in the publishing field as well as diversify into other areas." "There are many reasons," he says, "for the growth of our company. I think the most important is our belief in a management philosophy which we call 'The Climate of Excellence.'"

An "editorial preview" is a regular Cahners editorial practice. Every month, each Cahners publication is scrutinized before presstime. Each article and layout and cover is displayed and the editor summarizes the issue's chief objectives. Then each departmental editor explains how his material fits in. General discussion follows with Cahners corporate executives participating. Changes are frequently made if it seems desirable, to tighten heads, revise layouts, re-edit articles.

Cahners publications are produced by more than 700 men and women working in a score of offices throughout the nation. They reach a primary audience of a million and a half, represent a marketplace in which more than 3,000 advertisers invest around $40 million annually. Headliners in circulation among the Cahners group are *Design News*, 97,300; and *Institutions*, 84,000.

Conover-Mast, which started with *Mill & Factory* in 1928, has as its pacesetter *Volume Feeding Management* with 71,000 circulation.

This is the Cahners empire—coverage of building, metalworking and plastics, food and purchasing, boats and aeronautics—the activities of modern industry and modern life.

Chairman of the Board: Norman L. Cahners, 221 Columbus Ave., Boston, Mass. 02116.

Chilton Company

Progressive in ideas and management, Chilton Company of Philadelphia has established an enviable record since its founding in 1955 in developing its properties and policies. Taking its name from a passenger on the Mayflower, Chilton owns two famous magazines established before the Civil War—*Hardware Age* and *Iron Age*, both born in 1855. But it also became a pioneer in 1959 by adopting and publicly announcing statements of corporate and editorial responsibility, thereby enhancing its position as one of the largest specialized publishers and setting a standard for all publishing.

Chilton is one of the major companies with an integrated operation, with the Newton Falls Paper Mill, Inc., as a 50 per cent owned subsidiary, and its own Printing Division for its own and outside commercial production, the great majority by offset.

Topics Publishing Company, Inc., is another Chilton subsidiary, also 50 per cent owned, and printing *Drug Topics*, founded in 1857; *Drug Topics Red Book*, and *Drug Trade News*. In 1965 it purchased the Instruments Publishing

244

Company of Pittsburgh known today as the Rimbach Publishing Company, publishers of four properties in electronics and automation as well as two buyer guides. The same year it bought *Architectural & Engineering News* and *Contractor News*. Today Chilton produces 25 publications and several directories, as well as research services, direct-mail marketing, book, and educational divisions, for an annual gross of $30 million.

But it also rightly prides itself on the many awards and prizes it has won —for example, the Jesse H. Neal Awards to *Jewelers' Circular-Keystone* whose annual gold and diamond issues are outstanding examples of excellence in graphic arts. And also on its contributions to ever higher standards for the profession of specialized publishing.

Chairman of the board: G. C. Buzby, Chestnut & 56 Sts., Philadelphia, Pa. 19139.

Condé Nast Publications, Inc. (Street & Smith, subsidiary)

When Sam Newhouse bought Condé Nast and Street & Smith in 1959 for a reported price of $9,000,000 plus stock options he added magazines to his already imposing empire of newspapers and broadcasting. Today Condé Nast publishes such diverse specialized books as *Air Progress, Analog Science Fact and Science Fiction, Bride's Magazine, Glamour, House & Garden, Mademoiselle, Vogue,* and family service and athletic annuals, 29 publications in all counting the annuals and seven foreign editions.

Condé Nast, a St. Louis boy, started with *Collier's* at $12 a week, worked up to $40,000 a year, and decided to become a publisher for himself in 1909 by buying *Vogue* and *House and Garden*. Nast aimed at the elegant and upper-class and achieved his goals until Depression 1930 wiped out much of his money. British publishing pounds bailed him out but the company ran into renewed trouble in the 1950's until Newhouse took over.

Street & Smith had been a pulp stronghold in the 1890's and early 20th century but the westerns and romances, printed on coarse paper, lost public appeal and the firm then converted in 1949 to slicks. So the company which had put out dime novels before the Civil War sold to Newhouse and ended its century-long life.

Executive Vice President: Perry L. Ruston, 420 Lexington Ave., New York 10017.

Davis Publications, Inc.

The second half of another publishing firm, B. G. Davis, left Ziff-Davis in 1955 to found his own publishing venture, one with seven monthly and bi-monthly titles today and 26 annuals and semi-annuals. Davis Publications' best known books are *Science & Mechanics*, circulating 300,000, *Ellery Queen's Mystery Magazine* with 200,414, and *Camping Journal*, 175,000. That also will give an idea of the variety of reading entertainment and how-to properties of this fast-moving firm. It has magazines for boating and camping and trailering, all related to the outdoor life, as well as electronic, woodworking, and other home hobby do-it-yourselfers. Davis gets most of its sales from the newsstands and emphasizes striking covers to get 'em. Most of its magazines also are oriented to men and boys. Davis has a different way of developing publications. If an annual sells, they may try it as a semi-annual; if that's profitable, then monthly publications might be attempted. The Ellery Queen books (there's a semi-annual too) are edited by Ellery Queen, and Davis claims it's the oldest magazine in the mystery field.

Executive Vice President: Joel Davis, 229 Park Ave. South, New York 10003.

Dell Publishing Company

Dell's mass distribution record in magazines, paperbacks, and hardcovers has been setting records through the years since George T. Delacorte founded the firm in 1919. They sold nine million copies of " Peyton Place " in paperback but that's another story. In popular publications, they sell 1,763,534 copies of Dell Modern Group, four titles such as *Modern Romance* and *Modern Screen*; 851,576 of *Ingenue*; and 310,661 of Dell Men's Group, *Inside* and *Frontpage Detective*. Dell also has quite a few women executives. There's Helen Meyer, president; M. J. Jossel, promotion director; Jeanne Alexander, publicity director; Rosalie Barrow, production head. Subsidiaries include Delacorte Press, The Dial Press, Inc., and Mayflower Books, Ltd., in England.

One of the first Dell successes was *Ballyhoo*, a humor book which went through the roof with 3,000,000 copies by its fourth issue. That was back in the 1930's and the jokes were bathroom and being broke. *Ballyhoo* was a skyrocket. When it came down, Dell already had six others out. " We've published more magazines under more titles than any publisher in the United States," Delacorte asserts. Quick moves and fast ins and outs are a Dell technique. It distributes its millions of books through warehouses from coast to coast and in Canada. This is a mass magazine business with the emphasis on mass.

"Our philosophy is to gamble," says Mrs. Meyer. "We are the largest mass-market publisher in the world. We are the only publisher with mass-market paperbacks, higher-priced quality paperbacks, hard cover books, magazines, comics, and even purse books."

President: Mrs. Helen Meyer, 750 Third Ave., New York 10017.

246

Reuben H. Donnelley Corporation (Dun & Bradstreet, Inc.)

Allied today with the major financial publishing house of Dun & Bradstreet, Inc., Reuben H. Donnelley Corporation was founded by the son of the Richard R. Donnelley who established a major printing firm in Chicago in 1864 (the two companies today have no connection). That was the year Reuben H. Donnelley was born, the man who inaugurated this company which today operates under its Magazine Publishing Division the five groups which in turn produce 18 publications as well as several directories and airline guides. Dun & Bradstreet, which became parent company in 1961, is also known of course, as the publisher of financial and business periodicals.

Reuben H. Donnelley's other major operating divisions include the telephone directory company, a marketing department, and transportation service. In the Magazine Publishing Division, there's a Municipal Group producing *Fire Engineering*, and *Water and Wastes Engineering*; the Yorke Medical Group with the three American *Journals of Cardiology, Medicine*, and *Surgery*; a Construction Group issuing *Roads and Streets*, and *Rural and Urban Roads*; and the Transportation Group with its *Air Travel* and *Official Airline Guides*. Offices in 40 locations help supply the information and are staffed by 200 men and women. Combined circulation is more than a million. Donnelley attributes its success to the principle that an honest and forthright editorial policy will attract loyal readers who, in turn, will form a market to whom advertisers wish to direct their selling messages.

General Manager: Charles S. Mill, 866 Lexington Ave., New York 10036.

Fairchild Publications, Inc. (Capital Cities Broadcasting)

The Fairchild brothers, Edmund W. and Louis E., got experience gathering news for a grocery publication and then, in 1890, bought a men's wear periodical. On this foundation they built today's business news-gathering and publishing organization with 837 reporters and correspondents in 39 U.S. and 33 foreign bureaus. The Fairchild publications, produced by 1,500 full-time employees, include eight specialized magazines and daily papers, and numerous trade directories, business books, and market research services.

In 1968, Fairchild became a subsidiary, through merger, of Capital Cities Broadcasting but will continue as a major publishing operation. Capital Cities owns and operates AM, FM, and TV in nine cities in New York, North Carolina, West Virginia, Texas, Michigan, California, New Jersey, and Rhode Island. Men's and women's wear are the principal business activities covered by the Fairchild Publications which include *Women's Wear Daily*, the *Daily News Record*, and *Home Furnishings Daily* as well as *Footwear News, Men's Wear, Electronic News, Metalworking News*, and *Supermarket News*. All of

247

these, except *Men's Wear*, the magazine founded in 1890, are in tabloid newspaper format and style.

President: John B. Fairchild, 7 E. 12 St., New York 10003.

Fawcett Publications, Inc.

Capt. Billy's Whiz Bang, a pocket-sized book of privies and rough humor, has been parlayed by the Fawcett family into a major magazine domain with seven publications, innumerable specials, and a half-dozen yearbooks. The seven magazines sell approximately 11,325,000 copies a year and include such respectable titles as *Woman's Day*, *True*, *Mechanix Illustrated*, and *Electronics Illustrated*. A couple of detective books, Christmas and other specials round out the list.

Captain Billy, the magazine, and its original Capt. Wilford H. Fawcett, have both passed on but four sons continue the family tradition. The original joke book came out after World War I where Captain Fawcett got his rank. The Fawcett ball really began rolling with *True Confessions* (now belonging to Macfadden-Bartell) in 1922, picked up momentum with *Mechanix Illustrated* in 1928, and was really flying when *True* hit the newsstands in 1936. Then Fawcett bought *Woman's Day* in 1958 and made the big time with something for both sexes. They are all big sellers with *Woman's Day*, originally a supermarket exclusive, now selling 6,610,509 copies. *True*, packed with vigorous real-life adventure, circulates 2,477,333. The third Fawcett book to make the magic million-dollar circle is *Mechanix Illustrated*, 1,489,135 circulation. All are milestones in mass merchandising of magazines.

President: W. H. Fawcett Jr., 67 W. 44 St., New York 10036.

Haire Publishing Company

Two brothers, Alphonsus P. and Andrew J. Haire, started the Haire Publishing Company in New York City in 1910 and launched their first periodical, *Dress Essentials*, the next year. Two years later, *Corset & Underwear Review* (later sold to Harcourt, Brace & World), and *Notion & Novelty Review* were added. At intervals, new properties joined the Haire parade until today there are 9 periodicals and at least an equal number of directories and show specials. *Medical Lab* was added in 1968. Thomas B. Haire, a son of Andrew, also joined the company, in 1934, and today is president.

The Haire properties range from women's apparel to accessories, from housewares to luggage, from notions to wire. Two seeming mavericks are *Medical Lab* and *Wire and Wire Products*. *Product News International* is issued jointly with The American Express Company, going to Europe, Africa, Asia in odd-numbered months and to Latin America in the even-numbered. The circulation total for the regular periodicals is approximately 113,500, divided almost equally among paid, non-paid, and mixed circulation.

Vice President and Editorial Director: Cyrus Bernstein, 111 Fourth Ave., New York 10003.

Harcourt, Brace & World, Inc. (Harvest, Ojibway, subsidiaries)

One of the world's largest publishers of books has now become one of the world's largest publishers of specialized publications. Harcourt, Brace & World acquired full ownership of Home State Farm Publications in 1967, thus taking over five state farm periodicals and two trade magazines, renaming them The Harvest Publishing Company. Then in 1968 it purchased two more state farm publications by buying Nebraska Farmer Company, publishers of the *Nebraska Farmer* and *Colorado Rancher & Farmer*. These will continue to be published by the Nebraska Farmer Publishing Company as a subsidiary.

The 1968 expansion also included other fields such as publications for education, medical practice, novelties, and apparel. Harcourt, Brace & World acquired Byrum Publications (*Physicians Management*), Brookhill Publishing (four electronics books), F. A. Owen Publishing (educational), Scott Periodicals (plumbing and home maintenance), and four apparel and novelty properties from Haire Publishing.

The major acquisition in 1968, on the basis of titles, however, was Ojibway Press, of Duluth, Minnesota, and its three subsidiaries, owners of 27 properties in 13 industries. Thus, in two years, HB&W became a major magazine publisher of at least 42 specialized publications—one, *Sponsor*, however, has been discontinued. Total circulation amounts to approximately 1,300,000. The periodical publications division of Harcourt now is known as Harbrace.

Two executives especially have contributed to HB&W and Home State. William Jovanich, head of Harcourt, Brace and World, has moved it ahead (it was founded in 1919) with a distinguished list of trade and text, fiction and non-fiction hard cover and paperbacks. James Milholland, Jr., before becoming president of Home State in 1961, had been a director of that corporation as well as a HB&W editor. One of the farm magazines, the *Pennsylvania Farmer*, was founded by his grandfather in 1877. Milholland has also been president of the Agricultural Publishers Association and a director of the Audit Bureau of Circulations, and is now president of Harbrace Publications, Inc.

The two non-farm periodicals of Harvest are *Pest Control Magazine* and *Weeds Trees and Turf*. All but one of the seven state farm publications is published in the state whose name it bears. This is a fundamental publishing principle to which Harvest adheres. They all are long-lived, ranging in age from

249

the *Michigan Farmer*'s birth in 1843 to 1877, except for the Colorado book which dates back to 1947. Total circulation of the farm publications is 641,530, with the five books of the Home State group adding up to 509,234. *Pest Control* and *Weeds Trees and Turf*, contribute 43,264 more in circulation, making a total, without counting Ojibway, of 787,494.

At its northern headquarters in Duluth, Ojibway and its subsidiaries operate marketing, research, and merchandising services and the Davidson Printing Company as well as the many specialized publications in such fields as baking and meat processing, drive-ins, gas engineering and appliances, flooring and roofing, food management, office products and paper products. Its oldest publication is *Gas Age*, founded in 1883, and the largest is *Electronic Technician*, with a paid circulation of 83,839. The Ojibway magazines include both paid and controlled circulation; total circulation is nearly 350,000.

Harcourt, Brace & World, in addition to its newly acquired specialized publications, has other subsidiaries including Longmans Canada Ltd. of Toronto and Guidance Associates of Pleasantville, N.Y.

Harcourt, Brace & World, Inc. President: William Jovanich, 757 Third Ave., New York 10017.

Harbrace Publications, Inc. President: James Milholland, Jr.

Hearst Corporation

While William Randolph Hearst may be best known to journalistic history for his chain of newspapers, there is also a formidable group of Hearst magazines and radio-TV properties. The millionaire's boy not only helped to make "yellow journalism" a byword, but he also built a very substantial list of 16 general and specialized periodicals, with total circulation of 12 million.

The Hearst general magazines are *Cosmopolitan* and *Good Housekeeping*; specialized publications are *Motor, Motor Boating, American Druggist, Sports Afield, Bride and Home, eye, Science Digest, Harper's Bazaar, House Beautiful, Town & Country*, and *Popular Mechanics* . . . women's books, reading for girls and women, for boys and men, and sportsmen. The first Hearst magazine was *Motor* in 1903. Several, however, antedate Hearst as a magazine publisher—*American Druggist* goes back to 1871, and *Good Housekeeping, Cosmopolitan*, and *Sports Afield* were founded in 1885, 1886, and 1887 successively. The oldest by far, however, is *Town and Country*, established in 1846 as *Home Journal*. The five largest circulations are those of *Good Housekeeping*, 5,660,468; *Popular Mechanics*, 1,654,373; *Sports Afield*, 1,370,123; *Cosmopolitan*, 1,031,722; and *House Beautiful*, 977,079. Hearst bought, sold, combined, or killed a variety of his properties, depending on the state of his fortunes or whims. A half-dozen international editions are published abroad. There are also a number of annuals and "specials."

250

The "really rich" are the market for *Town and Country* and *Harper's Bazaar*, mass appeal is the pitch for *Cosmopolitan* and *eye* (a new teen-ager started in 1968) and *Good Housekeeping*. Famous magazine editors like Ray Long, Herbert Mayes, Charles Hanson Towne, Carmel Snow have shaped policies and bought big-name writers and artists ranging from Fannie Hurst to Will Durant to Salvador Dali. Hearst publishers set trends and social reforms, as with the Good Housekeeping Institute and Seal of Approval, protecting the consumer and policing advertising. Hearst editors appealed to the chi-chi and the hoi polloi. In magazines as in life, the word for Hearst was—and is—paradoxical.

President, Hearst Magazines: Richard E. Deems, 250 W. 55 St., New York 10019.

Johnson Publishing Company, Inc.

Negro publishing had a hard time attracting advertising support for primarily ethnic magazines until John H. Johnson came along. On the mythic few hundred dollars from a friend, he got out the *Negro Digest* and it went well, *Ebony*, a black *Life*, really made the grade when he founded it in 1945, the advertisers answered, and today circulation is more than a million. Next was *Tan*, for Negro women, which Johnson established in 1950 and built to more than 120,000. The 1951 Johnson venture was *Jet*, miniature news-picture magazine, which acquired more than 450,000 readers. Against tough tradition, Johnson made his magazine successful as no other Negro publisher had until he came along. His home base is Chicago.

President: John H. Johnson, 1820 S. Michigan Ave., Chicago, Ill. 60616.

Since then, *Sepia*, a *Life*-type book with more general content, has also done well. Published in Fort Worth, Texas, originally in 1954, it circulates to 63,346. It is owned by the Good Publishing Company.

Macfadden-Bartell Corporation (Bartell Media Corporation)

Out of the successes and excesses of Bernarr Macfadden, a poor Illinois farm boy who found sensational publishing riches in sensation, arose the publishing house of Macfadden-Bartell. Macfadden's first love and magazine, *Physical Culture*, gave him the bankroll which fostered *True Story* and *True Detective* and then he imitated them with others bearing similar titles. Management difficulties and the depression forced Macfadden out (he died in 1955), and in 1962 the Bartell Broadcasters, Inc. took control and changed the corporate name to Macfadden-Bartell Corporation. This company has continued the magazines and the basic editorial appeal today, when it lists 16 publications with a circulation of 8,500,000. Both Macfadden-Bartell and Bartell Broadcasters are subsidiaries of Bartell Media Corporation. Bartell

251

Broadcasters operates radio stations in New York, San Diego, Calif., Milwaukee, Wisconsin, and two television stations in the Netherlands Antilles.

Eleven Macfadden-Bartell properties are for women: *True Story*, founded in 1919 and with a circulation of 2,228,842; *True Confessions*, purchased in 1963 along with *Motion Picture* from Fawcett; *True Romance, True Experience, True Love, Photoplay*, established in 1911 and most famous of the film magazines; *TV Radio Mirror, Inside TV, Silver Screen, Screenland.* Total circulation for this Women's Group, 6,440,400.

Macfadden-Bartell explains that these books are edited "specifically to working class women—sometimes called 'blue collar' or 'wage earner' women. They are largely from the homes of hourly paid workers . . . there are a number of readers geared to the working class way of life who, in government statistics, would be classified with 'white collar' or middle class groups . . . her home life, environment and sociological outlook would be part and parcel of the working class . . . the working class woman brings to her problems and conflicts an emotional rather than a logical approach."

Men and boys are the readers sought for Macfadden-Bartell's *Sport*, and men form the audience for the true factual crime story published in *True Detective*, founded in 1924 as the first of its kind. Today it has partners among the Macfadden-Bartell books in *Official Detective* and *Master Detective.* Circulation for *Sport*, established in 1946 in pioneer anticipation of the great boom in athletic interest, is 1,120,424. The total figure for the three detective periodicals is 518,205.

Pageant is the one Macfadden-Bartell property which might be classified as a general circulation magazine, edited as a blend of digest, pictorial, and Sunday feature, and selling 412,668 copies.

Vice President, Advertising and Marketing: Lloyd C. Jamieson, 205 E. 42 St., New York 10017.

McGraw-Hill, Inc.

A name synonymous with specialized publishing, that's McGraw-Hill. Where did it begin and how, this corporation which holds acknowledged first place with 48 magazines and three daily construction newspapers, with trade and technical book divisions, with information and research services that extend throughout the world, with 800 full-time staffers, 4,000 correspondents, and 20 news bureaus in the United States and abroad?

In western New York State in Chautauqua county, where James H. McGraw grew up and became a young schoolteacher. But his old high school principal who was now working for an early railroad publication lured him to New York City. There he promptly became vice president in the little publishing house when it had a financial crisis and he raised $1,000 to help. This was in 1886. (In 1967, consolidated operating revenue for McGraw-Hill was $328,284,260 and net income, $27,418,834.) By 1889, McGraw bought the publication.

Meanwhile in Wisconsin, John Hill grew up and became a locomotive engineer and did writing for a machinist magazine as a sideline. By 1888 the magazine hired him to edit the new *Locomotive Engineer*. Within eight years he owned it.

The two young publishers met while helping to form the Audit Bureau of Circulations, united their book departments in 1909, and finally consolidated all operations in 1917 when the firm of McGraw-Hill was born. Since then it has taken over many another company, large and small, and grown itself into one of the world's great publishing houses. Among its subsidiaries are the Gregg Publishing Division, the F. W. Dodge Company, Dodge Publishing Services, Information Systems Company, and the financial leader, Standard & Poor's Corporation, and six foreign operations in England, Australia, Canada, South Africa, and Latin America.

Engineering, design, building, production, maintenance, purchasing, selling—these are the major fields which McGraw-Hill publications cover. *Engineering & Mining Journal* is McGraw-Hill's oldest publication, dating back to 1866. Two others, *Textile World* and the *Real Estate Record and Builders Guide*, were started just two years later while several—*American Machinist*, *Electrical World*, and *Engineering News-Record*, were established in the next decade. *Business Week* is at the top of the list in circulation with 578,600. High circulations are also recorded for *Engineering News-Record, Chemical Week*, and *American Machinist*. Total circulation for McGraw-Hill publications is more than 2,750,000.

This is McGraw-Hill which has made an enviable record in specialized publishing, has repeatedly won top awards for its editing and coverage, and which continues to move ahead. In 1967, for example, McGraw-Hill added *33*, serving the primary-metals industry, published by Opec, Inc., which has now also become a McGraw-Hill subsidiary.

McGraw-Hill Publications, Vice President, Editorial: J. R. Callaham, 330 W. 42 St., New York 10036.

Magazines for Industry, Inc. (Cowles Communications, Inc.)

This subsidiary of Cowles Communications, Inc., publishes 18 magazines (total circulation 612,851) and 3 internationals, 4 newsletters, 2 publications in which it has a 50 per cent interest (Chilton Company has the other half), and 6 annuals and directories. Most of its periodicals are consumer-oriented—

candy, soft drinks, food and drugs, glass, medicine, packaging. Cowles itself is the operator of *Venture*, the giant *Family Circle*, and the well-known *Look*, as well as many newspapers and radio-TV stations.

Another Cowles subsidiary is Dental Survey Publications, Inc., which publishes three dental books—*Dental Survey*, *Dental Industry News*, and *Dental Laboratory Review*, which have a total circulation of 106,280.

Magazines for Industry, Inc. was launched by Don Gussow in 1944 with *Candy Industry* as his first publication. Then he added *Soft Drink Industry*, spun off a section of *Candy Industry* into *The Candy Marketer*, *Food & Drug Packaging*, *Hard Goods & Soft Goods Packaging*, as well as four others. Merger with Cowles Communications, Inc., took place in 1966. *Modern Medicine*, *Journal-Lancet*, *Geriatrics*, *Neurology*, and *Nursing Homes* were purchased by Cowles in 1967 and joined with Magazines for Industry. In 1968, three books of Bettendorf Publications, Inc., all dealing with packaging and containers, were added to Magazines for Industry. Largest circulation among the group belongs to *Modern Medicine* with 212,427.

The president of both Magazines for Industry (for which he also edited two books for 15 years) and of Cowles Business and Professional Magazines is Don Gussow, thus continuing as executive in the same multiple group which he initiated. 777 Third Ave., New York 10017.

Marvel Comic Group

Millions of comics pour from the presses and to represent this publication mammoth, we've selected Marvel Comic Group, publishers of more than 22 comic magazines plus annuals and special collections. Their most popular books are *Amazing Spider Man* and *The Fantastic Four*, and all 22 produce a total circulation of more than seven million copies, or more than 80 million annually.

Marvel Comics is a wholly owned subsidiary of Magazine Management Company, Inc., and was founded in 1939. Marvel gives chief credit for creation and development of a new line of comics, which it calls a "specialized art form for sophisticates" transformed from "a mass vehicle for children of all ages," to Stan Lee, its editor-in-chief. Lee decided in 1961 that comic superheroes should resemble real people and not just be cardboard characters. New titles were created for "sympathetic" rather than superhuman heroes.

Goodman Publishing Company, which produces the Marvel books, also publishes the Complete Adventure Group, Complete Men's Group, Complete Women's Group, My Romance Group, and Screen Stars Group, as well as cross-word puzzle periodicals.

Major comic publishers also include the Archie Comic Group, Charlton

Comics Group, Harvey Comics Group, National Comics Group, American Comics, Dell Comic, Gold Key Comics.

Editor-in-chief, Marvel Comics: Stan Lee, 625 Madison Ave., New York 10022.

Meister Publishing Company

"Growth of large-scaled specialized farms has increased the need for specialized farm publications such as we publish," says Richard T. Meister, editorial director and general manager of Meister Publishing Company.

Meister produces five specialized farming magazines and two annuals, circulates not only in the United States but also in many foreign countries. The main office is in Willoughby, Ohio. Its *American Fruit Grower* has been published continuously since 1880 and has a paid circulation of 72,921 in this country and in more than 65 foreign nations. *American Vegetable Grower*'s paid circulation of 41,850 also has many readers overseas. A third magazine, *Cotton*, is published in Memphis, Tenn., in four editions, while *Cotton International* is an annual going to 88 countries. *Farm Chemicals* and *Farm Technology*, as well as *Cotton*, have controlled circulations.

E. G. K. Meister brought publishing skill in the difficult 1930 depression years to *American Fruit Grower*, founded by Charles A. Green, a Rochester, N.Y., fruit grower and nurseryman, who edited the book for 37 years, first under the name of *Green's Fruit Grower*. Later it also absorbed two other fruit growing magazines. Today the Meister publications furnish specialized information to the specialized farmers they serve.

Editorial Director and General Manager: Richard T. Meister, 37841 Euclid Ave., Willoughby, Ohio 44094.

Meredith Corporation

A small farming paper which a 19-year-old youth received as a wedding present started a publishing career which has blossomed into a major communications enterprise. The paper was the *Farmer's Tribune*, the year was 1895, and young E. T. Meredith built it into a successful business in seven years. Then he sold it so he could establish a farming magazine, *Successful Farming*, in 1902, to serve agriculture primarily in the Middle West, the center of successful American farming.

By 1922, Meredith started another magazine which was first called *Fruit, Garden, and Home*. To fit its editorial concept of family service, it was renamed *Better Homes and Gardens* and began a phenomenal circulation rise. It reached a million copies by 1928, but that was just the beginning. Oriented to complete coverage of all family activities, the magazine really skyrocketed

255

after 1950, climbing from 3,509,000 to 7,412,669 in mid-1968, issuing as many as 78 regional and state editions for a single monthly issue. In addition, Better Homes and Gardens annuals evidenced such demand that they became Special Interest Publications, a separate department, with seven annuals selling two million copies in 1967. Meanwhile *Successful Farming* moved ahead, focused on farm management in 1968, and established a circulation of 1,329,299.

Meredith Corporation itself has expanded and diversified. Today the Magazine Division has been joined by a huge Printing Division which handles not only Meredith production but also a large volume of commercial contract work. Other divisions include Consumer Books, which sold 9.5 million copies in 1967; the Broadcasting Division with AM, FM, and TV stations in four states and a cable television operation; the Geographical Globe Division; and an Educational Division operating Lyons and Carnahan, and Appleton-Century-Crofts among its other activities. Meredith revenues in 1967 were $110,358,000 and net earnings $7,007,000.

Profits, however, are not the only measure of Meredith achievement. E. T. Meredith served his country as Secretary of Agriculture—at his death, management was left in the hands of his son, E. T. Meredith Jr. and Fred Bohen, chairman of the board. The ideal of service also has been followed by substantial support for the 4-H program for farm youth—and has been rewarded by citations for distinguished journalism.

General Manager, Magazine Division: Robert A. Burnett, 1716 Locust St., Des Moines, Iowa 50303.

Miller Publishing Company

Continuously published since 1873, *The Northwestern Miller* is the bellwether for Miller Publishing Company's 16 publications in specialized agricultural and related fields. *Feedstuffs*, a weekly international newspaper for the animal feeding industry, has parented several other Miller vertical agricultural magazines since its establishment in 1929.

Convinced that farming has become highly specialized, Miller, along with other companies in agricultural publishing, has concentrated on specialized farming publications. But it also publishes in other fields, baking, dairy products, milling, nursing, and for sporting goods dealers. Miller founded about half its present properties, the other half was acquired by purchase. In 1966 Miller bought the four magazines of Western Farm Publications, Inc., and four others from a Milwaukee company. Miller has founded magazines in the 1960's and plans steady, stable growth in the future. Total circulation of Miller publications is 285,254, with *Farm Store Merchandising* the leader at 32,572.

President: W. E. Lingren, 2501 Wayzata Blvd., Minneapolis, Minn. 55440.

256

Peacock Business Press

Peacock represents a smaller company in number of titles but one which works a single field intensively. Alliteratively, paper and Peacock go together for it has four publications concentrating on paper and packaging, two monthlies, an annual purchasing directory, and a convention paper. Founded in 1920 as Howard Publishing Company, the firm's first was *American Paper Merchant*, which today is a monthly with mixed paid and non-paid circulation of 12,000. Then in 1932 the company purchased *Paper, Film and Foil Converter*, originally established in 1927. This monthly, with 93 per cent controlled circulation out of a total of 14,768, also absorbed *American Box Maker* when it was purchased in 1945. Its assistant editor was John Ochotnicky, one of our graduates. The company, which also publishes *Building Specialties and Home Improvements*, came under new ownership when purchased by Joseph S. Peacock in 1949.

President: Joseph S. Peacock, 200 S. Prospect, Park Ridge, Ill. 60068.

Penton Publishing Company

Steel and *Foundry* are the two heavy-industry magazines which have made the name of Penton Publishing Company known throughout the industrial United States. They started from the fascination of an iron molder from Sarnia, Ontario, with printer's ink and the development of his own trade. John A. Penton had been active in founding the Brotherhood of Machinery Molders, serving as its president for six years and initiating a small paper known as the *Machinery Molders Journal*. He decided that the foundry industry, which had no publication, needed one and so he founded *The Foundry*, publishing its first issue in 1892, ignoring the discouraging warnings of friends.

That also was the first step toward establishing the Penton Publishing Company, incorporated in 1904. Through stock exchange and purchase, in its first year the company became the publisher of *Marine Review, Iron Trade Review*, and *The Patternmaker*, as well as *The Foundry*. Several of these have disappeared or been swallowed up in the magazine *Steel*, which took that name in 1930 although it can trace the origin of its absorbed ancestors back perhaps to 1868. John Penton not only founded a publishing company, he took an active role in establishing many industry associations.

Today Penton has eight publications, with total circulation of 426,255, plus directories of foundries and Great Lakes vessels. In addition to *Steel* and *Foundry*, there are: *New Equipment Digest*, with the top circulation of 103,750; *Machine Design*, a close second with 99,516 circulation; *Automation, Printing Production, Book Production Industry*, and *Packaging Digest*, all operating on a controlled circulation basis. The Penton pioneers, *Foundry* and *Steel*, have circulations respectively of 25,031 and 81,151.

257

These properties are produced in a completely integrated operation from idea to printed page, as Penton has its own, newly-constructed printing plant. Penton has won 74 national awards for editorial excellence and prides itself also on the long services of its employees who own more than 75 per cent of the company's stock.

Vice President, Marketing: David C. Kiefer, Penton Bldg., Cleveland, Ohio 44113.

Petersen Publishing Company

A 21-year-old, movie publicity man lost his job in 1947 and so he got together with a buddy and published a new magazine, calling it *Hot Rod*. Starting with a stake of $400 and his first issue of 10,000 copies in 1948, Robert Petersen has run it up to 11 publications, 10 of them in the car-hobby-recreation field. Petersen also publishes books and annuals, holds stock in an automotive racetrack, runs a film production company, owns a 470,000-acre cattle ranch and Los Angeles real estate.

The Petersen properties are built, like Petersen, around the active life. His latest book is *Wheels Afield*, for people who own camp trailers and pickup campers. He also publishes *Skin Diver Magazine*, *Guns & Ammo*, *'Teen* for 13-to-16 girls, *Hot Rod Cartoons*, and *Cartoons*. *Hot Rod*, the early favorite, is still out in front of the automotive books with 787,233 circulation despite lots of competition. Total circulation for the Petersen books is more than 3,000,000.

Owner: Robert Petersen, 5959 Hollywood Blvd., Los Angeles, Calif. 90028.

Prairie Farmer Publishing Company

While the three publications of the Prairie Farmer Publishing Company represent a total paid circulation of approximately 712,000 and serve basically the four states of Illinois, Indiana, Iowa, and Wisconsin, they cast in age, reputation, and influence one of the longer shadows in farm publishing.

The *Prairie Farmer* and its circulation of 357,802 have been active in Illinois and Indiana since its founding in 1841. *Wallaces Farmer* bears the name of a famous family in agricultural publishing, dates back to 1855, and circulates 220,590 copies chiefly in Iowa. The *Wisconsin Agriculturist* was established in 1849 and serves 132,341 farmers in that state.

Together with two other farm periodicals, *The Farmer* and the *Nebraska Farmer*, they are represented by the Midwest Farm Paper Unit for the joint sale of advertising.

Vice President and Editorial Director: Paul C. Johnson, 1230 Washington Blvd., Chicago, Ill. 60607.

Reinhold Publishing Corporation (Subsidiary of Litton Publications, Inc.)

Reinhold Publishing is active in chemical publishing, not only through its own chemical catalogues but also as the advertising sales management for the 16 periodicals of the American Chemical Society. The company began in 1915 when Ralph Reinhold and two associates formed the Chemical Catalog Co., Inc., to publish "Chemical Engineering Catalog." Four years later Reinhold organized Pencil Points Press, Inc., to publish *Pencil Points*, known today as *Progressive Architecture*. The two companies were merged in 1933 as Reinhold Publishing Corporation.

In 1966, Reinhold merged with Medical Economics, Inc., to form a new parent corporation, Chapman-Reinhold, of which the two are now subsidiaries. European and British branches were spun off as a new subsidiary, Chapman-Reinhold (Nederland) N.V., in 1967, while the book division became Reinhold Book Corporation, with more than 650 titles in science, technology, and other fields. The two Reinhold companies employ nearly 350 and have total sales of about $11 million.

Chapman-Reinhold itself became part of the giant conglomerate Litton Industries, Inc., in 1968 when the publishing house was added to Litton's more than 50 other divisions which include such diverse activities as Monroe Calculating, bank equipment, a school for computer programmers, and Great Lakes shipping lines.

Reinhold Publishing's main properties are *American Artisan*, *Heating, Piping and Air Conditioning*, *Materials Engineering*, and *Progressive Architecture* plus two annuals. Reinhold magazine circulation totals 154,141. Medical Economics, Inc., operates *Hospital Physician*, *Medical Economics*, *Medical-Surgical Review*, and *RN*, with an over-all circulation of 735,819.

Litton Publications, Inc. President: William L. Chapman, Jr.

Simmons-Boardman Publishing Corporation

"I've been working on the railroad" might be a popular line around the offices of Simmons-Boardman where many of the editorial staff have had railroad experience prior to joining this premier publisher of railroad magazines, six of them.

Simmons-Boardman traces its beginnings back to 1889 in Chicago when a young clerk named E. A. Simmons began checking exchanges for the *Railway Age-Gazette* for $5 a week. Ten years later he was getting $20 as an ad salesman for the same publication. Another magazine offered to double his salary and he told his boss, W. H. Boardman. That brought a proposition for him to buy into the business and Simmons-Boardman was born.

Its publications are considerably older than the firm. *Railway Locomotives and Cars* goes back to 1832, certainly giving it a claim to being the oldest of all existing specialized publications. That was just four years after the Baltimore & Ohio Railroad was begun as the first public railroad in the United States! The other Simmons-Boardman railroad publications also are long-established: *Railway Age* was founded in 1856; *Railway Track and Structures*, in 1884; *Railway Signaling and Communications, Railway Purchases and Stores*, both founded in 1908. *International Railway Journal* serving 114 countries, is comparatively new, established in 1960.

The other Simmons-Boardman journals for the marine and light construction industries are: *Marine Engineering/Log*, established in 1878; and *American Builder*, 1868. The company also produces several annuals and reference books. Total circulation, all paid for the railroad books and combined controlled and paid for the other two, is 205,276.

Vice President, Operations: Robert G. Lewis, 30 Church St., New York 10007.

Standard Rate & Data Service

How communication agencies and advertisers ever got along without the Standard Rate & Data Service Catalogs is a mystery we'll let someone else try to figure out. This writer considers them indispensable. There also is *Media/scope*, the SRDS magazine for ad agencies as well as advertisers. And the advertising directories. The story behind SRDS is almost as incredible as the 6,000 listing changes they process every month in their beautiful and efficient plant at Skokie, Illinois.

Basically it's the story of Walter E. Botthof who started it all. He began working as a boy of 15 on a clerical job, then selling violins even though he couldn't play one or read a musical note. Book-learning came from night school, training as a court reporter, and some day school when it could be fitted in. He got a job as salesman for the *Farmer's Weekly Dispatch*—his first contact with specialized publications but not his last! Then to *The Moving Picture World*, and then a couple of advertising agencies. Another move took him to Peoria, Illinois, as advertising manager of the "Transcript," a morning paper. G. Logan Payne, who sent him there, represented 75 newspapers. Next to Detroit to manage a new sales office for Payne.

Along the way, Botthof was finding out that there simply wasn't a reliable source for basic information about markets, rates, circulations. Botthof decided to compile the data for all the papers he represented and also for all newspapers in those cities. SRDS had been created. The year was 1919. Now there was the first high-speed information system containing data on all media of interest to buyers of national advertising space. As new media came to the fore, SRDS produced separate monthly editions for radio, for TV, until today there are 10 such services and catalogues: for Business Publications, Consumer Magazines and Farm Publications, Network, Newspaper Circulation Analysis, Newspaper Rates and Data, Spot Radio, Spot Television, Transit Advertising, Weekly Newspaper, Direct Mail Lists. For the first seven catalogues alone, more than 18,000 listings are necessary.

Similar services are provided in Canada, Mexico, France, Italy, and West Germany, the European activity as a joint venture with MacLean-Hunter Company of Canada, largest publishing house north of the border. Other SRDS subsidiaries include the Standard Directories of Advertisers, and Advertising Agencies, issued in several editions, by a subsidiary, National Register Publishing Company; the SRDS Data Division; and the Consumer / Audience Profile Service.

Media/scope's first issue went to press in 1957 and now serves a controlled circulation of 19,940.

All this from the 15-year-old boy who says modestly at 80, "In every success story, there is that magical element known as plain, everyday luck and frankly, lady luck accompanied me arm in arm on many occasions and played a very important part in the success of Standard Rate & Data Service."

Chairman of the Board: Walter E. Botthof, 5201 Old Orchard Rd., Skokie, Ill. 60076. President: C. Laury Botthof.

Watt Publishing Company

Watt Publishing Company is a perfect example of a publisher who has built on the basis of single-minded dedication to one specialized field—in this case, poultry. Back in 1917, J. W. Watt and A. A. Yoder bought the *Poultry Tribune* which had been established in 1895 by R. R. Fisher. The Watt Publishing Company had begun.

Two more books, dealing with poultry, were added by 1934. The company was growing and Leslie A. Watt returned from *Outdoor Life*, where he had been circulation manager, to supply added publishing experience. Six other competitors were added and merged, often under new titles. Today Watt has nine publications, five domestic, two international, and two directories. *Poultry Tribune*, the first Watt property, has the largest circulation, 71,314, and is devoted entirely to eggs. It has four regional editions. *Poultry Meat*, with three editions, has 12,057 circulation. Two periodicals in related fields, *American Dairy Review* and *Farm Supplier*, now are published. The two international properties, *Industria Avicola*, printed in Spanish, and *Poultry International* circulate in Latin America, Portugal, Spain, and in Europe, Asia, Africa, and Australasia, respectively. Total Watt's circulation is 161,515.

President: Leslie A. Watt, Sandstone Bldg., Mount Morris, Ill., 61054.

261

Williams & Wilkins Company

Major name in medical publishing, Williams & Wilkins Company of Baltimore produces 32 medical publications while also serving as publisher or printer for other specialized areas. Its fascinating story begins with a boy getting a toy printing press for Christmas. This so stimulated John H. Williams that he persuaded his father to buy him a real press. On it, John went into business in reality, too. The year was 1890. When he needed money for expansion, he found a friend, Henry B. Wilkins, to invest and Williams & Wilkins had been established. They brought in another young man, Edward B. Passano, as a salesman at $75 a month.

Passano not only could sell, he was a born publisher and by 1907 he became the sole owner of Williams & Wilkins. The next major step was two years later when, at the request of a Johns Hopkins professor, the company printed its first medical publication, *The Journal of Pharmacology and Experimental Therapeutics* . . . which still is published by W & W! More medical and technical publications came fast, spurred by the close proximity of the university with its famous medical school. Williams & Wilkins became the publisher of many of them in its own name, establishing a staff of expert medical editors.

They issued their first hard-cover book, a treatise on hydrogen ions, in 1920, of hundreds they were to produce. The printing plant was so busy, it split off as Waverly Press, Inc. Actually Waverly owns all common stock of Williams & Wilkins and one share of preferred, and the Passano family owns all common stock of both corporations and much of the preferred. Waverly's book operations expanded with the purchase of medical books from Little, Brown and Company and from Thomas Nelson and Sons, as well as the complete firm of William Wood and Company.

The medical publications of W & W are led by the *Journal of Nervous and Mental Diseases*, founded in 1874, and *Current Medical Digest*, established 60 years later and heading the list with a controlled circulation of 146,086. Total circulation for the company is nearly 300,000. Great care and exactness is the key to medical publishing, even when circulations are small as they are apt to be with exceedingly specialized journals.

President: William M. Passano, 428 E. Preston St., Baltimore, Maryland 21202.

Ziff-Davis Publishing Company

The modern American with plenty of time for recreation and plenty of money in his pockets is the target for the Ziff-Davis magazines which zero in on the active life. Is skiing your way of life? Then *Skiing* will help you schuss.

262

Do you sail your own boat, fly your own plane? Then *Boating* and *Flying* will add to your zest.

Ziff-Davis publishes specialty magazines not only for the active participant but also for the retailer who serves them as customers and also for the professional businessman. There's *Airline Management and Marketing* plus *Business and Commercial Aviation* for industry (and a Flying annual), as well as *Skiing Trade News*, and *Skiing International Yearbook* for ski entrepreneurs. And to help those who help you get there, *Travel Weekly* for operators of travel agencies.

Less strenuous recreation also is in the picture for Ziff-Davis with *Popular Photography*, the best selling photo book at 444,354; or if you listen to records, try *Stereo Review* or *Popular Electronics* if you're a do-it-yourselfer (there's *Electronics World* for the professional). Or if you do prefer the open road, *Car and Driver*; while *Boating* is for the water-bug. There's one that may belong in one of these categories but we'll let you figure out which one—*Modern Bride*.

Fast-moving Americans have made a fast-moving business for Ziff-Davis with a total circulation of 2,680,211.

Executive Vice President: W. Bradford Briggs, 1 Park Ave., New York 10016.

From A to Z we've made a tour of multiple publishers of specialized publications, hitting the high spots to give a bird's-eye view of major companies which have led the way in years past and who will be in the front rank of this parade for the future. Now let's survey the professional associations of these publishers through which they've united to strengthen and advance their performance, both for higher revenues and for improved service to communication in our society.

Associations of Specialized Publications

American Business Press, Inc.

One organization, American Business Press, Inc., stands out as the unifying alliance of "specialized business publications serving specific industrial, business, service or professional audiences, not including general business or business news magazines." That's the association's own description of its membership which in 1968 included 500 publications and was still growing. ABP was formed in 1965 from the union of Associated Business Publications and National Business Publications.

Associated Business Publications, tracing its roots back to 1906, was organized in 1916 by paid circulation publications. National Business Publications was established in 1940 and its members chiefly utilized controlled circulation, free to a selected list. Today American Business Press maintains a New York headquarters and offers a wide variety of editorial and advertising services to its members, plus an effective speakers' bureau and education committee to encourage journalism training for careers on industrials.

Representative American Business Press members are Buttenheim Publishing Corporation, Chilton Company, Geyer-McAllister Publications, Haire Publishing Company, McGraw-Hill, Inc., Peacock Business Press, Inc. A total of 117 publishing firms maintain memberships. "Eligible for membership are independently-owned publications which pay corporate income tax (as opposed to tax-free society or association magazines); whose circulations are audited by independent, non-profit auditing bureaus governed by tripartite boards (representatives of advertisers, agencies, and publishers)."

There are active moves, as this is written, for a single audit for all business publications, regardless of whether they circulate on a paid or controlled basis.

American Business Press has moved ahead vigorously to sell the value of advertising in specialized publications and to promote the quality of that advertising. Each year since 1941 it has given awards for outstanding advertisements and campaigns. Each year since 1954 it has recognized editorial achievement through the Jesse H. Neal awards. Its educational committee carries on a continuous program of career advice and summer internships. Publishing management, editorial, circulation, production—these are other ABP divisions. As a major service to its members, ABP operates the Business Press Advertising Bureau. Active and positive communication is the hallmark of American Business Press today to tell the remarkable story of its members.

Manager of Member Services: Dave Bennett, 205 E. 42 St., New York 10017.

Vice President, Operations: Bill O'Donnell.

Executive Vice President: Hazen Morse.

President: John B. Babcock.

Magazine Publishers Association
American Society of Magazine Editors

Representing chiefly the large consumer magazines, the Magazine Publishers Association, formed in 1919, has steadily worked for higher standards of publishing and to forward the use of magazine advertising. Despite its orientation toward the consumer periodical, a considerable proportion of its members also publish specialized publications.

264

Its membership roll in 1968 numbered 115 different publishers of 365 magazines and included such houses as Curtis Publishing Company, Farm Journal, Inc., Harper's Magazine, McCall Corporation, and Parents' Magazine Enterprises, Inc. Its Magazine Center headquarters in New York, also houses its affiliated organizations:

The Periodical Publishers Association, a credit information agency which secures financial reports from advertising agencies doing business with MPA members.

The Magazine Advertising Bureau which works to sell magazines as an advertising medium through research, promotion, and advertising. The Bureau has been responsible for the full-page institutional ads which have appeared in many magazines in their own interest.

The Central Registry of Magazine Subscription Solicitors which acts to protect and police publishers' door-to-door sales.

The Publishers Information Bureau which provides statistical information about general magazine advertising.

The American Society of Magazine Editors which includes the editors of nearly 100 American magazines. It was founded in 1963, holds quarterly meetings, and an annual editorial conference in Washington. In cooperation with MPA, it sponsors magazine internships, seminars, and a National Magazine Award. In the MPA educational program, research grants are made both to educators and students.

The Magazine Publishers Association has five formal objectives:

To provide its members with services and information concerning every phase of magazine publishing, and to assist them in solving their common problems.

To develop a better understanding among magazines and groups with allied interests, such as advertisers and advertising agencies, national and local business organizations, educators and students, local, state, and national civic or public bodies and organizations.

To ensure their recognition that magazines are a continuing source of education for all, and that magazines provide the information, inspiration and entertainment upon which Americans everywhere base many of their thoughts, their tastes and their actions.

To stimulate greater use of magazines by readers through a program designed to show them how magazines can help them live better, and to sponsor programs that increase the circulation of magazines through constructive selling.

To promote a greater use of magazines by advertisers and their agencies through a program that emphasizes the penetration and permanence of the printed word and the advantages of magazines as a printed advertising medium.

These are the goals which motivate magazine publishers who do a business with a volume of $1,626,000,000 a year, $779,000,000 paid for magazines by readers, and $847,000,000 spent by advertisers according to 1964 estimates by the Magazine Advertising Bureau and Association of National Advertisers, and Publishers Information Bureau.

Executive Vice President, Magazine Publishers Association, Publishers Information Bureau, Periodical Publishers Association, and Secretary, American Society of Magazine Editors, Robert E. Kenyon Jr. Magazine Center, 575 Lexington Ave., New York 10022.

International Council of Industrial Editors

The International Council of Industrial Editors, as described by one of its presidents, is "a federation of industrial and organizational journalists and communicators." Translating that definition into the writer's own language, it's an association chiefly of company publication editors. The ICIE defines industrial publications as those "issued periodically by private sponsors: business and industrial companies and various kinds of associations. . . . In almost all cases they are free-circulation media; and in very few cases do they carry paid advertising. They fall into three general classifications: internal, for circulation primarily or only among the employees of the sponsor; external, for circulation among the sponsor's customers, prospects, dealers, salesmen, stockholders, among so-called thought leaders and other interested persons; and combinations of the two."

To belong to ICIE, you have to belong to one of its affiliated associations which operate in various cities and countries. It's an association of associations; editors accepted for membership by local groups automatically become members of ICIE. Today it reaches a total individual membership internationally of more than 6,500 and includes some 60 affiliated associations in the United States and 10 international affiliated associations. The international affiliates are in Canada, Great Britain, Denmark, Sweden, Norway, the Netherlands, India, Japan, the Phillipines, and Venezuela. More than 3,000 Americans are members; there are more than 3,500 international individual memberships.

This far-flung organization came into being in 1941 as the National Council of Industrial Editors Associations with 600 members in 11 associations. Its oldest affiliate still in existence is the American Railway Magazine Editors Association, founded in 1922; the second was the Industrial Editors Association of Chicago, in 1925. In 1946, with the affiliation of the Canadian Industrial Editors Association, the name became International Council of Industrial Editors.

ICIE's original constitution declared its purpose was "to foster and encourage the profession of industrial editing through the cooperation and exchange of ideas among editorial association; to build prestige for the pro-

fession; and to work for the betterment of all types of industrial publications."
It has conducted many activities to accomplish these ends, none more efficiently or usefully than its Central Office in Akron, Ohio, managed by Executive
Secretary, Geraldine Keating. Another attractive assist is its monthly magazine, *Reporting*, edited by Lawrence Ragan, and giving professional quality and
leadership to the members. Periodic questionnaire surveys of the membership
have produced valuable data. A Placement Service for members and job-
seekers has organized what previously was only a hit-and-miss effort by individuals. A monthly "Idea File" of reprints, suggestions, and case histories,
also has been circulated. An annual evaluation of members' publications is
tied in with annual awards. Education committees have been active both
through local associations and the national organization.

Executive Secretary: Geraldine Keating, 2108 Braewick Circle, Akron,
Ohio 44313.

American Association of Industrial Editors

Admitting both individual members and affiliated associations, the American Association of Industrial Editors was formed in 1938. Today it is approaching the 500 mark in individual memberships and has 11 affiliates with
700 additional members, making a total of more than 1,200. It is the only
national company editors' group admitting individual members and many
of its services are designed especially for them.

Most of its American affiliated associations are located in the Eastern
United States although it has individual members in other sections and
countries. In 1966, the Canadian Industrial Editors Association became an
affiliate. AAIE was a charter member of ICIE until 1946, withdrawing when
ICIE barred individual memberships. In 1969, it seemed likely that the two
organizations would reunite—on July 1, 1970—as the result of a favorable
vote by the executive committees of both AAIE and ICIE, to be ratified by
their memberships.

The AAIE Constitution states—

The objectives of the American Association of Industrial Editors are to help its
members increase their professional skills in and deepen their understandings of the
purpose and practice of written communications.

The Association shall seek to raise the standard of editorial presentation in
industrial publications, and to stimulate, inspire and enlighten its member companies
and their individual representatives so their communications will contribute more
fully to the effectiveness of understanding and the progress of the American economy
and society.

The Association shall provide a means of mutual exchange of ideas among its
members and shall provide practical services to assist its members in accomplishing
the objectives.

267

Services of AAIE are extensive and include newsletters and other special mailings, periodic analysis of member publications, an excellent awards program for publications, writing, photography, and layout. There is a thorough and professional bi-monthly, *Editor's Notebook*, edited by Walter G. Anderson. Its Central Office is located in Buffalo, New York.

Executive Secretary: Donald W. Boyd Jr., 802 Kenmore Ave., Buffalo, N.Y. 14216.

Comics Magazine Association of America

In the wake of World War II and the development of the comic book industry (as contrasted to the newspaper comic strips), a growing tumult of criticism came from sociologists and psychologists, from law enforcement and church officials. In response, a number of comic book publishers formed the Association of Comics Magazine Publishers in 1948 to act as an industry self-regulatory body. Its effectiveness was hampered however, because publishers of approximately 70 per cent of comic books turned thumbs down on the idea.

As criticism continued, a new attempt was made through formation of the Comics Magazine Association of America which now consists of 90 per cent of all publishers, distributors, printers, and engravers engaged in the industry. A stringent self-regulatory code was adopted and a code administrator appointed who literally had to put his seal of approval on every art panel and line of copy prior to publication.

The Code applies both to editorial and advertising matter. Its standards state that "in every instance good shall triumph over evil and the criminal be punished for his misdeeds." Horror and terror comics are banned, language shall be in good taste, sexual exploitation of the human figure is outlawed. Nudity is prohibited, dress must be "reasonably acceptable to society," salacious or suggestive postures are prohibited, and "females shall be drawn realistically without exaggeration of any physical qualities." Attacks on religious or racial groups are not permissible. Respect for the family shall be fostered. There shall be no advertising of liquor, tobacco, sex books or pictures, guns, knives or other weapons, gambling equipment, or questionable health or medical products.

Efforts of the CMAA have been successful in winning public approval from Protestant and Catholic church bodies, from officers of the National Congress of Parents and Teachers, and various civic and educational leaders. National awards have been received from the United States Chamber of Commerce and the American Society of Association Executives "for its success toward achieving one of the most difficult objectives of any industry—a workable self-regulation program."

268

Despite the best efforts of the Association, the Code, and public acclaim of its achieved results, a minority of comic book publishers continues to circulate considerable quantities of tasteless books emphasizing sex and violence and presumably only social mores and the courts can completely police such offenders.

The eight publisher members of CMAA are: Archie Comics Publications, Charlton Press, Inc., Country Wide Publications, Inc., Harvey Publications, King Features Syndicate, Magazine Management Company, National Periodical Publications, Inc., and Tower Comics, Inc. The four distributor members are: The Capital Distributing Company, Independent News Company, Macfadden-Bartell Corporation, and Publishers Distributing Company.

President: John L. Goldwater, 300 Park Ave., New York 10010.

Associated Church Press

The Associated Church Press is an association of more than 190 Protestant, Anglican, Orthodox, and Catholic publications in the United States and Canada, with a combined paid circulation of more than 23,700,000 families and individuals. Formed in 1912, its stated goal "is to promote acquaintance and fellowship, to foster helpfulness among editors and publishers of its member publications, and to stimulate higher standards of religious journalism in order to enable its member publications to render more useful service and to exert a more positive and constructive Christian influence on contemporary civilization."

A full-time executive headquarters in Chicago handles ACP editorial and business activities as well as services which include research, religious journalism workshops, personnel placement, an annual directory, a special syndicate, and editorial and layout analyses for all members without charge. A quarterly trade publication covers membership news and special features. Annual awards of merit are given to prize-winning member publications which, in recent years, have included *Motive, Scope, Christianity and Crisis, The Baptist Record, The Lutheran,* and *Youth.*

Executive Secretary: Alfred P. Klausler, 875 N. Dearborn St., Chicago, Ill. 60610.

Other Religious Associations

Two other major religious publisher associations exist, the Catholic Press Association, and the Evangelical Press Association. The Catholic Press Association at 432 Park Ave., South, New York 10016, has James A. Doyle as executive director. It was founded in 1911 and has 310 members—160 magazines, 140 newspapers, and 10 general publishers of books and pamphlets.

269

Two Protestant denominations operate their own organizations, the Methodist Press Association and the Southern Baptist Press Association. A number of weekly Jewish newspapers belong to the American Jewish Press Association.

More Magazine Associations

While perhaps not as well known outside of their own specialized fields, significant associations related to specialized publications include: the Association of Industrial Advertisers, the Agricultural Publishers Association and the American Agricultural Editors Association; the American Society of Business Press Editors and the Society of Business Magazine Editors; the American Association of Publication Production Managers, the Bureau of Independent Publishers and Distributors, the National Association of Science Writers, the Association of Screen Magazine Publishers, the Educational Press Association, and the American Association of Medical Writers. For a complete list and addresses, see the Appendix.

Educational Press Association of America, founded in 1895, has 600 members associated with educational journals. Its headquarters at Syracuse University, New York, provides a monthly newsletter, organizes national and regional workshops, and makes annual awards to educational publications.

Circulating the Copies

Until advertisers and publishers finally got together, for years circulation claims were exactly that and nothing more. Advertisers had paid for hopes and dreams; publishers claimed what they wanted. Independent circulation audits changed most of that . . . although much remains to be done.

"Almost two-thirds of business publications have no audits at all," commented Carroll J. Swan in a 1968 issue of *Media/scope*. "ABC audits 271 business publications and is limited to serving only those with 70 per cent or more of their circulation paid. BPA audits 635 business publications. This leaves 1,697 with neither a BPA nor an ABC audit."

What we call industrial publications are the ones Swan is talking about. He further declared that the unaudited get only 30 per cent of business press ad dollars and therefore tend to be less important for advertisers. "But they are so numerous that they still present a king-size problem in analysis to the advertiser and his agency."

As mentioned earlier in this chapter, strong moves are being made to arrive at a single audit based on a single standard of comparability, using the Standard Industrial Classifications and Standard Job Classifications. Much has been achieved, however, even if much remains to be done.

270

Just before the turn of the century, advertisers tried to establish circulation audits. But it was 1914 before they achieved their goal, the Audit Bureau of Circulations, known familiarly as ABC (not the radio-TV networks!). ABC considers itself an "industry-sponsored audit bureau" and states that 85.06 per cent of all U.S. magazine circulation is audited and reported in accordance with "industry-sponsored standards." When ABC achieved acceptance for its procedures, it completed audits for 26 general magazines, 52 farm publications, and 61 business periodicals in its first three months of operation.

Today, nearly 4,100 companies hold membership in ABC. Its board of directors is composed of representatives of the publications, both magazine and newspaper, the advertisers, and advertising agencies. Publisher members must file semi-annual "Publisher's Statements" of their circulations. These are verified or corrected in annual Audit Reports published by ABC and based on findings of an ABC field circulation auditor. To be eligible for membership, a publication must qualify at least 70 per cent of total distribution as paid—although, in 1969, modification of this provision was under consideration. "Publications with at least 50 per cent paid circulation may apply for provisional membership, provided that the publisher agrees to reach the 70 per cent level within 3 years after applying for association membership."

Business Publications Audit of Circulation, Inc., to audit business publications only, was formed in 1931 first under the name of Controlled Circulation Audit which it bore until 1954. BPA is based largely on the fact that most business publications practice "qualified" circulation which means specifically: (1) "clear conception and definition of the 'circulation boundaries'"; (2) "periodic review of mailing list to ensure conformance to the circulation boundaries so defined." Circulation is defined on the dual basis of "Field Service" (by type of businesses) and "Recipient Qualification" (by types of individuals). Three reports are made annually; two are semi-annual BPA Publisher's Statements and a third, the annual BPA Audit Report. Both paid and non-paid circulation are reported on a single form, using SIC number and reporting qualification sources.

Business Publications Audit is controlled by a board of directors consisting of 7 advertisers, 7 advertising agencies, and 7 publishers. When first established, BPA had 39 publication members; now it serves more than 600. Annual dues for publication members are $200 and auditing charges, based on circulation size, range from $357.50 for 8,000 copies or less to $986.50 for more than 200,000.

Verified Audit Circulation Corporation operates for profit as a non-membership company—both ABC and BPA serve members only. It will audit a publication whether paid or non-paid, regardless of the field it serves. It

271

"operates on the principle that every publication soliciting advertising (and every advertiser and agency purchasing advertising space) should have available an audit, whatever the circulation method, which provides accurate and valid measurements of the size, composition and quality of its circulation." VAC checks the validity of circulation by surveys based on random sampling of persons listed as receiving a publication. It issues two semi-annual reports based on publisher's statements and an annual audit, and uses local Certified Public Accountants to conduct its audits.

 Office of Certified Circulation Inc., was established by the Interamerican Press Society to certify circulations of Latin American publications. Like the other circulation audits, it relies on a triple structure of advertisers, agencies, and publishers. OCC has approved 10 international accounting companies to examine publishing records and certify accuracy. It distributes two reports annually: a sworn statement gives geographic distribution of net paid, and a certified OCC report with daily average circulation for an entire year. In 1968, it was serving approximately 30 publications.

Post Office 2nd class mailing regulations (39 U.S. Code 4354) require publication once a year (October) of "the extent and nature of circulation of the publication, including, but not limited to, the number of copies distributed, the methods of distribution, and the extent to which such circulation is paid in whole or in part; . . ." The same regulation calls for a statement of ownership.

Closely related to circulation but dealing with distribution rather than audits is the Bureau of Independent Publishers and Distributors, established in 1948. Its membership includes 13 national distributors and more than 600 local wholesalers of magazines, paperbacks, comics and children's books sold at U.S. and Canadian newsstands and produced for mass market distribution. See the Appendix for the list of national distributors.

Multiple Magnitude

While no book of this length can give a complete picture of the multiple publishing houses and associations in the magazine industry—the magnitude and complexity would call for an encyclopedia and the SRDS catalogues are closest to it, this chapter has presented a careful selection which, at least, indicates where deeper spadework can begin.

Cahners Publishing Company

Cover from a Cahners booklet; courtesy of Cahners Publishing Company.

Design in this cover from the Cahners Publication, *EDN*, is intricate and simple for its design-engineer readers. Copyright, 1968, by Cahners Publishing Company.

Fashion also means shoes and jewelry and Chilton has publications for men who sell both. This advertisement for a Chilton fashion publication is used by courtesy of Chilton Company.

Chilton Company, Chestnut and Fifty-Sixth Streets, Philadelphia, Pa. 19139

Cover of Chilton Company's annual report; by courtesy of Chilton Company.

Career booklet prepared and distributed by Standard Rate & Data Service, Inc., in cooperation with the Educational Committee of the Magazine Publishers Association, Inc. Used by permission of the Magazine Publishers Association.

Promotion material for *Jewelers' Circular-Keystone*. Copyright, 1968, the Chilton Company.

These Publications Give Business People the Specialized Information They Need

Covers of American Business Press member publications. Used by permission of American Business Press, Inc.

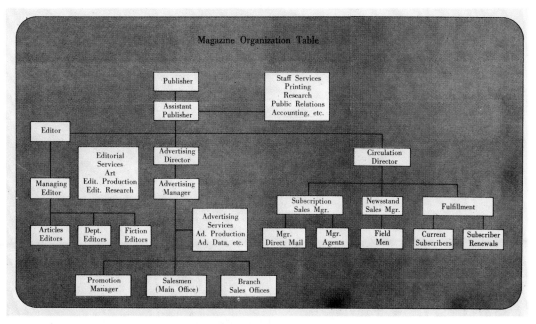

Magazine Organization Table

Magazine organization table from *Magazines in the U.S.A.,* showing chains of command. Used by permission of the Magazine Publishers Association.

Money market barometer. McGraw-Hill Correspondent Daniel da Cruz (left) checks the reverberating effects of the failure of a leading Beirut bank on the always-present demand for gold. Beirut's gold market responds to fluctuations in the international money market with mysterious swiftness. Reporter da Cruz is one of several hundred "stringers" (part-time correspondents) who augment McGraw-Hill's 32 full-time news bureaus and editorial offices around the world.

McGRAW-HILL REPORTING FROM

BEIRUT

McGraw-Hill surrounds your advertising
with readers by surrounding the world with reporters.

McGRAW-HILL
market-directed®
PUBLICATIONS

B. MOUGHANNI & FILS

Trade advertisement for McGraw-Hill; by permission of McGraw-Hill Publications.

12. All Aboard for Tomorrow!

I N the whirling universe of communications spins a magnificent celestial system, unknown to most men, even when they see it daily . . . the ever-expanding galaxies and constellations, the brilliant single stars, of specialized publications. On our first page we bid you welcome and invited you to visit this shining world with us. Through it we've traveled together and before we leave it, let's take one last journey on the time machine and look at the magazine of tomorrow.

If there's a favorite indoor sports for writers, it might be called writing the last chapter or where do we go from here! But for professionals and beginners alike, it's tempting to try to see something in the crystal ball for tomorrow's specialized publications—or for the printed word of any kind. It may well be that we're all looking through the glass darkly and happily so, perhaps, just in case electronics forever kills the alphabet. Me, I say use those ether waves and computer juke boxes just as we've used type stuck into little metal boxes, so long as we eventually come up with a page over which man can reflect.

Consider what some magazine men have predicted. William I. Nichols, publisher of *This Week*, declares, "The specialty magazines are booming. Whether you are a New Yorker, a pornographer, a skin diver or a raiser of Nubian goats—somewhere there is a specialty magazine made just for you." This, as one of his picks of emerging trends in the future communications.

"The increased need for specialized information will probably contribute to the introduction of more business and industrial publications," according to Wade Fairchild, of Fairchild Publications, Inc.

Hear John R. Callaham, vice president, editorial, of McGraw-Hill Publications. "I suspect that new publications will more than make up for the discontinuance of these weaker ones. The basis of my prediction for this increase stems largely from the explosive growth of knowledge and from increasing specialization in business, industry and technology."

Where and how will the expansion come? In new processes of production and distribution. In deeper reporting, in clearer, simpler writing. In layouts that have more initial appeal, that tantalize the reader to continue reading with mounting interest. In art that represents a happy wedding with words. In staff with imagination and more freedom to create. And in a blend of all the best elements of all media into immediate communication.

But I can hear you say, "Those are easy generalities—how about a few specifics."

That's harder, but I'll try.

For production we already have photo- and sound-activated composition, electro-chemical printing, home TV recorders, satellites for facsimile transmission. Apply these and the specialized publication of tomorrow is possible today. We also have the communication conglomerates right now ready and able in TV and print and what you will. We'll still have weeklies and monthlies for contemplative digestion, written by a staff whose assignment is to think and interpret, looking for meanings beyond the obvious. But we'll also have more specialized publications produced on an hourly and daily schedule, operating around the clock as the press associations do today.

When you roll out of bed, you'll turn the knob and get your Morning Magazine exactly as you ordered it the night before. While you shave and watch the viewer's recap of the news, the Instant-Fac will be running off your own special issue, expanding on the items for which you punched the button while watching. By the time breakfast is over, your own hand-tailored specialized Morning Magazine will be ready for you to read on your way to the office.

Any hour during the day, you'll be able to get an updated, up-to-the-minute supplement, while the evening edition will be waiting for your homecoming, exactly as you've requested during the day. If you want, the recorder attached to your Instant-Fac will give you a playback or simulcast so you can see and hear for yourself just what you've been reading about. You can select the top news, the interpretation, the specialized summary of what happened today in textiles, as well as baseball highlights and the fifth at Aqueduct. If there's a new angle in that textile that Eastman's making from sea-water, you can order your own extra and the Instant-Fac will deliver it, printed with pix and swatches, for you to look at and feel before you check in for another night.

Those pix will be in 3-D and color, of course. And if you want a whiff of the new perfume the model's wearing, the fragrance will whirl around you until your wife turns up her nose.

Never-never land? Want to bet!

Specialized communicator houses will prepare and transmit their own specialized publications to meet every taste and necessity. Just as Meredith, Cowles, and Time, Inc. are practically prepared to do already. All of them have radio-TV, book, and other communication interests. RCA has Random House and NBC. CBS has Holt, Rinehart and Winston which has books and magazines, and CBS has education films and the N.Y. Yankees. To conserve the public interest, there will be more communication satellite corporations with public ownership shared with private, and presided over by the Federal Communications Commission. While multiple and conglomerate operations may be deplored by some as anti-social interest, with mounting costs and technical complexity we'll have more mergers of communication companies and facilities.

Reporting can and will improve in quality. Too much coverage today is superficial and focused on the spectacular or so-called "controversial." Specialized publications have money to employ experts who can take the time necessary to do a first-class job . . . and who will understand what they are doing. More reporting will be done by teams of reporters and photographers and mobile electronic units. Combining talents and skills, there will be more synthesis of effort and fewer frantic one-man solos spread thin.

Just as editorial direction will be less haphazard and whimsical, so will editing be directed toward specified goals. Copy will be judged on how it advances definite objectives in coverage, not on an isolated "gee whiz" or "how does that grab you" caprice. Demographic data will mean articles hand-tailored to the audience for which they're intended, instead of turned loose on a hit-or-miss, continent-wide basis. Indeed, national and international editions will be discarded, as magazines already are using regional and demographic production custom-tailored to fit the customer.

Advertising, of course, will be placed on the same basis. And, speaking of advertising, ever stricter standards will be applied, not only to prevent fraud and deception but also to encourage quality service and products. Very likely, with increasing demand, advertising space will have to be rationed, which again will put a premium on guaranteed merchandise. There will also be less shot-gun advertising; it will follow increasingly selective placement according to a carefully researched pattern.

Controlled circulation long has been a major means of publishing and distributing industrial publications and company externals. Now it is part of the consumer magazine scene also, as well as extending its influence into other regions of specialized publishing. Metromedia, through its O. E. McIntyre Division, in 1968 launched a 10,000,000 controlled circulation monthly, *Home-makers' Digest*, for housewives. College students are the goal of *Dare*, which will put free copies into dormitories, fraternity houses, student unions. Communications Research Machines Inc. added *Careers Today*, with an initial circulation of 300,000, among college seniors and graduate students, in 1968 to its paid circulation *Psychology Today*. These free books will put increased pressure on the old-time properties sold by subscription and newsstand.

For the Instant-Fac home-delivered magazine, layout and art will have to be designed to fit distribution direct to the reader's home for immediate as well as delayed consumption. Greater legibility, larger body type and more white space, will be needed for the less-perfect human eye and improved longevity. Splashy covers for eye-catching newsstand sales certainly may continue but on a diminished scale, and newsstand circulation itself will greatly decrease. People will prefer their own personal publications. Mass communications will be personalized for the individual.

Color's wonderful appeal will not lessen although it will be used with more discrimination and sophistication, augmented also by three-dimensional effects with tactile and olfactory accompaniment. The sensory expert will accompany the reporting team and be a member of it.

Staff will be educated more thoroughly and to develop individual abilities. The average present-day journalism school, wearing its blinders of newspaper orientation, trots down the old dirt road of the past, teaching the poor kids formulas a half-century old. "Nuts and bolts" courses should disappear—no more spending a month learning how to write a stereotyped lead. Each story will make its own rules.

The rest of the university will be part of the journalism school, too. As it is, liberal arts training has been stressed, quite properly, if without sufficient attention to individual interests. As the bedrock of professional training, history and political science and philosophy will be integrated with journalism courses. Greater attention must be paid to grammar and composition as essential for writing. Background also in reading, literature of course and some authors, it's to be hoped, beside 19th century American or English. Sciences must receive much more attention—physics and chemistry and biology. They've produced our modern civilization and yet the usual journalism student takes only what he has to.

At the same time, the magazine major analyzes a variety of publications, writing and selling articles, preparing a complete dummy, doing the art work and designing the layouts, as an individual and with a team of other editors-to-be. To learn by doing, by personal initiative, to create original expression—

276

this is more than sitting in a classroom and listening to lectures by the hour.

Closer relations will be maintained with communications media to allow more on-the-job apprentice training—although less, we hope, at the expense of the consumer. That means better teachers, with more imagination, more professional experience of greater breadth.

This will take four years, maybe five, but then, with the aid of a company's personnel division and his new colleagues, the novice staff member will absorb perspective and begin to comprehend his publishing responsibilities. Of course, pay must be commensurate with training and talent. Each day will be a continuing seminar for the challenging career he or she has chosen. Does it work? More than 50 former students, with a total of one to 20 years with specialized publications, can speak for themselves. Names on request.

How can this be achieved? Already the cordial cooperation of magazine associations—the MPA, ABP, ICIE, and AAIE—has been unique among communications media. Even when journalism departments obviously demonstrated their newspaper preferences, the organizations of specialized publications and magazines have welcomed professors as members, offered them and their students internships and subsidies for travel. ABP established special research awards. *Mademoiselle* started its College Board program in 1937; *Reader's Digest* offered its travel funds in 1961. Individual ICIE chapters sent speakers to the campus, at their own expense; reduced meeting fees and dinner charges to cost to encourage students to attend, gave scholarships. MPA created an extensive program of summer internships.

Hardly a page of this book could have been written without the astonishing and whole-hearted cooperation of many magazine publishers and editors. They have opened their records, prepared special illustrations, talked freely and enthusiastically. Just as often they have supplied an infinite amount of material to magazine students for their projects and taken the time to write double-paged, single-spaced letters to answer their questions. But most of all, they have recruited with enthusiasm and zest, offering competitive salaries and unlimited opportunity.

Challenge to the imagination and the creative spirit is implicit in specialized publications. If we write about them with enthusiasm, it is because we believe in them wholeheartedly. This universe of communications, so little known and recognized, is a constant part of our daily lives. Specialized publications greet us in childhood, we grow up with them. They are chosen companions for our teens. On our jobs they are daily advisers. Their channels of communication move industry forward, inform the doctor in his profession, the housewife in her kitchen. At the close of day we relax with them. This is the universe all about us and through it we live and work and dream.

277

Appendix
Acknowledgments
Index

**Production Schedules for *Better Homes and Gardens.*
Courtesy of Meredith Corporation**

December

To:	Bob Jolley	Wes Booth	Laird Macdonald	Jim Lesac	REVISED
	Bill Fritz	Bob Tungland	Ivan McDonald	Ron Huggins	Bob Hefner
					Dick Dickey
From:	Suzanne Stevens				Leila Cornelison
					Katie Norris
					Noble Gammel

BETTER HOMES & GARDENS MASTER PRODUCTION SCHEDULE

Howard Smith
Ken Zosel
Ken Hill

	APR.	MAY	JUNE
Order for Non-Standard Units (4c)	12/27	1/26	2/27
Book Size–Preliminary	1/ 2	2/ 1	3/ 1
Order for Non-Standard Units (2c)	1/ 5	2/ 5	3/ 5
Final Regional Editorial Manuscripts & Engravings	1/22	2/22	3/22
Six Month Forecast	1/25	2/26	3/25
Cover Lineup and Engravings	1/26	2/27	3/27
Final Advertising Engravings	→ 2/12	3/12	4/12 ←
Final Editorial Manuscripts and Engravings	1/29	2/28	3/28
Final Delivery Counts	1/29	2/29	3/29
Final Release–Cover	2/ 1	3/ 1	4/ 1
Final Book size and Print Order	2/ 5	3/ 5	4/ 5
Final Regional Ad Engravings	2/ 2	3/ 1	4/ 2
Regional Page Lineup	2/ 1	3/ 1	4/ 1
Ad and Editorial Lineup-4c	2/ 6	3/ 6	4/ 5
Final Release-Regional pages-Editorial	2/ 2	3/ 4	4/ 2
Final Release-Regional pages-Advertising	2/ 2	3/ 5	4/ 3
National Page Lineup	2/ 8	3/ 8	4/ 8
Final Release-National pages-Editorial	2/12	3/12	4/12
Final Release-National pages-Advertising	2/12	3/12	4/12 a.m.
Filler Release	2/13 Noon	3/13 Noon	4/12 Noon
Finish Composing	2/14	3/14	4/15
Start Rotary Presses-National	2/17	3/18	4/17
Start Binding	2/24	3/25	4/24
On Sale Date	3/14	4/16	5/14
Estimated Book Size	170	156	144

MAGAZINES FOR MILLIONS

Page 1 of 3

2nd <u>REVISED</u> PROPOSED PRODUCTION SCHEDULE

PUBLICATION: BETTER HOMES & GARDENS

ISSUE: June

EST. PRINT ORDER: 7,900,000
FINAL PRINT ORDER DUE: April 5, 1968
FINAL BOOK SIZE DUE: April 5, 1968

DATE: March 29
PAGES: 126 Plus Regionals
and Special Units

RECEIVE PAGE LINEUP   Cover 3-27
Edit. 4-5
Reg'l. 4-1
Nat'l. 4-8

	C		FINAL DATES				
Form - - - - - - - - - - - - - -	COVER		F	G	H		
	4		7	10Reg1 4Natl	2		
Press- - - - - - - - - - - - - -	Hoe 30		H-26	C5	Clay		
Shopping by Mail molds due in D. M. -	--		4-2	4-2	4-2		
Final Advertising Engravings - - - -	3-12		4-2	4-2	4-2		
Final Editorial Manuscripts & Engr. -	3-28		3-22	3-22	3-22		
Final Release - Editorial - - - - - -	4-1		4-2	4-2	4-2		
Final Release - Advertising - - - - -	4-1		4-3	4-3	4-3		
Final Release - Filler - - - - - - -	--		--	--	--		
Start Press MR- - - - - - - - - - - -	4-4		4-9	4-9	4-9		
Start Bindery MR- - - - - - - - - - -	4-24						
Start Mailroom- - - - - - - - - - - -	4-26*						
On Sale Date- - - - - - - - - - - - -	May 14, 1968 (Tuesday)						

Furnished Material Due to Bindery - April 18, 1968

*Summer POPULAR GARDENING & Summer/Fall #60 NEW HOMES GUIDE ship w/this issue.

REGIONAL PAGES

	EDIT DUE IN	ADV DUE IN	EDIT PROOF OUT	ADV PROOF OUT	EDIT FINAL RELEASE DUE IN	ADV FINAL RELEASE DUE IN
100%	3-22	4-2	3-28	4-3	4-2	4-3
80%	3-19	--	3-26	4-1	--	4-2
70%	--	--	3-25	--	4-1	--
60%	--	3-27	--	3-29	--	4-1
50%	3-14	--	--	--	--	--
40%	--	--	--	3-29	--	4-1

282

2nd REVISED PROPOSED PRODUCTION SCHEDULE

PUBLICATION: BETTER HOMES & GARDENS

ISSUE: June

EST. PRINT ORDER: 7,900,000
FINAL PRINT ORDER DUE: April 5, 1968
FINAL BOOK SIZE DUE: April 5, 1968

DATE: March 29
PAGES: 126 Plus Regionals
and Special Units

RECEIVE PAGE LINEUP: Cover 3-27
Edit. 4-5
Reg'l. 4-1
Nat'l. 4-8

FINAL DATES

Form	A	B	D		E		
	56	28 Dup	24 Dup		10 p. Gatefld		
Press	G-71	G-72	H-24		H-25		
Shopping by Mail molds due in D. M.	4-10	4-10	4-10		SEE		
Final Advertising Engravings	3-12	3-12	3-12		ATTACHED		
Final Editorial Manuscripts & Engr.	3-28	3-28	3-28		SHEET		
Final Release - Editorial	4-12	4-12	4-12				
Final Release - Advertising	4-12	4-12	4-12				
Final Release - Filler	4-12 Noon	4-12 Noon	4-12 Noon				
Start Press MR	4-17	4-17	4-17				
Start Bindery MR	4-24						
Start Mailroom	4-26*						
On Sale Date	May 14, 1968 (Tuesday)						

Furnished Material Due to Bindery - April 18, 1968

*Summer POPULAR GARDENING and Summer/Fall #60 NEW HOMES GUIDE ship w/this issue.

	EDIT DUE IN	ADV DUE IN	EDIT PROOF OUT	ADV PROOF OUT	EDIT FINAL RELEASE DUE IN	ADV FINAL RELEASE DUE IN
				NATIONAL PAGES		
100%	3-28	4-12	4-4	4-12	4-12	4-12 Noon
94%	--	--	--	--	--	--
90%	3-25	4-10	4-1	4-11	4-11	4-11
80%	3-22	4-9	3-29	4-10	4-10	4-10
70%	3-19	--	3-27	4-9	4-9	4-9
60%	--	4-5	3-26	4-8	4-8	4-8
50%	--	4-2	3-25	--	--	--
40%	--	--	--	--	--	--

MAGAZINES FOR MILLIONS

<u>2nd</u> <u>REVISED</u> PROPOSED PRODUCTION SCHEDULE

DATE: March 29

JOB: EDITORIAL GATEFOLD

FROM: Central Planning

ISSUE: June

COLORS: 4/c

EST. QUANTITY: 7,900,000

PRESS: Hoe 25

TRIM SIZE: 9 1/2" x 12 1/2"

PAGES: 10 pages

<u>SCHEDULE</u>

RECEIVE PRINT ORDER	HAS BEEN RECEIVED
ORDER STOCK	HAS BEEN ORDERED
RECEIVE COPY & ENGRAVINGS	March 28
PRE-PRESS INFORMATION DUE	March 28
SET TYPE	March 29 – April 3
PROOF OUT	April 4
RECEIVE FINAL RELEASES	April 9
RECEIVE STOCK	April 10
PRESS DATE	April 15 – May 1
START BINDING	April 24

284

**Copy Flow Schedule for *Better Homes and Gardens*.
Courtesy of Meredith Corporation**

JUNE

NATIONAL PAGES

	Editorial				Advertising		
	Due In	Proof Out	Final Release Due In		Due In	Proof Out	Final Release Due In
100%	3/28	4/ 4	4/12	100% 94%	4/12 a.m.	4/12 a.m.	4/12 Noon
90%	3/25	4/ 1	4/11	90%	4/10	4/11	4/11
80%	3/22	3/29	4/10	80%	4/ 9	4/10	4/10
70%	3/19	3/27	4/ 9	70%	–	4/ 9	4/ 9
60%	–	3/26	4/ 8	60%	4/ 5	4/ 8	4/ 8
50%	–	3/25	–	50%	4/ 2	–	–
40%	–	–	–	40%	–	–	–

REGIONAL PAGES

	Editorial				Advertising		
	Due In	Proof Out	Final Release Due In		Due In	Proof Out	Final Release Due In
100%	3/22	3/28	4/ 2	100%	4/ 2	4/ 3	4/ 3
80%	3/19	3/26	–	80%	–	4/ 1	4/ 2
70%	–	3/25	4/ 1	60%	3/27	3/29	4/ 1
50%	3/14	–	–				
40%	–	–	–	40%	–	–	–

Letter to Writers for *The Christian Home.*
Courtesy of Mrs. Helen F. Couch, editor, *The Christian Home.*

201 Eighth Avenue, South
Nashville, Tennessee 37203

Dear Writer:

We are happy to know of your interest in writing for THE CHRISTIAN HOME. Here is a brief listing of our needs:

Articles: 1500-1800 words in length, directed to parents, and dealing with all aspects of family living. Each issue is developed on a specific theme and the majority of theme-related articles are solicited. However, many free lance materials are used. No biography or nostalgic pieces, please. We prefer queries on article ideas. Usual payment two and one-half cents a word.

Fillers: Serious, humorous, inspirational filler material of 500-800 words. Payment by arrangement with author.

Poems: A number of poems are used in each issue, preferably under 16 lines, not published previously. Also, use four- to eight-line humorous verse as filler material. Payment: fifty cents a line.

Fiction: We buy stories for adults 1500-3000 words in length. Please, no children's stories and no stories about the overworked, misunderstood husband or wife. Payment usually runs two and one-half cents a word.

Photographs: We buy sharp 8 1/2 x 11 glossies as illustrations for articles. We like to see these submitted with the article. Payment varies.

Cartoons: Most cartoons are done on assignment, however, we are happy to look at ideas.

We do not read carbon copies or mimeographed material. We look at all other material with a view to possible use. However, because of the great number of unsolicited manuscripts received, we do not have the time to enter into correspondence about a particular manuscript or give criticism.

Please include return postage and a self-addressed envelope on unsolicited manuscripts; otherwise they cannot be returned.

Best wishes to you in your writing.

Yours sincerely,

Helen F. Couch, Editor
THE CHRISTIAN HOME

286

Information Sheet for Writers for *The Christian Home.*
Courtesy of Mrs. Helen F. Couch, editor, *The Christian Home*

INFORMATION SHEET FOR WRITERS OF

"DEVOTIONS FOR THE FAMILY," THE CHRISTIAN HOME

The section "Devotions for the Family" is prepared as a guide for parents who wish to make worship in the home a part of their family life. This material probably has its widest usage by parents who have had limited experience with family worship and, therefore, need something of a pattern to follow until they discover a more creative approach for their particular families. On the other hand, many parents use these devotions regularly as basic material, expanding, enriching, and adapting to the needs of their families.

CONTENT--GENERAL

1. Material for each day should contain (1) one or more Scripture references, (2) a meditation, and (3) a prayer or suggestion for prayer.

2. Material should not be too elementary or too difficult. In general, material prepared to interest the child aged 9 to 12 years is best--this can be simplified by parents for younger children. Often it can be adapted for older members of the family group.

   If at all possible include brief directions "For Families With Older Children." These might be additional and longer scriptural readings, more provocative discussion questions, more advanced poems or anecdotes, and so forth. These directions may be set off at the close of the devotion or included in general directions. For example: Read 1 Corinthians: 4-5. (Older children may read the entire chapter.)

TERMINOLOGY

1. Remember you are writing material to be used by a family. Undoubtedly ages and background will vary widely. Do not confuse children (and often adults, too) by using terms that are not clear in meaning, such as: Lamb of God, the Word, the Kingdom, Father of Lights, angels of peace, Son of Man, eternity, hand of God, King of kings, the Evil One, Devil, Lord of lords, the chosen people, and so forth.

2. Avoid using terms that must be seen to be understood, that is, they depend on quotation marks or italics for their meaning. (Example: Some people are afraid of these "dangers.")

QUOTED MATERIAL

1. If stories, poems, prayers, or other material is quoted, please quote accurately.

2. Indicate the source--page number and name of book or publication, page number, author, publisher in a footnote. This is essential, so that the editor can secure necessary copyright clearance.

3. Indicate all quotations with the use of double quotation marks.

PRAYERS

1. Prayers should always be addressed to God, not to Jesus. This is true of both original and quoted prayers.

2. Avoid using to in petitions. For example: Help us understand, not help us to understand.

3. Prayers should be short and should relate to the meditation for the day.

4. A prayer written by the author is not always necessary. The writer may suggest a number of variations: silent prayer, sentence prayers, directed prayer, passage of Scripture, poem, hymn, and so forth.

SCRIPTURE REFERENCES

1. At least one Scripture reference should be included in the material for each day, although in some instances several may be appropriate. For obvious reasons, brief references are preferable.

2. Suggestions for use of the Scripture should be varied. For example, instead of "Read Psalms 100" at the beginning or ending of the meditation, you might want to suggest that the entire family read a particular passage in unison, responsively, or silently, or by turns, or from different translations. Or you might say something like: "Let us see what Jesus had to say about this (reference)," or "Here is a story from the Bible about _____ (reference)." Or, you might suggest that a family member paraphrase a passage which has been read previously.

3. Scripture references should relate to the meditation or serve a specific purpose in worship for the day. For example, if the meditation is concerned with honesty, you would not suggest Psalms 23 as the Scripture reading for the day. In some instances, however, passages of Scripture may be used as calls to worship, prayers, for moments of praise, and the like, and will not be directly related to subject of the meditation.

4. Except for special purposes (comparison, calling attention to special wording, and so forth) please use the Revised Standard Version of the Bible.

288

5. Spell out the names of books of the Bible.

6. In quoting poetry from the Bible, type it as poetry, except in the case of a single line, which may be run in.

LENGTH

Meditations will vary in length depending on subject matter. Copy for each day should average 40 - 50 lines typed on 35 characters.

MANUSCRIPT PREPARATION

1. Type your manuscript 35 characters (letters, spaces, punctuation marks) to the line.

2. Double-space all copy, including quotations.

3. Use a well-inked typewriter ribbon and 8 1/2 x 11 bond paper.

4. Prepare 1 original and 1 carbon copy to submit to the editor, originals and carbons assembled separately.

5. Number pages of original and carbon consecutively at the top.

6. Type each meditation separately, beginning each on a fresh sheet.

7. If pages are fastened together, use paper clips, not staples.

8. "X" out words rather than erase them.

9. Footnotes indicating sources of quotes should be numbered and typed at the bottom of the page on which quoted material appears.

10. Indicate the day of the week and the date at the beginning of each meditation thus: SUNDAY, May 19.

ADDITIONAL MATERIAL

1. Prepare a few brief paragraphs--about 50-60 lines--under the title "This Month...." These paragraphs will alert parents to some of the experiences that can be anticipated for their families during the month, some of the special emphases of the Christian year, how the family can make these devotions especially meaningful, and so forth. (See "Devotions" in past issues.)

2. Prepare a brief filler--about 30-50 lines, on a specific topic suggested by the editor.

BIOGRAPHICAL NOTE

Please give us information about yourself--the size of your family, your responsibilities in the church, your occupation, and so forth.

PLEASE CHECK THE ABOVE LIST BEFORE MAILING

Mail materials to: Mrs. Helen F. Couch, Editor
THE CHRISTIAN HOME
201 Eighth Avenue, South
Nashville, Tennessee 37203

E Where the Money Goes; a Ten-Year Summary of Financial Data for The Penton Publishing Company.
By permission of The Penton Publishing Company

FINANCIAL DATA—ten year summary

	Publication Income	Printing and Rent	Total Income	Income Before Federal Taxes	Income Taxes	Net Income	Per Cent of Total Income	Net Income per share*	Dividends Paid per share	Working Capital	Additions to Plant and Equipment	Number of Employees	Number of Share-holders
1967	$15,605,126	$ 38,800	$15,643,926	$1,519,307	$ 660,000	$ 859,307	5.49	$ .90	$.50	$4,254,156	$1,345,699	693	890
1966	15,397,042	5,952	15,402,994	2,129,526	1,020,000	1,109,526	7.20	1.16	.50	3,464,163	446,543	666	845
1965	13,619,963	14,783	13,634,746	1,685,615	800,000	885,615	6.50	.92	.47½	3,123,032	170,581	660	786
1964	12,768,788	37,624	12,806,412	1,640,228	782,000	858,228	6.70	.89	.45	2,657,620	216,432	656	777
1963	11,312,855	86,763	11,399,618	1,428,899	738,000	690,899	6.06	.74	.37½	2,237,463	95,847	624	773
1962	10,669,457	193,038	10,862,495	1,351,835	678,000	673,835	6.20	.72	.30	1,814,982	186,431	623	780
1961	9,845,415	164,686	10,010,101	1,014,019	533,000	481,019	4.80	.51	.25	1,475,039	114,458	612	654
1960	10,067,611	379,132	10,446,743	1,378,539	701,000	677,539	6.49	.72	.31¼	1,236,014	441,554	619	650
1959	8,496,442	339,643	8,836,085	926,284	479,000	447,284	5.06	.48	.31¼	1,164,065	78,549	579	646
1958	7,992,754	252,766	8,245,520	840,638	430,551	410,087	4.97	.44	.32½	1,025,782	503,953	552	597

Net income and dividends paid adjusted for 2 for 1 stock split.
*On average number of shares outstanding during each year.

***Instructor* Hints.**
By permission of F. A. Owen Publishing Company

WHO SHOULD SUBMIT

Teachers, supervisors, administrators, professional and free-lance authors who are familiar with the educational goals and programs for today's elementary schools.

THE INSTRUCTOR CAN USE MANUSCRIPTS THAT

1. Describe classroom or all-school activities OR give solutions to school problems.

2. Report science, social studies, or language arts units.

3. Show art projects, including samples of the children's work with brief descriptions.

4. Relate new ideas, teaching devices, recent research or innovations.

5. Pertain to holidays, special events, or any day--quality songs, stories, poems, or plays.

THE EDITORS

Base acceptance on several factors:
1. Quality of ideas and material submitted.
2. Amount of similar material already accepted.
3. General plans for monthly content of the magazine.

Notify author that manuscript is:
1. Accepted
2. Held for longer consideration
3. Rejected

Hold Seasonal material until 3rd month prior to use month.

Hold nonseasonal material up to 6 months without additional notification.

Reserve the right to edit.

IF MANUSCRIPT IS ACCEPTED

A contract is sent to contributor prior to publication.

Amount paid depends on quality of thought and writing, length, and proposed use. (Prices for contributions not quoted in advance.)

Payment is made within 30 days after author returns signed contract.

291

<u>AUTHORS SHOULD</u>

<u>Send</u> manuscripts to only one publication at a time.

<u>Submit</u> manuscripts on an approval basis.

<u>Sell</u> all publication rights unless otherwise stipulated.

<u>Permit</u> reasonable editing.

<u>Send</u> seasonal material 6 months in advance (April for October).

<u>PHOTO REQUIREMENTS</u>

<u>Dramatic closeups</u>--sharply focused, b&w, glossy--5" x 7" or 8" x 10".

<u>Color prints or transparencies</u> are NOT satisfactory.

<u>Pictures should</u> show action and should be unposed.

<u>Group scenes</u> are RARELY dramatic. Focus on 1 to 3 children!

<u>Professional photographers</u> take the best pictures.

<u>HOW TO SUBMIT MATERIAL</u>

1. Type--double space--one side--8½" x 11" paper--keep carbon copy.

2. Indicate number of words submitted.

3. Length:

400 to 800 words	.	Primary Stories
800 to 2000 "	.	Upper-Grade Stories
800 to 1500 "	.	Articles
1500 to 1800 "	.	Units
1500 to 2000 "	.	Plays

4. Name and address on each page. Use given name. Indicate if Miss, Mrs., Mr., or pen name.

5. Give teaching position: grade or subject, name and location of school.

6. Put name and address on each photo, drawing, or sample. Pack them adequately and securely for mailing.

7. Enclose return postage for manuscript and other materials, if rejected.

8. Mail contributions, postage prepaid to: THE INSTRUCTOR, Editorial Department, Dansville, New York 14437

**Editorial Tips for Writers of *NEA Journal* (name changed to *Today's
Education*).
By permission of the *NEA Journal***

SUGGESTIONS FOR AUTHORS SUBMITTING MATERIAL FOR THE NEA JOURNAL

Picking a subject

The Journal covers all educational areas from nursery school to adult education. It's usually a good idea to limit your topic rather than attempt too sweeping a subject; the average Journal article is 1000 to 2000 words. Lively descriptions of successful practices are greatly preferred to mere theorizing about what should be going on. Timeliness is a factor; don't wait to write about something until it is "old hat." Remember, also, that articles take a long time to be processed—August is not too early to submit a Christmas story or article. Before starting work on an article, read over back issues of the Journal to make sure the topic has not been covered in recent months.

Writing the article

Have a plan of attack worked out before you begin to write. An outline is a great boon to getting your ideas sorted out in advance and helps you decide which are the main points to be highlighted. If you're definitely allergic to outlining at the start, try writing a rough draft first and then see if you can make an outline from it. If it refuses to resolve itself into any sensible pattern, some rewriting is undoubtedly needed.

Don't feel that you have to be technical and formal—in fact such an approach is almost guaranteed to send your reader into a spasm of yawns. Long paragraphs likewise have a soporific effect. Term papers bristling with (1), (2), (3)'s and bewhiskered with fringes of footnotes seldom make the grade.

Use crisp, simple English and avoid cliches. Use unexpected or imaginative words or phrases to add flavor to your writing. A dash of humor now and then is also good seasoning. There's definite reader appeal in using human-interest stories to make a point.

Bits of natural-sounding dialogue give a feeling of authenticity and have the added advantage of making the page look light and inviting by breaking up solid blocks of prose. Vary sentence structure both as to length and type.

Don't ramble and digress, or you'll lose your reader at the second left-hand turn. If there are too many meaningless side trips the editors can't figure out where you're going and give up in despair. Never use more words than necessary to tell the essential story.

Preparing the manuscript

Manuscripts should be typed, double-spaced, on one side of the paper, using at least your second-best ribbon. Submit the original (with return postage) and keep a carbon.

Be sure that facts, dates, and names are accurate. If you use a quotation, give the source, which may be edited out of the final version, but is a great boon to the harassed checker. Bibliographies are helpful for the same reason. Proofread your article, or better yet, have someone else do it for you. A manuscript burgeoning with misspelled words and typographical errors is not calculated to make friends and influence editors.

Submit your labor of love to only one magazine at a time. If it is excellent, several of them may decide to use it, and you'll be in a really embarrassing spot. If, on the other hand, it's not usable, sending it to 20 editors won't get you anywhere. If possible, submit glossy finish photographs with your manuscript. Good ones may make your contribution irrestible. Identify each photo and give credit line, if any.

Don't be discouraged if your manuscript is rejected. Some interesting and well-written contributions are returned because of overcrowded schedules. What one magazine rejects may be exactly what another has been seeking. So, try and try again. However, after each round-trip, improve your material if you can.

MAGAZINES FOR MILLIONS

ABP Member List.
By permission of American Business Press, Inc.

ABP American Business Press, Inc. Member Publications
The Association of Specialized Business Publications

Actual Specifying Engineer
Adhesives Age
Administrative Management
Advertising Age
Advertising & Sales Promotion
Air Cargo
Air Conditioning, Heating & Refrigeration News
Air Conditioning, Heating and Ventilating
Air Engineering
Airport Services Management
American Artisan
American Aviation
American Building Supplies
American City, The
American Dairy Review
American Druggist
American Fur Breeder
American Gas Journal
American Journal of Cardiology, The
American Journal of Medicine, The
American Journal of Surgery, The
American Machinist
American Metal Market
American Paint and Wallpaper Dealer
American Paint Journal
American Painting Contractor
American Perfumer and Cosmetics
American School Board Journal, The
American School & University
Amusement Business
Apparel Manufacturer
Appliance Manufacturer
Architectural & Engineering News
Architectural Record
Arizona Beverage Journal
Armed Forces Management
Assembly Engineering
Automation
Automation in Housing
Automotive Industries
Automotive News
Aviation Week & Space Technology
Bakers Review
Bakers Weekly
Baking Industry
Beer Distributor
Billboard
Biscuit and Cracker Baker
Blast Furnace and Steel Plant
Boating Industry, The
Book Production Industry
Boot & Shoe Recorder
Boxboard Containers
Brick & Clay Record
Business Automation
Building Construction
Building Materials Merchandiser
Building Specialties and Home Improvements
Building Supply News
Buildings
Business Abroad
Business Advertising
Broadcasting
Business Education World
Business Publication Rates and Data
Buyers Purchasing Digest
Butane-Propane News
Candy Industry and Confectioners Journal
Candy Marketer, The
Canner/Packer
Catholic Market
Catholic School Journal
Ceramic Industry
Chemical Engineering
Chemical Equipment
Chemical Week
Coal Age
Coal Mining & Processing
College and University Business
Combustion
Commercial Car Journal
Concrete Products
Construction Equipment and Materials
Construction Methods and Equipment
Construction News (Public Works Issue)
Consumer Advertising
Consumer Magazine and Farm Publication Rates and Data
Contractor
Contractor News
Contractors' Electrical Equipment
Contractors and Engineers
Control Engineering
Corset & Underwear Review
Croplife
Data Processing Magazine
Datamation
Department Store Economist
Design News
Diesel Equipment Superintendent
Display World
Distribution Age
Domestic Engineering
Drive-In Management
Drive-In Restaurant
Drug Topics
Drug Trade News
Editor & Publisher
EDN-The Electronic Engineer's Design Magazine
Educational Screen and Audiovisual Guide
EEE-Circuit Design Engineering
Electric Light and Power
Electrical Construction and Maintenance
Electrical Equipment
Electrical South
Electrical West
Electrical Wholesaling
Electrical World
Electronic Component News
Electronic Design
Electronic Engineer, The
Electronic Procurement
Electronic Products
Electronic Technician

Electronics
Electro-Technology
Engineering and Mining Journal
Engineering News-Record
Factory
Farm Store Merchandising
Fast Food
Feedlot
Feed & Farm Supplier
Feedstuffs
Fire Engineering
Fleet Owner
Food & Drug Packaging
Food Engineering
Food Topics
Forest Industries
Foundry
Gas
Gas Age
Gas Appliance Merchandising
Gasoline Retailer
Geyer's Dealer Topics
Gift & Tableware Reporter
Gifts & Decorative Accessories
Glass Digest
Glass Industry, The
Glass Packer-Processor
Government Product-news
Graphic Arts Buyer
Grinding and Finishing
Handbags & Accessories
Hard & Soft Goods Packaging
Hardware Age
Hearing Dealer
Heating & Air Conditioning Contractor
Heating, Piping & Air Conditioning
Hog Farm Management
Home and Auto Retailer
Home and Garden Supply Merchandiser
Hosiery and Underwear
Hospital Management
Hospital and Nursing Home Food Management
Hospital Physician
Hospitality: (American Motel-Hotel-Resort Lodging Combination)
Hospitality: American Restaurant (Restaurant Combination)
Hospitality (Food and Lodging Combination)
Hotel Management-Review & Innkeeping
House & Home
Housewares Review
Hydrocarbon Processing
Ice Cream Field & Ice Cream Trade Journal
Ice Cream Review
Incentive-Magazine of the Premium Industry
Industrial Arts and Vocational Education
Industrial Bulletin
Industrial Design
Industrial Distribution
Industrial Equipment News
Industrial Gas
Industrial Marketing
Industrial Research
Industrial Water Engineering
Inland Printer/American Lithographer
Institutional Distribution
Institutions Magazine
Instrument & Apparatus News
Instruments and Control Systems
Interior Design
Interiors
International Science and Technology
Iron Age
Jewelers' Circular-Keystone, The
Jobber Executive
Journal of Plumbing, Heating & Air Conditioning, The
Knitter, The
Law and Order
Lighting
Linens & Domestics
LP-Gas
Luggage & Leather Goods
Machine Design
Machine and Tool Blue Book
Machinery
Manufactured Milk Products Journal
Manufacturing Confectioner, The
Marine Products
Mart Magazine
Materials in Design Engineering
Meat
Media/scope
Medical Economics
Merchandising Week
Metal/Center News
Metal Finishing
Metal Products Manufacturing
Metals Week
Metalworking
MicroWaves
Milk Dealer, The
Mill & Factory
Mobilehomes Merchandiser
Modern Beauty Shop
Modern Brewery Age
Modern Converter
Modern Floor Coverings
Modern Hospital, The
Modern Machine Shop
Modern Maintenance Management
Modern Materials Handling
Modern Medicine
Modern Nursing Home Administrator
Modern Packaging
Modern Plastics
Modern Railroads
Modern Tire Dealer
Motor
Motor/Age
Motor Service Magazine
Municipal South, The
Musical Merchandise Review
National Petroleum News
Nation's Schools
Nation's Schools/Board Member Edition

Network Rates and Data
New England Electrical News
New Equipment Digest
Newspaper Rates and Data
Notion & Novelty Review
Nucleonics
Nursery Business
Oceanology International
Office Appliances
Office Design
Office Products Dealer
Oil and Gas Equipment
Oil and Gas Journal, The
Oil, Paint and Drug Reporter
Optical Journal and Review of Optometry, The
Oral Hygiene
Pacific Logger & Lumberman
Package Engineering
Packer, The
Paint and Varnish Production
Paper, Film and Foil Converter
Paper Sales
Paper Trade Journal
Paperboard Packaging
Pet Shop Management
Petro/Chem Engineer
Petroleum and Chemical Transporter
Petroleum Engineer
Pipeline Engineer
Pipe Line Industry
Pit and Quarry
Plant and Business Food Management
Plant Engineering
Plastics Technology
Plastics World
Plumbing-Heating-Air Conditioning Wholesaler, The
Postgraduate Medicine
Poultry & Eggs Weekly
Poultry Meat: Broiler Combination-Turkey Combination-Complete Poultry Meat
Poultry Tribune
Power
Power Engineering
Practical Builder
Premium Practice-The Magazine of Incentive Merchandising
Printers' Ink
Printing Impressions
Printing Magazine/National Lithographer
Printing Production
Produce Marketing
Product Design & Development
Product Engineering
Production
Production Equipment
Products Finishing
Professional Nursing Home
Progressive Architecture
Progressive Grocer
Public Utilities Fortnightly
Pulp & Paper
Purchasing
Purchasing Week
Quality Assurance
Quick Frozen Foods-Retail Edition Combination
Quick Frozen Foods-Trade Edition
Reinforced Plastics
Rent-all
Reproductions Review
Research/Development
Restaurant Equipment Dealer
RN-National Magazine for Nurses
Roads & Streets
Rock Products
Rubber Age
Rubber World
Rural & Urban Roads
Sales Management
School and College Food Management
Screen Process Magazine
Service Station Management
Signs of the Times
Soft Drink Industry
Soft Drinks
Soft Serve & Drive-In Field
Southern Automotive Journal
Southern Engineering
Southern Hardware
Southern Hospitals
Space/Aeronautics
Spectator, The
Sponsor
Sports Age
Spot Radio Rates and Data
Spot Television Rates and Data
Steel
Technology Week
Television
Textile Bulletin
Textile Industries
Textile Services Management
Textile World
Tobacco
Tobacco Leaf, The
Tooling & Production
Toys and Novelties
Traffic Management
Traffic World
Transit Advertising Rates and Data
Transportation & Distribution Management
UnderSea Technology
Variety Department Store Merchandiser
Vend
Volume Feeding Management
Water & Sewage Works
Water and Wastes Digest
Water and Wastes Engineering
Weekly Newspaper Advertising Rates and Data
Western Advertising
Western Electronic News
Western Farm Equipment
Western Plastics

Western Underwriter-Life Edition
Western Underwriter-Property and Casualty Edition
What's New In Home Economics
Wood & Wood Products
Woodworking Digest
World Oil

INTERNATIONAL AFFILIATES

Alan Attijarat
Architecture-Batiment-Construction
Automotive World (English & Spanish editions)
Batiment
British Columbia Lumberman
Building Supply Dealer
Bus & Truck Transport in Canada
Canadian Advertising Rates and Data
Canadian Architect, The
Canadian Automotive Trade
Canadian Aviation
Canadian Builder
Canadian Chemical Processing
Canadian Consulting Engineer
Canadian Controls & Instrumentation
Canadian Electronics Engineering
Canadian Farm Equipment Dealer
Canadian Forest Industries
Canadian Gas Journal
Canadian Grocer
Canadian Hotel and Restaurant
Canadian Industrial Photography
Canadian Interiors
Canadian Jeweller
Canadian Machinery and Metalworking
Canadian Metalworking/Machine Production
Canadian Nuclear Technology
Canadian Packaging
Canadian Paint & Finishing
Canadian Petroleum
Canadian Plastics
Canadian Printer & Publisher
Canadian Pulp and Paper Industry
Canadian Shipping and Marine Engineering News
Canadian Transportation
Canadian Wood Products Industries
Cites et Villes
Civic Administration
Climatisation, Chauffage et Plomberie
Construction West
Design Engineering
Drug Merchandising
Electrical Contractor and Maintenance Supervisor
Electrical Equiment News
Electrical News & Engineering
Electronics & Communications
Energy International
Engineering & Construction World
Engineering and Contract Record
Equipment Industriel
Executive
Financial Post, The
Financial Times of Canada
Food in Canada
Food Service & Hospitality
Furniture & Furnishings Magazine
Genie-Construction
Hardware Merchandising
Heating/Plumbing/Air Conditioning
Heavy Construction News
Hebdo-Construction
Home Goods Retailing
Hospital Administration in Canada
Industria Avicola
Industrial Products & Equipment
Industrial World (English & Spanish editions)
Ingenieria Internacional Construccion
International Business Automation
International Electronics (English & Spanish editions)
Iron Age Metalworking International
Journal of Commerce Weekly
La Papeterie
Lawn & Garden Merchandising
Le Bureau
L'Entrepreneur en Plomberie-Chauffage
L'Epicier
Le Pharmacien
Le Quincaillier
Marketing
Materials Handling in Canada
Mechanical Contracting & Plumbing
Medical Post, The
Men's Wear of Canada
Mining in Canada
Modern Power & Engineering
Modern Purchasing
Office Administration
Office Equipment & Methods
Oilweek
Packaging Progress
Photo Trade
Plant Administration & Engineering
Poultry International
Product Design and Value Engineering
Progressive Plastics
Pulp & Paper International
Revue-Moteur
School Administration
School Progress
Shoe and Leather Journal
Southam Building Guide
Stationery & Office Products
Style
Sugar y Azucar
Transport Commercial
Water & Pollution Control
Western Business and Industry
Western Pharmacist
World Construction
World Mining
World Petroleum
World Wood

The Specialized Business Press—Your Direct Line To Big Buying Power.

List of Specialized Publishing Associations

Agricultural Publishers Association
333 N. Michigan Avenue
Chicago, Illinois

American Agricultural Editors Association
Box 3665
Harrisburg, Pennsylvania   17105

American Association of Industrial Editors
802 Kenmore Avenue
Buffalo, New York   14216

American Association of Medical Writers
P.O Box 267
Arlington, Va. 22210

American Business Press, Inc.
205 E. 42nd Street
New York, New York   10017

American Railway Magazine Editors Association
c/o John J. Knifke
80 East Jackson Boulevard
Chicago, Illinois

American Society of Business Press Editors
1012 14 Street N.W.
Washington, D.C.   20005

American Society of Magazine Editors
575 Lexington Avenue
New York, New York   10022

Associated Church Press
875 N. Dearborn Street
Chicago, Illinois   60610

Association of Publication Production Managers
c/o Conde Nast Publications
420 Lexington Avenue
New York, New York   10017

Association of Screen Magazine Publishers

Bureau of Independent Publishers and Distributors
10 East 40th Street
New York, New York   10016

Catholic Press Association
432 Park Avenue South
New York, New York   10016

Comics Magazine Association of America
300 Park Avenue South
New York, New York 10010

Educational Press Association of America
Newhouse School of Journalism
Syracuse University
Syracuse, New York 13210

Evangelical Press Association
Box 277, La Canada, Calif. 91011

International Council of Industrial Editors
2108 Braewick Circle
Akron, Ohio 44313

Magazine Advertising Bureau, Inc.
575 Lexington Avenue
New York, New York 10022

Magazine Publishers Association, Inc.
575 Lexington Avenue
New York, New York 10022

National Association of Boating Magazines
P.O. Box 1750
Annapolis, Maryland

National Association of Science Writers
75 Bayview Ave.
Port Washington, N.Y. 11050

Periodical Publishers Association
575 Lexington Avenue
New York, New York 10022

Publishers Information Bureau
575 Lexington Avenue
New York, New York 10022

Society of Business Magazine Editors
919 10th Street
Washington, D.C.

List of National Distributors.
By permission of Bureau of Independent Publishers and Distributors

Bureau of Independent Publishers and Distributors

<u>National Distributors</u>

Russell Barich
Ace News Co.
1120 Ave. of the Americas
New York, N. Y. 10036

Louis Fein
Capital Distributing Co.
Division St.
Derby, Conn. 06814

William Gipe
Dell Publications, Inc.
750 Third Ave.
New York, N. Y. 10017

Jack Adams
Fawcett Publications, Inc.
Fawcett Bldg.
Greenwich, Conn. 06830

Harold Chamberlain
Independent News Co.
575 Lexington Ave.
New York, N. Y. 10022

A. A. Rachoi
ICD-Hearst Magazines, Inc.
250 W. 55th St.
New York, N. Y. 10019

Mose Diehl
Kable News Co.
777 Third Ave.
New York, N. Y. 10017

S. N. Himmelman
Macfadden-Bartell, Inc.
205 E. 42nd St.
New York, N. Y. 10017

Mr. Ira Moshier
Popular Publications, Inc.
   (no small books)
205 E. 42nd St.
New York, N. Y. 10017

Raymond Fiore
Publishers Distributing Corp.
401 Park Ave., South
New York, N. Y. 10016

Dwight Yellen
Select Magazines, Inc.
229 Park Ave., South
New York, N. Y. 10003

Frank Walston
Curtis Circulation Co.
Independence Sq.
Philadelphia, Pa. 19105

David Lichtenberg
Triangle Publications, Inc.
TV GUIDE
Radnor, Pa. 19087

Good housekeeping
Suggestion system
Vocational training
Technical explanations

COMPANY POLICY
Hours and wages
Bonus and incentive plans
Union relationships
Recruitment of new employees
Supervisory training
Litigation affecting company status
Rules and regulations
Striking and insubordination
Vacations and sick leave
Solicitation on company property
Contributions to community welfare
Board of directors meeting reports

BUSINESS AND FINANCIAL INFORMATION
Balance Sheet
Profit and Loss statement
Earnings
Taxes
Wages (laws affecting)
Costs of operation
Business conditions
New property and equipment
Dividends
Financing
Investments
Prices
Sales
Markets
New products

EMPLOYEE RECOGNITION
Service awards
Promotions
Heroism
New employees
Retired employees
Obituaries
Service anniversaries
Hobby stories
Family stories
Personals
Birthdays, weddings, births
The old timer
Community contributions
Unusual performance
Exemplary activities

EMPLOYEE WELFARE
Health and nutrition
Safety
Venereal disease
Medical and dental facilities

GENERAL STORIES
Economic information
Community activities
Citizenship
Adult education
Income taxes
Social security
Legislation affecting the company
Politics (local and national

GENERAL INFORMATION ABOUT THE COMPANY
  Seniority and age groups
  New officers and directors
  Mergers
  Raw material sources
  Customers
  Exports
  Company history
  Departments and branch plants
  Corporate structure
  Plant expansion
  Advertising
  Public relations
  Contests
  Stockholders

INFORMATION ABOUT INDUSTRY
  Contribution to industry
  Relative position
  Industry as economic factor
  Contribution to other industries
  What other members of industry think about company
  Competitive and non-competitive aspects
  Inter-industry personalities
  The industry and government

EMPLOYEE BENEFITS
  Hospitalization
  Insurance
  Credit union
  Company's publications
  Stock ownership
  Library
  Cafeteria
  Pension plan
  Profit sharing
  Recreational facilities

MISCELLANEOUS
  Fiction
  Children's page
  Comics
  Fashions
  Interior decorating
  Recipes and homemaking
  Sons and daughters of employees
  Classified ads
  Crossword puzzles, bridge, chess
  Cartoons and jokes
  Inspirational articles
  Poetry
  Prize contests
  Questions and answers
  Other quiz-type features
  Reader's forum
  Religious material

299

Acknowledgments

TO the many editors and publishers, writers and photographers, who granted permission to use their work, we gratefully acknowledge in detail, chapter by chapter, their contributions, arranged alphabetically.

Circulation figures are based in most cases on Standard Rate & Data Service catalogues for Business Publications, and for Consumer Magazines and Farm Publications, as of November, 1968. Editorial policy descriptions are drawn in many instances from "Editorial Profiles," appearing in the same directories, all by permission of Walter E. Botthof, chairman of the board, Standard Rate & Data Service, Inc. In a few situations, editorial descriptions are revised from material appearing in The Writer's Market, 1968, by permission of Kirk Polking, editor.

Chapter 2. The Affluent Home and Family

Audit Bureau of Circulations, Publisher's Statement for Dec. 31, 1967, *Better Homes and Gardens*, by permission, C. O. Bennett, manager, public relations, Audit Bureau of Circulations, jointly with the Meredith Corporation, by permission, Robert S. Clark, public relations department.

Meredith Corporation: interviews and data on Meredith Corporation and *Better Homes and Gardens* from Bert Dieter, editorial director; James A. Riggs, editor, *Better Homes and Gardens*; Kenneth McDougall, director of editorial corporate public relations; Ray Deaton, research associate, Robert Jolley, production manager; by permission, Robert S. Clark, all courtesy of Meredith Corporation.

Meredith Corporation: circulation growth bar chart, production schedules, photostatic page layouts, editorial content schedules, sales promotion piece and questionnaire, pressroom photograph, copy flow schedules, all for *Better Homes and Gardens* and by courtesy of Meredith Corporation.

Meredith Corporation: cumulative schedule of editorial content records, courtesy of Meredith Research Division special tabulation based on The Lloyd H. Hall Company data.

Meredith Corporation: *Better Homes and Gardens*, June, 1968, cover, copyright, Meredith Corporation, 1968, all rights reserved.

Chapter 3. The Juvenile Revolution

Comics Magazine Association of America, history and promotional material, by permission, John L. Goldwater, president.

Journalism Quarterly, information based on "Content and Readership of Teen Magazines," by Janice S. Stewart, Autumn, 1964, vol. 41, no. 4, pp. 580-583.

Macfadden-Bartell, history, by permission, Lloyd C. Jamieson, vice president advertising and marketing.

Marvel Comic Group, history and promotion material, by permission, Joseph Field Associates, Joseph Field, president.

Trade advertisement for Boys' Life, by permission, Robinson, Donino & West, Inc. and *Boys' Life*.

Triangle Publications, advertisement and promotion material, *Seventeen*, by permission, George E. Johnston, promotion director, *Seventeen*.

Western Publishing Company, Periodicals Department, *The Golden Magazine*, company history, promotion material, and questionnaires, "Cracky," copyright by *The Golden Magazine*, by permission, Larry Adler, director of marketing and advertising.

Chapter 4. The Long, Leisurely Weekend

Eastman Kodak Company, cover, Kodak Bulletin, copyright by Eastman Kodak Company, by permission, C. E. Fitzgibbon, manager, editorial and graphic services, public relations department.

Inside front-cover spread. Copyright, 1964, Eastman Kodak Company, C. E. Fitzgibbon, Manager, Editorial and Graphic Services, Public Relations Department.

Macfadden-Bartell Corporation, advertisement for *Sport*, by permission, Lloyd C. Jamieson, vice president advertising and marketing.

National Wildlife, cover, copyright by National Wildlife, by permission, R. B. Kirkpatrick, executive editor.

Chapter 5. The Role of Religious Magazines

Methodist Publishing House, curriculum units, production schedules, schedule of themes, suggestions for writers, *The Christian Home*, by permission, Mrs. Helen Couch, editor, and interview.

Methodist Publishing House, chart of church school publications, organization chart, Board of Publications, by permission, Carolyn Hite, rights and permissions, Board of Publications.

Methodist Publishing House, covers for *Three/Four* and *Accent on Youth*, copyright by Methodist Publishing House Board of Publications, by permission, Carolyn Hite.

motive, "When Stokely Met the Presidents: Black Power and Negro Education," by Vincent Harding; "The Latest Inscriptions," by James den Boer; reprinted from *motive*, January, 1967, by permission, Ron Henderson, managing editor.

Southern Baptist Convention, statement from "Church Literature Guidebook," by James L. Sullivan, executive secretary-treasurer, The Sunday School Board, quotation from *Storytime*, by permission, Clifton J. Allen, editorial secretary; interview with Lucy Hoskins, editor, *Church Administration*.

Chapter 6. The Giant Galaxy of Company Publications

Armco Steel Corporation, illustration, "Raindrops of Understanding," by permission, Robert W. Hawk, editor, *Armco Today*.

Cities Service Company, quotation from "Bell, Gong and Whistle," *Service*, January, 1960.

Crucible Steel Company, copy and illustrations, "Reporting the News," by permission, Inez Artico, editor, *Steelman*.

Direct Advertising / Paper Makers Advertising Association, quote from "Allis-Chalmers Solves Communications Commotion with Internal Publications," by A. R. Tofte, advertising manager, Allis-Chalmers Company, from *Direct Advertising Magazine*, copyright, *Direct Advertising Magazine*, by permission, Fred S. Van Voorhis, editor and executive secretary.

Dow Chemical Company, Midland, Michigan, material from "Dow Fibers in Detroit," *Dow Diamond*, by permission, James Shahlin, editor.

Dun's Review, "The Employee Publication: A Report on Objectives," by William C. Lewis, editor, *Dun's Bulletin*, copyright, 1957, Dun & Bradstreet Publications Corporation, reprinted by permission, Raymond Brady, editor.

Eastman Kodak Company, information on publications, by courtesy, C. E. Fitzgibbon, manager, editorial and graphic services, public relations department.

Fluor Corporation, quotation from "Frozen Frontier," *Fluor-o-scope*.

International Council of Industrial Editors, quoted material and information from *Reporting*; "ICIE Career Booklet;" "The ICIE File," by William

J. Cadigan, copyright, 1961, by International Council of Industrial Editors; "Operation Tapemeasure;" copyright by International Council of Industrial Editors, by permission, Geraldine T. Keating, executive secretary.

Monsanto Magazine, publication schedule, editorial plans, layout plan and dummy, cover, copyright, 1965, by *Monsanto Magazine*, by permission, Leonard A. Paris, editor.

New York State School of Industrial and Labor Relations, Cornell University, material from "Cornell Conference Report on Mutual Problems of Company Editors and Their Managements," by permission, Charlotte H. Gold, assistant director of publications.

Ohio Bell Telephone Company, "The Inquiring Reporter," from *The Ohio Bell*, November–December, 1964, by permission, Norm Treadon, editor.

Philip Morris, Inc., copy and illustrations, "Why Our Company Magazine?", by permission, Thomas V. Reilly, manager, employee communications.

Public Relations Journal, quotation from "Where the Editor Can Go," by Carlton E. Spitzer, June, 1964, by permission, Milton Fairman, editor.

Quill, "The 'House Organ' Grows Up," by Robert Newcomb; "Why Corporations Publish Periodicals," by John Earl Davis, April, 1955, quotations printed by permission, Clarence O. Schlaver, editor.

S. D. Warren Company, quotations from "The Company Publication," by permission, John H. Thwaits, manager, publishing division.

Shield, United Air Lines, quotation from "Yes, Michael, There Is a Santa Claus," January, 1962, by permission, Marguerite Welch, managing editor.

Southwestern Bell Telephone Company, copy and illustrations, *Scene*, by permission, Paul Maranto, editor, and Dave Park, information supervisor.

Travelers Insurance Company, quotations from *The Traveler's Record*, March, 1865.

Chapter 7. The Voice of Industry

American Business Press, Inc., history, "Fast Facts," "ABP Info / File '67," "Careers in the Business Press," promotional booklets, promotional advertising supplement, illustrations, by permission, Dave Bennett, manager, member services.

Baird, Russell N., and Turnbull, Arthur T., "Industrial and Business Journalism," Chilton Company, 1961.

Business Press International, Inc., publisher's statement, *Business Automation*, December, 1967, used with joint permission of Business Publications Audit of Circulation, Inc., by permission, R. E. Marx, vice president.

Business Publications Audit of Circulation, Inc., publisher's statement, *Business Automation*, December, 1967, used with joint permission of Business Press International, Inc., by permission, Delmar C. Woodcock, vice president.

Cahners Publishing Company, promotional booklet, by permission, Ned Johnson, administrative vice president.

Chilton Company, "Chilton Responsibilities and Policies," Chilton Annual Report, 1967, "This Is Chilton," "The Chilton Publisher," cover of *Jewelers' Circular-Keystone*, Chilton promotional advertisements and charts, by permission, W. B. Williams, corporate advertising and sales promotion manager; and interview with William A. Barbour, editor and publisher, *Hardware Age*.

Elfenbein, Julien, "Business Journalism," Harper & Brothers, 1960.

Fairchild Publications, history and promotional material, by permission and interview with James W. Brady, publisher, *Women's Wear Daily*, and Joseph P. Hanley, director of syndication and public relations.

Haire Publishing Company, promotional advertisement, company history especially prepared and by permission, Cy Bernstein, vice president.

McGraw-Hill Publications, Annual Report, 1967, charts and illustrations, photographs, promotional advertisements, by permission, Donald A. Moser, associate, public affairs and communications department; Richard LaBonte, director of promotion; William P. Giglio, director of public services; interviews with John R. Callaham, executive vice president publications, and A. J. Fox, editor, *Engineering News-Record*.

Media/scope, quotations from editorial material and Association of Industrial Advertisers analysis of editorial content by Lloyd H. Hall Company, Inc., by permission, Carroll Swan, editor, and Fritz Landmann, publisher.

Penton Publishing Company, charts and graphs, Annual Report, 1967, illustrations and publication covers, by permission, David C. Kiefer, vice president-marketing.

Reuben H. Donnelley Corporation, history, "This Is Donnelley," "Pocket Guide," by permission, Edward B. Wintersteen and Charles S. Mill, vice president and general manager; interview with Harold J. McKeever, editor, *Roads and Streets*.

Chapter 8. The Siamese Twins—Business and Labor

"Directory of National and International Labor Unions in the United States," Bulletin No. 1493, U.S. Department of Labor, April, 1966.

International Union, United Automobile, Aerospace & Agricultural Implement Workers of America, cover and materials from *UAW Solidarity* and *UAW New Technology*, by permission, Joseph Walsh, director of public relations.

McGraw-Hill Publications, advertisements for *Business Week*, by permission, Richard LaBonte, director of publications.

Wall Street Journal, advertisement, by permission, William McSherry, manager, news department services.

Chapter 9. Professions and Associations

American Chemical Society, history and background, from Dr. Richard L. Kenyon, director of applied publications.

American Institute of Physics, history and background, H. William Koch, director.

American Medical Association, history and background, from Russell H. Clark, director, management services division.

Daniel Starch and Staff, cover and material from "Here Are the Vital Facts Concerning the NEA Journal," by permission, Howard A. Stone, president.

Decker Communications, information from Frederic C. Decker, president.

Department of the Army, Office of Chief of Information, information and background on Military publications, by courtesy of Lt. Col. S. H. McKenty, Acting Chief, Command Information Division, by authorization of Major General Wendell J. Coats, Chief of Information, Department of the Army, The Pentagon.

Durbin, John, photograph, Tokyo staff of "Stars and Stripes," by permission.

F. A. Owen Publishing Company, quotation from "What Instructor's Contributors Need to Know," by permission, E. Stanley Copeland, president.

International Council of Industrial Editors, cover, *Reporting*, by permission, Geraldine T. Keating, executive secretary.

Media/scope, cover, by permission, Carroll Swan, editor; Fritz Landsmann, publisher.

National Education Association, cover and material from "Here Are the Vital Facts Concerning the NEA Journal," "Suggestions for Authors Submitting Material for the NEA Journal," by permission, Walter A. Graves, associate editor; interview with Mildred S. Fenner, editor, *Today's Education*; information from Ruth Skewes Ford, former production editor, *NEA Journal*.

Teachers Publishing Corporation, cover, booklet for *Grade Teacher*, by permission, Allen A. Raymond, president, Teachers Publishing Corporation.

William & Wilkins Company, information from history, "After Seventy-Five Years," by permission, William M. Passano, president.

Chapter 10. Down on the Farm

Future Homemakers of America, information, Millie A. Stolbach, editor, *Teen Times*.

Harvest Publishing Company, illustrations from promotional booklet, by permission, Kenneth H. Constant, vice president, advertising.

Meister Publishing Company, history and information, by permission, Richard T. Meister, editorial director and general manager.

Meredith Corporation, cover, advertising copy, illustrations, reader questionnaire, *Successful Farming*; cover, June, 1968, copyright, Meredith Corporation, 1968, all rights reserved; interview with Richard Hanson, editor, *Successful Farming*, courtesy of Meredith Corporation, by permission, Robert S. Clark, public relations department.

"My First 80 Years," by Clarence Poe, history of *The Progressive Farmer*, University of North Carolina Press, 1963.

Oklahoma Publishing Company, history and information, by permission, Ferdie J. Deering, editor and manager, *The Farmer-Stockman*.

Prairie Farmer, history and information, by courtesy of Vern Anderson, vice president, and Paul C. Johnson, editorial director.

Progressive Farmer, history and background, by permission.

Vance Publishing Company, history, by courtesy of George L. Milne, vice president and publishing director.

Watt Publishing Company, illustrations and information from booklet, "dedicated to the next 50 years," by permission, Don Welch, sales promotion manager.

Chapter 11. Land of the Giants

Company and publication history and background by courtesy of—

American Association of Industrial Editors, Donald W. Boyd, Jr., executive secretary.

American Aviation Publications, Wayne W. Parrish, president.

American Business Press, Inc., Dave Bennett, manager, member services, and chart and illustrations from promotional supplement, New York Times, also by permission. Information also by courtesy Hazen Morse, executive vice president.

American Chemical Society, Dr. Richard L. Kenyon, director of applied publications.

American Institute of Physics, H. William Koch, director.

American Medical Association, Russell H. Clark, director, management services division.

Associated Church Press, Alfred P. Klausler, executive secretary.

American Society of Magazine Editors, Robert E. Kenyon, Jr., secretary.

Audit Bureau of Circulations, C. O. Bennett, manager, public relations; also ABC logotype, Trade Mark Registered, by permission.

Bill Publications, Harlan Lang, director of special projects.

Bureau of Independent Publishers and Distributors, Alan P. Fort, executive director.

Business Publication Audit of Circulation, Delmar C. Woodcock, vice president; also BPA logotype, Trade Mark Registered, by permission, Peter L. Chamberlin, manager, administrative service.

307

Cahners Publishing Company (including Conover-Mast), Ned Johnson, administrative vice president; also cover.

Catholic Press Association, James A. Doyle, executive director.

Chilton Company, W. B. Williams, corporate advertising and sales promotion manager; also promotional advertisements, by permission.

Condé Nast Publications, Inc. (including Street & Smith), Perry L. Ruston, executive vice president.

Davis Publications, Inc., Joel Davis, executive vice president.

Dell Publishing Company, Inc., Nancy Meranus.

Reuben H. Donnelley Corporation, Edward B. Wintersteen and Charles S. Mill, vice president and general manager.

Educational Press Association, Ronald W. McBrine, executive secretary.

Fairchild Publications, Inc., Joseph P. Hanley, director of syndication and public relations.

Fawcett Publications, Inc., W. H. Fawcett, Jr., president.

Haire Publishing Company, Cy Bernstein, vice president.

Harcourt, Brace & World, Inc. (including Harvest Publishing Company and Ojibway), Leo. W. Nist, advertising services manager; Kenneth H. Constant, vice president, advertising; James Milholland, Jr., president, Harbrace Publications, Inc.

Hearst Corporation, Hearst Magazines, Richard E. Deems, president.

International Council of Industrial Editors, Geraldine T. Keating, executive secretary.

Johnson Publishing Company, Inc., John H. Johnson, president.

Macfadden-Bartell Corporation, Lloyd C. Jamieson, vice president, advertising and marketing.

McGraw-Hill Publications, John R. Callaham, vice president, editorial; Richard LaBonte, director of promotion; William P. Giglio, director of public service; Donald A. Moser, associate, public affairs and communications department; also advertising and illustrations, by permission.

Magazines for Industry, Inc. (subsidiary of Cowles Communications, Inc.), Don Gussow, president.

Magazine Publishers Association, Robert E. Kenyon, Jr., executive vice president; chart and cover, "Magazines in the U.S.A."

Marvel Comic Group, Stan Lee, editor in chief.

Meister Publishing Company, Richard T. Meister, editorial director and general manager.

Meredith Corporation, Bert Dieter, editorial director, *Better Homes and Gardens*; Kenneth McDougall, director of editorial corporate public relations; Richard Hanson, editor, *Successful Farming*; Robert S. Clark, public relations.

Miller Publishing Company, W. E. Lingren, president.

Office of Certified Circulation, C. F. Rork, managing director; also OCC logotype, Trade Mark Registered, by permission.

308

Peacock Business Press, Joseph S. Peacock, president; John Ochotnicky, editorial assistant.

Penton Publishing Company, David C. Kiefer, vice president, marketing.

Petersen Publishing Company, Robert Petersen, owner.

Prairie Farmer Publishing Company, Paul C. Johnson, vice president and editorial director.

Reinhold Publishing Corporation, Fred P. Peters, executive vice president.

Simmons-Boardman Publishing Corporation, Robert G. Lewis, vice president-operations.

Standard Rate & Data Service, Inc., Walter E. Botthof, chairman of the board.

Verified Audit Circulation Corporation, also VAC logotype, Trade Mark Registered, by permission.

Watt Publishing Company, Leslie A. Watt, president; Don Welch, sales promotion manager.

Williams & Wilkins Company, William M. Passano, president.

Ziff-Davis Publishing Company, W. Bradford Briggs, publisher, *Skiing*.

Also special permissions as follows:

Book Production Industry, "The Story of Dell Publishing Co., Inc.," vol. 80, no. 5, by permission, Joel A. Roth, managing editor.

Writer's Digest, information from article on Davis Publications, by A. R. Roalman, by permission, Kirk Polking, editor, *Writer's Digest*.

Appendix

American Business Press, Inc., ABP members list.

Bureau of Independent Publishers and Distributors, List of National Distributors, by permission, Alan P. Fort, executive director.

F. A. Owen Publishing Company, "What Instructor's Contributors Need to Know," by permission, E. Stanley Copeland, president.

Meredith Corporation, production schedules for *Better Homes and Gardens*, courtesy of Meredith Corporation, by permission, Robert S. Clark, public relations department.

Methodist Publishing Company, "Editorial Tips for the Free-Lancer," for *The Christian Home*, by permission, Mrs. Helen Couch, editor.

Penton Publishing Company, "Financial Data—10-year Summary," by permission, David C. Kiefer, vice president, marketing.

National Education Association, "Suggestions for Authors Submitting Material for the *NEA Journal*," by permission, Walter A. Graves, associate editor.

U.S. Plywood-Champion Papers, Inc., "House Magazine Copy," by K. C. Pratt. Copyright, 1946, by permission, C. J. Wedding, public affairs.

Index

Association publications (*continued*)

Massachusetts Horticultural Society, 29; Men's Garden Clubs of America, 29; American Museum of Natural History, 34, 45; National Wildlife Federation, 34, 45; American Society of Cinematographers, 44; American Society of Magazine Photographers, 44; Photographic Society of America, 44; Professional Photographers of America, 44; Academy of Natural Science of Philadelphia, 45; National Audubon Society, 45; Sierra Club, 45; Doll House Clubs of America, 46; Society for the Preservation and Encouragement of Barber Shop Quartet Singing in America, Inc., 49; National Rifle Association, 54; National Geographic Society, 57–58; American Automobile Association, 58, 62; National Association of Trailer Owners, 61; Travel Trailer Clubs, 61; Automobile Legal Association, 62; National Safety Council, 62; Paper Industry Management, 113; United States Chamber of Commerce, 114, 140–41; American Association of Petroleum Geologists, 116; American Chemical Society, 116, 117, 159, 212–13, 241–42; National Tire Dealers and Retreaders Association, 122; American Cooperage Association, 134; National Association of Insurance Agents, 134; American Banking Association, 142; CUNA International, Inc., 143; National Education Association and affiliates, 156–59 *passim*; state education associations, 158–59; American Association of Physics Teachers, 159; American Association of University Professors, 159; American Economic Association, 159; American Psychological Association, 159; Association for Childhood Education International, 159; Illinois Education Association, 159; National Council of Churches, 162; Phi Beta Kappa, 162; American Alumni Council, 163; American Library Association, 164; Association of College and Research Libraries, 164; College Undergraduate Magazines, Inc., 164; Catholic Library Association, 165; Special Libraries Association, 165; National League of Cities, 166; National Municipal League, 166; Fraternal Order of Police, 168; International Association of Chiefs of Police, 168; National Sheriff's Association, 168; National Association of Counties, 169–70; National Association of Postmasters, 171; American Foreign Service Association of the Department of State, 172; United Nations Association, 172; Alpha Delta Sigma, 175; American Marketing Association, 175; National Newspaper Association, 177; International Conference of Weekly Newspaper Editors, 178; American Radio Relay League, 183; Society of Broadcast Engineers, 183; American Association of Schools and Departments of Journalism, 184; American Society of Journalism School Administrators, 184; Association for Education in Journalism, 184; Sigma Delta Chi, 184–85; Theta Sigma Phi, 184–85; American Bar Association, 185; Columbia Scholastic Press Association, 185; National Scholastic Press Association, 185; National School Yearbook Association, 185; Quill and Scroll Foundation, 185; American Judicature Society, 186; American Law Institute, 186; American Heart Association, 189; American Society for Microbiology, 189; American Society of Abdominal Surgeons, 189; Registry of Medical Technologists of the American Society of Clinical Pathologists, 189; American College of Physicians, 189, 191; American Society of Anesthesiologists, 190; American College of Radiology, 191; American College of Surgeons, 191; American Public Health Association, 191; Massachusetts Medical Society, 191; American Hospital Association, 193; American Nursing Home Association, 193; California Nurses' Association, 194; National League for Nursing, 194; American Dental Association, 195; American Academy of Optometry, 196; American Dental Hygienists' Association, 196; American Optometric Association, 196; Guild of Prescription Opticians of America, 196; National Association of Certified Dental Laboratories, 196;

317